"A rich, diverse and significant collection of essays on the texts, commentaries, parliamentary acts, court cases – even the cartoons – that have most powerfully sought to define or intervene in Britain's unwritten constitution. The experts brought together in this landmark volume tell a compelling story about the evolution of the British constitution, and its legacy elsewhere."

Professor Alice Hunt, *University of Southampton, UK*

"This collection revives the old tradition of lawyers doing constitutional history, but without the distortion of the old 'Whig interpretation'. Sir William Blackstone was not a Whig, as the book shows. In an outstanding chapter, Baroness Hale shows why *Entick* v. *Carrington* (1765) was as important a curb on executive overreach as her own judgments in *Miller I* and *Miller II*. In another, Anne Twomey shows how the long shadow of British constitutional law still lies over the common-law former Dominions. The book should be carefully read by historians and political scientists as well as by lawyers."

Professor Iain McLean FBA FRSE, *Senior Research Fellow, Nuffield College, University of Oxford, UK*

"This is a wonderfully eclectic miscellany. Every chapter is erudite, insightful and thought-provoking. The collection will be of great interest to anyone with a serious curiosity about British constitutional history."

Professor Brice Dickson, *Emeritus Professor of International and Comparative Law, Queen's University Belfast, UK*

"The essays in the book, brought together under the expert editorship of Dr Chris Monaghan, are a fascinating mixture of studies of 'works' of three kinds. First, there are chapters examining the raw materials and foundational phenomena of the UK's constitution, including Magna Carta, the Petition of Rights, Instrument of Government, Toleration Act, Act of Settlement, union with Scotland, Government of India Act, and the classic judgment in *Entick v. Carrington*. Secondly, there are essays on major commentaries on the constitution by people who made more or less important contributions to understanding and developing it, such as Sir John Fortescue, Bolingbroke, Blackstone, De Lolme, Wollstonecraft, Burke and Erskine May. Finally, contributors look at other ways of representing or understanding the constitution, including caricatures and comparative perspectives.

The topics and contributors have been well chosen, providing both expertise and an unexpected take on a history too often taken for granted. Every essay offers fresh perspectives, new understandings and a thought-provoking, entertaining read. Each chapter opened my eyes to new ideas and put my previous understanding (or misunderstanding) of the constitution in a new light. For example, the fascinating chapter on Mary Wollstonecraft as a constitutional thinker makes a strong case for regarding her as a significant contributor to the cultural history of the constitution. The text is a tour de force of editorial planning and authorship. Participants have produced a valuable asset for both students and scholars of our historical constitution. It will enrich the thinking and writing of all who use it. I am delighted to recommend the book."

Professor David Feldman KC (Hon), FBA, *Emeritus Rouse Ball Professor of English Law, University of Cambridge, UK*

Leading Works in the History of the Constitution

This collection brings together academic analysis of leading contemporary accounts of the British Constitution with key constitutional documents and sources while also offering analysis of the leading histories of the Constitution.

The works in question represent examples of the constitutionally most significant legislation, judicial decisions and commentaries by scholars and key actors. Its scope is the 700 years of English and then British history from the Magna Carta to Britain as an imperial power grappling with the question of how to govern India.

The contributors, presenting a balance of established academics and early career researchers, present an original and succinct account of the significance of each leading work. They draw upon the context in which it was written, contemporary literature and more modern academic analysis of the work and its author(s).

Presenting a complement to standard texts on the history of the Constitution, the book will be of interest to researchers and academics working in the areas of Constitutional Law and Politics, Public Law and Legal History.

Chris Monaghan is Principal Lecturer in Law at the University of Worcester.

Analysing Leading Works in Law

Series Editor: Russell Sandberg
Cardiff University, UK

In an age where legal education is undergoing considerable change and facing a number of challenges, the *Analysing Leading Works in Law* series is designed to explore how the study of Law and legal sub-disciplines have developed so far and their likely future. The purpose of the series is to fire critical light at the way in which sub-disciplines within Law understand themselves and perpetuate their identity.

Each book focuses upon a different legal sub-discipline. It asks leading and emerging scholars in the field to select and analyse a 'leading work'; one which has contributed internationally to the development of the sub-discipline as a whole. The chapters explore the likely implications and applications of the leading work upon the sub-discipline in question. The discussion may be in part autobiographical, exploring how the work in question has impacted upon the contributor's own scholarship and understanding of the sub-discipline in question.

The books in this series are intended to assess the development of the sub-discipline in question and examine its potential future development. The leading works chosen are not meant to be exhaustive; they are simply illustrative and a means by which the contributors reflect upon the often unspoken question about how and why a sub-discipline has developed in the way that it has and the way in which it could develop in the future.

Titles in this series:

Leading Works in Public Law
Edited by Patrick O'Brien and Ben Yong

Leading Works in the History of the Constitution
Edited by Chris Monaghan

For more information about this series, please visit: https://www.routledge.com/Analysing-Leading-Works-in-Law/book-series/ALWIL

Leading Works in the History of the Constitution

Edited by Chris Monaghan

Routledge
Taylor & Francis Group
LONDON AND NEW YORK

First published 2026
by Routledge
4 Park Square, Milton Park, Abingdon, Oxon OX14 4RN

and by Routledge
605 Third Avenue, New York, NY 10158

Routledge is an imprint of the Taylor & Francis Group, an informa business

British Library Cataloguing-in-Publication Data
A catalogue record for this book is available from the British Library

Library of Congress Cataloging-in-Publication Data
Names: Monaghan, Christopher editor
Title: Leading works in the history of the constitution / edited by Chris Monaghan.
Description: Abingdon, Oxon [UK] ; New York, NY : Routledge, 2026. | Series: Analysing leading works in law | Includes bibliographical references and index.
Identifiers: LCCN 2025007528 (print) | LCCN 2025007529 (ebook) | ISBN 9781032658612 hardback | ISBN 9781032658711 paperback | ISBN 9781032658698 ebook
Subjects: LCSH: Constitutional history—Great Britain | Constitutional law—Great Britain
Classification: LCC KD3934 .L43 2026 (print) | LCC KD3934 (ebook) | DDC 342.4102/9—dc23/eng/20250307
LC record available at https://lccn.loc.gov/2025007528
LC ebook record available at https://lccn.loc.gov/2025007529

ISBN: 978-1-032-65861-2 (hbk)
ISBN: 978-1-032-65871-1 (pbk)
ISBN: 978-1-032-65869-8 (ebk)

DOI: 10.4324/9781032658698

Typeset in Galliard
by Apex CoVantage, LLC

Contents

Table of cases

Australia

Preface

An edited book is very much a collective endeavour, and there would have been no book without the willingness of the contributors to support the project and to write their chapters. I have been grateful to have worked with such a supportive and kind team of contributors who have made the planning and editing process such a positive experience. Thank you very much to the contributors: Glenn Burgess, Robert Craig, N.C. Fleming, Baroness Hale, Angus Harwood Brown, Mark Goldie, Colin Lee, Paul Raffield, Max Skjönsberg, Sylvana Tomaselli, Robert Thomas, Anne Twomey, Ian Ward, Elizabeth Wicks and Blair Worden.

For those who research the long eighteenth century, Professor Harry Dickinson is a name associated with scholarly excellence and a long-standing contribution to our understanding of Georgian Britain. Latterly the Emeritus Professor of British History at the University of Edinburgh, Professor Dickinson had authored a number of leading books, including *Walpole and the Whig Supremacy* (London, 1973), *Bolingbroke* (London, 1970), *Liberty and Property: Political Ideology in Eighteenth Century Britain* (London, 1977) and *The Politics of the People in Eighteenth-Century Britain* (London and New York, 1994 and 1995). He also edited a number of books, such as *A Companion to Eighteenth-Century Britain* (Oxford, 2002) and *Britain and the American Revolution* (London, 1998). Professor Dickinson had kindly agreed to contribute a chapter on Sir William Blackstone's *Commentaries on the Laws of England.* It was with sadness that Professor Dickinson passed away on 24 January 2024. In an obituary written by Alvin Jackson in *The Scotsman*, Jackson paid tribute to Harry Dickinson and described him as "ferociously able, energetic and hard-working and these qualities, when allied with a sharp intellectual vision and ambition, produced some formidably wide-ranging and important work." I am grateful to Professor Dickinson's colleague, Frances Dow, who informed me of Harry's passing and, along with Harry's family, were very supportive of including a contribution in this book on Blackstone's *Commentaries on the Laws of England* that would be written by another historian.

I am grateful to have worked with and have been supported throughout my academic career to date by some amazing individuals who have been generous with their time and constant with their encouragement. This support is appreciated and, in particular, I would like to acknowledge Robert Blackburn, Matthew Flinders and Sean Thomas. Thank you to Russell Sandberg, the series editor of *Analysing Leading Works in Law*, who has always given his full support and encouragement. I would like to thank Alison Kirk, Anna Gallagher and Heather Doquiatan at Routledge, Elamurugan Anbarasan and those colleagues who helped during the production of the book. As always, my colleagues at the University of Worcester have been encouraging and supportive. I am grateful to Robin Eagles, Josie Welsh and Michael Lane for casting their eyes over my own chapter. Finally, I would like to thank my wife Nicola and my family for their unceasing support.

Chris Monaghan
Worcester, January 2025

Contributors biographies

Glenn Burgess is a Professor of Early Modern History at the University of Hull. His research interests have mostly been in the history of Tudor and Stuart England, the history of political thought and philosophy and the theory of history. His major publications include *The Politics of the Ancient Constitution: An Introduction to English Political Thought 1603–1642* (1992); *Absolute Monarchy and the Stuart Constitution* (1996); *British Political Thought 1500–1660: The Politics of the Post-Reformation* (2009); and, as editor, *The New British History: Founding a Modern State 1603–1715* (1999); *English Radicalism, 1550–1850* (2007) and *European Political Thought 1450–1700* (2009).

Robert Craig is a Senior Lecturer in Law at the University of Bristol. His publications include "Casting Aside Clanking Medieval Chains: Prerogative, Statute and Article 50 after the EU Referendum," [2016] 79(6) MLR, 1041–1063, in the Modern Law Review which was cited by Lord Reed in Miller at paragraph [201]. A second article was cited with approval in the case of Privacy International, again by the Supreme Court. "Ouster clauses, separation of powers and the intention of parliament: from Anisminic to Privacy International" [2018] Public Law 570–584.

N.C. Fleming is Professor of Modern History, University of Worcester. He is the author or editor of eight books, including *Britannia's Zealots, Volume I: Tradition, Empire and the Forging of the Conservative Right* (2019) and *Aristocracy, Democracy and Dictatorship: The Political Papers of the Seventh Marquess of Londonderry* (2022). He was called to the Bar by the Inner Temple in 2002, and he is a fellow of the Royal Historical Society and an associate fellow of the Institute of Commonwealth Studies, University of London.

Mark Goldie is Emeritus Professor of Intellectual History at the University of Cambridge. He is an Honorary Professor at the University of Sussex. He was previously Vice-Master of Churchill College and departmental chair of the History Faculty. His publications include *Roger Morrice and* *the Puritan Whigs* (2016) and *Contesting the English Polity, 1660–1688: Religion, Politics, and Ideas* (2023). He has co-edited a number of books, including *The Cambridge History of Eighteenth-Century Political Thought* (2006) and *The Cambridge History of Political Thought, 1450–1700* (1991) and *The Politics of Religion in Restoration England* (1990).

Rt Hon the Baroness Hale of Richmond DBE retired as President of the Supreme Court of the United Kingdom in January 2020 after a varied career, first as an academic lawyer at the University of Manchester (also qualifying and practising for a while as a barrister in Manchester), then as the first woman member of the Law Commission and finally as a Judge. She has taken part in many notable cases, most famously the "prorogation case" in September 2019. In retirement, she has spent her time in good works, speaking and writing – her memoir, *Spider Woman, A Life*, was published in 2021.

Angus Harwood Brown is a Harper-Schmidt Fellow in the Society of Fellows in the Liberal Arts and a Collegiate Assistant Professor at the University of Chicago, where he teaches and researches the history of political and constitutional thought. He is currently working on a book on debates about constitutional guardianship in the late eighteenth century.

Colin Lee is Clerk of Legislation in the House of Commons and has served as Clerk in the House of Commons for more than 36 years. He was an Assistant Editor of the 25th Edition of *Erskine May's Treatise on The Law, Privileges, Proceedings and Usage of Parliament* (2019). He co-edited *The Papers of John Hatsell* (2020) and is the author of various articles and contributions to books on the historical development of parliamentary procedure and on financial procedure.

Chris Monaghan is a Principal Lecturer in Law at the University of Worcester. He is the author of *Accountability, Impeachment and the Constitution: The Case for a Modernised Process in the United Kingdom* (2022) and co-edited *British Origins and American Practice of Impeachment* (2024) and *Questions of Accountability: Prerogatives, Power and Politics* (2023). He is a Fellow of the Royal Historical Society and is currently co-editing a volume on the impeachment of Warren Hastings.

Paul Raffield is Professor Emeritus in the School of Law, University of Warwick. He is the author of *Shakespeare's Strangers and English Law* (2023), *The Art of Law in Shakespeare* (2017), *Shakespeare's Imaginary Constitution: Late Elizabethan Politics and the Theatre of Law* (2010) and *Images and Cultures of Law in Early Modern England: Justice and Political Power, 1558–1660* (2004). Paul co-founded the journal *Law and Humanities*, of which he is a consultant editor. He is an Honorary Research Fellow at Birkbeck Law School, University of London.

Max Skjönsberg is Assistant Professor of Humanities in the Hamilton School of Classical and Civic Education at the University of Florida, USA. He is the author of *The Persistence of Party: Ideas of Harmonious Discord in Eighteenth-Century Britain* (2021), the editor of Catharine Macaulay, *Political Writings* (2023) and the co-editor of *Adam Ferguson's Later Writings: New Letters and an Essay on the French Revolution* (2023).

Robert Thomas is a Professor of Public Law at the University of Manchester and works on administrative law and administrative justice. Key publications include *Administrative Justice and Asylum Appeals* (2011); *Administrative Law in Action* (2022); *Immigration Judicial Reviews* (2021, co-authored with Joe Tomlinson); *Public Law* (5th ed, 2024, co-authored with Mark Elliott); and *The Oxford Handbook of Administrative Justice* (2022, edited with J Tomlinson, R. Kirkham and M. Hertogh).

Sylvana Tomaselli is a Fellow of St John's College, Cambridge. She has contributed to numerous works on eighteenth and nineteenth-century political theory and intellectual history, including: "Peace, Genre, and War" in *A Cultural History of Peace in the Enlightenment* (1648 – 1815) Stella Ghervas & David Armitage (eds.) 2020; "A Vindication of the Rights of Men," in *The Wollstonecraftian Mind*, Sandrine Bergès, Eileen Hunt Botting and Alan Coffee (eds.) 2020; "The Philosophes," in *Mary Wollstonecraft in Context*, Nancy E. Johnson and Paul Keen (eds) 2020. Her *Wollstonecraft: Philosophy, Passion, and Politics* appeared in 2021. She joined the Advisory Board of the International Society for Intellectual History (ISIH) in 2024.

Anne Twomey is Professor Emerita at the University of Sydney, where she taught Constitutional Law and Public Law for decades. She has previously worked for the High Court of Australia, the Commonwealth Parliamentary Research Service, the Senate Legal and Constitutional Committee and The Cabinet Office of NSW. She continues to do consultancy work for governments, Parliaments and inter-governmental bodies and is a consultant to Gilbert + Tobin lawyers.

Ian Ward is Professor of Law at Newcastle University. His principal area of research expertise lies at the intersection of law, literature and history. His previous publications include *Writing the Victorian Constitution* (2018), *English Legal Histories* (2020), *Sex, Crime and Literature in Victorian England* (2014) and *The Trials of Charles I* (2022).

Elizabeth Wicks is Professor of Human Rights Law and Co-Director of the Centre for Rights and Equality in Health Law (CREHL) at the University of Leicester. Her research expertise focuses on issues of human rights in health care, medical law and constitutional history. She is the author of five monographs and dozens of book chapters and articles. Her books include *The Evolution of a Constitution: Eight Key Moments in British Constitutional*

History (2006), *The Right to Life and Conflicting Interests* (2010) and, most recently, *Suicide and the Law* (2023). She is currently part of an interdisciplinary working group on "Deliberate Dying," is co-editing a *Research Handbook on Human Rights Law and Health* and is planning a monograph on introversion and the law.

Blair Worden was a Fellow and Tutor in Modern History at St Edmund Hall from 1974–1995. He was made an Emeritus Fellow of the College in 2003. Blair Worden is an expert in the history of the English Civil War as well as on the wider early modern period. Blair Worden was elected a Fellow of the British Academy in 1997. His principal publications include *God's Instruments. Political Conduct in the England of Oliver Cromwell* (2012), *The English Civil Wars 1640–1660* (2009), *Literature and Politics in Cromwellian England: John Milton, Andrew Marvell, Marchamont Nedham* (2007), *The Sound of Virtue: Philip Sidney's 'Arcadia' and Elizabethan Politics* (1996) and *The Rump Parliament 1648–1653* (1974).

Introduction

The focus of *Leading Works in the History of the Constitution* begins with Magna Carta and ends with the Government of India Act 1858. It is intended to offer an analysis of leading constitutional works in the form of statute and the common law, as well as the works by contemporary commentators that sought to explain the historical development of the constitution. For the purposes of this book, within the *Analysing Leading Works in the Law* series, the works in question represent examples of the constitutionally most significant legislation, judicial decisions, and commentaries by scholars and key actors. Its scope is the 700 years of English (and then British) history that have flowed from the banks of the River Thames at Runnymede to Britain as an imperial power grappling with the question of how to govern India. The decision to stop at 1858 is twofold.[1] The first reason was the practicality of giving appropriate space to leading works from prior to the nineteenth century, a problem given the large number of texts, statutes, and common law decisions that could have been included within this book. The second reason was to avoid duplicating the contributions covering key constitutional texts by AV Dicey and Sir Ivor Jennings in Patrick O'Brien and Ben Yong's excellent volume *Leading Works in Public Law.*[2]

The focus in this book is on the development of the constitution from an English and then British perspective. Unfortunately, word count and circumstance meant that there would inevitably be omissions, such as the Declaration of Arbroath and the Act of Union with Ireland.

The British constitution is often contested, with scholars such as FF Ridley infamously arguing that there was no such thing. More recently, Lord Neuberger of Abbotsbury, the then President of the Supreme Court, questioned whether the United Kingdom truly possessed a

1 Although there is a chapter considering the comparative perspectives in the historical legacy of the English constitution which looks far beyond 1858.

2 (Routledge 2025).

DOI: 10.4324/9781032658698-1

Constitution.[3] His successor as President, Baroness Hale of Richmond, was of the view that:

> Allegedly, the United Kingdom is one of only four countries in world not to have a written Constitution – the others are said to be Israel, New Zealand and Isle of Man. This does not mean that we do not have a Constitution. Everyone does. The UK played large part in framing the modern Constitutions of much of the common law world. So it must have had some idea of what a Constitution is and what it should do.[4]

The idea is that Britain possesses an evolutionary constitution which has settled on fundamental principles such as Parliamentary Sovereignty as a result of the events of 1688 and the Bill of Rights 1689. Despite the importance of the Glorious Revolution in settling a century of constitutional conflict between the monarchy and Parliament, the constitution's origins extend further back to before the invasion of England by William, Duke of Normandy, in 1066. As Philip Norton observes:

> The constitution has taken shape over centuries, the basis of the constitution being confirmed in 1688. Prior to then, the form and acceptance of the constitution had evolved. One can see its origins in the coronation oath of the tenth century, which included the words 'that I forbid all rapine and injustice to men for all conditions.'[5]

In his highly influential monograph, *Our Republican Constitution*, Adam Tomkins begins his first chapter by stating that '[t]he British Constitution is a remarkable creation. It is no exaggeration to say that there is nothing quite like it anywhere else in the world.'[6] It fascinates and divides scholars, is often the first thing that undergraduates on a law degree learn about in their Public Law or Constitutional and Administrative Law modules, and begs the question of whether it is ripe for reform, outdated, or durable enough to weather future yet unknown constitutional crises.[7] How we understand the constitution and draw upon history is a moot point, with critics of the traditional English focus (in spite of the existence of a union between England and Scotland

3 Lord Neuberger, 'UK Supreme Court Decisions on Private and Commercial Law: The Role of Public Policy and Public Interest' (for Commercial Law Studies Conference 2015, 4 December 2015) <https://jcpc.uk/uploads/speech_151204_ac906d4392.pdf>

4 Lady Hale, 'The United Kingdom Constitution on the Move' (The Canadian Institute for Advanced Legal Studies' Cambridge Lecture, 7 July 2017).

5 Philip Norton, *Governing Britain: Parliament, Ministers and Our Ambiguous Constitution* (Manchester University Press 2020) 3.

6 Adam Tomkins, *Our Republican Constitution* (Hart Publishing 2005) 1.

7 Andrew Blick, *Stretching the Constitution: The Brexit Shock in Historic Constitution* (Hart Publishing 2019).

since 1707) questioning whether the Scottish contribution has been unduly neglected. Reflecting on the influence of AV Dicey on constitutional scholars, Iain McLean, in his monograph, *What's Wrong with the British Constitution?*, notes that 'they continue to take his theories as their starting point. One problem is that he seemed to know very little about Scotland.'[8] Hence, our understanding of the constitution is flawed. McLean sees the constitution as being incoherent because, in 1707, 'two constitutional traditions were awkwardly merged.'[9] This is problematic as it has meant a focus on English constitutional principles since 1707 rather than a restart with the creation of Great Britain. An example of this is Parliamentary Sovereignty, an English principle that is at odds with Scottish constitutional tradition and has been explicitly rejected by the Scottish Government in its proposed interim constitution for an Independent Scotland. In 2023's 'Building a New Scotland: Creating a modern constitution for an independent Scotland,' it states that

> The founding principle of the UK's constitutional arrangements is parliamentary sovereignty, where ultimate power and authority rests with the 'Crown-in-Parliament' at Westminster. Independence would allow Scotland to create a new, modern, codified constitution that replaces the doctrine of Westminster sovereignty with the Scottish constitutional tradition of popular sovereignty, where power and authority rest with the people of Scotland.[10]

This approach reiterated the Declaration of Arbroath of 6 April 1320.[11]

The aim of this book, written for academic lawyers, historians, and undergraduate and postgraduate students, is to offer a useful resource that seeks to support the understanding of the development of the constitution and the significance of how we write its history. Given the range and number of leading works that could have been included, *Leading Works in the History of the Constitution,* attempts to offer a cross-section of the most important. This,

8 Iain McLean, *What's Wrong with the British Constitution?* (Oxford University Press 2009).

9 ibid 5–6.

10 'Creating a Modern Constitution for an Independent Scotland' (Scottish Government, June 2023) <https://www.gov.scot/binaries/content/documents/govscot/publications/research-and-analysis/2023/06/building-new-scotland-creating-modern-constitution-independent-scotland/documents/creating-modern-constitution-independent-scotland/creating-modern-constitution-independent-scotland/govscot%3Adocument/creating-modern-constitution-independent-scotland.pdf> 12.

11 See the translation <https://www.nrscotland.gov.uk/learning-and-events/the-declaration-of-arbroath/transcription-of-the-declaration-of-arbroath/>. The key words are 'Yet if he [the King of Scots, Robert the Bruce] should give up what he has begun, seeking to make us or our kingdom subject to the King of England or the English, we should exert ourselves at once to drive him out as our enemy and a subverter of his own right and ours, and make some other man who was well able to defend us our King; for, as long as a hundred of us remain alive, never will we on any conditions be subjected to the lordship of the English.'

of course, is subjective, as it is difficult to include all those texts, legislation, or judicial decisions that scholars may regard as leading. In editing this book, I have aimed to ensure that there is a consistent coverage of the key events and turning points in constitutional history.

The book is intended to be read alongside established histories and new accounts of the constitution and to offer something different from the traditional commentary model that combined original sources and academic commentary by opting to focus not on an entire century or reign but on the leading works themselves, the author and the historical context.

For those with an academic interest in British constitutional history, a number of excellent books have been published in recent years, which includes Ann Lyon's *Constitutional History of the UK*,[12] which permits the constitution to be taught at the undergraduate level through a highly accessible textbook format; Peter Cane and H Kumarasingham's excellent and comprehensive two volume *The Cambridge Constitutional History of the United Kingdom*,[13] the highly accessible *The Evolution of a Constitution: Eight Key Moments in British Constitutional History*[14] by Elizabeth Wicks, John Allison's *The English Historical Constitution: Continuity, Change and European Effects*,[15] and Sir Stephen Sedley's *Lions under the Throne: Essays on the History of English Public Law*.[16] Also of importance to constitutional historians is Sir John Baker's excellent *The Reinvention of Magna Carta 1216–1616 (Cambridge Studies in English Legal History)*[17] There are also classic accounts such as SB Chrimes' *English Constitutional History*,[18] Henry Hallam's *Constitutional History of England*,[19] FW Maitlands' *The Constitutional History of England*,[20] Sir Thomas Erskine May's *Constitutional History of England*, and William Stubbs' *The Constitutional History of England*.

I am grateful to those colleagues who agreed to contribute and write chapters. The chapters represent a broad range of views, interpretations of the constitution and historical events, and outstanding analysis. *Leading Works in the History of the Constitution* brings together legal scholars and historians from around the globe, a parliamentary researcher and official, and the former President of the United Kingdom Supreme Court. It is hoped that the reader will find that each chapter adds something to the existing literature and a unique commentary on the leading work. The chapters are intended to stand alone in the sense that each author has adopted their own distinctive perspective,

12 (Second edition, Routledge 2016).
13 (Cambridge University Press 2023).
14 (Hart Publishing 2006).
15 (Cambridge University Press 2007).
16 (Cambridge University Press 2015).
17 (Cambridge University Press 2017).
18 (Opus Books 1967).
19 (Eight edition, John Murray 1867).
20 (Cambridge University Press 1919).

which thus permits them to take the reader through the historical context and explain why their chosen work has proven, after hundreds of years, to be regarded as a leading work. The chapters within the volume reflect the author's expertise and interest and offer the reader an insight into the politics and history of that period.

The chapters within the book begin with Robert Craig's chapter on Magna Carta. In Chapter 1, Craig recounts the historical context in which Magna Carta arose, the reasons for the baronial revolt against King John, and why Magna Carta is the soul of the constitution. He observes that

> [t]he document itself is, to this day, treated with deep reverence by public officials and the general public alike. It appears to have secured its place as the mystical emblem underpinning the freedoms of the people, and there is no sign of its status diminishing.

In Chapter 2, Paul Raffield looks at two works by Sir John Fortescue, who was the Chief Justice of the King's Bench during the reign of Henry VI. The works are *De Laudibus Legum Angliae* and *The Governance of England*. He explores the intellectual origins of Fortescue's belief in the common law as having sovereignty. Raffield is clear about the fundamental importance of Fortescue in advancing the idea that the law placed limits on the powers of the monarch. His influence was seen in the writings of Edward Coke in the decisions of the *Case of Proclamations* and *R (on the application of Miller) v The Prime Minister (No 2). As Raffield concludes,* ‛[t]he legacy of Fortescue's *De Laudibus Legum Angliae* and *The Governance of England* is long-lasting, influential, and ineradicable.

In Chapter 3, Glenn Burgess explores the significance of Sir Edward Coke's The Second Part of the Institutes of the Laws of England. It examines why Coke's work has proved so important, both at the time he wrote and in our understanding of the development of constitutional thought. The chapter looks at the cases that Coke gave judgments in and how his views on the prerogative developed. Ian Ward examines the importance of the Petition of Right in Chapter 4. Ward's chapter looks at the context behind the drafting of the Petition of Right and how it was a response to immediate concerns over the conduct and policies of King Charles I. He recounts the significance of *Darnel's Case* and the refusal of individuals to pay forced loans to the king, the unpopularity of this attempt to raise a form of taxation without parliamentary approval, and how this led to the drafting of the Petition. As Ward observes, Charles was obliged to agree to the Petition, as unless he did so, ‘there would be no money,’ which would equate to ‘five subsidies worth £300,000.’

In Chapter 5, Blair Worden explores the Instrument of Government of 1653 and is clear from the outset about its constitutional significance, as ‘[i]n modern terms the Instrument was the nation's first codified or written constitution and, with the Humble Petition, its only one.’ Worden's chapter looks at how historians have varied in their treatment of the Instrument of Government, with David Hume referring to it as a 'motley [text which was]. . . crude and undigested,' Henry Hallam's dismissal of the document as unworthy of consideration, and the far more positive assessment made by SR Gardiner. The chapter recounts the history and the wider political context that led to the drafting of the Instrument of Government. He notes that '[t]he classification of legislature and executive was a consequential innovation' and the similarities that this had with the United States Constitution,

> for the formula would reappear in the American Constitution, though not in any intervening constitution. There are other resemblances of principle and categorisation between the two documents: in the provisions (though they are never identical) for the exercise by the single ruler of a qualified veto and of the power of pardon; for the command of the army; for the appointment of office-holders; for the power to make war or peace.

However, Worden observes that '[t]he American framers knew nothing' of the Instrument of Government.

In Chapter 6, Mark Goldie explores the Toleration Act 1689 and the Confessional State. Goldie argues that the Toleration Act

> marked a caesura in the historical relationship between religion and civil society. Hitherto, the Church of England had perpetuated the medieval Catholic concept of the unity of the Christian faith and the duty of temporal rulers to enforce religious uniformity. Accordingly, England before 1689 was a persecuting society.

As Goldie argues, the Toleration Act did not apply to Catholics, and following the enactment of the Act, there was further legislative discrimination against Catholics, such as An Act for the Further Preventing the Growth of Popery 1700. Goldie notes that the Toleration Act was further limited in its scope, for example, as it 'extended only to worship and not to public office' and it 'did not exempt Quakers.' Goldie's chapter considers how further religious toleration and the removal of legislative discrimination occurred in the centuries that followed the Toleration Act. In Chapter 7, the significance of the Act of Settlement 1701 is examined by Chris Monaghan. In the chapter, he looks at the events that led to the enactment of the Act of Settlement 1701 and, in particular, the need to ensure the Hanoverian succession in England and the exclusion of the Catholic House of Stuart. The chapter considers the lasting legacy of the Act for Catholics living today in the United Kingdom (i.e., someone who is Catholic cannot become the monarch) and why the Act was so important as a landmark in securing judicial independence and security of tenure for senior judges.

Elizabeth Wicks explores the importance of the 1707 Union Between England and Scotland in Chapter 8. She *inter alia* argues that '[t]he significance of the Union has not always been fully appreciated' and the Acts were often seen as just regular Acts of Parliament. On the other hand, Wicks is critical of those who regard the Acts of Union 'as a Constitution in their own right' and therefore meaning that the new British Parliament was therefore 'born unfree.' Wicks is clear that the state, Great Britain, which was established by both the English and Scottish Acts of Union, was

> not a party to the 'Treaty of Union' [and while] . . . it may well be bound in constitutional terms by its constitutive documents, but in international law terms, it could not be bound by the terms of a treaty to which it was not a party. Nor could either the English nor Scottish Acts of Union have legal status within the new state.

The chapter notes that whilst the Union between England and Scotland was voluntary, England was the dominant party, and Scotland had a clear incentive to have the 'economic advantages in joining with its more prosperous southern neighbour.' Finally, Wicks considers the legacy of the Union in light of the movement for Scottish independence.

In Chapter 9, Max Skjönsberg offers an account of why Viscount Bolingbroke's *Remarks on the History of England* and *Dissertation upon Parties* is a leading working in constitutional history. Commenting on the significance of Bolingbroke's *Remarks on the History of England,* Skjönsberg contends that 'it is arguably unmatched in its sophisticated blending of the principles of the separation of powers and checks and balances in eighteenth-century constitutional thought, prior to the *Federalist Papers* in 1787–88.' He argues that in *Dissertation upon Parties,* Bolingbroke regarded the constitution as being one of mixed government that brought together the three estates ('democracy, aristocracy and monarchy'). In terms of Bolingbroke's view of the constitution, Skjönsberg observes that 'Bolingbroke contended that the constitution finally regained its balance during Elizabeth I's reign.'

Baroness Hale's chapter on the decision in *Entick Carrington*[21] explores the constitutional significance of Lord Camden's judgment. In Chapter 10, Baroness Hale takes the reader through why the decision is significant and provides a close analysis of Camden's judgment. She is clear, though, that 'it is hard to see the saga as a triumph for freedom of speech' but that the legacy is 'to alert, not only the British public, but also the people of the American colonies, to the importance of free speech among the liberties of the subject.' In terms of where the decision was significant, Baroness Hale observes that 'More plausibly, it was a triumph for freedom from improper search and seizure.'

In Chapter 11, the significance of William Blackstone's *Commentaries on the Laws of England* is explored by Max Skjönsberg. From the outset, he is

21 (1765) 19 St Tr 1029.

clear that whilst Blackstone is now 'synonymous with Whiggery,' in his lifetime, Blackstone 'contributed to the Toryism that dominated the University of Oxford.' Skjönsberg sees Blackstone's political career as 'mediocre' and argues that Blackstone's academic writing in his '*Commentaries* became a constitutional and legal encyclopaedia that different people used for various purposes.' As a lawyer, Skjönsberg notes that Blackstone, just like Sir Edward Coke, 'did not justify English law solely on the basis of history but also natural law.'

Angus Brown explores Jean-Louis de Lolme's book *The Constitution of England* in Chapter 12. This seminal text was written in 1775. Brown offers a detailed analysis of de Lolme's interpretation of the constitution. Brown is clear that his aim in writing the chapter is not to 'vindicate or disprove de Lolme's theory of the British Constitution as a historical account, but rather to offer it up as a clarifying alternative to our prevailing Parliamentarian mythology.' Brown discusses de Lolme's concerns, such as the declining role of the aristocracy, which in England had proved to be a force for good. As Brown notes,

> We live in the world which de Lolme feared. In the United Kingdom today, the representatives of the people do not share in the executive power, but dominate it entirely, leaving only a vestigial and largely 'ceremonial' monarchy in the place of the constitutional Kingship which de Lolme admired.

In Chapter 13, Sylvana Tomaselli looks at Mary Wollstonecraft on the Constitution. To Tomaselli, Mary Wollstonecraft, whilst not producing 'a leading work on constitutions,' crucially offered a critical and effective rebuttal to Edmund Burke's defence of the English constitution. As Tomaselli argues, 'she raised a simple but nonetheless crucial question about the legitimacy of this constitution in the first *Vindication*.' Tomaselli explains why Wollstonecraft was shocked by Burke's response to the French Revolution when he had been supportive of American independence and of the Federalists. In terms of a critique of Burke's writing, Tomaselli sees the response as being 'not concerned with being a fair reader of Burke's corpus of speeches, and criticising not just Burke, but also Dr Richard Price who was 'a highly esteemed leader of the Dissenting community.'

Edmund Burke's *Thoughts on the Cause of the Present Discontents* is the subject of Chapter 14. Max Skjönsberg regards this pamphlet as being 'the most notable among Edmund Burke's early political pamphlets.' He outlines the context in which *Thoughts on the Cause of the Present Discontents* was written and the influence of John Wilke's attempt to become the Member of Parliament for Middlesex. Burke, as a supporter of the Marquis of Rockingham, was critical of King George III and the system of a so-called 'double cabinet' that saw the King's friends discuss government policy and act as an alternative to the cabinet. Skjönsberg argues that 'Although Burke's attack on the "double cabinet" as a conspiracy against the constitution was naturally exaggerated, it represented a genuine attempt to grapple with the meaning of George III's accession, and Britain's uncodified constitution.'

The importance of caricature as a way of understanding the British constitution is explored in Chapter 15 by Chris Monaghan and Robert Thomas. They argue that caricatures created by James Gillray and his contemporaries help us to understand how big constitutional questions and political controversies were depicted at the time. The chapter covers themes such as King George's pivotal role in the fall of the coalition government between Lord North and Charles James Fox, the impeachment of Warren Hastings, the first governor-general of Bengal, and the regency crisis caused by King George III's illness. Drawing on academic literature, contemporary accounts, and an analysis of the caricatures, Monaghan and Thomas argue that not only do they serve as a way to understand how people may have understood the late eighteenth-century constitution, but they also highlight the role of state propaganda (i.e., government pensions for caricaturists), the demands of the consumer, and the incredible freedom enjoyed by caricaturists to poke fun at leading figures from the king downwards.

In Chapter 16, Colin Lee looks at Thomas Erskine May's *A Treatise Upon the Law, Privileges, Proceedings and Usage of Parliament.* In his chapter, Lee outlines the career of Erskine May and the history behind the creation of what would become the leading book on parliamentary procedure. He considers what happened after Erskine May's death in terms of how successive editors gradually felt confident to develop the book rather than just edit it. Lee is clear about the position impression that Erskine May's book had on his contemporaries such as William Gladstone. As Lee notes, '[t]he most enduring testament to the status of the *Treatise* was its continuation after his death.'

N.C. Fleming assesses the impact of the Government of India Act 1858 in Chapter 17. The Act was the British state's response to the Indian Mutiny or War of Independence and the perceived failures of the governance of India by the East India Company. Fleming argues that the Act 'has long been overshadowed' by Queen Victoria's proclamation that followed the Act. The Government of India Act 1858 brought to an end the governance of India by the East India Company and the notional rule of the Mughal emperor. To Fleming, it 'swept away all ambiguity about sovereignty; the British crown was now unequivocally the singular source of all constitutional and judicial authority, and the basis of British relations with the princely states.' The Act followed nearly a century of British legislation to regulate the governance of India through the East India Company, an early example being Lord North's Regulating Act of 1773, which created the position of governor-general (the first holder being Warren Hastings).

Finally, in Chapter 18, Anne Twomey considers the Comparative Perspectives on the Historical Legacy of the English Constitution. Twomey does this by looking at the influence in Australia and New Zealand of Magna Carta, Sir William Blackstone's *Commentaries on the Laws of England,* James Bryce's

The American Commonwealth and Thomas Erskine May's *Treatise on the Law, Privileges, Proceedings and Usage of Parliament*. She is clear that 'English constitutional history forms part of the constitutional history of many former British colonies across the globe' and '[k]nowledge of that history can give context to these provisions and enrich understanding of them, although it cannot dictate their meaning and operation today.'

1 Magna Carta

The soul of the British constitution

Robert Craig

1.1 Introduction

Magna Carta is 'rightly' regarded as the 'sacred text' of the British constitution.[1] It remains a tabula rasa on which successive generations project their evolving constitutional priorities. A hagiographical paean to easily the most famous document ever produced on these isles might appear to be a *sine qua non* of a collection on the leading works of the constitution. The document itself is, to this day, treated with deep reverence by public officials and the general public alike. It appears to have secured its place as the mystical emblem underpinning the freedoms of the people, and there is no sign of its status diminishing.

The celebrations to mark the 800-year anniversary of Magna Carta were on a considerable scale, with Her Majesty the Queen and the Prime Minister, David Cameron, attending a commemorative ceremony on 15 June 2015. A slew of speeches, articles and books by judges, commentators, academics and politicians were a testament to the enduring legacy of this legendary text. There was much hyperbole. The prime minister described Magna Carta as 'revolutionary, altering forever the balance of power between the governed and the government'.[2] In a speech a few days later, Lord Neuberger, the head of the Supreme Court, said that Magna Carta 'represents the United Kingdom's greatest contribution to the world – the rule of law and democratic government'.[3]

Stirring stuff. Magna Carta is commonly believed to be the foundational constitutional document of the United Kingdom. It is said by many lawyers to underpin the origins not only of the rule of law but also the separation of powers, jury trial, *habeas corpus*, access to justice, governance by consent

1 F Pollock and FW Maitland, *The History of English Law before the Time of Edward I*, vol I (Cambridge University Press 1989) 184.

2 <https://www.gov.uk/government/speeches/magna-carta-800th-anniversary-pms-speech>.

3 Lord Neuberger, 'Magna Carta – The Bible of the English Constitution or a Disgrace to the English Nation?' (Speech at Guildford Cathedral, 18 June 2015) <https://supremecourt.uk/speeches/lord-neuberger-at-guildford-cathedral> accessed 27 January 2025.

DOI: 10.4324/9781032658698-2

and parliamentary sovereignty. Some more historically minded commentators take a rather different view, including a famous article by Jenks describing the 'myth' of Magna Carta.[4] Many are highly sceptical, suggesting that it was a backwards-looking document, which did not mention the rule of law, parliament or the constitution at all, nor even jury trial and *habeas corpus*.[5] Instead, it was aimed at restoring some of the ancient privileges that had been lost over decades of legal reforms implemented by Henry II and exploited by Richard I and John. These included detailed rules governing, for example, escheats, scutages and seisin – all irrelevant and meaningless to modern eyes.

Magna Carta may even have provided cover for one of the foundational myths that helped to form the United States, which is that their rebellion was against being ruled by a hereditary King, rather than the reality, which was that the rebellion was against a relatively advanced representative parliament (by contemporary standards). One of the key demands of the rebels, which might be thought to be in some tension with the claim of rebellion against an unaccountable hereditary monarch, was 'no taxation without representation'. The latter phrase is frequently traced back to chapters 12 and 14 of Magna Carta, which stated that 'no scutage or aid' could be levied 'unless by common counsel of our kingdom' except where it was to pay ransom or to pay for the king's eldest daughter to get married. Quite a stretch, one might think, to bring such a clause to bear on the dispute between the Americas and Great Britain. Nonetheless, the refusal to grant rights of representation in parliament was an infamous source of friction that led to the conflict. So, it is not just the United Kingdom that has arguably rooted its foundational constitutional myths on contestable interpretations of Magna Carta.

1.1.1 Magna Carta in context

It seems almost churlish to rain heavily on the perennial Magna Carta parade, but it is undeniable that the modern perception of Magna Carta is starkly at odds with the contemporaneous view and the circumstances and context of its creation. This is to take nothing away from its importance as a symbolic representation of some central constitutional concepts. Nonetheless, the Whiggish projection of those ideas back onto Magna Carta is in many ways more interesting than if the original had actually mentioned any of the core constitutional principles that underpin modern theory. Butterfield himself, who is rightly credited with first challenging the 'over-simplification' of adopting a

4 Edward Jenks, 'The Myth of Magna Carta' (1904) Independent Review 260.

5 Lord Sumption, 'Magna Carta Then and Now: Address to the Friends of the British Library' (9 March 2015) <https://supremecourt.uk/speeches/lord-sumption-at-the-friends-of-the-british-library-agm> accessed 27 January 2025.

linear model of history, even uses debunking Magna Carta ('a feudal document in a feudal setting') as an early example of

> disillusioning us concerning something in the past which we had assumed to be too like something in the present.[6]

Magna Carta is sufficiently malleable that it functions as an excellent cypher for some of the core attributes of the constitution because both that document and the constitution itself are endlessly contested, flexibly interpreted and highly political. Magna Carta is an eternal metaphor for the political constitution of this country from which current fashionable constitutional precepts are shamelessly reverse-engineered.

It is not even clear if Magna Carta should be treated as a 'statute, treaty, private compact or declaration of rights', as it was sealed before the concept of parliamentary statutes was really established.[7] Indeed, charters were always *sui generis*. Magna Carta was sealed in mid-June 1215, although there is some dispute as to whether it was 15 or 19 June at Runnymede. Lord Sumption describes the counterparties, with some poetic licence, as a group of 'muscular conservative millionaires from the north of England', who had invited Prince Louis of France over to England after losing all patience with the rule of King John.[8] The King had recently returned from a disastrous attempt to recover lands in France in 2014, which had completely failed. Punitive taxation had preceded that expedition, and with that money lost, the prospect of further tithes loomed large in the minds of the barons who ruled their personal fiefdoms around the country. His popularity plummeted as a result, and he added the nickname 'John Softsword' to his previous nickname of 'John Lackland', both acquired in comparison with his brother Richard Lionheart, held in considerably greater esteem to this day.

It was John and Richard's father, King Henry II, who had laid the groundwork for the far more centralised and controlling state they inherited in the late 12th and early 13th centuries. Henry II was an administrative genius who was hyperactive with it. The 'reforms ordained by the king' during his rule mean that his reign has been described as 'of supreme importance in the history of our law'.[9] Lord Neuberger rightly credits Henry II with the founding of the common law, although it might be more accurate to describe it as 'Royal Law' because it was the 'the agency of courts whose jurisdiction extended over the whole kingdom' that 'made the King's law "common"' in

6 H Butterfield, *The Whig Interpretation of History* (Norton & Co 1965) 14, 10.
7 CH McIlwain, *The High Court of Parliament and Its Supremacy* (Oxford University Press 1910) 54.
8 Sumption (n 5) 18.
9 Pollock and Maitland (n 1) 145.

the first place.[10] Henry II's judges were responsible for 'the growth of a body of common law, uniform through the length and breadth of England'.[11] Henry II was certainly responsible for a considerable reduction in the revenue of the barons through his startling success in persuading the polity that all serious criminal offences were automatically to be treated as being against his peace, personally, and therefore such proceedings, and crucially the revenue accruing, should be brought in his courts and not to the local baronial courts that characterised the previous legal regime.

Henry II also successfully instituted sweeping reforms in civil law, not least by introducing circuit judges whose job it was to administer the realm and execute the royal will. It seems strange to modern eyes to think of judges beginning as administrators, but it is important to recall that matters of state look considerably more fluid from a modern perspective. Some fluidity can be positive. Even today, senior members of the executive are drawn from within parliament, and tribunals operate in a grey area between administrative awards of public funds and the determination of legal rights and entitlements. Henry II developed the system of writs that framed and shaped the common law for many centuries, but his real genius was that he 'threw open the doors of his royal Courts of Law . . . and provided – always in return for hard cash, be it said – a better article in name of justice than could be procured elsewhere in England'.[12] This resulted in the hegemony of royal law across the country, although it took many decades and multiple reigns to be successful and for the royal judges to institute and embed universal common law across the realm.

It was the legacy of the great reforms set in train by Henry II that were inherited by his two sons: Richard and John. The reactionary barons were still resisting some of the changes, and detailed consideration of Magna Carta quickly reveals how some reforms were deemed irreversible, whereas John's poor decisions that resulted in the humiliation of Runnymede emboldened the negotiators to attempt to reverse others, however temporarily. Indeed, Magna Carta constituted something of a 'last stand' by the barons in a number of areas, and this 'has left its traces in several chapters of Magna Carta'.[13] Far from being a forward-looking statement of constitutional principles and individual rights, large parts of Magna Carta were deeply reactionary in attempting to *reverse* centralising reforms of the court system painstakingly introduced in previous decades. On the other hand, as we have seen, Henry II had been 'completely successful' in establishing that 'heinous crimes were . . . admitted on all hands to be . . . reserved exclusively for royal jurisdiction'.[14] Far from being the starting point of our constitutional history, Magna Carta was part of

10 McIlwain (n 7) 43.
11 William McKechnie, *Magna Carta* (James Maclehose and Sons 1914) 12.
12 Ibid.
13 Ibid 87.
14 Ibid 89.

an ongoing and disputed legal discourse that was vigorously contested before and afterwards. The royal courts were victorious in the end, however.

The charter sealed in 1215 was not even called Magna Carta at the time, only becoming so known by contrast with the charters of the Forest that were distinct from the later issuances of Magna Carta. Nor was Magna Carta the first such charter. Henry II had issued charters as well – indeed, Stephen Langton, the Archbishop of Canterbury, has been credited with drawing the attention of the barons, at a surreptitious meeting, of a previous set of claims which could usefully be used as a basis for drafting the demands that led to the 1215 Charter.[15] Nor were many of the provisions that novel, indeed, '[o]n the whole, the charter contains little that is absolutely new. It is restorative'.[16] There were some surprising innovations, but many provisions were simply lifted from previous proclamations and charters.

1.1.2 The disastrous final years of John's reign

The negotiations to settle the terms of Magna Carta were deeply humiliating and infuriating for John.[17] He had granted a charter to the City of London in an attempt to keep them onside, but this had not prevented the gates being opened to Prince Louis and the rebels, which put him in an impossible position.[18] While it is true that the barons were cautious in some areas in their demands, there are provisions in Magna Carta which were genuinely startling in their import. Chapter 61 is one such. It lays down that in the event of a breach of the terms of the charter, 25 nominated barons would have the right to distrain the King to secure a remedy.

This provision was unique to Magna Carta, never appearing in any other charter, and is sometimes erroneously taken to be evidence of a nascent parliamentary body. Instead, it was simply a codification of an accepted feudal right, in the event of a serious dispute, for a formal renunciation of the oaths of allegiance. This has little or nothing to do with the actual origins of the Houses of Parliament, which began as extensions of the King's Curia ('Council') that expanded and grew significantly over the centuries. The idea of the 25 barons sitting in judgment on the King was ridiculed on the continent and significantly damaged the reputation and standing of the English monarchy.

Nonetheless, John agreed to the terms of the charter agreed in June 1215. He had resolved a bitter dispute with Archbishop Langton earlier in the decade but had been forced to swear allegiance to the Pope as part of the settlement of that conflict, which had resulted in him being temporarily excommunicated. This gave John an easy way to challenge the terms of the charter that

15 McKechnie (n 11), 33.
16 Pollock and Maitland (n 1) 183.
17 Ibid 33.
18 Ibid 35.

he had so solemnly sworn to uphold. He appealed to the Pope to annul the charter, which Innocent III duly did within a matter of six weeks, throwing in some choice words about how inappropriate it was for the barons to have challenged the monarch in the way they had at Runnymede.[19] That might have been the end of the story as far as Magna Carta 1215 was concerned, but for the fact that the repudiation sparked an immediate and furious reaction from the barons, who took up arms immediately, precipitating an invasion by the French into the bargain.

The death of John in 1216 left the country in a precarious position. His son, Henry III, was hastily crowned at Gloucester. The legendary Sir William Marshal was appointed Regent and promptly issued a fresh charter in the King's name known as Magna Carta 1216.[20] Marshal then rallied the troops against the French invasion, eventually buying off Prince Louis for an enormous 10,000 marks, a sizeable chunk of annual regal income. This was followed by a fresh charter being issued in 1217.[21] McKechnie suggests that the new charters 'incidentally rather than deliberately' left out 'such constitutional machinery as had found a place in John's Great Charter'. Finally, a much-shortened charter was issued in 1225, when the young King reached majority, and it was the latter that became the default version of Magna Carta in the ensuing centuries. So much for the foundational constitutional document of the United Kingdom.

1.2 Constitutional principles

The role of Magna Carta as a blank slate on which successive generations inscribe their core values has a long and storied history.

> There is scarcely one great principle of the English constitution of the present day . . . which has not been read by commentators into the provisions of Magna Carta.[22]

The commentators in 2015 did not disappoint in their own projections of current values onto the mythical canvas represented by the ancient charter. Lady Hale purported to locate the origins of representative government in Magna Carta based on the 'no taxation without representation' fallacy, for example. Even the generally highly sceptical Lord Sumption argued that Magna Carta was a significant milestone in the development of the rule of law by contrast with monarchical rule.[23] Lord Neuberger is noticeably cautious

19 Ibid 45–46.
20 Ibid 139–44.
21 Ibid 145.
22 Ibid 156.
23 Lady Hale, 'Magna Carta: Our Shared Heritage' (Historical Society Annual Lecture 2015) <https://supremecourt.uk/speeches/lady-hale-gives-the-supreme-court-historical-society-annual-lecture-2015-washington-dc> accessed 27 January 2025. Sumption (n 5).

but still claimed to detect the 'green shoots . . . on which modern, civilised society rests', citing specifically 'democratic government' and 'the rule of law', amongst other core modern ideals.[24] The temptation to project is indeed a powerful one and appears to remain undimmed.

1.2.1 Parliamentary sovereignty

The claim that Magna Carta can be understood as foundational to parliamentary sovereignty, representative government or government by consent can be swiftly addressed. Parliament in the modern sense can be traced back only so far as the Glorious Revolution and the transfer of the supreme constitutional authority of the country from the monarch to the Crown-in-Parliament that occurred in the late 17th century. Pragmatically, historically and politically, it was those events that underpin the doctrine of parliamentary sovereignty.

True it is that the struggles in previous centuries provide the essential backdrop to that momentous change, but a revolution it most certainly was, and there is a high risk of colouring our perception of 800 years ago through the lens of what happened constitutionally only 350 years ago. Indeed, even that lens is distortive. As Butterfield pointed out, the 'controversialists of the 17th century who made a too direct reference of Magna Carta to their own day' ended up 'arguing in a circle' and, worse, 'making their history confirm some of their misconceptions concerning their own present'. We risk doing the same.

One famous allegedly parliamentary provision in Magna Carta was chapter 61, mentioned earlier and described as a 'wild scheme' by McKechnie.[25] In addition, chapters 12 and 14 are frequently cited as grounding the alleged first flowering of accountability of the monarch to parliament. These latter provisions purport to lay down limits on the power of the king to levy a scutage or aid other than for highly particular purposes. They further appear to require the summoning of the barons and others before such impositions could be imposed. Neither of these provisions survived into the 1216 edition, never mind the 1225 version of Magna Carta. They are, therefore, thin ice on which to build a claim to originating the notion of sovereignty of parliament. That has not stopped heroic attempts to rely on these provisions to reverse engineer the green shoots of a notion of sovereignty rooted in taxation and representation.

McIlwain is clear that 'not its true interpretation, but the glosses made on it by after generations that have given Magna Charta its place'.[26] Well, quite. On no sensible view of the history of the constitution can it be said that parliamentary sovereignty had its roots in 1215. Its earliest beginnings could, at

24 Lord Neuberger, 'Magna Carta and the Holy Grail' (Speech at Lincoln's Inn, 12 May 2015), [29] <https://supremecourt.uk/uploads/speech_150512_c7b57cef4d.pdf> accessed 27 January 2025.

25 McKechnie (n 11) 163.

26 McIlwain (n 7) 56.

a stretch, be located in the reign of Edward I in the late 13th century, but the real work was done by brave souls, including John Cooke, chief prosecutor of Charles I, who paid for the privilege by being executed in the most horrific way some decades later.[27] It is human nature to look for patterns and pleasing narratives, but attempting to root parliamentary sovereignty in Magna Carta might be thought to underplay the magnitude of the 17th-century ructions and the courage of those heroes who laid the foundations of the modern constitutional settlement at sometimes immense personal cost.

1.2.2 Separation of powers

The doctrine of the separation of powers is also of recent vintage, at least in terms of Magna Carta. Montesquieu traced the origins of the classical three branches back to the constitutional structure of the United Kingdom, somewhat ironically given that the pure vision he lays out fails to match the UK in multiple ways.[28] In particular, Bagehot's 'efficient secret' remains the 'near complete fusion of executive and legislative powers' as ministers are drawn from parliament but wield ultimate executive authority as well.[29] There are many functional overlaps as well, with ministers passing secondary legislation and tribunals operating in a grey area between executive and judicial decision-making.

Adam Tomkins offers a radically different view, claiming that a more accurate historical account of the separation of power, not powers, would reflect a binary division between the Crown and Parliament, with the courts historically rooted in the Crown.[30] Tomkins himself traces the narrative of that separation back to Magna Carta, pointing out that at 'the time of Magna Carta, there was no Parliament', but claiming that the charter 'long remained the most important constitutional document' eventually grounding the claim that the 'Crown ruled, but Parliament held the purse strings'.[31] It is true that in the ensuing centuries, these ideas took hold but, as Tomkins himself acknowledges, the idea that there was a Parliament at all, never mind that it controlled the purse strings, or the King, in 1215 requires the by now familiar poetic legal licence to be accepted. The problem with Tomkins' characterisation of the separation of power is that, arguably since the Act of Settlement 1701, and certainly since the Judicature Acts 1873–5, the jurisdictional authority of the courts is rooted

27 A genuine legal hero whose story is memorably and beautifully told by Geoffrey Robertson, *The Tyrannicide Brief: The Story of the Man Who Sent Charles I to the Scaffold* (Pantheon 2005).

28 Montesquieu, *The Spirit of the Laws* (first published 1748, A Cohler, B Miller and H Stone eds, Cambridge University Press 1989).

29 Walter Bagehot, *The English Constitution* (first published 1867, P Smith ed, Cambridge University Press 2001) 8–9.

30 Adam Tomkins, *Public Law* (Oxford University Press 2003) 46.

31 Ibid 41.

in statute, not the Crown. On no sensible view can any version of the modern separation of power doctrine be traced back to Magna Carta.

Lady Justice Arden (later promoted to the Supreme Court) is convinced that despite the general view that the concept of separation of powers is of comparatively recent vintage, Magna Carta can, in fact, be shown to illustrate an early flowering of the notion that the courts should be separate from the King. In a speech shortly before the 800-year anniversary, she claimed that the requirement in Clause 17 that the court of Common Pleas should be held 'in a fixed place' is important because it 'laid the foundation for the doctrine of the separation of powers'.[32] This was achieved because 'the separation of the judges from the King's court made clear that judges were to operate independently of the King'.[33]

Lady Arden also claims that Clause 45, which mandated that judges needed to 'know the law of the realm and mean to observe it', meant 'requiring judges to apply . . . the law of the realm as opposed to the law of the king' which she claims was 'the law of the people or, as it was and is called: the common law'.[34] This is a paradigm example of the common tendency, painstakingly detailed by McKechnie and others, of reading Magna Carta through a modern lens. As we saw earlier, confirmed by Lord Neuberger, John's father, King Henry II, is credited with founding the common law. It was 'common law' because it was imposed across the country by the king's judges in a uniform way, supplanting the bewildering variety of local and baronial laws that peppered the counties across the realm. Common law was *royal* law. It remained so for centuries until the courts became creatures of statute by virtue of the Judicature Acts 1873–5.

Far from illustrating the separation of powers, Magna Carta illustrated a major *concession* by the barons that the royal takeover of the justice system and the installation of a new legal system was irreversible. Their submission to these extraordinary changes, which significantly reduced their revenue and power, was such that Magna Carta actually *recognised* the permanence of the new system by asking for the Common Pleas court to be settled in one place for ease of access and so that claims could be brought to it more easily. McKechnie expresses some astonishment at how pliant the barons were, saying that it 'is a cause for wonder . . . that their demands were not more sweeping . . . in their hour of triumph' – instead, they 'accepted cordially one half of the royal innovations'.[35]

32 Lady Justice Arden, 'Magna Carta and the Judges – Realising the Vision' (Speech at Royal Holloway, June 2011, 5) <https://intranet.royalholloway.ac.uk/aboutus/documents/pdf/magnacarta/magnacarta8711.pdf> accessed 27 January 2025.

33 Ibid.

34 Ibid 5–6.

35 McKechnie (n 11) 91.

Nor is it sustainable to claim that the evolution of the court of Common Pleas indicated a separation of the judges from the king. Nothing could be further from the reality at the time. The courts were the king's courts, and the judges were the king's judges. Not only was this manifestly the case in the 13th century, but it also remained the case for many centuries afterwards. All modern lawyers are familiar with the *Case of Proclamations* and *Case of Prohibitions* in the 17th century.[36] It is alleged in these two cases that Coke sought to lay down a fundamental separation between the monarch and the courts even though he did not publish brief but explosive reports of his decisions until many decades later. Less well-known is just how radical Coke's position was even in the 17th century, never mind the 13th century.

A far more accurate 17th-century perspective is available by considering the epic *Ship Money* case, which is hundreds of pages long and decided by all 12 judges at the time sitting together.[37] Only two of those judges overtly found against the King, with three others hiding behind a technicality. Fully seven of the judges found for the King, some of them in the most trenchant terms, making clear that they were the King's judges applying the King's law. Lord Berkley said, famously, that 'I never heard that Lex was Rex, but it is common and most true that Rex is Lex'.[38] Lord Jones held that 'we are judges deputed, but our judgment flows from him . . . he is the fountain of justice'.[39] This is radically inconsistent with a claim that the separation of the judiciary from the monarch began with Magna Carta.

1.2.3 The rule of law

The separation of powers, in much of constitutional theory, is commonly linked to the concept of the rule of law as part of a broader notion of constitutionalism. It is one of the ironies of Magna Carta that it is almost universally touted as a paradigm early example of the imposition of the rule of law on the monarch. This is despite the fact that the rule of law is a relatively recent concept, particularly in the modern sense and it is surprisingly difficult to locate intelligible references to it before Dicey's famous exposition in the late 19th century.[40] The unstated assumption that appears to underlie these claims is the notion that the monarch at the time of Magna Carta operated entirely without restraint, without any reference to legal claims. Lord Sumption is quick to

36 *Case of Prohibitions* (1607) 12 Co Rep 63; 77 ER 1342, *Case of Proclamations* (1611) 12 Co, Rep. 74; 77 ER 1352.

37 *R v Hampden (Ship Money)* (1637) State Trials 825.

38 Ibid 1098.

39 Ibid 1181.

40 AV Dicey, *An Introduction to the Study of the Law of the Constitution* (8th edn, Macmillan 1927).

squash this view, pointing out that the 13th century operated in an 'intensely law-minded age'.[41]

Bracton is commonly cited as holding that the King was always subject to the law because the law makes the king.[42] This is also highly contested. Kantorowicz argues persuasively that to the extent that the king was 'below' the law, he was equally 'above' the law.[43] This was because the law that applied to the king was God's law, not positive law. The king was thus bound but not in any temporal court or any temporal law. Nevertheless, the king was expected to abide by the norms and precepts of the society. John's political failures in relation to the Church and his abortive excursion across the Channel led to his demands for ever more revenue, but those claims by the king on his subjects were highly formalised and rooted in long legal history. Even the processes by which such claims could be contested were governed by strict forms, culminating in a formal defiance of the authority of the king which then had to be negotiated and the consequences and pardons agreed.

The claim that Magna Carta, therefore, illustrated the very *beginnings* of the notion of the rule of law is not tenable. The core problem with the idea that common law was above the king has already been canvassed, which is that the king was the source of common law in the first place. It remained an insuperable difficulty that in disputes between the king and the barons, the king was the final arbiter. This meant that he was judge in his own cause, a breach of natural justice that does indeed persist as unacceptable to this day. Nor was there any succour to be found in the fact that John had resolved his differences with the Pope by formally declaring his allegiance to the Pope as his superior. As we saw earlier, both sides appealed to the Pope once Magna Carta was signed, but to no avail from the point of view of the barons.

The Pope's decision to annul Magna Carta forms a counterpoint to the almost universal claim that the document was a constitutional high point because it was a check on the unlimited power of the king and further that, as a legal document, the alleged check can be read as an early example of the rule of law precisely because that check was done in legal form. But this is just the start of the problems with the claim that Magna Carta represented a tussle between the rule of law and the monarch. As we have seen, the *monarch* was responsible for the generation of a common set of uniform rules across the country, replacing the myriad of local, disparate and baronial courts that littered the country. Every freeholder of land had their own court, and the fiefdoms were somewhat variable in their allegiance and loyalty to the centre. McKechnie claims that the attempt to revive the writ of *praecipe*, laid down in Clause 34, was a last desperate attempt by the barons to restore some of the rights lost by their courts. It failed. Not only was it unsuccessful, but

41 Sumption (n 5) 5.
42 Ernst Kantorowicz, *The King's Two Bodies* (Princeton University Press 1957) 156.
43 Ibid 158.

as McKechnie and Jenks make clear, circumventing its terms – or rather the future editions of Magna Carta that perpetuated its terms – complicated the law for many years afterwards.[44]

The claim that in truth Magna Carta represented a strike *against* the advent of a uniform common law across the country may appear startling, not least because of the extent to which it cuts against the dominant narrative that has held sway for so long. Nonetheless, Magna Carta was reactionary, not progressive, representing an attempt to reverse the reforms of King Henry II and his sons and restore baronial, local, dispersed judicial power. The astonishing social, economic, cultural and constitutional benefits that accrued to the country by virtue of having a reasonably stable, settled set of generally agreed rules on contract, land, tort and the rest could not have happened without the visionary work of Henry II – even if John did his level best to ruin the progress through his disastrous rein. Unpleasant though it was for the barons to lose a significant proportion of their income by losing their courts, it was a significant boon at the national level. Magna Carta was but a stage in that political and constitutional discourse between the rulers and the ruled, but had the barons achieved through Magna Carta what they aimed to achieve, the rule of law – such that it was at that time – would have been significantly *weakened*.

1.3 Chapter 39, jury trial and habeas corpus

It might be thought somewhat puzzling to claim that Magna Carta cut *against* the rule of law in many ways, not least because of the most famous clause included in the charter, which is said to remain in force to this day. It is worth setting it out in full.

> Nullus liber homo capiatur, vel imprisonetur, aut disseisiatur, aut utlagetur, aut exuletur, aut aliquo modo destruatur, nec super eum ibimus, nec super eum mittemus, nisi per legale judicium parium suorum vel per legem terrae.
>
> No freeman shall be taken or imprisoned or disseised or exiled or in any way destroyed nor will be go upon him nor send upon him except by the lawful judgment of his peers or by the law of the land.

McKechnie sets out Sir Edward Coke's famous claims that this clause underpins 'a guarantee of trial by jury' as well as also 'prohibiting arbitrary commitment', which was taken to mean *habeas corpus*.[45] Both claims are excellent examples of the tendency to project whatever was the dominant legal view onto the *tabula rasa* that is Magna Carta. As Pollock and Maitland point out,

44 McKechnie (n 11) 351. Jenks (n 4) 270.

45 McKechnie (n 11) 376. Paul D Halliday, *Habeas Corpus: From England to Empire* (Harvard University Press 2010) 15.

it was only possible to 'worship the words' in chapter 39 precisely 'because it was possible to misunderstand them'.[46]

Jury trials did not even begin for many decades after Magna Carta, and arguably well into the next century. Even then, it was radically different from its modern conception. Pollock and Maitland somewhat ruefully point out that 'it is now generally admitted that the phrase *iudicium parium* does not point to trial by jury'. *Habeas corpus* is even less relevant. Halliday flatly denies a direct link, arguing that 'we must drop our expectation that there is a long story to tell' instead claiming that '*habeas corpus* was made into a powerful writ by judges responding to the volatile mix . . . before and after 1605'.[47] He lays out in detail the actual history of *habeas corpus*, which effectively began in the 17th century as the judges developed the writ to control other public bodies and force them to account for their actions.[48]

Many of these bodies were regional and local, with little connection to the central government and monarch, so the writ is another example of the mythical assumption that powerful developments in the protection of individuals must necessarily be grounded in some kind of rebellion, resistance or counter to royal power. In fact, *habeas corpus* was the royal courts seeking to control and moderate the actions of public bodies who had strayed outside their boundaries, and successful applications were to the credit, not detriment, of centralised royal control. As it happened, this centralisation and normalisation of legal accountability by the king's courts were *despite* Magna Carta and its legacy, which, it will be recalled, sought to roll back the reforms whereby the royal courts had accrued significant power and control on behalf of the king. As Halliday states, based on Hale, as the centuries went by, it was accepted by all parties that 'all jurisdictions – even church courts – derived from the crown'.[49]

Nonetheless, the wording of Chapter 39 has a very modern resonance, particularly in the notion that consequences for a 'liber homo' should be restricted to where there has been a judgment of peers or the law of the land. Coke was much taken with this language, describing the clause as constitutional 'dust, threads, or shreds of Gold'.[50] Coke, however, was possibly the most guilty of all in terms of the projection of his own views onto the Magna Carta canvas. Lord Sumption is scathing about Coke's treatment of the terms of Magna Carta as if they were to be understood through the legal lens of his own time centuries later.[51] Jenks is scarcely less so, writing in 1915 about Coke's 'powerful if somewhat unscrupulous intellect', which meant that even contemporaries

46 Pollock and Maitland (n 1) 184, footnote 124.

47 Halliday (n 45), 18.

48 Ibid 80–82.

49 Ibid 78.

50 Sir Edward Coke, *The Second Part of the Institutes of the Laws of England.*

51 Sumption (n 5) 14–15.

knew he was 'mingling his politics with his historical research'.[52] Jenks himself directly accuses Coke of imposing his 'ingenious but unsound historical doctrines and claims that 'zeal for historical truth is apt to pale before the fiercer flame of zeal for political victory'.[53]

It is easy to be beguiled by the bewitching, enchanting, even magical words of chapter 39 as they float towards us over countless centuries. Who could fail to be moved by the apparent commonality between us and nameless 'free men' who sought to defend themselves from being imprisoned or attacked by an arbitrary monarch without due process of law or the protection of numbers inherent in the right to appeal to your own? The superficial meaning of the words clearly affected Coke, as we have seen already. We might even forgive the fact that the agreement was in large part between the king and the barons (although there was a general saving clause later in the document that could be read more widely) precisely because these kinds of concessions can be extended over time.

The problem, as ever with Magna Carta, is that the *prima facie* meaning – however evocative, moving and fascinating – begins to crumble when put into its contemporaneous context. The first few words, 'nullus liber homo' ('no free man'), calls to mind the battle for freedom over many centuries that makes instinctive sense in the modern era. Unfortunately, 'liber homo' had a distinct meaning which was a freeholder of land or, as Powicke put it, 'to speak more accurately, the free tenant'.[54] This is rather less glamourous and, in stark contrast to its superficial meaning to modern eyes, refers to a tiny subclass of the population that were freeholders who held their land as tenants from the king or a superior lord.[55] These were powerful, autocratic and usually rich despots within their own domains. Later versions spoke of 'liber tenementum', rather than 'liber homo', removing all the potential romance in the meaning. Be that as it may, the genius of Magna Carta is, and remains, its fluidity and ambiguity such that it can – and has – been read to mean something quite different by later generations.

Nisi per legale judicium parium suorum vel per legem terre.[56]

Much controversy surrounds most of the final line, but particularly, the use of the word 'vel' ('or') instead of 'et' ('and'). This creates a dilemma for modern eyes. If a defendant could only be subjected to any of the serious consequences listed in chapter 39 'by lawful judgment of his peers' how can that

52 Jenks (n 4) 272.
53 Ibid 272–73.
54 F Powicke, 'Per iudicium parium vel per legem terrae' in *Magna Carta Commemoration Essays* (Royal Historical Society 1917) 109.
55 Jenks (n 4) 269.
56 'Except by the lawful judgment of his peers or by the law of the land'.

be an *alternative* to the 'law of the land'? McKechnie, as well as Pollock and Maitland, claimed that 'vel' must be read as something akin to 'and/or'.[57] McKechnie cites the use of 'aut' (which also translates as 'or') elsewhere in the same clause and in the charter as a whole, which is a stronger indication of an intention to indicate alternative options.[58]

For McKechnie, the use of vel not aut proves that a more equivocal conjunctive preposition was, in fact, intended in the particular context of judgment by peers. He bases his argument on the fact that the 'law of the land' (lex terrae) did not mean 'law of the land' as we would understand it today. On the contrary, the narrow technical contemporary meaning of lex is 'test'. So, people were 'put' to their 'law' by their innocence or guilt being tested as part of the proceedings. These ceremonies were run by a priest because God would step in to vindicate or condemn the defendant – 'a miracle, if necessary, would attest the just claim of the innocent'.[59] The 'test' took place after the judgment, or 'doom', had been handed down.[60] So law came *after* the judgment. This is deeply counterintuitive from any modern perspective.

There were three types of test at the time: ordeal, compurgation, or battle – the latter being introduced by the Normans and William the Conqueror. Trial by compurgation was a highly formalised ritual involving 'witnesses' (not in the modern sense) where one slip or word out of place was fatal, sometimes literally. Trial by ordeal consisted of either trial by fire, where the defendant had to walk a certain distance with a hot iron burning their arms, or the even more dreaded trial by water, involving the retrieval of a stone from boiling water. The healing (or not) of the skin after the test was indicative of divine intervention and determinative of guilt. These tests were 'except in the case of battle, entirely one-sided'.[61] It was also, obviously, completely corrupt if the subject 'had arranged matters properly with the priest who presided'.[62]

McKechnie's clever point about the use of vel was that the doom or judgment was inevitably connected to the test which came after it. Therefore, it made little sense to say that it was one *or* the other when it was one *and* the other. Elsewhere, however, McKechnie acknowledged some difficulties with treating vel as conjunctive rather than disjunctive. One issue was that the particular circumstances of Magna Carta had been preceded by the king physically going against the barons personally, with his military in tow. This caused consternation, and it was only the urgings of the Archbishop, Stephen Langton, that he should follow due process that calmed the King down. Chapter 39 was, therefore, a direct response to the King's behaviour and constituted a

57 McKechnie (n 11) 381. Pollock and Maitland (n 1) 184 footnote 124.
58 Ibid.
59 Ibid 85.
60 Ibid 84.
61 Ibid 85.
62 Ibid.

promise that he would not simply attack a recalcitrant baron without at least holding a curia first. Since barons could then demonstrate their innocence even after a judgment by insisting on trial by battle ('lex terrae'), chapter 39 provided a real remedy against King John directly.

Indeed, the words 'in mea curia' ('in my court') had been dropped from an earlier draft when 'liber homo' had been substituted for 'barones' at the start of the clause. It would make no sense to say that all freeholders could have their curia in front of the king personally when many of them were beholden to their particular baron – so they were lower down the pecking order. One way to think of a genuine 'curia' in front of the king is as a precursor to Acts of Attainder, for barons at least. So a 'judicium parium' could be issued that rendered a baron an outlaw ('utlagetur'), which is frequently translated as 'disseised' but was particularly feared because it allowed anyone to kill the outlaw for a hefty reward.

There is a further twist if focus is placed on the possibility of being declared an outlaw. An outlaw would clearly not be eligible to claim their 'lex terrae', by definition. This may, therefore, provide an alternative explanation for the use of 'vel' not 'et' ('and') in this clause. In other words, the use of vel may have been accurately disjunctive because a declaration that a subject is an outlaw would not lead to a subsequent 'test'. The drafter would have known and reflected this fact in the decision to use vel not et. The underlying assumption that in other circumstances, a judgment/doom would lead inexorably to a test would have been understood and assumed by the legal experts at the time.

These historical realities, while fascinating, simply illustrate the amorphous nature of Magna Carta yet again. The more you delve into the actual legal context and circumstances, the clearer it becomes that the meaning and purpose of the document bears little or no relationship to anything that makes legal sense to us today. That is, of course, its genius because its *tabula rasa* qualities are what permit later generations to impose their prejudices, viewpoints and peccadilloes onto this shape-shifting blank slate, thereby holding up a constitutional mirror for future generations to understand and assess their own legal values.

1.4 Conclusion

Magna Carta is a perfect avatar for the constitution of this country. Centuries of analysis have in no way diminished its fascination for succeeding generations. The celebrations of its 800-year anniversary were lavish in their scale and publicity, which is perhaps appropriate for what remains one of the most important exports this country has contributed to the culture of the world. The complexity of its terms and the opacity of its meaning today make it the ideal receptacle for the ever-changing legal and political normative culture of the constitution. Current constitutional fashions include a deepening commitment to the rule of law, democracy, separation of powers and parliamentary sovereignty. These more recent additions to the constitutional firmament have taken their place alongside longer-standing traditions of jury trial, habeas corpus, no taxation without representation and the protection of private property.

All these conceptual shibboleths have been variously argued to have their roots in the charter sealed by King John in Runnymede in 1215. None of them, in fact, do so. This amazing fact is the key to understanding the incredible longevity of this astonishing document. It is the very expression of the geist – the 'spirit' or soul – of the constitution of the United Kingdom. No doubt, as future constitutional fashions develop over time, we will see further convoluted attempts to retrofit novel constitutional concepts back onto the utterly alien mores, legal climate and political ructions of a culture that has little or no resonance with ours today. As LP Hartley famously said, 'the past is a foreign country: they do things differently there'.[63] It is deeply ironic that one of the most important uniting features of the British constitution is the messianic attempt to manufacture links over many centuries to a charter issued over eight centuries ago.

Bibliography

Arden (Lady Justice), Magna Carta and the Judges – Realising the Vision', speech at Royal Holloway, June 2011

Bagehot W, *The English Constitution* (1867), (P Smith ed, Cambridge University Press 2001)

Butterfield H, *The Whig Interpretation of History* (Norton & Co 1965)

Coke E, *The Second Part of the Institutes of the Laws of England* (1628)

Dicey AV, *An Introduction to the Study of the Law of the Constitution* (8th edn, Macmillan 1927)

Hale (Baroness), Historical Society Annual Lecture 2015, 'Magna Carta: Our Shared Heritage'

Halliday PD, *Habeas Corpus: From England to Empire* (Harvard University Press 2010)

Hartley LP, *The Go-Between* (Penguin 1953)

Jenks E, 'The Myth of Magna Carta' (1904) *Independent Review* 260

Kantorowicz E, *The King's Two Bodies* (Princeton University Press 1957)

McIlwain CH, *The High Court of Parliament and Its Supremacy* (Oxford University Press 1910)

McKechnie W, *Magna Carta* (James Maclehose and Sons 1914)

Montesquieu (Baron), *The Spirit of the Laws* (first published 1748, A Cohler, B Miller and H Stone eds, Cambridge University Press 1989)

Neuberger (Lord), 'Magna Carta – The Bible of the English Constitution or a Disgrace to the English Nation?', Speech at Guildford Cathedral, 18 June 2015

Neuberger (Lord), 'Magna Carta and the Holy Grail', Speech at Lincoln's Inn, 12 May 2015

Pollock F and Maitland FW, *The History of English Law Before the Time of Edward I*, Vol I (Cambridge University Press 1989)

Powicke F, 'Per iudicium parium vel per legem terrae' in *Magna Carta Commemoration Essays* (Royal Historical Society 1917)

Robertson G, *The Tyrannicide Brief: The Story of the Man Who Sent Charles I to the Scaffold* (Pantheon 2005)

Sumption (Lord), 'Magna Carta Then and Now: Address to the Friends of the British Library', 9 March 2015

63 LP Hartley, *The Go-Between* (Penguin 1953).

2 Sir John Fortescue, *De Laudibus Legum Angliae* and *The Governance of England*

Paul Raffield

2.1 Introduction

> [N]or the laws of any Christian kingdom, are so rooted in antiquity. Hence there is no gainsaying nor legitimate doubt but that the customs of the English are not only good but the best.[1]

For Sir John Fortescue, Chief Justice of the King's Bench between 1442 and 1460, nominal Lord Chancellor to Henry VI following the deposition of the Lancastrian King in 1461, and author of *De Laudibus Legum Angliae* (from which the previous quotation is taken), the laws and customs of England were coextensive and indivisible. Fortescue identified three separate forms of human or municipal law: these were 'either law of nature, customs, or statutes', and when customs and the law of nature 'have been reduced to writing' and received royal approval, then they 'are changed into a constitution or something of the nature of statutes.'[2] Of these three (supposedly indisputable) sources of English law, custom was arguably the least susceptible to irrefutable definition, and it is, therefore, something of a paradox that Fortescue was an exemplar of late-medieval judicial authority expressing the opinion that custom was a singular, defining, and unique feature of common law.

It is the main purpose of this chapter to examine and analyse the contribution made by Fortescue to the juridical notion of custom in relation to the institutional foundations of common law. I concentrate primarily on juristic ideas of custom attendant on the theories espoused by Fortescue in *De Laudibus Legum Angliae* (written *c.* 1470) and *The Governance of England*.[3] His

1 Sir John Fortescue, *De Laudibus Legum Angliae* (SB Chrimes ed and tr, CUP 1942) 41, c. XVII. Fortescue's other major work, *De Dominio Regali et Politico*, was published in 1715 as *Difference Between an Absolute and Limited Monarchy*, and in 1885 under its more familiar title *The Governance of England* (Charles Plummer ed, OUP 1885).

2 Fortescue, *De Laudibus* 37, c. XV.

3 The date of composition of *The Governance* is uncertain, although Lockwood states that 'an updated and revised version was presented to Edward IV after 1471': Sir John Fortescue, *On the Laws* and *Governance of England* (Shelley Lockwood ed, CUP 1997) Introduction xix.

DOI: 10.4324/9781032658698-3

political and constitutional theories were adopted and expanded by lawyers in the first half of the sixteenth century, notably by the barrister and jurist Christopher St German, author of *Dialogus de fundamentis legum Anglie et de conscientia*, more commonly known as *Doctor and Student*, published in English in 1530. In passing, I consider the gradual change in the juridical meaning of *consuetudo*, from that intended by the Chief Justiciar of England Ranulf de Glanvill and the cleric, justice, and jurist Henry de Bracton,[4] to its meaning as recorded in the decisions of judges, handed down in the courts of common law. The judiciary adopted for themselves a didactic and rabbinical role, in accordance with the description of them by Fortescue as *sacerdotes* (priests): 'For a priest is by etymology said to be one who gives or teaches holy things'.[5] Like Fortescue, they were trained in the arcane practices and rituals of the English legal system at the Inns of Court and rehearsed their calling as utter barristers or counsellors and subsequently as serjeants-at-law in the law courts at Westminster prior to their elevation to the ranks of the judiciary.

2.2 Custom, kings, and *lex regia*

In order to understand more completely the contribution of Fortescue to the formulation of political and constitutional theory and practice, it is important to consider the significance of customs to the governance of England in the early medieval period. Of great relevance in this respect are the works of the medieval jurists Ranulf de Glanvill (d. 1190) and Henry de Bracton (d. 1268). The contribution of Glanvill and Bracton to a body of constitutional theory provides the contextual background to my later discussion of Fortescue. There is compelling documentary evidence that from the end of the sixth century to the middle of the eleventh (starting with the reign of Æthelbert of Kent in *c.* 589 and ending with the reign of Cnut, 1016–35), laws and ordinances were introduced by successive kings.[6] During the seventh and eighth centuries, affirmation was provided of forms of communal justice based upon regional customs: folk-rights or *folcriht*. Contemporaneous documents refer to the Kentish *gemot* (or moot) of the eighth century: a folk-assembly at which local grievances were aired; but this could hardly be termed a formal court of law (Pollock and Maitland describe the *folc-gemot* as 'any public court whatever, greater or less').[7] Similar to the gemot in form and informality was the feudal manorial court, presided over by the lord of the manor or his steward, at which minor disputes were resolved and rural

4 See *Tractatus de legibus et consuetudinibus regni Anglie*, completed *c* 1189, of which Glanvill was the attributed, albeit disputed, author; and Henry de Bracton, *De Legibus et Consuetudinibus Angliae*, completed *c.* 1235.

5 Fortescue, *De Laudibus* 8, 9, c. III.

6 Sir Frederick Pollock and Frederic William Maitland, *The History of English Law Before the Time of Edward I*, 2 vols (CUP 1911) vol I: 27.

7 Ibid 1: 40.

customs effected.[8] The king's justice or *lex regia* was dispensed by means of the hundred courts and county courts, the former sitting every four weeks and the latter biannually.[9] These courts were often controlled by lords but were subject to supervision by the king's officials, known as reeves. The court of the hundred was regulated at the county level by the king's representative, the shire-reeve (sheriff).[10]

Following the Danish invasion of the ninth century, there were three systems of law extant in England: the laws of Wessex, Mercia, and Danelaw.[11] But by the tenth century, England was a single kingdom, and as J.H. Baker suggested, when the Norman invaders arrived in 1066, they found a relatively sophisticated legal and governmental system, 'as well developed as anything they had left in Normandy.'[12] Despite the irrefutable fact of the Norman Conquest, Fortescue claimed that 'the realm has been continuously ruled by the same customs as it is now'.[13] These customs prevailed, he argued, because their antiquity was the guarantor of their legitimate authority: '[I]f they had not been the best, some of those kings would have changed for the sake of justice or by the impulse of caprice, and totally abolished them.'[14]

Central to the development of custom as a recognisable feature of English law was the increased concentration of power in the person of the king under the Norman monarchs and (especially) their Angevin successors, beginning with the reign of Henry II in 1154.[15] Near the start of the twelfth century, the compiler of *Leges Henrici Primi* (*c.* 1118) emphasised the importance of the royal court in preserving 'the use and custom of its law at all times and in all places and with constant uniformity',[16] lending credibility to the thesis that, before the establishment of an independent legal profession, the custom of the realm was defined and determined by the king and his court. At the latter end of the twelfth century stood Glanvill and his insistence that common law was essentially the king's law (*lex regia*), which custom or *consuetudo* supplemented and resembled. The king was 'guided by those of his subjects most learned in the laws *and* customs of the realm whom he knows to excel all

8 JH Baker, *An Introduction to English Legal History* (Butterworths 2002) 4, 8–9.

9 See Sir William Dugdale, *Origines Juridiciales, or Historical Memorials of the English Laws* (F and T Warren 1666) 26.

10 Pollock and Maitland, *History of English Law*, vol I: 42; Baker, *Introduction to English Legal History* 9.

11 Ibid 3.

12 Ibid 12.

13 Fortescue, *De Laudibus* 39, c. XVII.

14 Ibid.

15 Paul Brand, '*Multis Vigiliis Excogitatam et Inventum*: Henry II and the Creation of the English Common Law' (1990) 2 Haskins Society Journal 197–222; Christopher Harper-Bill and Nicholas Vincent (eds), *Henry II: New Interpretations* (Boydell Press 2007).

16 *Leges Henrici Primi* (LJ Downer ed, Clarendon Press 1972) 109.

others in sobriety, wisdom and eloquence'.[17] Some 50 years after the completion of Glanvill's *Tractatus* (*c.* 1187), Henry de Bracton's *De Legibus et Consuetudinibus Angliae* was completed, *c.* 1235. The exact contribution made by Bracton to this work is uncertain: his main input was probably to update text compiled and written by Justice William de Raley (Raleigh), whom Bracton served as a clerk.[18] Like his predecessor Glanvill, Bracton associated common law with *lex regia*. At the start of Book I of *De Legibus*, Bracton stated that English law was unwritten but that, despite the absence of codification, common law had 'the force of law' because it had 'the authority of the king or the prince preceding.'[19] The pervasive influence of Roman law is immediately apparent in Bracton's claim that unwritten law was legitimated by the tacit command of the monarch. *The Institutes* of the Byzantine emperor Justinian I expounded the principle that the will or pronouncement of the prince had 'legislative force', because the populace yielded all its authority to him through its acceptance of *lex regia*.[20] This was not to say that, for Bracton, the king was above the law. He explicitly states that 'the king himself ought not to be subject to man, but subject to God and to the law, for the law makes the king' (*Ipse autem rex, non debet esse sub homine, sed sub Deo et sub lege, quia lex facit regem*);[21] but the subjection of the king to law and not to man had the inevitable juridical consequence that the monarch (and his delegates) remained the ultimate arbiter of what constituted custom.

As far as custom is concerned, for Bracton (as for Glanvill) it was synonymous with local or regional practices and mores: 'There are also in England several and divers customs according to the diversity of places.'[22] In Bracton's juridical scheme (as in Glanvill's), custom supplemented *lex regia*, although it might also on occasion be taken for the law itself: 'Custom, also, is sometimes observed for law in parts, where it has been approved by habitual usage, and it fills the place of law, for the authority of long usage and custom is not slight.'[23] It was during the period in which Glanvill was active in shrieval and judicial office (he was Sheriff of Yorkshire and one of the royal justices in the north of England during the reign of Henry II, 1154–89) that the royal court started to play a major role in regulating local activities on a regional basis. If *lex regia* was to extend over the whole of the realm, then its successful administration

17 Ranulf de Glanvill, *Tractatus de legibus et consuetudinibus regni Anglie qui Glanvilla vocatur* (GDG Hall ed, T Nelson 1965) 'Prologue' 2b, emphasis added.

18 See Henry de Bracton, *De Legibus et Consuetudinibus Angliae*, 6 vols (Travers Twiss ed, CUP 2012) vol I: Introduction, xxiv–xxv; also, JL Barton, 'The Mystery of Bracton' (1993) 14 Journal of Legal History 1–142.

19 Bracton, *De Legibus*, vol I: 3, Bk. I.I.

20 *Justinian's Institutes* (Peter Birks and Grant McLeod tr, Duckworth & Co. 1987) 37, Bk. I.II ('*De Iure Naturali et Gentium et Civili*'). vi.

21 Bracton, *De Legibus* vol I: 39, Bk. I: VIII.

22 Ibid vol I: 3, Bk. I.I.

23 Ibid vol I: 13, Bk. I.III.

and enforcement could not depend solely on the person of the king. The writ system was instrumental in enforcing commands of the king throughout the realm, and judicial delegates or deputies of the king were appointed to the role of justiciar (Glanvill became Chief Justiciar in 1180) to ensure that the king retained control of justice across the entire country. Itinerant justices were sent from the royal household to dispense justice in the shires. 'Wandering justices' (*justiciae errantes*) were organised into circuits and became known as 'justices in eyre' (*justiciae in itinere*) or the 'general eyre'. As well as exercising the functions of a court of law (in civil and criminal matters), the eyre served as an itinerant form of central government, exercising a supervisory and regulatory role over local government and local customs.[24]

The justices of the eyre during this period were politicians and servants of the Crown, often members of the clergy (like Bracton) or knights of the shires (like Glanvill). Although known by the title *justiciarii*, these men were not professional judges (in the sense of having trained and practised as pleaders prior to holding judicial office), and complaints about the arbitrary nature of justice dispensed by the eyre led to the creation by Henry II of a permanent *curia regis* at the Palace of Westminster. The first of these courts, the Exchequer (dealing with the control of the king's revenue), had been established at Westminster in 1130, during the reign of Henry I. Of great importance to the centralisation of the legal institution and the gradual emergence of an independent legal profession, was the decision of Henry II towards the end of his reign that, although itinerant justices would continue to judge cases on a circuit around the realm, at any time five of his judges should remain stationary and sit in *curia regis* at Westminster. Hence, foundations were laid for the emergence of the courts of King's Bench and Common Pleas, the former dealing with pleas of the Crown (such as treason and felonies) and the latter with private litigation.[25] Coextensive with the centralisation of the legal institution at Westminster was the emergence of a secular legal profession. The chronicler Matthew Paris recorded that as early as 1230, there was a class of 'forespeakers of the bench', commonly known as *narratores*.[26] The Latin noun *narratores* referred to the recitation by the pleader of the plaintiff's count or *narratio*, but it has inevitable connotations also of a storyteller, chronicler or historian, relating and narrating the supposedly immemorial customs of common law.

2.3 Custom, common law, and the legal profession

An ordinance of Edward I in 1292 (20 Edward I) was at least partly responsible for the emergence of the Inns of Court as the physical and spiritual home of the legal community. The ordinance prohibited members of the clergy from

24 Baker, *Introduction to English Legal History* 15–16.

25 Sir Edward Coke, *The Fourth Part of the Institutes of the Laws of England, Concerning the Jurisdiction of the Courts* (E and R Brooke 1797) 73, 98.

26 Matthew Paris, *Chronica majora*, 7 vols (Henry Richards Luard ed, Longman & Co 1876) vol III: 619.

acting as pleaders in temporal actions, thus enabling the development of a secular profession. In the same year, Edward I ordered the Chief Justice of the Common Pleas (John of Mettingham) and his fellow justices to 'provide and ordain, from every County, certain Attorneys and Lawyers, of the best and most apt for their learning and skill, who might do service to his Court and people.'[27] This decision, together with the establishment of a permanent *curia regis* at Westminster, prompted the 'Attorneys and Lawyers' to congregate as members of unincorporated associations in London, in close proximity to the royal court, the city, and the courts of common law. By the time Fortescue had written *De Laudibus*, the oldest of the four Inns of Court had been in existence for approximately 130 years, the Inner Temple and Middle Temple having been inhabited by lawyers from the 1340s onwards. Gray's Inn was leased to the apprentices of law during the same period. There is no record extant that Lincoln's Inn served as an honourable society of lawyers prior to 1417 (Fortescue was a member of Lincoln's Inn by 1420 and served the Inn as a Bencher from 1425). The Inns of Chancery were less elevated in status than the Inns of Court. It was at the Inns of Chancery that attorneys acquired rudimentary principles of common law, mainly through the study of the writ system. They were established in the same period as the Inns of Court: when *De Laudibus* was written, there were ten Inns of Chancery in existence, each of which was affiliated with one of the Inns of Court.

The primary contribution of the Inns of Court to the development of English law during this period was their role as autonomous educational institutions, where the technicalities and procedures of common law were disseminated to and assimilated by law students (inner barristers) through a variety of disputatious oral exercises. These consisted of readings (cases presented by senior utter barristers to members of their particular Inn and subsequently argued by utter barristers, Benchers, and judges), moots (formal arguments between rival inner barristers over points of law),[28] and more informal oral disputations, known as bolts. As self-governing municipal authorities, the governing bodies of the Inns thereby ensured that the common law was systemised and rationalised solely through the agency of the legal profession. Decisions of the courts, recorded on the Plea Rolls and collated in the Year Books (prior to the mass publication of law reports from the mid-sixteenth century onward), were no longer in the charge of clerics such as Bracton. These decisions formed the basis for the system of precedent (*stare decisis*), which developed in the sixteenth and early seventeenth centuries. Interpretation of law became the exclusive domain of judges and serjeants-at-law, all skilled practitioners in and knowledgeable guardians of the arcane, technical procedures of common law. These men were the new custodians and arbiters of common law and legal practice. Consequently, custom in its juridical context became associated with the pronouncements of judges in their capacity as independent interpreters of law. As far as the evolution of common law was concerned, *lex regia*, which

27 *Rotuli Parliamentorum* i.84, in Dugdale, *Origines Juridiciales* 141.
28 Ibid 159.

(according to Glanvill) custom had merely resembled or supplemented, was of diminished importance.

De Laudibus Legum Angliae serves one of its didactic functions as a paean to the Inns of Court and their honourable members, all of whom are depicted as brethren in a secular priesthood. I referred previously to the description by Fortescue of the judges as *sacerdotes* or priests, giving and teaching 'holy things', and noteworthy in this respect is the claim made by him that law students studied not only the technical aspects of common law but that 'after the divine services' they applied themselves to the study 'of Holy Scripture and of chronicles.'[29] Of course, as its title indicates, *De Laudibus* was a panegyric in praise of English secular law, but the relevance of religion to the evolution of common law cannot be ignored. In *De Laudibus*, the idealised description of judges as *sacerdotes* follows the assertion of Fortescue that, according to *the Book of Deuteronomy*, Moses 'invites you [the Prince of Wales] to strive zealously in the study of the law'. A few lines earlier, he notes the injunction of Justinian I that an emperor should be '*armed with laws*'.[30] The reference to Justinian I (and throughout *De Laudibus* to Roman law) marks a significant revision in political and juridical thought from the days of Glanvill and Bracton.

These two medieval jurists stood on either side of the Great Charter of 1215, which symbolised both the restricted powers of the Crown and the inalienable liberties of the subject. In so far as *Magna Carta* was a statement of privileges made available under the Angevin kings, as well as a statement of principles concerning organisation of the feudal state, then it may be argued that the Charter had recourse to local customs, common (with some regional variations) to the whole of western Europe. Despite its iconic status as a symbol of fundamental liberties, which accrued largely in the early seventeenth century as a response by common lawyers to the threat of Stuart absolutism, to a great extent, *Magna Carta* represented the will and self-interest of the barons. This group of nobles was asserting contended rights in a feudal society, such as those over title to a property, the correct form of judgment, and the rightful conduct of a king. Bracton reaffirmed the principle of the limited powers of kingship by stating that the king was under God and law, but, as I have noted previously, Book I of *De Legibus* starts with a rehearsal of the (apparently contradictory) principle of Roman law that the will of the prince has the force of law.

The invocation by Fortescue of Justinian I in the preceding passage from *De Laudibus* is highly significant, as the central constitutional argument of his treatise (and a signal development from Bracton) is precisely that the will of

29 Fortescue, *De Laudibus* 119, c. XLIX. On Fortescue's 'subtle blend of religious and secular ideas', see John Guy, 'Thomas More and Christopher St German: The Battle of the Books' in Alistair Fox and John Guy (eds), *Reassessing the Henrician Age: Humanism, Politics and Reform, 1500–1550* (Blackwell 1986) 95–120, 119.

30 Fortescue, De Laudibus 5, c. I.

the prince does not have the force of law unless it is compliant with the principles of common law. Fortescue was emphatic that the nature of government under an English king was 'not only regal but also political' (a thesis which he was to develop in *The Governance of England*), by which he meant that the king may not create, alter, or otherwise subvert any laws 'without the assent of his subjects',[31] because England was ***dominium politicum et regale***.[32] In the context of Fortescue's republican political thought ('republican' in the sense of the best interests of *res publica* or the common-weal), 'assent of his subjects' referred to 'the concession or assent' of the three estates of the realm: nobility, clergy, and commonalty, as represented in Parliament.[33] In other words, the king must govern in accordance with English law and its customs. Under an 'entirely regal' legal system, it would be permissible for a king to make whatsoever alterations he wished because, as under French civil law (Fortescue was at pains to point out), '*What pleased the prince has the force of law*.' For the avoidance of doubt, Fortescue stated unequivocally that 'The laws of England do not sanction any such maxim'.[34] Given that *De Laudibus* was written at least partly in France between July 1463 and April 1471, while Fortescue was accompanying the exiled wife of Henry VI, Queen Margaret, and acting as tutor to Edward of Westminster, Prince of Wales (killed later at the Battle of Tewkesbury in 1471), it should come as no surprise that he compared the customs of France with those of England (Fortescue had started his protracted period of exile in Scotland, following the decisive defeat of the Lancastrian forces at the Battle of Towton in March 1461: like France, Scotland was subject to civil law). Nor, given the polemical nature of *De Laudibus*, is it surprising that he should have attributed the hardship suffered by French subjects to the oppressive nature of civil law, as enforced by the absolute monarch Louis XI:

> Exasperated by these and other calamities, the people live in no little misery. They drink water daily, and they taste no other liquor unless at solemn feasts. They wear frocks or tabards of canvas like sackcloth. They do not use woollens, except of the cheapest sort, and that only in their shirts under their frocks, and wear no hose, unless to the knees, exposing the rest of their shins.

Meanwhile, in England (so Fortescue claimed), due to observance of and subjection to law by the king:

> Hence the inhabitants of that land are rich, abounding in gold and silver and all the necessaries of life. They do not drink water, except those who sometimes abstain from other drinks by way of devotional or penitential

31 Ibid 25, c. IX.
32 Fortescue, This is the Lockwood edition, cited in n 3, not the Plummer edition, cited in n 1. 83, c. I.
33 Fortescue, *De Laudibus* 87, c. XXXVI.
34 Ibid 25, c. IX; 79, c. XXXIV.

> zeal. They eat every kind of flesh and fish in abundance, with which their land is not meanly stocked.[35]

John Selden noted in the 1616 edition of *De Laudibus* that Louis XI 'governed, not according to the Ancient Constitution of *France*, by a General Assembly of the three Estates . . . They were ruled by Armies and Councils of Power, in which Royal Will and Pleasure only presided.'[36] The phrase 'Ancient Constitution' is closely associated with resistance by English common lawyers and parliamentarians of the seventeenth century (such as Selden) to excessive, unconstitutional, and (arguably) unlawful exercise of the royal prerogative by the monarch. Indeed, the eulogistic title *De Laudibus Legum Angliae* was given to Fortescue's work by Selden, presumably to imply the superiority of English common law to rival jurisdictions (as Fortescue had made clear in his comparison between the English and French legal systems). Its first publication in English (in a translation by Robert Mulcaster) was in 1567 under the title *A Learned Commendation of the Politique Lawes of England*, although as early as 1513, John Rastell had referred in descriptive (rather than titular) terms to it as 'de laudibus legum Anglie'. For Selden (and his contemporary Sir Edward Coke), the 'Ancient Constitution' was a succinct formulation of the principle that unwritten or customary law was of greater authority than statute or imperial edict because of its immemorial origins. Where Selden and Coke were responding to the burgeoning constitutional conflict between Crown and common law, Fortescue was writing at a time of immense political upheaval and uncertainty, during the dynastic struggle between the Houses of York and Lancaster, popularly known as the Wars of the Roses. As indicated previously, in *The Governance of England*, Fortescue developed the theory of political and regal dominion, under which a 'king may not rule his people by other laws than such as they assent to',[37] and the fact that a version of the work was presented to the Yorkist King Edward IV after his restoration to the throne in 1471, following the death of Henry VI, suggests that it may have been intended as a practical guide to kingship rather than a theoretical work solely of academic interest. It was expected by many that Fortescue would be executed after the accession of Edward IV to the throne, but his intellectual and propagandist skills were of evident use to the new regime. He was pardoned by the King and reinstated as a royal counsellor. He died peacefully in 1479.

Authority for the claim made by Fortescue for the juridical and constitutional sovereignty of common law derived from its antique origins and immutable nature, more ancient even than 'the civil laws of the Romans'

35 Ibid 83–84, c. XXXV; 87, c. XXXVI.

36 Sir John Fortescue, *De Laudibus Legum Angliae* (John Selden ed, R Gosling 1737) 77, n (a), c. XXXV.

37 Fortescue, Lockwood edition, n 3. 83, c. I.

and 'the laws of the Venetians, which are renowned above others for their antiquity – though their island was uninhabited, and Rome unbuilt at the time of the origin of the Britons.'[38] According to Fortescue, the professed sources of this much-lauded antiquity were to be found in an eclectic collection of Judaeo-Christian, classical, and medieval texts, including the Bible, the theological works of St Augustine and St Thomas Aquinas, *The Politics* and *The Nicomachean Ethics* of Aristotle, and *Historia Regum Britanniae* by Geoffrey of Monmouth. Fortescue thereby forged a link between the custom of common law and the historiography of the ancient and medieval worlds. It was to the *First Book of Samuel* (1 *Samuel* 8), as interpreted by Aquinas in *On Princely Government*[39] that Fortescue turned for validation of the proposition that God ruled his people 'under Judges "royally and politically"', until such time as they offended the Almighty Father by desiring to be ruled by a king 'who reigned upon them "only royally"'.[40] The impression created by Fortescue is one of a legal system in which judges played a supra-judicial role as counsellors or *amici principis*, constantly reminding the king of the primacy of custom in shaping the law. Hence, in Chapter 2 of *The Governance of England*, when Fortescue states that '*rex* is so called from *regendo* or ruling',[41] he is alluding to St Augustine, who notes that when the Romans 'found the domination of kings intolerable', they established authority in the form of 'two men, who were called "consuls", from *consulere* (to take counsel), not "kings" (*reges*), a word derived from *regnare* (to reign), or "lords" (*domini*), derived from *dominare* (to dominate).'[42]

2.4 Custom and the Tudor inheritance

The fusion of classical literature and philosophy with the tenets of Augustinian and Thomist political theology was a notable feature of *De Laudibus*. Fortescue reinterpreted the legend of the Trojan Brutus landing in Britain and founding the city of *Troynovant* (as narrated by Geoffrey of Monmouth in *Historia Regum Britanniae*)[43] to depict the descendant of Aeneas as an archetype of English nationhood and a symbolic origin of English law: 'the kingdom of England blossomed forth into a dominion regal and political out of Brutus's band of Trojans, whom he led out of the territories of Italy and of the Greeks.'[44] Fortescue presents Brutus as the iconic embodiment of

38 Fortescue, *De Laudibus* 39, 41, c. XVII.
39 Aquinas probably wrote only the first book of *On Princely Government* and the first four chapters of the second book; Ptolemy of Lucca is supposed to have completed the work.
40 Fortescue, Lockwood edition, n 3. 84, c. I.
41 Ibid 85, c. II.
42 St Augustine, *City of God* (Henry Bettenson tr, Penguin 2003) 197, Bk. V. c.12.
43 Geoffrey of Monmouth, *The History of the Kings of Britain* (Lewis Thorpe tr, Penguin 1966) 71–74, Pt i.15–18.
44 Fortescue, *De Laudibus* 33, c. XIII.

dominium politicum et regale, a form of polity which Fortescue was to analyse and propound in *The Governance of England.* It is arguable whether Fortescue blurred such distinctions as existed between mythology and history and between literature and law, but undeniable is the significance of Aristotelian civic republicanism both to *De Laudibus* and *The Governance of England*, and its subsequent influence over jurists in the first half of the sixteenth century. Such was the importance of Aristotle to the political thought of Fortescue that he referred to him throughout *De Laudibus* as 'the *Philosopher*'; and, in support of the argument that English law was derived from natural law (rather than from statute), he quotes approvingly from Book V of *The Nicomachean Ethics*: '*Natural law is that which has the same force among all men.*'[45] A similar emphasis on the relevance of *ordo naturae* to municipal order was made by Sir Thomas Elyot in *The boke named the Governour* (published in 1531), in which the author claims that the state 'is disposed by the ordre of equite and governed by the rule and moderation of reason.'[46]

The publication of Elyot's *Governour* was roughly contemporaneous with the publication in English of the Second Dialogue of St German's *Doctor and Student* in 1530 (the Latin version of the First Dialogue was published in 1523), a central theme of which was 'the ordre of equite' and the role of the court of Chancery in applying the Aristotelian principle of *epieikeia* or natural equity to the interpretation of English law. St German developed the theory espoused by Fortescue of a pre-existing customary law related to the law of God and the law of reason, which demanded the exercise of conscience by all subjects of the English legal institution. Conscience was founded in the law of God and the law of nature, and a human law was bad in conscience if it contradicted either of these laws. According to St German, the customs of the realm had been accepted by king and subject alike because they were necessary for the good governance of the state and were synonymous with common law itself. St German explains that the first ground of English law was the law of reason, the second ground was the law of God, and

> The thyrde grounde of the lawe of Englande standeth upon dyverse generall Customes of olde tyme used through all the realme: which have ben acceptyd and approvyd by our soveraygne lorde the kynge and his progenytours and all theyr subgettes.[47]

The role of statute or *leges scriptae* in the English legal system described by St German was merely to affirm customs and not to repeal them. Like Fortescue, St German argued for the sovereign authority of the judiciary in determining whether a custom was law: 'it shall alway be determyned by the Iustyces

45 ibid 39, c. XVI.
46 Sir Thomas Elyot, *The Boke Named the Governour* (Thomas Bertheleti 1531) sig Ar.
47 Christopher St German, *Doctor and Student* (Theodore Frank Thomas Plucknett, and John L Barton eds, Selden Society 1974) 45, 'First Dialogue', c. VII.

whether there be any suche *law or* generall custome *as alleged,* or not.' To this end, in the Coronation oath, the king swore his allegiance and subjection to law: 'that he shal cause all the customes of his realme faythfully to be observyd.'[48] At a time when the Crown was seeking to establish a sovereign, national jurisprudence, independent from and no longer subject to papal jurisdiction, St German was rehearsing the Bractonian principle that a king was subject to God and law (and by extension, to the customs of the realm) because the law made the king. The shadow cast by Fortescue was long and remained enduring. In his book on what he terms the 'constitutionalist revolution' of the early modern period in England, Alan Cromartie notes the similarity between Fortescue and Bracton but goes on to observe that 'What readers found in Fortescue, however, was unimpeachable authority – the word of a Chief Justice – for a range of near-republican opinions.'[49] The political and constitutional principle of the rule of law, which restricted the prerogative powers of the monarch, was initiated in embryonic form by Bracton. The theory of a king subjected to law provided Fortescue with the basis for his proposition of *dominium politicum et regale.* Bracton lacked Fortescue's institutional status: he was neither Lord Chief Justice nor Lord Chancellor. Although a member of *coram rege,* the pinnacle of his judicial career was as a justice of the assize in the southwestern counties of England, notably Devon, Somerset, and Cornwall, before his retirement in 1257.

The idea of a fundamental law of greater authority than a statute or imperial edict was expressed by Sir Edward Coke and others in the early seventeenth century. It derived from the political theory expressed by Fortescue in both *De Laudibus Legum Angliae* and *The Governance of England.* Fortescue made an unattributed contribution to a judgment of the UK Supreme Court in 2019 when ministers of the Crown were reminded that they could not override the law: the prerogative powers of the executive branch of government were always subject to and restricted by law. In their leading judgment in *R (on the application of Miller) v The Prime Minister,* Lady Hale and Lord Reed quoted from Coke's report of *Case of Proclamations* (heard in 1611 and included in Part 12 of *The Reports,* published in 1655), 'that "the King hath no prerogative, but that which the law of the land allows him",[50] indicating that the limits of prerogative powers were set by law and were determined by the courts.' Throughout *The Reports,* Coke implicitly acknowledged the debt owed to his fifteenth-century predecessor as Lord Chief Justice.[51] The legal limits to

48 Ibid 47.

49 Alan Cromartie, *The Constitutionalist Revolution: An Essay on the History of England, 1450–1642* (CUP 2006) 21.

50 *R (on the application of Miller) v The Prime Minister* [2019] UKSC 41, para 32.

51 For example, the belief propounded by Fortescue that common law was 'deduced from the *Law of Nature*' was a sentiment echoed by Coke in his report of *Postnati. Calvin's Case,* where he stated 'that the law of nature is part of the law of England': Fortescue, *De Laudibus,* 29; *Postnati. Calvin's Case,* Part 7 (1608) of *The Reports of Sir Edward Coke, Knt. In English,* 7 vols (George Wilson ed, Rivington 1777) vol IV: 1a, 12b.

monarchical power were delineated by Fortescue in his two encomia to the juridical, political, and constitutional sovereignty of common law, which he wrote during the Wars of the Roses. The legacy of Fortescue's *De Laudibus Legum Angliae* and *The Governance of England* is long-lasting, influential, and ineradicable.

Bibliography

Baker JH, *An Introduction to English Legal History* (Butterworths 2002)
Barton JL, 'The Mystery of Bracton' (1993) 14 Journal of Legal History 1–142
Bracton H, *De Legibus et Consuetudinibus Angliae*, 6 vols (Travers Twiss ed, CUP 2012) vol I
Brand P, '*Multis Vigiliis Excogitatam et Inventum*: Henry II and the Creation of the English Common Law' (1990) 2 Haskins Society Journal 197–222
Coke E, *The Reports of Sir Edward Coke, Knt. In English*, 7 vols (George Wilson ed, Rivington 1777)
Coke E, *The Fourth Part of the Institutes of the Laws of England, Concerning the Jurisdiction of the Courts* (E and R Brooke 1797)
Cromartie A, *The Constitutionalist Revolution: An Essay on the History of England, 1450–1642* (CUP 2006)
Dugdale W, *Origines Juridiciales, or Historical Memorials of the English Laws* (F and T Warren 1666)
Elyot T, *The Boke Named the Governour* (Thomas Bertheleti 1531)
Fortescue J, *De Laudibus Legum Angliae* (John Selden ed, R Gosling 1737)
Fortescue J, *The Governance of England* (Charles Plummer ed, OUP 1885)
Fortescue J, *De Laudibus Legum Angliae* (SB Chrimes ed and tr, CUP 1942)
Fortescue J, *On the Laws and Governance of England* (Shelley Lockwood ed, CUP 1997)
Geoffrey of Monmouth, *The History of the Kings of Britain* (Lewis Thorpe tr, Penguin 1966)
Glanvill R, *Tractatus de legibus et consuetudinibus regni Anglie qui Glanvilla vocatur* (GDG Hall ed, T. Nelson 1965)
Guy J, 'Thomas More and Christopher St German: The Battle of the Books' in A Fox and J Guy (eds), *Reassessing the Henrician Age: Humanism, Politics and Reform, 1500–1550* (Blackwell 1986)
Harper-Bill C and Nicholas V (eds), *Henry II: New Interpretations* (Boydell Press 2007)
Justinian's Institutes (Peter Birks and Grant McLeod tr, Duckworth & Co. 1987)
Paris M, *Chronica Majora*, 7 vols (Henry Richards Luard ed, Longman & Co 1876)
Pollock F and Maitland FW, *The History of English Law Before the Time of Edward I*, 2 vols (CUP 1911) vol I
St Augustine, *City of God* (Henry Bettenson tr, Penguin 2003)

3 Sir Edward Coke's *The Second Part of the Institutes of the Laws of England*

Glenn Burgess

Part I

Sir Edward Coke, after a long and controversial career as the leading English common lawyer of his generation, died in 1634 at Stoke House in Buckinghamshire. Not long before, his papers were confiscated by order of the Privy Council:

> In *September* following Sir *Edward Coke* died, but upon his Death-bed Sir *Francis Windebank* [Secretary of State] . . . by an Order of Council came to search for seditious and dangerous Papers, by virtue whereof he took Sir *Edward Coke*'s Comment upon *Littleton,* and the History of his Life before it, written with his own Hand, his Comment upon *Magna Charta,* &c. the Pleas of the Crown, and Jurisdiction of Courts, and his *11th* and *12th* Reports in Manuscript, and I think 51 other Manuscripts, with the last Will of Sir *Edward*. . . the Books and Papers were kept till seven Years after, when one of Sir *Edward*'s Sons in 1641, moved the House of Commons, that the Books and Papers taken by Sir *Francis Windebank* might be delivered to Sir *Robert Coke,* Heir of Sir *Edward,* which the King was pleased to grant, and such as could be found were delivered.[1]

Coke had by this time published 11 volumes of his *Reports* (1600–1615) and the first part of the *Institutes* ('Coke on Littleton', once an essential textbook on English land tenures, much feared by students), which had appeared in 1628. At that time, he indicated that the *Institutes* were 'an Introduction to the knowledge of the national lawes of the Realme', and that he had already completed writing the Second and Third Parts, while for the Fourth, 'we have only collected some materialls'.[2] The items confiscated included an annotated

1 Roger Coke, *A Detection of the Court and State of England During the Four Last Reigns and the Interregnum*, 2 vols (3rd edn, London 1697) 253.

2 Steve Sheppard (ed), *The Selected Writings of Sir Edwards Coke*, 3 vols (Liberty Fund 2003) vol II, 585–87.

DOI: 10.4324/9781032658698-4

volume of Littleton's *Tenures* in which he had written notes on key events in his life,[3] the manuscripts of the three later volumes of the *Institutes*, and the final volumes of the Reports (11 and 12 presumably being an error for 12 and 13). These were to be published in 1656 and 1659 and contained the most politically and ideologically contentious material in his case reports.[4]

Concerns about the possible publication of this material were not new. The king had already, in 1631, been worried about a book that Coke might publish 'to the prejudice of his prerogative'. Coke was 'an oracle amongst the people' who 'may be misled by anything that carries such an authority'.[5] After Coke's death, the king personally ordered Windebank to return to his house to confiscate further papers. In December, again at the king's command, Coke's chambers at the Inner Temple were raided, with further confiscations of manuscripts, and his study was sealed.[6] Coke struck fear, but one person's fear is another's hope. Coke's heirs sought the recovery of the confiscated manuscripts in December 1640, soon after the first meeting of the Long Parliament, and the Commons formed a committee to pursue the matter and to recover these 'monuments of the subjects' liberties'.[7] Eventually, the king ordered that 11 of Coke's books be sent to Sir Ranulph Crew (Coke's executor), and the house ordered them to be handed to Coke's son, Sir Robert Coke.[8] A motion was made that the remaining three parts of the *Institutes* should be published.[9]

Throughout the records of these events, reference is made to Coke's commentary on Magna Carta. This was the second part of the *Institutes*, his commentary on the *Statutes of the Realm*, which did indeed begin with a lengthy comment on the Statute that inaugurates that collection, Magna Carta, in the form it took in the last of several reissues by Henry III (9 Hen. 3 c. 2). The synecdoche of referring to Coke's Commentary on

3 Now BL Harvey MS 6687, and published as 'Sir Edward Coke's "Vade Mecum"' in *Collectanea Topographica et Genealogica*, vol VI (Society of Antiquaries 1840) 108–22.

4 Andrew Thrush, 'Coke, Sir Edward (1552–1634)' (*History of Parliament* 1604–29) <https://www.historyofparliamentonline.org/volume/1604-1629/member/coke-sir-edward-1552-1634>; also Catherine Drinker Bowen, *The Lion and the Throne: The Life and Times of Sir Edward Coke 1552–1634* (Hamish Hamilton 1957), chs. 34 & 35; Allen D Boyer, 'Coke, Sir Edward (1552–1634), Lawyer, Legal Writer, and Politician' (*Oxford Dictionary of National Biography*) <https://www.oxforddnb.com/view/10.1093/ref:odnb/9780198614128.001.0001/odnb-9780198614128-e-5826>.

5 *CSPD*, 1629–31, p 490.

6 *CSPD*, 1634–35, pp 165, 340–41, 348, 351 (the last of these is a list of confiscated manuscripts). See also *CSPD*, 1641–43, p 414 (possibly misdated?).

7 HMC Cowper, ii, 266; Wallace Notestein (ed) *The Journal of Sir Simonds D'Ewes* (Yale University Press 1923) 108.

8 Maija Jansson (ed), *Two Diaries of the Long Parliament* (Alan Sutton 1984) 85 & n; *Commons Journal*, ii, 80, 85.

9 Notestein (ed), *Journal*, 358; *Commons Journal*, ii, 80, 85, 144; Sheila Lambert (ed), *Printing for Parliament, 1641–1700* (List & Index Society 1984) 1. Copyright was later assigned firmly to Coke's heirs (*Commons Journal*, ii. 470, 554).

Magna Carta no doubt indicates one of the focal points for both the fears and the hopes circling his unpublished work (Coke himself had described the work in 1628 as 'a Commentarie upon the Statute of *Magna Charta*, *Westm. 1* and other old Statutes').[10] 'Pleas of the Crown' was the third part of the *Institutes* on criminal law, and the fourth part was on the jurisdiction of courts. Coke's *Second Part of the Institutes of the Laws of England* was published in 1642; the remaining volumes appeared in 1644. Anticipated by friend and foe alike, the *Second Part* appeared around the time England descended into civil war.

Part II

Coke's writing was the accompaniment to a long and distinguished legal and political career, the key milestones he picked out in his own *Vade Mecum*. His education at Trinity College Cambridge and admission to Clifford's Inn and the Inner Temple (1571) led to his being called to the bar in 1578. His career flourished locally with his appointment as Recorder of Norwich in 1586 and as a Justice of the Peace for Norfolk in the same year. Coke became a Bencher of the Inner Temple in 1590, and the focus of his career shifted to London. He was appointed Recorder of that city in 1591 and then Solicitor General in 1592. Early the following year, he became Speaker of the House of Commons after being elected, initially for Aldeburgh (1589), then as a member for Norfolk (1592/3). Coke became the queen's Attorney General in 1593; on the accession of James I, he was appointed to the same office by the new king and knighted, becoming a member of the king's privy chamber. It was as Attorney General that Coke, in 1603, prosecuted Sir Walter Raleigh for High Treason, which led to Raleigh remaining imprisoned in the Tower of London until 1616. In 1606 Coke became Chief Justice of the Court of Common Pleas before being promoted to Chief Justice of King's Bench and a member of the Privy Council in 1613. Through much of this, Coke was very much a senior government legal officer, firmly embedded both in the legal profession and in the royal administration.[11]

Coke's dismissal as Chief Justice of the Court of King's Bench was the result of the position he took in what is known as the *Case of Commendams* (1616), though this was perhaps the culmination of a series of irritations that he had presented to the king's government, most stemming from his insistence that the common law should determine the proper jurisdictional boundaries for other laws that operated in England, notably the equity courts and the

10 Sheppard (n 2) *Selected Writings*, vol II 586–87.

11 Nearly all of the information here is from 'Coke's "Vade Mecum"', his own selection of the highlights in his personal and professional life, supplemented occasionally from the sources listed in n.4, and from AGR Smith, 'Coke, Edward (1552–1634)' (*History of Parliament 1558–1603*) <https://www.historyofparliamentonline.org/volume/1558-1603/member/coke-edward-1552-1634>.

ecclesiastical courts, as well as the king's prerogative; and from his intertwined view that the expertise of those learned in the common law gave them a privileged position in determining these jurisdictional issues. Kings who were not learned in the common law were, of course, virtually present in their courts and were the source of legal authority, but only trained judges exercised that authority within the legal system. The king in person should not intervene in matters where the ordinary law held sway. As he told James I to his face, 'the King is alwaies present in Court in the Judgment of Law . . . But the Judgments are always given *Per Curiam,* [by the court]'. The king replied that, as he was possessed of natural reason as much as a judge was, then surely he could give judgment himself. To which Coke famously replied that, well-endowed with reason though the king undoubtedly was, he

> was not learned in the Lawes of his Realm of England, and causes which concern the life, or inheritance, or goods, or fortunes of his Subjects; they are not to be decided by naturall reason but by the artificiall reason and judgment of Law, which Law is an act that requires long study and experience, before a man can attain to the cognizance of it.[12]

In the *Case of Commendams* – temporary appointments to ecclesiastical benefices – Coke and the judges refused the king's request to delay a decision until they had heard his view since the case could have implications for the royal prerogative. Coke alone refused to submit to the king's reiterated request, arguing that it 'was a delay of justice, and . . . contrary to lawe and the Judges' oath'.[13]

Dismissal from the bench did not end Coke's public career. His eclipse was not total: Coke remained a privy councillor and sat in Star Chamber. But it was his parliamentary career that made him an 'oracle of the people' and someone to be feared even after death. He was elected to the Commons in 1621, 1624, 1625, 1626, and 1628, though in 1626, he was prevented from taking his seat after being tactically pricked as Sheriff for Buckinghamshire. This was but a temporary reprieve for the Crown, anxious to silence an outspoken critic, as Coke's role in the proceedings of 1628 that led to the Petition of Right was perhaps the finest moment of his parliamentary career. It is telling for Coke's priorities that he began this parliament willing to grant the king supply and to provide retrospective statutory recognition for the Forced Loan (a tax without parliamentary authority, in effect), provided that it was affirmed for the future that 'there shall be no taxation but by act of parliament'.[14] Eventually, the Peti-

12 *Prohibitions del Roy* (1607), In Conference before the King, 12 Co. Rep. 63–65, in Sheppard (n 2) vol I, 480–81. There has been much discussion of Coke's idea of 'artificial reason'.

13 *Acts of the Privy Council of England, 1615–1616*, 604–05.

14 Thrush (n 4) is an excellent summary of Coke's parliamentary career in the 1620s; more extensively, Stephen D White, *Sir Edward Coke and the Grievances of the Commonwealth* (Manchester University Press 1979). The quote is from *CD 1628*, ii. 74.

tion of Right sought to deal with that issue, alongside that of arbitrary imprisonment (which had been used to enforce payment of the so-called Loan), by other means, that is, by a petition that would recognise the principles in question as matters of right and not of the king's grace. Coke spoke eloquently throughout of the need for enforceable recognition of the key principles of common law registered by Magna Carta and other key statutes, which should not be weakened by any allowance for the king's overriding sovereign power.[15]

Part III

The Second Part of the Institutes is a commentary on English statutes. The commentary should be understood in relation to a matter that has been at the heart of much scholarly writing on Coke, namely his understanding of the authority of stature and of the institution that produced it, the King-in-Parliament. At least until the Civil War, it is important to remember, the English parliament was understood by all as an institution of which the king was an integral part and was a mode for the exercise of the king's sovereign authority in conjunction with the consent of the whole realm.

Coke's report of *Caudrey's Case* stated:

> '[B]y the ancient laws of this realm, this kingdom of England is an absolute empire and monarchy consisting of one head, which is the King, and of a body politic, compact and compounded of many . . .[and] the kingly head of this politic body is instituted and furnished with plenary and entire power, prerogative and jurisdiction to render justice and right to every part and member of this body, of what estate, degree, or calling so ever in all causes ecclesiastical or temporal'.

Coke believed both that England was an imperial monarchy – language rooted in the Henrician reformation – but also one in which much of the king's temporal judicial authority was exercised 'by the mouth of the Judges', who 'judge and determine the same by the temporal laws of England'.[16] Parliament, too, was an agency of imperial monarchy, comprising 'the Kings Majesty sitting there in his Royall politick capacity, and of the three Estates of the Realm'

15 *CD1628*, iii, 494–95, 497, 502–03. *CD 1628*, iii, 505 – these references are all records of the same speech – makes it clear that Coke's objection was to the word 'power', which had no legal definition. 'Prerogative' was the correct term for the king's discretionary authority (which was defined and limited in scope by the law): 'the Prerogative of the King is given to him by the Common Law, and is part of the laws of the Realm' (3 Co. Inst. 84; also 2 Co. Inst. 496). At the same time, on matters relating to the person of the king, his prerogative was absolute and could not be bound even by statute; on matters involving the property and rights of his subjects, however, the king could be bound by law (*Case of Non Obstante or Dispensing Power* (1607) 12 Co. Rep. 18–19, in Sheppard (n 2) *Selected Writings*, vol I, 423–25).

16 *Caudrey's Case* (1591) 77 ER 1, 5 Co. Rep. 9a, pp 10–11.

(i.e., the lords spiritual, the lords temporal, and the commons).[17] Acts or statutes could be made only by 'the consent of the Lords, the Commons, and the Royall assent of the King'.[18] Whereas other Courts were directed by common law (or, in some cases, civil or canon law), parliament followed its own laws and customs. Matters before it were decided '*secundum legem & consuetudinem Parliamenti* [according to the law and custom of parliament]'.[19] But the power of parliamentary acts 'is so transcendent and absolute, as it cannot be confined either for causes or persons within any bounds';[20] consequently, no parliament could bind its successors.[21]

As Coke notes, some statutes were 'introductory of a new law, and some be declaratory of the ancient law, and some be of both kinds'.[22] Magna Carta, which took pride of place in Coke's *Second Part*, he described as 'for the most part declaratory of the principall grounds of the fundamentall Laws of *England*, and for the residue it is additional to supply some defects of the Common Law'. He soon added that it was declared by a later act of parliament to 'be taken as the Common Law', which could mean either that it made common law or that it was a statement of pre-existing law (the latter seems more likely in this instance).[23] In general, the law of England consisted of 'the Common Law, which is the most general and ancient Law of the Realm', statutes, and 'particular Customes' (that is, local customs, for if they were national customs, they would be part of the common law).[24] While the common law had primacy as 'an Artificial perfection of reason', 'by long experience grown to such a perfection, to the government of this Realm, as the old rule may justly be verified of it . . . No man . . . ought to be wiser than the Law, which is the perfection of reason', it could nonetheless 'be abrogated or altered by Parliament' because parliament represented, like the common law itself, a collective wisdom of many.[25]

There were, though, some limits even to the parliament's 'transcendent' power.[26] For a start, certain parts of the royal prerogative not affecting the property of subjects were absolute and could not be bound by statute.[27] But just how far could parliament go in changing the common law itself?

17 4 Co. Inst. 1, p 1062.
18 4 Co. Inst. 25, p 1110.
19 4 Co. Inst. 15, p 1092.
20 4 Co. Inst. 36, p 1133.
21 4 Co. Inst. 42–43, pp 1144–47.
22 4 Co. Inst. 25, p 1111.
23 2 Co. Inst. Prologue, 148–49.
24 Co. Litt. 115b. (Sheppard (n 2) *Selected Writings*, vol II, 711).
25 Co. Litt. 77b; Co. Litt. 115b. (Sheppard (n 2) *Selected Writings*, vol II, 711).
26 For another use of this term Co. Litt. 110.
27 See refs in n 14. Also 2. Co. Inst. 36 (Sheppard (n 2) *Selected Writings*, vol II, 828).

The question has been much debated in relation to Coke's enigmatic comment that

> in many Cases, the Common Law doth controll Acts of Parliament, and sometimes shall adjudge them to be void: for when an Act of Parliament is against Common right and reason, or repugnant, or impossible to be performed, the Common Law will controll it, and Adjudge such Act to be void.[28]

The passage has sometimes been seen as an early statement of the idea of judicial review. The *locus classicus* for this view is a 1926 essay by the distinguished American legal historian Theodore FT Plucknett. Plucknett was well aware of Coke's ingenuity in using medieval justifications for legal and constitutional innovation. He credits Coke with 'the idea of a fundamental law which limited Crown and Parliament indifferently', and traces the reception of the idea that the law could judge statutes to be void, including Blackstone's considered rejection of it and its embrace by some American judges. Cautious though he was, Plucknett nonetheless recognised that Coke's words in *Bonham's Case*, at least as later interpreted, were one of the things to which 'we owe the bold experiment of making a written constitution which should have judges and a court for its guardians'.[29] Some have built on this foundation, perhaps most impressively Allen D Boyer;[30] others find the attribution of a nascent doctrine of judicial review to Coke anachronistic. The debate continues, and it may indeed be, as one recent commentator has put it, 'unlikely that agreement is possible over such an ambiguous passage'.[31] One plausible counterview is that Coke was expressing no more than the truism that laws breaching the fundamental principles of natural law (which he thought to be part of English law) were no laws at all. This would make his statement compatible with the 'transcendent' power of parliament because it did not amount to granting judges the right to disallow legislation.[32] On the other hand, he might have had something altogether different in mind, asserting either that, in some cases, a statute might not be applied or simply a principle of statutory interpretation.

28 8 Co. Rep. 118a (Sheppard (n 2) *Selected Writings*, vol I, 275).

29 Theodore FT Plucknett, '*Bonham's Case* and Judicial Review' in Allan D Boyer (ed), *Law, Liberty and Parliament: Selected Essays on the Writings of Sir Edward Coke* (first published 1926, Liberty Fund 2004) 151, 176, 178–83, 185. For a wider view of the idea of a controlling common (fundamental) law see JWF Allison, *The Historical English Constitution: Continuity, Change and European Effects* (Cambridge University Press 2007), ch. 6.

30 Allen D Boyer, '"Understanding, Authority, and Will": Sir Edward Coke and the Elizabethan Origins of Judicial Review' (1997) 39 Boston College Law Review 43–93.

31 Ian Williams, 'Edward Coke' in DJ Galligan (ed), *Constitutions and the Classics: Patterns of Constitutional Thought from Fortescue to Bentham* (Oxford University Press 2014), ch. 3, 100.

32 RH Helmholz, 'Bonham's Case, Judicial Review, and the Law of Nature' (2009) 1(1) Journal of Legal Analysis 325–54.

One reading of Coke is that he was addressing not the possibility of judicial review but the reality of dealing with statutes that were repugnant or impossible.[33]

All in all, Coke seems committed to the 'transcendent' power of parliament, while also believing that the common law formed (or was part of) a fundamental law within which English government or politics operated.[34] The 'artificial reason' possessed by the common law judges meant that they were best placed to understand how this worked. The two principles do not, on the face of it, seem reconcilable, hence the unending debate on Bonham's Case but, in so far as the *Institutes* were his final view on the matter, Coke himself believed that they were. We can see how he went about putting the pieces together in *The Second Part of the Institutes of the Laws of England.*

Part IV

As we have seen, the publication of Coke's *Second Part* seems to have been feared by the king and his advisors and just as eagerly anticipated by the king's opponents. It was printed in a country polarising for civil war. Coke did not, of course, ever imagine the situation famously diagnosed by Philip Hunton soon after the outbreak of war. England was 'a limited legal monarchy' in which 'there can be no stated internal judge of the monarch's actions if there grow a fundamental variance betwixt him and the community'.[35] The Civil War was just such a situation of 'fundamental variance'. Coke had devoted his career to ensuring that this 'variance' could not arise and that there would always be a judge for whatever contention might arise between the king and his subjects. The Civil War represented the failure of this constitution, a situation in which there was 'no legal constituted judge'.[36] Of course, though the circumstances in which his book was read after 1642 were very different from those in which he wrote it, this did not stop readers from appropriating from him whatever might serve their purposes. But did the king or his parliamentary enemies have the most to gain from the book?

The most significant section of *The Second Part* was its opening commentary on Magna Carta. Coke was a key figure in the 'reinvention' of Magna

33 The options are neatly laid out in Ian Williams, 'Dr Bonham's Case and "Void" Statutes' (2006) 27(2) Journal of Legal History 111–28, which interprets Coke as advancing a form of 'strict construction'. Also John V Orth, 'Did Sir Edward Coke Mean What He Said?' (1999) 16 Constitutional Commentary 33–38.

34 The constitutional significance of the choice between parliamentary sovereignty and the common law constitution is well brought out in Jeffrey Goldsworthy, 'The Myth of the Common Law Constitution' in Goldsworthy (ed), *Parliamentary Sovereignty: Contemporary Debates* (Cambridge University Press 2010), ch. 2.

35 Philip Hunton, 'A Treatise of Monarchy (1643)' in David Wootton (ed), *Divine Right and Democracy: An Anthology of Political Writing in Stuart England* (Hackett Publishing 2003) 187.

36 Ibid 209.

Carta in the late Elizabethan and early Stuart period, adopting and extending changes in the interpretation of the charter that can be traced back to the 1580s.[37] Justin Champion has, indeed, suggested that '[t]he idea that the Charter provided the constitutional bedrock of the legitimate institutions of government and justice originated with . . . Sir Edward Coke'.[38] While this may overplay Coke's originality, it accurately gauges his influence. The *Institutes* captured the understanding of Magna Carta (and other early statutes) as an affirmation of fundamental common law principles that could, in some cases, be traced to pre-Conquest roots,[39] already extensively deployed in the debates on the Petition of Right.

Already, the *First Part of the Institutes* had captured a key point.

> The Common Law hath no controller of any part of it, but the High Court of Parliament, and if it be not abrogated or altered by Parliament, it remains still . . . . The Common Law appeareth in the Statute of *Magna Charta* and other ancient Statutes (which for the most part are affirmations of the Common Law) in the original writs, in judiciall Records, and in our books of termes and yeers.[40]

The 'Proeme' to the *Second Part* stated that Coke would make use of the full range of historical records to 'discerne what the Common Law was before the making of every of those Statutes, which we handle in this work, and thereby know whether the Statute be introductory of a new Law, or declaratory of the old'.[41] The examination of statute was, in good part, a route to a proper understanding of the state of the common law.

Wherever he could, Coke reinforced the idea that the oldest statutes were declarations of the fundamental common law, and he did his utmost to build a common-law constitution for England. Its principles were changed only with peril. So he noted that it was allowed, contrary to the common law recognised

37 Much the fullest account is now Sir John Baker, *The Reinvention of Magna Carta 1216–1616* (Cambridge University Press 2017). Still impressive is Faith Thompson, *Magna Carta: Its Role in the Making of the English Constitution 1300–1629* (University of Minnesota Press 1948), which ends with a chapter on 'Coke's Commentaries'.

38 Justin Champion, 'Reinventing the Charter: From Sir Edward Coke to Freeborn John' (2015) 125 The Historian 16–21 at 16. See also the debate on Champion's essay 'Magna Carta after 800 Years: From liber homo to modern freedom' (May 2015), online <https://oll.libertyfund.org/publications/liberty-matters/2015-05-01-justin-champion-magna-carta-after-800-years-from-liber-homo-to-modern-freedom-may-2015>.

39 Ian Williams, 'The Saxon Constitution and Early-Modern Law' (Selden Society Lecture 2022) <https://discovery.ucl.ac.uk/id/eprint/10152415/>; and the examination of Coke's historical sources in Anthony Musson, 'Myth, Mistake, Invention? Excavating the Foundations of the English Legal Tradition' in Andrew Lewis and Michael Lobban (eds), *Law and History: Current Legal Issues 2003*, vol 6 (Oxford University Press 2004) 63–81.

40 Co. Litt. 115b (Shepperd (n 2) *Selected Writings*, vol I, 711.

41 2 Co. Inst, Proeme; Sheppard (n 2) *Selected Writings*, vol II, 752.

in Westminster 1 that certain local officials, including Sheriffs, to take fees, with the result that 'it is not credible what extortions and oppressions have thereupon ensured'. Coke commented: 'So dangerous a thing it is, to shake or alter any of the rules or fundamentall points of the Common Law, which in truth are the main pillars, and supporters of the fabric of the Common-wealth'.[42] Coke here refers the reader to the Preface to the Fourth Part of his *Reports*, where he says that 'it is a Maxime in policie' that alteration to 'any fundamental point of the ancient Common Lawes and customes of the realme' would be

> most dangerous; for that which hath been refined and perfected by all the wisest men in former succession of ages and proved and approved by continuall experience to be good & profitable for the common wealth, cannot without great hazard and danger be altered or chaunged.[43]

Coke was not unaware that parliaments could act unwisely and trusted perhaps the possibility that errors would be corrected with time. But what reconciled him to the role of parliament was that it, too, represented a collective wisdom superior to that of any individual (including the king alone).

> In this Court of Parliament the King is *Caput, principium & finis*. And as in the naturall body when all the sinews being joined in the head do join their forces together for the strengthening of the body, there is *ultimum Potentiae*: so in the politique body when the King and the Lords Spiritual and Temporall, Knights, Citizens, and Burgesses, are all by the Kings command assembled and joined together under the head in consultation for the common good of the whole Realm, there is *ultimum Sapientiae.*[44]

The common law was the collective wisdom of many generations; parliament, the collective and highest wisdom of the realm in the present. Coke embedded parliamentary sovereignty within a common law constitution by dint of this emphasis on collective wisdom,[45] along with the principle of minimal change and constant affirmation of core principles. It is comparable to Edmund Burke's view that the superiority of England lay in its ability to make only necessary and minimal changes, unlike the revolutionary French. Change preserves in general while modifying only what Burke referred to as 'the peccant part', the bit that no longer worked.[46]

42 2 Co. Inst, 74; Sheppard (n 2) *Selected Writings*, vol II, 927.
43 4 Co. Rep, Pref., Sheppard (n 2) *Selected Writings*, vol I 95.
44 4 Co. Inst. 3, Sheppard (n 2) *Selected Writings*, vol II 1067.
45 This builds on the insight of Williams (n 31) 'Edward Coke' 107.
46 Emund Burke, *Reflections on the Revolution in France* (first published 1790, JGA Pocock ed, Hackett 1987) 19.

Thus, the *Second Part*, especially in its commentary on Magna Carta, sketched a common law constitution, repeatedly pointing out that 'this Charter is declaratory of the ancient Law and Liberty of England'.[47] Key issues of contention in the political world of early Stuart England were resolved by reference to the principles inherent in Magna Carta and, thus, in the common law. From it could be learnt the principle, taken from Plowden, that 'the Common Law hath so admeasured the Prerogative of the King, as he cannot take, nor prejudice the inheritance of any'.[48] Monopolies, a subject of intense parliamentary debate involving Coke in 1621 and 1624, were generally 'against this great Charter, because they are against the liberty and freedome of the Subject, and against the Law of the Land';[49] they were also 'against divers other Acts of Parliament, *which are good commentaries upon this Chapter*', a telling phrase.[50] All unparliamentary taxation was prohibited. 'No charge shall be levied of the people, if it were not granted in Parliament'.[51] Therefore, the decision given in the Exchequer in *Bate's Case* (1606) that had allowed the king by prerogative to impose customs duties on imported goods – a decision that led to repeated parliamentary debate – 'was against Law'.[52] Though some 'impost' or impositions' are named

> in divers Acts of Parliament, the same are to be intended of lawfull imposition, as of Tunnage and Poundage, or other Subsidies imposed by Parliament, but none of those Acts or any other doe give the King power at his pleasure to impose.[53]

Coke's commentary on what is today regarded as the most important chapter of Magna Carta (Chapter 29 in the 1225 version he used; Chapter 39 in the 1215 Magna Carta)[54] was a resounding defence of the requirement for legal process in all essential things. No freeman – the term covered everyone including villeins except in respect of their Lords – could be tried, imprisoned, dispossessed of property, exiled, outlawed 'but *per legem terrae*, that is, by the Common Law, Statute Law, or Custome of England'. No Englishmen could lose that which belonged to him,

> by his free birth-right, unlesse it be by the lawfull judgement, that is, verdict of his equals (that is, by men of his own condition) or by the

47 2 Co. Inst. 3 (p 758).
48 2 Co. Inst. 36 (p 828); also 2 Co. Inst. 63 (p 886).
49 2 Co. Inst. 47 (p 852).
50 2 Co. Inst. 63 (p 887), italics added.
51 2 Co. Inst. 60 (p 880).
52 2 Co. Inst. 63 (p.886).
53 2 Co. Inst. 61.
54 David Carpenter (ed), *Magna Carta* (Penguin 2015) 4–8, 52–53.

> Law of the Land (that is, to speak it once for all) by the due course, and processe of Law.

This principle comprehended criminal trial 'at the Kings suite', whether in Kings Bench or elsewhere, which must also be 'by the judgment of his Peers . . . or according to the Law of the Land'.[55] Parliament's effort to allow some 'absolute, and partiall trialls by discretion' in the reign of Henry VII had led, as any breach of 'fundamentall Law' must, to 'horrible oppressions, and exactions, to the undoing of infinite numbers of people'. Fortunately, the collective wisdom of parliament was self-correcting, and the offending act was abolished at the beginning of the reign of Henry VIII.[56] Among the actions that were available to preserve these fundamental rights, one takes us directly back to the debates on the Forced Loan and the Petition of Right. By the terms of writs of *habeas corpus,* 'it manifestly appeareth, that no man ought to be imprisoned, but for some certain cause: . . . for otherwise how can the Court take order therein according to Law'. The Petition of Right, Coke noted, 'hath made an end of this question',[57] and thus affirmed the ancient principles of the common law. That was not the only battle of the past visible in Coke's pages. At issue in the *Case of Commendams* was the king's request to delay justice while he consulted the judges. That, too, was contrary to Magna Carta.

> [B]y no mean common right, or Common law should be disturbed, or delayed, no, though it be commanded under the Great seale, or Privie seale, order, writ, letters message, or commandement whatsoever, either from the King, or any other, and that Justices shall proceede, as if no such Writs [etc.] . . . were come to them.[58]

The commentary on Magna Carta was, of course, only a modest portion of the *Second Part.* Detailed work on Coke's writing as texts rather than as legal authorities is still embryonic, but two points relevant to my argument might be drawn from elsewhere in the volume. First, Coke laid great stress on the confirmation of Magna Carta and other early statutes, repeating the affirmation that this document represents the fundamental laws that long predated 1215 (or 1225). Edward I 'expressly confirmed' and 'excellently interpreted' the Charters, and in his discussion, Coke warned 'that when any ancient Law or Custome of Parliament is broken, and the Crown possessed of a precedent, how difficult it is to restore the Subject again to his former freedom and

55 2 Co. Inst. 46 (p 849).
56 2 Co. Inst. 51 (p 860).
57 2 Co. Inst. 53 (p 864). Also 2 Co. Inst. 55 (pp 868–70) for a fuller discussion of the remedies available in law in respect of this chapter of Magna Carta.
58 2 Co. Inst. 56 (p 871).

safety'.[59] The Act *de Tallagio non Concedendo* (34 Ed. 1) furthermore 'containeth a restitution generall to the Subjects of all their Lawes, Liberties and free Customes', not just those in Magna Carta or the Charter of the Forest but 'all other Laws, Liberties, or Freedomes, and free-customes whatsoever'.[60] The confirmation by Edward I did something else, too. It determined that 'whatsoever judgement is given against the Statute of Magna Charta, or of Charta de Foresta is made void by this Act, and may be reversed by write of Error, because the judgement is given against the Law'.[61] In his Preface, Coke had also made this point that by this Confirmation Magna Carta was to be 'taken as the Common Law', adding that 'all former Statutes made against either of those Charters are now repealed'.[62] Statute could be abused, but abuses were reversed; for the most part, it reinforced and repaired the common law.

A second point emerges from the discussion of Westminster 1 (3 Ed. 1). Coke emphasised the remedies available in cases of royal misgovernment (a situation not remote from that of 1642). It was a principle that 'all matters of judicature and proceedings in Law are distributed to the Courts of Justice, and the King doth judge by his Justices'. Anything done by 'the extrajudiciall commandment of the King, be against Magna Carta'. The king 'being a body politique cannot command but by matter of Record'. If these principles were breached, then action could be taken, not against the king, but against his agents. 'If the King command me to arrest a man, and accordingly I doe arrest him. He shall have his Action of false imprisonment against me, albeit he was in the Kings presence'.[63] Coke not only sketched a common law constitution. He was, as we have seen elsewhere, very interested in the question of what remedies were available for breach of the fundamental protections the common law gave to the rights and liberties of Englishmen.

Part V

It may be true, as McKechnie has said, that 'Coke, following his vicious method of assuming the existence, in Magna Carta, of a warrant for every legal principle of his own day, misled generations of commentators'.[64] It may also be true that Coke's *Second Part of the Institutes of the Laws of England* had, to a degree, missed its moment: finished by 1628, it addressed with some force the issues of the decades before this date. What could those who awaited its appearance do with it when it finally appeared? Their issues were different. The common law constitution was in abeyance. A little later, when the *Fourth*

59 2 Co. Inst. 525, 528.
60 2 Co. Inst. 535.
61 2 Co. Inst. 527.
62 2 Co. Inst. Proeme (pp 748–52).
63 2 Co. Inst. 187.
64 Willam McKechnie, *Magna Carta: A Commentary on the Great Charter of King John* (2nd edn, James Maclehose 1914) 358.

Part appeared, they might have reflected ruefully on Coke's account of 'the five Cases' in which parliament performed badly. '1. When the king hath been in displeasure with his Lords, or with his Commons. 2. When any of the Great Lords were at variance between themselves. 3. When there was no good correspondence between the Lords and the Commons. 4. When there was no unity between the Commons themselves. 5. When there was no preparation for the Parliament before it began'.[65] The 1640s ticked every box.

And yet, a reception history of Coke's *Institutes* during the English Revolution would surely make interesting reading. Coke transmitted a powerful vision of a common law constitution that embedded a sovereign parliament as its one institution of deliberate (but preferably cautious) change. The simplicity of the fundamental principles that this embodied was an asset, and so Coke's vision became a vessel into which could be poured the concerns of many others keen to resist arbitrary government. When the Leveller leader John Lilburne was tried in 1649, a woodcut of him in court showed him with a copy of Coke's *Institutes*.[66] Lilburne cited Coke repeatedly; other radical leaders both made use of Coke's defence of the liberties of freeborn Englishmen while becoming wary of too much reliance on the past. It helped, though, that Coke's ancient constitution was *both* historical *and* rational. What they could get from Coke and the *Second Part of the Institutes* was a sense of the importance of something like Magna Carta, which in Coke's capacious reading becomes almost a constitution for the realm embodying fundamental principles of reason, transmitting and preserving them through time. Even those who moved on to think that what England needed now was a new Magna Carta owed Coke a debt.[67] His *Institutes* helped to give its readers a sense of what a constitution was – and could be.[68]

Bibliography

Allison JWF, *The Historical English Constitution: Continuity, Change and European Effects* (Cambridge University Press 2007)

Baker J, *The Reinvention of Magna Carta 1216–1616* (Cambridge University Press 2017)

Boyer AD, '"Understanding, Authority, and Will": Sir Edward Coke and the Elizabethan Origins of Judicial Review' (1997) 39 Boston College Law Review 43–93

65 4 Co. Inst. 35 (p 1131).

66 Michael Braddick, *The Common Freedom of the People: John Lilburne and the English Revolution* (Oxford University Press 2018) 190–91. Also Geoffrey Robertson, 'Lilburne and the Law' in John Rees (ed), *John Lilburne and the Levellers: Reappraising the Roots of English Radicalism 400 Years On* (Routledge 2018), ch. 4.

67 John Witte Jr, 'A New Magna Carta for the Early Modern Law: An 800th Anniversary Essay' (2015) 30(3) Journal of Law and Religion 428–45.

68 See generally Janelle Greenberg, *The Radical Face of the Ancient Constitution: St Edward's Laws in Early Modern Political Thought* (Cambridge University Press 2001); Glenn Burgess, *The Politics of the Ancient Constitution: An Introduction to English Political Thought 1603–1642* (Macmillan 1992) 86–99, 226–29.

Boyer AD, 'Coke, Sir Edward (1552–1634), Lawyer, Legal Writer, and Politician', *Oxford Dictionary of National Biography*, 14 November 2018. Oxford University Press. <https://www.oxforddnb.com/view/10.1093/ref:odnb/9780198614128.001.0001/odnb-9780198614128-e-5826> accessed 5 May 2025

Braddick M, *The Common Freedom of the People: John Lilburne and the English Revolution* (Oxford University Press 2018)

Burgess G, *The Politics of the Ancient Constitution: An Introduction to English Political Thought 1603–1642* (Macmillan 1992)

Carpenter D (ed), *Magna Carta* (Penguin 2015)

Champion J, 'Reinventing the Charter: From Sir Edward Coke to Freeborn John' (2015) 125 *The Historian* 16–21

Coke R, *A Detection of the Court and State of England during the Four Last Reigns and the Interregnum*, 2 vols (3rd edn, London 1697)

Drinker Bowen C, *The Lion and the Throne: The Life and Times of Sir Edward Coke 1552–1634* (Hamish Hamilton 1957)

Goldsworthy J, 'The Myth of the Common Law Constitution' in J Goldsworthy (ed), *Parliamentary Sovereignty: Contemporary Debates* (Cambridge University Press 2010)

Greenberg J, *The Radical Face of the Ancient Constitution: St Edward's Laws in Early Modern Political Thought* (Cambridge University Press 2001)

Helmholz RH, 'Bonham's Case, Judicial Review, and the Law of Nature' (2009) 1(1) Journal of Legal Analysis 325–54

Hunton P, 'A Treatise of Monarchy (1643)' in D Wootton (ed), *Divine Right and Democracy: An Anthology of Political Writing in Stuart England* (Hackett Publishing 2003)

Musson A, 'Myth, Mistake, Invention? Excavating the Foundations of the English Legal Tradition' in A Lewis and M Lobban (eds), *Law and History: Current Legal Issues 2003 Volume 6* (Oxford University Press 2004)

Orth JV, 'Did Sir Edward Coke Mean What He Said?' (1999) 16 Constitutional Commentary 33–38

Plucknett TFT, '*Bonham's Case* and Judicial Review' in Allan D Boyer (ed), *Law, Liberty and Parliament: Selected Essays on the Writings of Sir Edward Coke* (first published 1926, Liberty Fund 2004)

Robertson G, 'Lilburne and the Law' in J Rees (ed), *John Lilburne and the Levellers: Reappraising the Roots of English Radicalism 400 Years on* (Routledge 2018)

Sheppard S (ed), *The Selected Writings of Sir Edwards Coke*, 3 vols (Liberty Fund 2003)

Thompson F, *Magna Carta: Its Role in the Making of the English Constitution 1300–1629* (University of Minnesota Press 1948)

Thrush A, 'Coke, Sir Edward (1552–1634)' in A Thrush and J P Ferris (eds), *History of Parliament: The House of Commons 1604–29*, 6 vols (Cambridge University Press 2010). Online: https://www.historyofparliamentonline.org/volume/1604-1629/member/coke-sir-edward-1552-1634

White SD, *Sir Edward Coke and the Grievances of the Commonwealth* (Manchester University Press 1979)

Williams I, 'Dr Bonham's Case and "Void" Statutes' (2006) 27(2) Journal of Legal History 111–28

Williams I, 'Edward Coke' in DJ Galligan (ed), *Constitutions and the Classics: Patterns of Constitutional Thought from Fortescue to Bentham* (Oxford University Press 2014)

Williams I, *The Saxon Constitution and Early-Modern Law* (Selden Society Lecture 2022)

Witte R, 'A New Magna Carta for the Early Modern Law: An 800th Anniversary Essay' (2015) 30(3) Journal of Law and Religion 428–45

4 The Petition of Right

Ian Ward

4.1 Introduction

The *Petition of Right* gained the assent of King Charles I on 7 June 1628.[1] Whether it needed it is moot, for whilst it was enrolled, it was published as a declaration rather than a statute of the realm, a curiosity to which we will return. But Parliament demanded the King's assent regardless, determined that his acquiescence should be apparent. It was necessary indeed to 'raise the dejected hearts of your loving subjects'.[2] It was not a long document, but it was, in the moment, remarkable. Declaring the existence of certain 'rights and liberties' enjoyed by all Englishmen, the *Petition* proceeded to articulate three closer provisions. The first, drawing inspiration from the *Statutum de Tallaglio non concendo* of 1297, confirmed that there could be no raising of taxes or loans without the 'authoritie of parliament'.[3] The second, articulated in sections 2 to 5, noted that subjects who had refused to contribute to these 'forced' loans had been 'imprisoned confined and sondry other waies molested and disquieted' by local commissioners, and that this was 'contrary to law'. The third provision, articulated in Chapter 6, made the complaint that soldiers had been 'dispersed' into the counties and billeted amongst unwilling householders 'to their great grievance and vexation'. This was also contrary to law. The closing two chapters looked back and forth. The seventh raised the spectre of *Magna Carta*, more particularly the revered due process clause in Chapter 39.[4] The eighth summated the grievances before closing in terms which, hindsight suggests, were rather over-optimistic; that if the laws of the land were properly respected, they will 'tender the Honor of Your Majestie and the prosperitie of this Kingdome'.

1 3 Cha 1.
2 In J Guy, 'The Origins of the Petition of Right Reconsidered' (1982) 25 Historical Journal 307.
3 25 Edw.1. Tallage was a feudal due which had long attracted criticism, condemned in *Magna Carta*.
4 Chapter 39 in the text of 1215; Chapter 29 in the statute of 1297. Sometimes known as the *lex terrae* clause.

DOI: 10.4324/9781032658698-5

Whilst its place in the longer history of the British constitution is sometimes contested, the place of the *Petition* in the closer political history of early Stuart England is not. A key moment, hindsight suggests, on the road to civil war and revolution. Our purpose is to revisit both the text and the context of the *Petition*, to consider its conception, its writing, and its reception.

4.2 Conceiving the Petition

The provisions of the *Petition* spoke to an immediate concern regarding the attempt by King Charles I to re-float his Exchequer by means of 'forcing' loans from some of his better-off subjects. We will consider this closer context shortly. At the same time, though, it is possible to 'trace' a longer conception. We might imagine the *Petition* in the context of the reformation settlement and its attendant difficulties. We might even follow the seventh chapter back to 1215. We will discover some historians of a more Whiggish bent falling prey to this temptation in due course. For now, though, we are going to alight on a couple of different moments.

A first returns us to the middle of the fifteenth century, and a text entitled *In Praise of the Laws of England* written by Sir John Fortescue, a former Lancastrian Chief Justice.[5] Our particular interest is drawn to Chapter 17 of Fortescue's treatise and the determination of ***dominum politicum et regale***: 'For the king of England is not able to change the laws of his kingdom at pleasure, for he rules his people with a government not only royal but also political'. And the critical example that follows. For a King of England, accordingly,

> [I]s not able to change the laws without the assent of his subjects nor to burden an unwilling people with strange impositions, so that, ruled by laws that they themselves desire, they freely enjoy their own goods, and are despoiled neither by their own king nor any other.[6]

In other words, an English King can only tax his subjects with the consent of Parliament. The upside, for the King, was that his people would 'rejoice'. The downside was that whenever he found himself short of money, he would be obliged to recall Parliament.

A second moment requires a shorter journey back in time. Just 18 years, in fact, to 1610 and the resolution of the *Case of Proclamations*.[7] The case is one of a series in which King James clashed with his judges over the reach of his prerogative, starting with the *Case of Prohibitions* in 1607 and ending with the *Case of Commendams* in 1616. The former tested the legality of proclamations

5 Written between 1468 and 1471 whilst the author was in exile in France.

6 S Lockwood (ed), *Sir John Fortescue: On the Laws and Governance of England* (Cambridge University Press 1994) 17.

7 (1610) 12 Co Rep 74.

issued under the royal prerogative which would today be termed executive ordinances. James liked ruling by decree, issuing over 100 during the first half dozen years of his reign. It saved what he called the 'pother' of Parliament. The case is chiefly remembered for the principle articulated by Chief Justice Sir Edward Coke, 'that the King hath no Prerogative, but that which the Law of the Land allows him'. It is possible here, as it is in Fortescue's commentary, to discern the spirit of a principle that would become familiar in modern public law: the evolution of the cherished *lex terrae* of Chapter 39 into a 'rule of law'.[8]

At the same time, it is easy to neglect the original reason why the *Case of Proclamations* reached court. The two proclamations under consideration related to the regulation of starch importation and building development. The starch business was lucrative for a variety of reasons, not least stiffening ruffs. The development in question was the conversation of multi-occupancy units for the purposes of running brothels. James was as approving of stiff ruffs as he pretended to disapprove of brothels.[9] But what really interested him was the income stream that the respective licensing regimes facilitated. The terms of incorporation for the Company of Starchmakers confirmed that the Crown would receive half of every importation 'fine'.[10] In simple terms, James wanted his cut.

The root of the *Petition* lay here, in a place familiar to scholars of the New Testament: 'For the love of money is the root of all evil'.[11] Not all the high-octane constitutional squabbles that consumed the King and his judges between 1607 and 1616 were animated by money, but most were. *Dr Bonham's Case* tested the authority of the College of Physicians to exact licensing fees from aspiring practitioners, a cut of which was supposed to go to the Exchequer.[12] Financial matters also lay behind the *Earl of Oxford's Case*, which followed in 1615,[13] as they did in the *Case of Commendams*, which moved around the legality of a writ intended to transfer benefices and tithes during periods when clerical livings were vacant.[14] The added significance of *Commendams* was that it brought an end to Coke's judicial career, suspended in spring and dismissed in November, having displayed his 'craturity' once too often.[15]

8 It was recently raised, for example, in *R (on the application of Miller) v The Prime Minister* [2019] UKSC 41, at para.32.

9 For the contextual background to the case, concerning both the starch industry and James's seeming disapproval of prostitution, see I Ward, *The Trials of Charles I* (Bloomsbury 2023) 19–23.

10 It also confirmed a manufacturing monopoly for the Company. Which would prove to be quickly unworkable and was accordingly revoked in 1619.

11 1 *Timothy* 6:10.

12 (1610) 8 Co Rep 113b.

13 (1615) 21 ER 485; I Ch Rep 1.

14 (1616) APC 1615–1616 596.

15 An aspersion credited to James in the wake of Coke's judgment in the *Case of Prohibitions* in 1607. The word, meaning cunning, is of Scots origins.

It might have been expected that Coke would ease himself into retirement and spend some more time with his grandchildren, perhaps. But he was not the retiring type, nor indeed much of a family man. More the wife-beating and child-abusing type, if rumours are to be believed.[16] At first, he tried to ingratiate himself back into royal favour. But when that did not work, Coke began to attach himself to an emergent parliamentary opposition. King James, meanwhile, died in March 1625. The hope that his son Charles might be a rather more conciliatory monarch proved to be fleeting.[17] As did the hope that he might be better able to balance the books. Repeated requests for parliamentary grants were denied, leading to the abrupt dissolutions of the so-called 'Useless' parliament in June 1625 and its successor 12 months later. The former was dissolved for having refused the customary practice of granting the King 'tonnage and poundage' for life, the latter for having spent much of its time complaining that the King had proceeded to levy the said duty under his prerogative.[18] Charles, in turn, was reported 'vexed' by the snub and not a little embarrassed by its consequence. In the moment, he was busy buying up the famed Gonzaga art collection, recently on the market, whilst also trying to fund the Duke of Buckingham's variously ill-conceived military ventures. Both cost money.[19] And so we arrive at 1627, in the familiar circumstance of a profligate King short of money and a fractious Parliament unwilling to give him any. All of which meant that history was about to repeat.

16 Coke's relationship with his wife, Elizabeth, was evidently unhappy. She was 26 years his junior. They married in 1598 and were reported to have separated by 1604. We can only speculate violence but given Coke's notorious temper and the manners of the moment, it would have been odd if it were not an abusive marriage. Coke's treatment of his daughter Frances was notorious. When she proved reluctant to marry the demented Sir John Villiers, it was reported that Coke had her 'tyed to the bed-poste and severely whipped into consent'. Coke was keen on the marriage, in the hope that it might ingratiate him with Sir John's brother George, Duke of Buckingham. The marriage eventually took place in September 1617, and proved to be predictably violent and unhappy.

17 The Earl of Dorset was confident in the prospect of a new 'covenant' between Charles and his subjects. A fawning Coke wondered if Charles might prove to be another Henry V. Sadly not. See R Cust, *Charles I* (Routledge 2007) 109, and Ward (n 9) 28.

18 Tonnage and poundage duty was originally conceived in the early fifteenth century, as an 'imposition' on wine importation. It had been granted to each monarch for life since the reign of Henry VI.

19 Charles purchased most of the Gonzaga collection in two instalments. A first, costing around £18,000, comprised lots of Titian, Raphael, and Caravaggio. The centrepiece of the second, at the cost of a further £10,000, was Mantegna's famed set of canvasses entitled *The Triumph of Caesar*. Much would be sold off in early 1649. Not the Mantegna though, especially admired by Cromwell. The Duke of Buckingham's ill-conceived ventures comprised a failed attempt to seize Spanish treasure ships at Cadiz in late 1625, followed by a similarly futile attempt to relieve the Huguenots bottled up in La Rochelle in 1527.

4.3 Writing the Petition

We will start our survey of the final months leading up to the presentation of the *Petition* back in court. On this occasion, we are interested in the *Case of the Five Knights*, or *Darnel's Case*, as it is more properly known; the 'first link in the chain of events leading to the petition', it has been suggested.[20] Absent an obliging Parliament, Charles had taken to the idea of a 'forced' loan during the summer of 1627. The *Case of the Five Knights* tested the legality of the policy, albeit obliquely. The royal proclamation which accompanied the writs gave the reason of 'necessitie to which no ordinarie course can give no lawe'. Even the King's closest supporters harboured doubts. The Archbishop of Canterbury kept his 'suppressed within my soul'.[21]

Others were less discreet. Thomas Crosfield, a fellow of Queens College Oxford, likened it to 'Spanish servility'.[22] Feeding the 'palate of power', the Earl of Clare was heard to remark. The gentlemen of Kent berated Lord Keeper Coventry at Maidstone Assizes, reminding him that such a tax was against the 'whole discourse of Fortescue'.[23] When the King intimated that non-payers might be prosecuted in court, Coventry advised against it. As 'far as he understood the law, none were liable to martial law but martial men'. Charles was though undaunted. If the courts refused to do his bidding, he would 'sweep all their benches'.[24] So he blundered on into a marketing disaster. In March 1627, writs were issued against six of the more 'refractory' non-payers, five knights of the shire, plus the Earl of Lincoln. The knights were despatched to the Fleet prison 'by special command of His Majesty'. Lincoln was sent to the Tower, as befitted his rank.

None of the five were charged with a crime. The contention was their detention. Charles was said to be 'much moved' when they petitioned for 'relief out of prison'; but evidently not enough. The five duly issued writs of *habeas corpus* at King's Bench, and the bailiff, unsure what to do, failed to present. It was the Attorney-General, similarly unsure, who then issued a second writ in the name of one of the confined, Sir Thomas Darnell. Leading for the knights, the famed John Selden sought familiar recourse to Chapter 39:

> No man is to be arrested, or imprisoned, or disseised, or outlawed, or exiled, or in any way destroyed, nor will go against him, nor will we send

20 Guy (n 2) 289.

21 R Cust, 'Charles I, the Privy Council, and the Forced Loan' (1985) 24 Journal of British Studies 219, 222.

22 K Sharpe, *The Personal Rule of Charles I* (Yale University Press 1992) 700. The slavery metaphor was commonly cited in parliamentary debate. See here S Willms, 'The Five Knights' Case and Debates in the Parliament of 1628: Division and Suspicion Under Charles I' (2006) 7 Constructing the Past 95.

23 D Smith, *Constitutional Royalism and the Search for Settlement c.1640–1649* (Cambridge University Press 1994) 34.

24 Cust (n 21) 225, 227–28.

against him, save by the lawful judgement of his peers or by the law of the land.

If the knights were not surrendered, Selden opined, their 'imprisonment shall not continue for a time, but forever; and the subjects of this kingdom may be restrained of their liberties perpetually'. An observation which, it was reported, elicited 'wonderful applause' in the galleries. Lord Chief Justice Hyde was less impressed and held that relief lay with the King who, being 'bound by law', would 'do what is right'.[25] The case was not over, though. A few weeks later, Selden stood up in the reassembled Commons and accused the Attorney-General of seeking to enrol an interlocutory 'judgement' of the court and thus fabricate a precedent 'for ever and ever'.[26] A dastardly subterfuge that persuaded the Commons to establish a committee to hear Selden's complaint. Amongst those who gave evidence before the committee, confirming that subjects could not be held at the King's 'pleasure' without charge was Sir Edward Coke.[27]

It was in this same excitable mood that the Commons passed four 'resolutions' to be conveyed to the King. A first deploring prerogative taxation and three more relating to conditions of detention, which could only be lawful, had to be under formal charge and was subject to the run of *habeas corpus*.[28] Summoned to the Lords to hear Lord Keeper Coventry, Members were assured that 'you shall find as much security in his Majesty's royal word and promise as in the strength of any law'.[29] Hardly convincing in the wake of Selden's 'discovery'. With Charles continuing to demur, the Commons decided that the 'resolutions' should be passed into law in the form of a statutory petition. The question of authorship was easily resolved. All they needed was a skilled lawyer, likely bearing a grudge, with time on his hands. And one name rather obviously suggested itself. On 8 May 1628, Coke presented a draft *Petition of Right* to the House of Lords. We have already noted its terms.[30] There was little new to be found in Coke's draft, which was precisely the point. Written in the spirit of the 'ancient' constitution and, more particularly, the hallowed 'liberties' of *Magna Carta*, the 'statute of statutes' as Francis Ashley had put it

25 M Kishlansky, 'Tyranny Denied: Charles I, Attorney-General Heath and the Five Knights Case' (1999) 42 Historical Journal 53, 61–64, 76.

26 See Guy (n 2) 296–301, and also Kishlansky (n 25) 56–58, and 74–75, wondering whether the accusation of duplicity might be better directed towards Selden.

27 An ironic moment, as the Solicitor-General noted, citing evidence of Coke saying precisely the opposite back in 1616. See Guy (n 2) 302–03, and Kishlansky (n 25) 73.

28 Arbitrary imprisonment being the 'principal grievance' according to both Guy (n 2) at 291, and L Reeve, 'The Legal Status of the Petition of Right' (1986) 29 Historical Journal 259–60, 259.

29 In Guy (n 2) 305.

30 The signal refinement in the *Petition* addressed grievances regarding billeting and, by insinuation, martial law. See here L Boynton, 'Martial Law and the Petition of Right' (1964) 79 English Historical Review 255–84.

in the febrile summer of 1616, 'worthy to be written in letters of gold'.[31] The *Petition* was dressed to impress.

Charles dithered. His first response was to offer to reaffirm *Magna Carta*. But that was not enough. *Magna Carta* did not need to be reaffirmed; its status was sacrosanct, already secured in the common law. The *Petition* was an assertion, not a plea, written to affirm immediate 'grievances' along with certain inalienable 'rights' which were in the care of Parliament, not the gift of the Crown. The lexicon had shifted over four centuries, the mood over the previous four months. It is possible to see here the birthing of another revered principle of British constitutional law, the sovereignty of Parliament. It certainly chimed with Coke's renowned commentary on the 'High Court of Parliament', which could be read in the fourth volume of his *Institutes*. Parliament governed itself, and it protected the 'liberties' and 'rights' of all Englishmen. The aligned insinuation, that it also enjoyed a supervening judicial capacity, would come in very handy in early 1649, as the senior officer corps of the New Model Army contemplated putting a King of England on trial. Most importantly, the *Petition* demanded a response and acquiescence.[32]

In the end, it was the money that talked. Absent the acquiescence, there would be no money. The idea of assenting to the *Petition* hardly appealed to the King. But the sweetener, five subsidies worth £300,000, did. Seeking the advice of his judges, Charles received some encouragement in the shape of an assurance that he would still retain the right to detain subjects in 'secrecy' for a 'convenient time' without cause if the circumstances justified it.[33] But still, he dithered, troubled by the absence of a statement on reserved prerogative powers and offended by the scarcely veiled insinuation that the grievances enumerated were a consequence of his folly. On 2 June, he issued a vague declaration that 'right be done according to the law of the realm', a seeming affirmation of an earlier promise that he would not infringe the liberties enshrined in *Magna Carta* except 'upon just cause'.[34] Parliament refused to budge. On 5 June, the Privy Council spent five hours discussing the *Petition*. Two days later, Charles assented. Sir Edward Hyde recalled the events in appropriately transactional terms, a *Petition* 'purchased'.[35] Coke expressed himself 'almost dead for joy'.[36]

31 J Baker, *The Reinvention of Magna Carta 1216–1616* (Cambridge University Press 2018) 1, 427–28.

32 See S Gardiner, *History of England from the Accession of James I to the Outbreak of the Civil War 1603–1642* (Cambridge University Press 1884/2011) 6.273–75.

33 See Gardiner (n 32) 6.294–95, and Reeve (n 28).

34 Sharpe (n 22) 40–41, and Cust, *Charles*, 74.

35 Earl of Clarendon, *History of the Rebellion* (Oxford University Press1853) 1.185–202 (get precise).

36 In T Royle, *Civil War: The Wars of Three Kingdoms 1638–1660* (Little Brown 2004) 21.

But any hope that the publication of the *Petition* might betoken a cessation in hostilities was quickly dispelled. Charles, it seemed, was up to his old tricks again.[37] A first publication of the *Petition* was halted by royal command, and when a second rolled off the presses, it was absent a statute number, notwithstanding the fact that it was enrolled. The King's printer had evidently erased it with a pumice stone. Instead, the *Petition* was published as a 'declaration'. It also came with an 'answer' drafted by the King or by his close adviser, William Laud, at least.[38] It confirmed that the King's 'meaning was not to grant any new privileges but to rectify your old'. Whilst confessing that the loan might, on reflection, have been an 'undue course', he reserved his right to do similar again, where 'necessity' should become the 'law', whilst also pointedly asserting his 'right' to collect 'tonnage and poundage'.[39] A few weeks later, the Exchequer Court dismissed the counterargument that the duty was now unlawful under the terms of the *Petition*. The Commons erupted, stalling payment of the subsidies. Robert Triplet, an Islington brewer, petitioned the King, who he held 'in my esteem like God'. Robert had a couple of pieces of advice. First, convert the Queen to Protestantism. Second, pay closer heed to Sir Edward Coke, 'as good a commonwealth man as you have in all your kingdom'.[40]

Unfortunately, Charles was not especially good at paying heed, and if he did, it was usually to the wrong people, like indeed the Queen, who had absolutely no intention of converting. It was Henrietta Maria, amongst others, who persuaded Charles that the time had come to close his third Parliament, so 'blinded' was it 'with popular applause'.[41] Needless to say, it was all rather messy. The Speaker was held in his chair by furious Members whilst the House passed a series of further resolutions condemning 'innovation in religion', the misuse of prerogative to 'break parliaments', and the illegal levying of 'tonnage and poundage'. Anyone who paid the latter, the House resolved, should be 'reputed a capital enemy to the kingdom and commonwealth'.[42] A horrified Sir Simonds D'Ewes recorded a 'tumultuary' day, the 'most gloomy, sad, and dismal day for England that happened in five hundred years'.[43]

37 For a comment here, suggesting an affinity between Charles's subterfuge here and the attempt to enrol the interlocutory judgment in the *Case of the Five Knights*, see J Morrill, *The Nature of the English Revolution* (Longman 1993) 289–90.

38 Shortly to be appointed Bishop of London.

39 For an overview, see R Cust, 'Charles I and a Draft Declaration for the 1628 Parliament' (1990) 63 Historical Research 143–61.

40 D Cressy, *Charles I and the People of England* (Oxford University Press 2015) 196.

41 The comment was made in his dissolution 'declaration'. See Smith (n 23) 27, and Sharpe (n 22) 59–60.

42 Cust, *Charles* (n 17) 118.

43 Sharpe (n 22) 56.

4.4 Receiving the Petition

The enactment of the *Petition* is, of course, merely the next stage in its history. We must also consider its reception. Here again, there is a shorter term and a longer one. The immediate consequence of the *Petition*, following the chaotic dissolution of Parliament, was a decade of 'personal rule'. Easier on the nerves, perhaps, but not on the Exchequer. Expenditure on the royal wardrobe doubled during the first decade of Charles's reign, from £13 million a year to £27 million. So many nice things to buy. And so many wars to engage too. Within months of his succession, Charles had asked Parliament for £700,000 to support his Uncle Christian IV of Denmark in his war with the perfidious Hapsburgs. To which could be added the Duke of Buckingham's variously fated endeavours. It was another war which, in due course, persuaded Charles to revisit the possibility of raising an extra-parliamentary levy.

The war this time was of the more notional variety, against pirates, the seventeenth-century equivalent of our similarly fantastical 'wars' against terrorism or a coronavirus. To counter this apparent threat, Charles issued writs for the collection of 'ship money' in October 1634, to be levied from London and certain seaports. There had been 'ship money' levies since the days of the Plantagenets, and Charles had himself attempted a levy it in the months following the dissolution of his third Parliament, only to quickly withdraw the writs when the extent of opposition had become apparent. Needs, however, pressed, especially as Charles had just agreed on a secret treaty with Philip IV of Spain to provide aid in his war against the Dutch. The Attorney-General obligingly confirmed the notional legality of the ruse, even during times of relative peace, further suggesting that it would not contravene the *Petition* as it was not, strictly speaking, a tax. And so the writs were issued along with a royal proclamation which confirmed their need 'for the good and safety of the Kingdom', whilst taking care to emphasise that 'in such cases' the King was the 'sole judge' of the 'danger'. In other words, the King had the absolute authority to determine the extent of his absolute authority. His father might have been impressed.

Too many of his subjects were not. The 'most deadly and fatal blow' inflicted on the 'liberty of the subjects of England' in 'five hundred years past', D'Ewes opined, before asking the familiar question: 'What shall free men differ from ancient bondsmen and villeins' if 'their estates be subject to arbitrary taxes?'[44] The Earl of Warwick counselled that it was squarely against the provisions of both *Magna Carta* and the *Petition*, adding the provocative rider that those who were refusing to pay should be considered 'patriots'. Charles was, however, undaunted, reminding his judges that the situation was simple.

44 Sharpe (n 22) 692.

In cases of 'peril . . . is not the King the sole judge . . . of the danger?'[45] The judges replied in emollient terms.

Twelve months later, the levy was broadened to include inland towns. Meanwhile, the courtrooms of England began to fill with fractious cattle-owners suing writs of *replevin* and their lawyers, looking for a fight and a decent fee. And dozens of non-payers, such as Sir John Corbett of Adderley in Shropshire, were summoned by Lord President of the Marches, in this instance, for refusing to contribute to a militia muster. Doubling down, Sir John cited the *Petition of Right*; a truculence that saw him despatched to the Fleet.[46] A culture of provincial recalcitrance was emerging, as Archbishop Laud noted, non-payers growing daily more 'bold'.[47] A perspicacious King might have paused for thought. Hyde strenuously argued against prosecuting non-payers, one particularly. But Charles, as we have already noted, was hardly perspicacious.

In the summer of 1637, the sheriff of Buckinghamshire returned a list of non-payers, which included the name of John Hampden. Hampden knew what was coming and was prepared. *Hampden's Case* arrived at the Court of Exchequer in early autumn 1637.[48] His counsel, Oliver St John, did not dispute prerogative power, but he did dispute the authority of the Crown to seize 'goods' without 'parliamentary assistance', contrary to the 'fundamental laws of England'. The Attorney-General deployed a metaphorical defence, surmising that the King 'is the first mover among these orbs of ours, and he is the circle of this circumference'. The King held a 'trust' which included a duty to do 'whatever tends to the preservation' of the realm at moments of 'danger' and, if need be, deal with instances of 'refractoriness'. The 12 justices in Exchequer found themselves at considerable odds. Four sided with the King on the ground the Attorney-General intimated. Two leant just as strongly the other way, most notably Justice Croke, who confirmed that 'no necessity can procure this charge without a parliament'. The others immersed themselves in technicalities regarding the execution of the writ, such as the differences between a tax and a 'service', commanding such a service, and receiving the benefit. In fact, so confusing were the respective opinions that no one was entirely sure of the result. Bulstrode Whitelock counted it ten to two for the King. The Venetian ambassador, Antonio Correr, thought it seven to four, with one abstention.[49]

But if the extent of the victory was uncertain, the identity of the loser was not. As Hyde had feared, *Hampden's Case* 'grew the argument of all

45 Sharpe (n 22) 719.

46 On Corbett's case, see M Braddick, *God's Fury, England's Fire: A New History of the English Civil Wars* (Penguin 2009) 65–66.

47 Sharpe (n 22) 728. By 1639 delinquency rates had risen to 80%.

48 (1637) St Tr 826.

49 B Whitelock, *Memorials of English Affairs, from the Beginning of the Reign of King Charles I to the Happy Restoration of King Charles II* (Oxford University Press 1853) 1.71–72, and Sharpe (n 22) 722–23.

tongues', and did far more 'credit' for Hampden than it did his King. At that moment, Hampden had the 'greatest power and interest' of any man 'in this kingdom'.[50] Hampden would go on to be a prominent critic of the King in both the 'Short' and 'Long' Parliaments before dying of wounds following the battle of Chalgrove Field in 1643. Charles meanwhile staggered on until another ill-conceived military venture finally brought an end to 'personal' rule. In truth, the first 'Bishops' war' was hardly a war at all. Frustrated by the refusal of the Scottish Kirk to accept his Prayer Book, Charles despatched an army north. By the time it reached Berwick, it was clear that it was in no condition to go further. The so-called 'pacification of Berwick' set the terms of a temporary cessation of hostilities. The following year, the Scots moved south, inflicting a humiliating defeat at Newburn before occupying Newcastle. The second Bishops' War ended with Charles agreeing, under the terms of the Treaty of Ripon, to pay £25,000 a month; in effect, protection money.

Worse still, he was obliged to recall Parliament to secure the necessary finance. The 'Short' Parliament, summoned at the end of February 1640, had sat for just three weeks, most of which was spent articulating various 'grievances', including alleged infringements of the *Petition of Right* and the 'false gloss' with which the King and his 'ill ministers' had sought to shade it.[51] Charles had ended it when it became apparent that it was not going to vote him any subsidies. Then came Newburn and Newcastle and the Treaty of Ripon. The 'Long Parliament' opened for business at Westminster in November, every bit as aggrieved. A few weeks in, it presented Charles with a *Grand Remonstrance*, enumerating 204 'grievances'. Uppermost in its collective mind was the imposition of *Ship Money* 'contrary' to associated parliamentary resolutions and 'the *Petition of Right*'.[52]

Parliament would eventually agree to pay off the Scots, to the tune of £300,000, under the terms of the Treaty of London in August 1641. By then, it had passed a *Triennial Act*, thereby securing its own existence, abolished the prerogative courts of High Commission, Star Chamber, and the Council of the North, declared *Ship Money* illegal, impeached Archbishop Laud, and executed the Earl of Strafford.[53] It also impeached a number of judges involved in *Hampden's Case*, those who were deemed to have given the wrong answers.[54] The following May, Parliament issued a document entitled *Nineteen Propositions*, one of which suggested that henceforth, any officer of state should be obliged to swear an oath to uphold the *Petition*. Three months later, Charles

50 Clarendon (n 35) 1.168.

51 The words of Sir Francis Seymour. Sharpe (n 22) 867.

52 Commons resolution of 7 December 1640, quoted in Smith (n 23) 70.

53 Under the terms of the *Triennial Act* (16 Cha 1 c1), parliament was to meet for a session of 50 days once every three years, at the least.

54 Having been identified in the *Grand Remonstrance*. See W Jones, *Politics and the Bench: The Judges and the Origins of the English Civil War* (Allen and Unwin 1971) 13–15, 137–43.

declared war on his own Parliament. We know how that story ends. The story of the *Petition of Right*, however, continues.

4.5 Reading the Petition

The *Petition* would continue to occupy a place in later histories of what Charles Dickens liked to term the 'great seventeenth century time'. Historians of a Whiggish hue were tempted to extract a greater significance, placing the *Petition* in a longer constitutional evolution from *Magna Carta* through to the *Bill of Rights* and beyond. Taking inspiration from the *caveat* inscribed in the draft 'Declaration of Rights', that it was 'not for making new laws but for declaring old'.[55] On these same terms, Hume recognised a 'memorable moment' in the history of 'English government', supposing that King Charles's assent to the *Petition* was 'almost equivalent to a revolution and by circumscribing, in so many articles, the royal prerogative gave additional security to the liberties of his subjects'.[56] Referring to the *Case of the Five Knights*, which had precipitated the Petition, he supposed that 'by raising as spirit of liberty in the nation', it 'went even to shake the foundations of Charles's throne'.[57] Blackstone, no more a Whig in his politics than Hume, likewise inclined to a Whiggish reading of the *Petition*. Situating his discussion in a chapter, 'Of the Absolute Rights of Individuals', Blackstone recognised a 'parliamentary declaration of the liberties of the people', which laid the path for the 'bill of rights' to follow in 1688.[58]

Regardless of their political bent, eighteenth and nineteenth-century historians inclined the same way. The *Petition of Right* was to be understood constitutionally as part of a much longer narrative of national determination. There may be certain regrettable moments on the road to this determination, such as the execution of King Charles, but its direction was sure. Henry Hallam, instinctively Whiggish, took the bull by the horns. Commenting on the regicide, he supposed that the *Petition of Right* removed any excuse that Charles may have had for his continuing 'violations of liberty'. Most importantly, he could not claim 'ignorance' of the common law of England. The entire event, encompassing the *Five Knights* as well as the *Petition*, had proved Charles to be a man of deep 'insincerity' and the 'kingdom' not to be 'in a temper to put up with tyranny'.[59] The road to the scaffold started in 1628, the road to the 'glorious' revolution, too. Samuel Rawson Gardiner adopted a similar

55 See here M Kishlansky, *Monarchy Transformed: Britain 1603–1714* (Penguin 1997) 285, and also Morrill (n 37) 437–38.

56 D Hume, *A History of Great Britain Under the House of Stuart* (A Millar 1759) 172.

57 D Hume, *A History of England, Abridged, from the Invasion of Julius Caesar to the Revolution on 1688* (J Buist ed, J&T Fairbairn 1793) 267.

58 W Blackstone, *Commentaries on the Laws of England* (Oxford University Press 2016) 1.124.

59 H Hallam, *Constitutional History of England from Henry VII to George II* (JM Dent 1800) 355, 362.

line, suggesting that Charles's reception of the *Petition* confirmed an instinct for casuistry, whilst its drafting described 'the severest censure to which any King of England had submitted since the days of Richard II'. Gardiner, like Hume, spotted the 'germs of a revolution'.[60] Winston Churchill's *A History of the English-Speaking Peoples*, Victorian in everything but publication date, assumed a predictably Whiggish tone. Parliamentary tactics were 'artful', the reader learns, but 'justified by their convictions', for it is in the *Petition* that 'the main foundations of English freedom' are to be found.[61]

The age of Whig history, its 'interpretation' at least, was, however, passing.[62] To be replaced by the age of the revisionist. In his account of the 'constitutional history' of England, Maitland concentrated his discussion of the *Petition* under the sub-heading of 'Taxation and Control over Finance' during the reigns of the early Stuarts, citing the *Case of the Five Knights* as the immediate animating factor. The very next paragraph goes on to trace the consequence of the *Petition* in *Hampden's Case*.[63] The broader context might be constitutional, but the immediate circumstance of the *Petition* is described by the pragmatics of political economy. A thesis revisited by Conrad Russell emphasising the alignment of parliamentary politics and economic crisis during the increasingly heated debates of 1641 and early 1642. Aggrieved MPs time and again invoked 'rights' now enshrined in the *Petition*, whilst increasingly given to suppose that their King was busy conjuring a 'malignant and popish' party for the purpose of returning the English to the 'yoke' of Rome.[64]

Revisionism prefers contingencies of circumstance and personality. Thus, John Guy ascribes the uproar which surrounded the enrolment of the decision in the *Five Knights* to 'a quirk of King's Bench book-keeping'.[65] In the case of the *Petition*, this means a greater interest in the pragmatics of parliamentary politics, the consequence of an empty Exchequer, and the chronic dithering of a King who kept on making the same mistakes.[66] Gardiner's Charles. There is no necessary incompatibility here, of course. The *Petition of Right* might be representative of immediate political and economic circumstances whilst also assuming a place in a longer history of constitutional evolution.[67] Conversely, it

60 Gardiner (n 32) 6.276, 285. The 'most scholarly of the Whig historians' in his interpretation of the *Petition*, according to Reeve. See his (n 28) 257.

61 W Churchill, *A History of the English Speaking Peoples* (Cassell 1974) 2.143–44.

62 The classic account of this passing is Herbert Butterfield's, *The Whig Interpretation of History* (Bell 1931).

63 F Maitland, *Constitutional History of England* (Cambridge University Press 1919) 306–08.

64 C Russell, *Parliaments and English Politics* (Oxford University Press 1979) 321, 330–31, 338–40, 380, C Russell, *The Causes of the English Civil War* (Oxford University Press 1990) 137–43, and C Russell, 'Parliament and the King's Finances' in C Russell (ed) *The Origins of the English Civil War* (Macmillan 1973) 113–14.

65 Guy (n 2) 294.

66 On the changing perception of the *Petition*, see (n 46) 46.

67 For a commentary along these lines, focussing more closely on the place of economics in Coke's mind, and the constitution he shaped, see B Yandle, 'Sir Edward Coke and the Struggle for a New Constitutional Order' (1993) 4 Constitutional Political Economy 263–85.

might, with hindsight, be adjudged nothing more than a 'half-effective measure', a curiosity bred of a very curious moment in English political history; not entirely forgotten, but very nearly.[68] An essentially 'cosmetic' exercise at a variant, a gesture of parliamentary frustration.[69] A collateral concern here moves around the legal status of the *Petition*. Does it assume statutory authority notwithstanding Charles's skullduggery? It certainly went through a legislative process and was commonly treated as a statute by later generations, not least in *Hampden's Case*. The alternative is that it should be treated as a declaration, the constitutional authority of which is discovered by judicial *fiat*.[70] History is about making choices.

In terms of modern readings of the *Petition*, there is something else we might consider in closing. It has become fashionable in contemporary conversation to wonder about the significance of so-called 'constitutional statutes'. Such statutes are not irrepealable, but it might be that conditions attach to the 'manner and form' of their repeal. Such statutes may, for example, need to be expressly, rather than merely impliedly, repealed. The possibility evidently runs against Dicey's renowned supposition that all statutes carried equal weight; thus, 'neither the Act of Union with Scotland nor the Dentists Act 1878, has more claim than any other to be considered a supreme law'.[71] A century and a quarter of international law and globalisation have, however, rendered Dicey otiose. Much of the contemporary conversation has been energised by the UK's accession to the EU and its legal consequence. Lord Justice Laws intimated the idea of a 'constitutional statute' in *Thoburn*, the case of the so-called 'metric martyrs', which moved around the implementation of a European Union directive intended to harmonise weights and measures. Laws defined a 'constitutional statute' as one which affects the 'conditions the legal relationship' of citizen and state', or 'enlarges or diminishes the scope of what we would now regard as fundamental constitutional rights'.[72]

The UK has now left the EU, of course. But the conversation is still active, as is the consequential parlour game, identifying possible 'constitutional' statutes. More recently conceived candidates include the Human Rights Act 1998, the devolution statutes, and the Constitutional Reform Act 2005. Lord Bingham was certainly of the opinion that the former might enjoy an enhanced status, more especially because of its peculiar relation with the rule of law.[73] At this point, the idea of constitutional statutes aligns with that of a 'common law' constitution. The opinion of Lord Steyn in *R (on the application*

68 For this resolution, see Morrill (n 37) 410. A similar sentiment can be read into John Baker's recent reassessment of *Magna Carta*, in which the *Petition* is relegated to a passing footnote quotation of someone else's comparative disdain. See Baker (n 21) at 449.

69 Guy (n 2) 311.

70 For a discussion here, favouring the 'legislative' option, see Reeve (n 28) 257–77.

71 A Dicey, *An Introduction to the Study of the Law of the Constitution* (Macmillan 1959) 145.

72 [2003] QB 151, at para.62.

73 T Bingham, *The Rule of Law* (Allen Lane 2010) 66–72.

of Jackson) v Attorney General lent this way. In 'exceptional circumstances', where a Parliament looked to 'abolish' a 'constitutional fundamental', the 'new Supreme Court may have to consider' the possibility of striking down that legislation.[74] The implication was clear. As Vernon Bogdanor noted, in 'such exceptional cases, the rule of law may trump parliamentary supremacy'.[75] A 'silent step' towards a British *Marbury v Madison*, Sir Stephen Sedley teases.[76] Whilst all laws might be procedurally 'equal', some are 'constitutionally more equal than others'.[77] The 'cornerstone' of a 'new constitution'?[78]

Or maybe an old, revitalised 'historical constitution'.[79] The same parlour game invites suggestions from a sometimes distant past. *Magna Carta*, the Bill of Rights 1689, the 'great' Reform Act of 1832, or perhaps that of 1867, which, in truth, mattered so much more. And, just possibly, the *Petition of Right*.[80] Lord Bingham includes the *Petition*, along with the *Case of Five Knights*, in his confessedly 'impressionistic' account of 'milestones' in British constitutional history. 'A lineal descendent' of *Magna Carta*, he suggests, in slightly Whiggish terms.[81] After which comes the Habeas Corpus Amendment Act of 1679, the Bill of Rights, and the Act of Settlement 1701. Sedley likewise credits the *Petition* as representing an 'important stage in the history of the royal prerogative', more closely reading the *Petition* as a prologue to the abolition of Star Chamber. After which, once again, came the same Bill of Rights and Act of Settlement.[82] Despite the ravages of revisionism, the longer narrative evidently retains its charm. It is for each historical generation to gauge the extent to which it wishes to be enchanted. But, however sceptical we might wish to be regarding history as if 'told by strolling minstrels', as Herbert Butterfield famously put it, it would be a strange history of the Anglo-British constitution which did not at least pause for a moment in 1628.[83]

74 [2005] UKHL 56, para.102. By way of example, Steyn cited any attempt to abolish judicial review. For discussions here, see S Sedley, *Lions Under the Throne: Essays on the History of English Public Law* (Cambridge University Press 2015) 145–46, and also T Allan, 'Questions of Legality and Legitimacy: Form and Substance in British Constitutionalism' (2011) 9 International Journal of Constitutional Law 156, 156–57, 161–62.

75 V Bogdanor, *Beyond Brexit: Towards a British Constitution* (Tauris 2021) 164.

76 See Sedley (n 74) 149. Allan prefers a more abrasive metaphor, suggesting that Steyn was 'driven to threaten a judicial revolt'. In T Allan (n 74) 156.

77 Sedley (n 74)118.

78 J McConalogue, *The British Constitution Resettled: Parliamentary Sovereignty Before and After Brexit* (Palgrave 2020) 47–48.

79 J Allison, *The English Historical Constitution: Continuity, Change and European Effects* (Cambridge University Press 2007) 221–28.

80 Even if it was not, as we noted earlier, technically a statute of the realm.

81 Bingham (n 73) 17–20.

82 Sedley (n 74) 185–86.

83 Butterfield (n 62) 11–13, 64.

Bibliography

Allan T, 'Questions of Legality and Legitimacy: Form and Substance in British Constitutionalism' (2011) 9 International Journal of Constitutional Law 156
Allison J, *The English Historical Constitution: Continuity, Change and European Effects* (Cambridge University Press 2007)
Baker J, *The Reinvention of Magna Carta 1216–1616* (Cambridge University Press 2018)
Bingham T, *The Rule of Law* (Allen Lane 2010)
Blackstone W, *Commentaries on the Laws of England* (Oxford University Press 2016)
Bogdanor V, *Beyond Brexit: Towards a British Constitution* (Tauris 2021)
Boynton L, 'Martial Law and the Petition of Right' (1964) 79 English Historical Review 255
Braddick M, *God's Fury, England's Fire: A New History of the English Civil Wars* (Penguin 2009)
Butterfield H, *The Whig Interpretation of History* (Bell 1931)
Churchill W, *A History of the English Speaking Peoples* (Cassell 1974)
Clarendon (Earl of), *History of the Rebellion* (Oxford University Press 1853)
Cressy D, *Charles I and the People of England* (Oxford University Press 2015)
Cust R, 'Charles I, the Privy Council, and the Forced Loan' (1985) 24 Journal of British Studies 219
Cust R, 'Charles I and a Draft Declaration for the 1628 Parliament' (1990) 63 Historical Research 143
Cust R, *Charles I* (Routledge 2007)
Dicey A, *An Introduction to the Study of the Law of the Constitution* (Macmillan 1959)
Gardiner S, *History of England from the Accession of James I to the Outbreak of the Civil War 1603–1642* (Cambridge University Press 1884/2011)
Guy J, 'The Origins of the Petition of Right Reconsidered' (1982) 25 Historical Journal 307
Hallam H, *Constitutional History of England from Henry VII to George II* (JM Dent 1800)
Hume D, *A History of Great Britain Under the House of Stuart* (A Millar 1759)
Hume D, *A History of England, Abridged, from the Invasion of Julius Caesar to the Revolution on 1688* (J Buist ed, J&T Fairbairn 1793)
Jones W, *Politics and the Bench: The Judges and the Origins of the English Civil War* (Allen and Unwin 1971)
Kishlansky M, *Monarchy Transformed: Britain 1603–1714* (Penguin 1997)
Kishlansky M, 'Tyranny Denied: Charles I, Attorney-General Heath and the Five Knights Case' (1999) 42 Historical Journal 53
Lockwood S (ed), *Sir John Fortescue: On the Laws and Governance of England* (Cambridge University Press 1994)
Maitland F, *Constitutional History of England* (Cambridge University Press 1919)
McConalogue J, *The British Constitution Resettled: Parliamentary Sovereignty Before and After Brexit* (Palgrave Macmillan 2020)
Morrill J, *The Nature of the English Revolution* (Longman 1993)
Reeve L, 'The Legal Status of the Petition of Right' (1986) 29 Historical Journal 259
Royle T, *Civil War: The Wars of Three Kingdoms 1638–1660* (Little Brown 2004)
Russell C, 'Parliament and the King's Finances' in C Russell (ed), *The Origins of the English Civil War* (Macmillan 1973)
Russell C, *Parliaments and English Politics* (Oxford University Press 1979)
Russell C, *The Causes of the English Civil War* (Oxford University Press 1990)
Sedley S, *Lions Under the Throne: Essays on the History of English Public Law* (Cambridge University Press 2015)
Sharpe K, *The Personal Rule of Charles I* (Yale University Press 1992)

Smith D, *Constitutional Royalism and the Search for Settlement c.1640–1649* (Cambridge University Press 1994)
Ward I, *The Trials of Charles I* (Bloomsbury 2023)
Whitelock B, *Memorials of English Affairs, from the Beginning of the Reign of King Charles I to the Happy Restoration of King Charles II* (Oxford University Press 1853)
Willms S, 'The Five Knights' Case and Debates in the Parliament of 1628: Division and Suspicion Under Charles I' (2006) 7 Constructing the Past 95
Yandle B, 'Sir Edward Coke and the Struggle for a New Constitutional Order' (1993) 4 Constitutional Political Economy 263

5 The Instrument of Government of 1653

Blair Worden

The document that we know as the Instrument of Government was a list of provisions which Oliver Cromwell swore to observe when he was installed as Lord Protector on 16 December 1653. It supplied the rules of his regime until July 1657, when it was replaced by a modified version of it, the Humble Petition and Advice, which survived Cromwell's death in 1658 but fell with the protectorate in 1659, a year before the restoration of the monarchy. In modern terms, the Instrument was the nation's first codified or written constitution and, with the Humble Petition, its only one. No one remarked on that novelty at the time.[1] There is striking originality in the Instrument, but its framers did not aspire to replace the accumulation of ancient laws and customs that we think of as the nation's unwritten constitution, though its relationship to them was unstated and clouded in ambiguity. The text was a pragmatic and hastily devised solution to a political crisis which must be recounted if the document is to be understood.

If we seek revolutionary architecture in the contests over forms of government in the 1650s, we must look elsewhere: to the programme announced in James Harrington's *Oceana* in 1656 and to the debates it provoked in 1659–60. Outside the circles of power, the Instrument attracted less attention. Contemporaries were more interested in the fact of Cromwell's acquisition of power than in the terms of it. So has posterity been. The text of the Instrument, which the new government nervously got printed in inconspicuous and ephemeral form,[2] became durably accessible from 1682 when it was included in the first of a series of collections of texts from the civil wars.[3] Yet

1 The Instrument was not even called a constitution, a noun which had shifts and shades of seventeenth-century meaning that rarely match our own usage. It was likelier to signify either the setting up or the existence of arrangements of power than the arrangements themselves. Here we need the noun, and the adjective constitutional, as shorthand, but must be alive to the anachronism.

2 *The Government of the Common-Wealth as it was publicly declared at Westminster* (London 1653[-4]).

3 Bulstrode Whitelocke, *Memorials of the English Affairs* (London 1682). In the eighteenth century it was included in the widely read *Somers Tracts* and *The Parliamentary or Constitutional History of England*.

DOI: 10.4324/9781032658698-6

its availability did not enhance its reputation, which was tied to the impermanence of Cromwellian rule and to the obloquy directed at its memory. The most influential historian of the eighteenth century, David Hume, called the Instrument a 'motley' text, 'crude and undigested', the work of men radically deficient in 'the spirit of legislation'.[4] In 1800 Henry Hallam, the pioneer of modern constitutional history, judged it not 'worth while' to 'pay much attention' to the document.[5]

Over the course of the nineteenth century the Instrument attracted more interest. The protectorate, which, like Cromwell himself, was now more favourably viewed, was drawn into the evolutionary approach which Hallam had led. By 1890, the Instrument could be analyzed among 'the constitutional experiments of the Interregnum'.[6] In the previous year, S.R. Gardiner, the great historian of civil-war England, published his collection of *Constitutional Documents of the Puritan Revolution*, where the Instrument has been most often studied. His commentary contains the most considered judgment to have been passed on the Instrument. Though he thought the document was doomed by its political context, he reversed Hume's judgment of its quality and declared it 'impossible not to be struck with the ability of its framers'. Gardiner's tribute was just. Yet his Whiggish perspective impelled him to a mixed verdict. With the Humble Petition, the Instrument was 'interesting as anticipating in many respects the constitutional and political development of England and the United States of America', but the two texts contained 'too much in advance of the general intelligence' to endure.[7]

Gardiner correctly characterized the Instrument as a 'middle course' between two alleged tyrannies: that of Charles I, and that of the Parliament which opposed and replaced him. In 1653, it was the parliamentary 'tyranny' that confronted Cromwell, the lord general of the army that had defeated Charles I. Before the civil wars, Parliament had been an occasional body, called and dissolved at the Crown's will. No one imagined that it ought to have the functions or powers of an executive. The breakdown of royal authority from 1640 transformed its character. Having extracted from the king an act forbidding him to dissolve it without its own consent, it raised an army against him and went into permanent session. With no authority to restrain it, it developed striking theories of parliamentary sovereignty. From the king's defeat in 1646, it ran the country. Complaints of parliamentary tyranny rose not only among royalists but on Parliament's own side, where army officers and

4 David Hume, *The History of England*, 6 vols (Philadelphia 1795–96), v, 311–12.

5 Henry Hallam, *The Constitutional History of England*, 3 vols (1884 edn), ii, 245.

6 Edward Jenks, *The Constitutional Experiments of the Interregnum* (Cambridge University Press 1890).

7 SR Gardiner (ed), *The Constitutional Documents of the Puritan Revolution, 1625–1660* (Clarendon Press 1889) liii–lxiv. The texts of the two documents are at pp 405–17, 447–49.

Levellers pressed for measures to make Parliament accountable to the nation it represented.

The Parliament did not mean its monopoly of rule to be permanent. The doctrine of parliamentary sovereignty was devised to define the assembly's relationship with Charles I, not to remove him. Parliament vindicated its actions against him and its continuous session as a response to a national emergency that had arisen from his betrayal of his trust and his declaration of war on his people. Most MPs wanted peace terms that would disable him from repeating his crimes but not prevent the lawful exercise of royal authority by his successors. They were thwarted by the Cromwellian army, which in the later 1640s emerged as a semi-autonomous political force, aggrieved at mistreatment by the assembly which had appointed it and animated by political, social, and religious resentments for which it held Parliament as much as the king to blame. In the winter of 1648–9, angered by what seemed to it fresh betrayals by the king and Parliament alike, the army forcibly expelled the parliamentary majority and, through the minority that was prepared to work with it, had Charles tried and executed in 1649. In the following months, the remnant of the Parliament, the Rump as it came to be called, abolished kingship and the House of Lords and declared England to be a 'Commonwealth and Free State'.

Under the Rump, the *de facto* parliamentary government of the civil wars was institutionalized. The business of government was deputed to a subordinate council of state chosen by Parliament, mostly from its members, and answerable to it. Yet the proclamation of a free state was hesitant and gingerly. Though there were those in the 1650s who argued that the old government had been 'dissolved' in 1649 and that a new one must be created, the now unicameral Parliament normally thought of itself as a continuation of a form of government which king, Lords, and miscreant MPs had deserted. In its own view, the Rump was entitled to rule without the other two estates not because England had exchanged monarchical for republican rule but because the Commons was the elected representative of the people, who are the origin of all just power.

In accordance with that principle, and with proposals by the army, the Rump drafted a scheme for an overhaul of the electoral system as far-reaching and as fatal to rotten boroughs as the Reform Act of 1832. It would be implemented by the Instrument in the elections of 1654 and 1656.[8] The Rump itself, which governed a nation that neither was nor wished to be represented by it, had not dared to hold the elections it designed. There was wide agreement that royalists could justly be disenfranchised for many years, a premise which the Instrument would again enforce. But what of the body of parliamentarian and neutral opinion which had been revolted by the revolution of 1649 and which, if it regained representation at Westminster, could be expected to turn on the regicides and reopen the wounds of the 1640s?

8 See my *The Rump Parliament* (Cambridge University Press 1974), ch 8.

In April 1653, when the Parliament had sat for 13 years, Cromwell forcibly expelled it. Its authority, he claimed, now 'devolved' to him as its general.[9] What would he do with it? He had no intrinsic interest in forms of government. They were 'as Paul says dross and dung in comparison of Christ',[10] whose service was Cromwell's driving purpose. The principle of representation mattered to him only because of its hold on colleagues and followers and because he knew that no settlement would be attainable without parliamentary endorsement. Though he used the Rump's reluctance to hold elections as the pretext for its expulsion, he too knew their peril and postponed the prospect of them. He had been unable to get his and his restless army's programme of social and religious reform through the Rump. Yet he had wearied not of its form of rule, only of the people who ran it. In its aftermath, he introduced a change of personnel, not of machinery. He replaced the Rump with another single-chamber assembly, 'Barebone's', as it was nick-named, chosen not by the electorate but by him and his fellow officers. Like the Rump, it entrusted executive power to a subordinate council answerable to it.

Yet Cromwell, who had endorsed the Rump as a makeshift regime in 1649, looked to Barebone's too as a temporary one. He had, and would retain, a dual goal: godly reformation and conditions of peace and settlement in which it could thrive. His challenge was to persuade the nation to share his perception of the two aims as complementary rather than conflicting. He wanted Barebone's to set the godly reformation in motion and to draw the nation to it. Unhappily for him, the assembly took to extremes the reforms which the Rump had refused. In the ensuing social panic, the survival of the Puritan cause, even the preservation of public order, came into question. On 12 December, allies of Cromwell secured the resignation of Barebone's, which returned its powers to him.

Out of that emergency, the Instrument of Government emerged four days later. Now Cromwell ended the undivided parliamentary rule he had endorsed since 1649. Now there would again be a single ruler who would share power with Parliaments, an arrangement he believed to be the 'most agreeable to the general sense of the nation'.[11] The Instrument had been drafted, perhaps over two months, by army officers, maybe in conjunction with civilian allies of Cromwell. It was the brainchild of the officer John Lambert, whose 'cunning pencil' and 'subtle working brain' were acknowledged by adversaries of the Instrument.[12] He had cut his teeth as a political thinker in 1647 when he helped to draw up the peace terms which the army had at that time wanted to

9 John Morrill (ed), *The Letters, Writings, and Speeches of Oliver Cromwell*, 3 vols (Oxford University Press 2023) ii, 686.

10 Ibid i, 465.

11 Ibid ii, 142.

12 Bulstrode Whitelocke, *Memorials of the English Affairs* (London 1682) 257; JT Rutt (ed), *Diary of Thomas Burton*, 4 vols (London 1828) iv, 61.

be submitted to Charles I and which prefigure provisions of the Instrument. When it was first shown to Cromwell, the Instrument offered him the title of king in Charles's place. The army was divided and inconsistent about kingship. In refusing the title, Cromwell yielded to the body of military opinion which opposed the 'lordly interest' of monarchy and was predisposed to regard any elevation of his political authority as the sacrifice of their cause to his ambition. But there were others in the army who would have been happy for Cromwell to be king, provided he was the army's king. They proposed the crowning of him in 1653 but bitterly opposed parallel moves by their civilian adversaries four years later.

The title he chose in 1653, lord protector, had previously been held by rulers acting temporarily on behalf of kings who inherited the throne as minors. But the Instrument did not intend Cromwell's rule to be temporary. He was characteristically and adroitly ambiguous about the implications of his title. He quietly assumed rights and observed practices that had belonged to the Crown. But was his office a redefinition, under a change of name, of the office of king, or was it a break with it? Analogous uncertainties ran through the Instrument, which half-created, half-restored.

The final content of the Instrument was hammered out in hectic discussions that preceded Cromwell's installation. At that low-key and rapidly improvised ceremony the document was read out but was not submitted in written form. The text was printed only on 2 January, as 'The Government of the Common-wealth of England, Scotland, and Ireland, and the Dominions thereunto Belonging'. Ireland and Scotland had been conquered by Cromwell on the Rump's behalf in 1649–51. The Instrument extended parliamentary representation to them, as the Rump had intended to do, but in practice the elections would be controlled from England. Many of the provisions of the Instrument were ill-suited or irrelevant to conditions in Ireland and Scotland. England's arrangements of power were the document's focus.

The gap in time between Cromwell's proclamation and the publication reveals unease within the regime at the risk or impropriety of its affront to legal and civilian practices of government.[13] It also reveals divisions about the desirability and efficacy of the text. Some clauses of the document that Cromwell swore to observe were silently amended before publication. In neither the spoken nor the printed form of the Instrument was there any explanation or vindication of its existence, for what sanction of legitimacy could have been invoked? There was no agreed name for the document. Though it was sometimes colloquially called 'the Instrument of Government', or simply 'the Instrument', it had no distinctive claim to that title. For convenience, I inescapably call it 'the Instrument', but an 'instrument' was a means of conveying

13 Blair Worden, 'Oliver Cromwell and the Instrument of Government' in Stephen Taylor and Grant Tapsell (eds), *The Nature of the English Revolution Revisited* (Boydell Press 2013) 123–50. I there describe the evolution and drafting of the Instrument.

or establishing authority, not the authority itself.[14] Spokesmen for the document of 1653 and their opponents referred to it most commonly not as an 'instrument' but as 'the government', though sometimes as 'the establishment' or 'the form of government' or 'act of government' or 'frame of government'. Only with Gardiner, who needed his own shorthand, did it become automatic to call the text 'the Instrument of Government'.

The devisers of the Instrument had as much eye to political exigency and calculation as to principles of constitutional design. The Instrument included five clauses independent of the arrangements for the distribution of authority prescribed by the other 37. One of them, clause 40, assuaged the soldiery by guaranteeing the observation of articles of surrender which the army had negotiated in the wars but which, to its indignation, Parliament had overruled. The other four (clauses 35–8) cover, in cagey and slippery wording, profoundly divisive issues of religion. They insist on liberty of conscience, the dearest of all of Cromwell's aims.[15] It was no less dear to religious groups inside and outside the army whose support he needed to retain and who regarded the illegal origins of the Instrument as a price worth paying for the enshrinement of the principle. Liberty of conscience, to which seventeenth-century Parliaments were never sympathetic, had been fundamentally resisted by the bulk of the parliamentarian opinion which Cromwell now sought to restore to the political fold. The Instrument gave parliamentarians notice that their return would be conditional on their acceptance of an inimical principle.

Alongside his commitment to liberty of conscience, Cromwell retained the reforming goals which the Rump had resisted and Barebone's exceeded. His aim to combine reform with settlement persisted. The Instrument, which followed the act of 1641 in arranging for Parliaments to meet triennially even if the ruler had not summoned them, stipulated that the first Parliament would meet after nine months, in September 1654. In the interim, the Instrument entitled the protector and his council to pass 'ordinances' and to implement them until the Parliament reviewed them. He used the provision to make changes, extensive but not immoderate, to the running of the Church and of the legal system. The settlement would come from the readmission to public life of the people and opinions which had constituted the core of the parliamentarian cause but which had been excluded since the regicide.

The imposition of the Instrument was an act of naked illegality. Yet, as the judges and law officers who sanctioned it saw, it offered a route back to legality,

14 Cromwell used an 'instrument' to devolve power to Barebone's (Morrill (n 9) ii 705). In 1657, in addressing Parliament on the Humble Petition and Advice, the document through which it intended to replace the text of 1653, Cromwell repeatedly called the new version 'the' or 'this' or 'your instrument' (Morrill (n 9) iii 356, 389, 406). After the revolution of 1688, the Conventions of England and Scotland, evidently unaware of the Cromwellian precedent, transferred power to William and Mary by 'the Instrument of Government'.

15 Blair Worden, *God's Instruments. Political Conduct in the England of Oliver Cromwell* (Oxford University Press 2012), 63–90.

for if parliamentary opinion could be persuaded to accept the provisions of the document, it would find a way of legalizing them. The document made short-term provisions, which allocated power and initiative to the protector, for the entrenchment of the regime and the stabilizing of the country, and long-term ones to meet the goals pursued by Parliament before the regicide: the limitation of the ruler's authority; the guarantee of regular Parliaments; government by law rather than by arbitrary will. If Parliament were to be persuaded to accept the Instrument, indignation at Cromwell's coups would have to be parried and proud objections overcome. Yet where else could MPs go? Few of them wanted to return to undivided parliamentary rule. Most of them had fought or worked against the now-exiled Stuart dynasty. They knew the danger to themselves of its return, against which Cromwell's standing army, huge and expensive as it was, was the bulwark. However much MPs resented Cromwell's past actions against them, they and their successors recognized that, in the words of one MP, 'It is not easy to wrest a club out of Hercules' hands'.[16]

*

The political necessities of which the Instrument was born proved a mother of invention. The text laid down a premise which had not been stated in any previous constitutional proposal. It distinguished between 'legislative' authority, which was to be shared between the protector and Parliament, and 'executive' authority, which was to lie with the protector. The concrete prescriptions of the document did not need those terms. The Instrument could simply have listed the roles of protector and Parliament, as the peace proposals of the 1640s had listed those of king and Parliament. But king and Parliament were historic identities whose status and actions were habitually understood in terms of custom and precedent that could not validate Cromwell's new office. Instead, the Instrument explained the office in terms of its function, the 'executive' role, which, as propaganda for the new government would explain, had been transferred from kingship and re-designed to the nation's advantage.

The classification of legislature and executive was a consequential innovation. It is in the definition of the two by the Instrument that, as M.J.C. Vile observed, we first 'find the doctrine of the separation of powers standing on its own feet'.[17] We may add that the Instrument helped re-cast the concept of the executive. The executive's function, in so far as it had been apprehended, had normally been regarded as the implementation of laws passed by the legislature. That perspective had found little room for the wider role of government, its management of affairs of state, which is the executive's role in the Instrument. Perhaps a better phrase for 'separation of powers' would be 'distinction of powers', for the arrangements of power laid down by the

16 *Burton* (n 12) iii 260.
17 MJC Vile, *Constitutionalism and the Separation of Powers* (Oxford University Press 1967) 3.

Instrument depended as much on the interaction of legislature and executive as on the division between them. Sometimes the distinction fades, for the framers who made it were not concerned with establishing an unimpeachable doctrine. They used the categories to posit solutions to the constitutional issues which had divided king and Parliament and were bound to face protector and Parliament: the ruler's 'negative voice' or veto, control of the armed forces, and the relationship of the ruler to his council.

The council, the successor to the royal privy council, had a critical role in the Instrument. The neglect or perversion of conciliar government was a long parliamentary complaint. The Instrument gave the council a series of formal roles and obliged the protector to rule with its advice and consent. It is in addressing the composition of the council that the requirements of the Instrument are most ingenious and innovative, and there, too, that the arrangements are most interactive. The Instrument named the initial councillors, all followers of Cromwell, but when a vacancy arose, a shift would begin. The sitting or next Parliament would submit six names to the council itself, which would choose two of them, from whom the protector would name one.

Legislative power is defined in the first clause of the Instrument, and executive power in the second. Here, Gardiner's Whiggish perspective is vindicated, for the formula would reappear in the American Constitution, though not in any intervening constitution. There are other resemblances of principle and categorization between the two documents: in the provisions (though they are never identical) for the exercise by the single ruler of a qualified veto and of the power of pardon; for the command of the army; for the appointment of office-holders; for the power to make war or peace. The American framers knew nothing of the English ones. The parallels arose from the correspondence of experience. In both countries, the rejection of a royal 'despotism' had provoked a lurch to the opposite extreme, the monopoly of the legislative body: in England by an unlimited Parliament, in America by the uncontrolled powers of the Congressional Congress and state legislatures.[18] Both documents attempted to balance the two branches. In defending the Instrument, Cromwell would commend the 'true and equal balance' between his office and Parliament.[19]

Yet the achievement of balance, which exercised the delegates at Philadelphia in the sweltering summer of 1787, may have been a last-minute aspiration in the winter of 1653. There survive drafts of the Instrument, or of provisions to be included in it. Though sometimes hard to interpret and date, they give

18 Blair Worden, 'Checks and Balances: The Cromwellian Origins of the Presidency' in Ben Lowe (ed), *Political Thought and the Origins of the American Presidency* (University Press of Florida 2021) 19–52. A shorter version of that paper is 'Checks and Balances; The Birth of a Vocabulary' in Paul Hammond and Andrew Hadfield (eds), *Words at War. The Contested Language of the English Civil War* (Oxford University Press 2024) 297–309.

19 Morrill (n 9) iii 142.

us glimpses of the evolution of the document in the days before and after the end Barebone's. During that time the role envisaged for the protector seems to have been strikingly enlarged, under pressure from Cromwell. We cannot draw firm conclusions from the absence of the word 'executive' from the drafts, for the texts merely abbreviate or summarize proposals. Even so, the drafts do not give the protector the balancing role to which, in the final version, the word executive points. Their wording indicates how entrenched the practice of parliamentary rule had become and how large a mental step was needed to break through it.

In framing their peace terms in the 1640s, Parliament and the army had faced a dilemma. Although they believed the Parliament's practical exercise of sovereign power against Charles I to have been justified by emergency, they knew it to have been unusual. In normal circumstances, they would not have wanted MPs to be full-time politicians. Anyway, no one argued that large assemblies were ideal for executive decision-making. So peace-seekers expected or called for 'intervals' between Parliaments.[20] But how should executive power be exercised during them? So long as Charles I was alive, it was agreed, there must be commissioners or a council appointed by Parliament to observe and restrain the king on its behalf. When, in the late 1640s, the army began to envisage the removal of the king or at least the radical attenuation of his powers, it called for a similar body to hold power on behalf of the outgoing Parliament until the meeting of the next one, to which it would report and be accountable. The Rump, in designing the elections it was reluctant to hold, made a similar arrangement.[21]

'Intervals' between Parliaments reappear in the drafts and, very differently, in the Instrument. At the drafting stage, powers of the protector, such as the making of peace or war, were to be held only in the intervals. Everyone knew Cromwell's capacity for exceeding his official political roles. He had overshadowed Barebone's even though he was not a member of it. The extent and limits of his formal powers were nonetheless of essential importance. The role envisaged for him in the drafts seems to have been merely that which in the late 1640s and in the Rump had been expected of an interim council or commissioners. Only in the final version does the protector emerge as Parliament's partner rather than its subordinate.

*

In February 1654, the new regime published an apologia for the Instrument, 17,000 or so words long, with the title *A True State of the Case of the Commonwealth*. It was written anonymously by Cromwell's in-house thinker, Marchamont Nedham, on whose arguments and propaganda Cromwell was heavily reliant. The alliance was as incongruous as it was effective. Nedham, 22 years

20 Gardiner (n 7) 51, 284, 304, 317, 368.
21 Worden (n 8) 372.

Cromwell's junior, was a shameless trimmer whose hired pen served a succession of masters and regimes, parliamentarian, royalist, Puritan, anti-Puritan. Yet he was at one with Cromwell in his readiness to regard 'forms of civil administration (being but as the shell to the kernel)' as 'subordinate and inferior to the ends of government' (p. 8). *A True State* is an able exposition of 'this government now established' (which it never calls an 'instrument') (p. 40). The document is portrayed as a return to sense and 'practical convenience' (p. 37), which supplies a government 'well bounded on both sides against anarchy and tyranny' (p. 52).

Nedham, who was close to the centre of events during the birth of the Instrument, is the obvious source of its distinction between legislative and executive power. He had already used the formula on another political front, in propaganda of 1652 which he recycled in *A True State.*[22] M.J.C. Vile, in identifying the document as a landmark in which the separation of powers becomes 'a coherent theory of government, explicitly set out', quotes a passage of *A True State*[23] where Nedham attacks the practice of the Rump in combining 'the supreme powers of making laws, and of putting them in execution', for

> placing the legislative and executive powers in the same persons is a marvellous in-let of corruption and tyranny: whereas [in] the keeping these two apart, flowing in distinct channels, . . . there lies a grand secret of liberty and good government.
>
> (10)

The tract produced another linguistic innovation, which likewise had a long future.[24] *A True State*, in denouncing the undivided rule of the Rump, objected that its procrastinated plans for future Parliaments had supplied 'no manner of balance or check' upon them. Copies of Nedham's tract were handed to members of the first Parliament of the protectorate, where, in debates on the Instrument, the vocabulary of checks and balances began to evolve. Evidently under Nedham's coaching, Cromwell took it up first in defending the Instrument and then, when he had lost hope of it, in calling for its revision. We associate the emergence of the language of 'checks and balances' with eighteenth-century debates on, and celebrations of, the English or British constitution, but it was Nedham and Cromwell who launched it.

In both men's eyes, constitutions were to be measured by their fruits, not by their antiquity. *A True State* does not adopt the conventional premise

22 Worden (n 11) 'Checks and Balances: *The Cromwellian Origins of the Presidency*' 19–52, at 35.
23 Vile (n 16) 53–56.
24 For this paragraph, see Worden (n 18) 'Checks and Balances; The Birth of Vocabulary' 297–309.

that England had an ancient and continuous set of laws and customs. Constitutions, it seems, came and went. The Instrument would 'establish this Commonwealth upon a better and more sure basis of government, than hath been enjoyed by our ancestors for many generations' (2). The document is superior because it answers to principles of constitutional design. Silently, Nedham borrows from the text of 1642, *The King's Answer to the XIX Propositions*,[25] in which Charles I had sought to recover support by abandoning, momentarily as it would prove, his claim to absolute rule. He had represented himself, as Nedham represents the protector, as the defender, against the tyrannical aspirations of Parliament, of a mixed constitution which brought together the virtues of monarchical, aristocratic, and democratic forms. Essential to Nedham's argument was the role of Cromwell's council. The *Answer to the XIX Propositions* had presented the House of Lords as the aristocratic component of the constitution. Now the Lords, too royalist or anyway too opposed to the regicide to survive, had been abolished. Nedham gives its role to the council, an aristocracy not of rank but of wisdom. It has another role, which helps Nedham explain that the 'foundation' of the new government is 'laid in the people'. Not only will the people choose the 'legislative' power, but 'executive' power also 'doth flow from the community' and so 'stands upon a fairer account than in former times' (28–9). For the authority of the executive council, whose future members will be chosen from candidates nominated by the people's representatives, will 'flow indeed originally' from the people. So will the election of future protectors, which will lie with the council and so 'take its rise originally and virtually from the people' (28–9, 45, 51).

Cromwell greeted the Parliament that met in September 1654 in a buoyant mood. From the chaos of December 1653, order had returned. The absence of a Parliament had lowered the political temperature. Cromwell reminded MPs of the electoral 'indenture' which had obliged MPs to accept 'the government as it is now settled in a single person and the parliament'. Although the Instrument did not oblige him to seek parliamentary ratification for the text, his rule could never attain legitimacy without it. His representatives in the Commons wanted Parliament to endorse the Instrument quickly and proceed to enact his reforming agenda. Instead, the Instrument came under bitter attack. After 12 days came another military purge. MPs could remain in the House only if they pledged themselves to the formula which the electoral indenture had prescribed. The purge removed almost all those who wanted to restore the Rump and who would never have accepted Cromwell's rule. But a much greater number, consisting of men who had ceased to sit in Parliament in 1648–9 or who shared their outlook, mostly swallowed scruples and concurred.

25 Worden (n 18) 30.

The formula 'as it is now settled' was deliberately ambiguous. Did it require acceptance of the whole Instrument or merely of the principle of rule by a single person and Parliament? Cromwell was willing to compromise. He distinguished between 'fundamentals' on which he would not budge and 'circumstantials' on which he might.[26] Somewhere in his mind, there seems to have lain the concept of fundamental law, which lays down principles beyond the scope of man-made law.[27] Yet he never found a formula for raising the Instrument above statute. There was no equivalent in the Instrument to the Leveller insistence in 1647 on 'native rights' which the people had 'reserved' from intrusion by the Parliaments they elected.[28] Cromwell did remember the 'fundamental' law of Magna Carta. Parliamentary statutes had enshrined it, but its provisions were unalterable only if they were agreed to lie beyond statutes, for no Parliament can bind its successor. Cromwell told the MPs of 1654 that 'in every government there must be somewhat fundamental, somewhat like a Magna Carta, that should be standing, and unalterable'.[29] To carry his followers in the army and in the congregations, he encouraged them to think of the Instrument as a Magna Carta.[30] He also insisted that one of the 'fundamentals', 'liberty of conscience', was 'a natural right'.[31] Yet his inference was that law ought not to curb it, not that it could not. He did not indicate how supra-statutory provisions could be established. His distinction between fundamentals and circumstantials was a strategy of negotiation, not a philosophical claim. Fundamental meant non-negotiable.

The Instrument's provisions for liberty of conscience, which the Parliament attempted to restrict, were one of the two features of the document which did most to damage Cromwell's relations with the assembly. The other was control of the armed forces, which was always the toughest constitutional issue of the period because all else depended on it. It provided the basic dividing line of 1642 when Parliament went to war. During the war, it was the one issue on which Parliament, in proposing peace terms, demanded permanent rather than temporary restrictions on the Crown's powers.[32] In 1654, the difficulty of the issue was exacerbated by disagreements about the size of the standing army, for which the Instrument stipulated a 'constant yearly revenue' that was not to be remitted without the protector's consent. Cromwell acknowledged that requirement, which he justified as necessary to the preservation of the Puritan cause, to be the 'most hard' claim for Parliament to swallow.[33]

26 Morrill (n 9) I iii 93–96.
27 JW Gough, *Fundamental Law in English Constitutional History* (Clarendon Press 1961).
28 Gardiner (n 7) 334; cf. 368.
29 Morrill (n 9) iii 94.
30 Worden (n 13) 46; John Nickolls (ed), *Original Letters and Papers of State* (London 1743) 134.
31 Morrill (n 9) iii 94.
32 Gardiner (n 7) 294–95.
33 Morrill (n 9) iii 143.

Rather than offer a veil of legitimacy to the Instrument by formally debating it, the Parliament proceeded on a fiction. It silently took provisions from the document and included them, in amended form, in a bill to be prepared for submission to the protector for consent, 'declaring and settling the government of the Commonwealth of England, Scotland, and Ireland'. In accepting the conversion of the Instrument into a bill, Cromwell implicitly recognized that he could rule only on the alterable basis of statute. The amendments to the Instrument shifted the balance of power in Parliament's favour. For example, the making of war and peace, which the Instrument allocated to the protector and council, required Parliament's consent in the bill of 1654. The Instrument gave the protector an absolute veto on any bill which altered the provisions of the Instrument and a suspensive veto on other bills. In the Parliament's version, he was to have a merely suspensive veto on any bill. The detailed haggling between Cromwell's supporters in Parliament and their critics was often ill-tempered. Yet the debates demonstrated the success of the Instrument in supplying a framework which corresponded to the parliamentarian aims of the civil wars. A leading stickler for parliamentary authority power in the debates would remember that the Instrument, 'in the bowels of it', 'took away' Parliament's 'rights', and yet that it 'had much good in it'. At least in retrospect, he wished that agreement had been reached.[34]

Relations between Cromwell and the Parliament were soured by an underlying division of premise. Like the Parliament of the 1640s, the assembly of 1654 was ready to allow powers to a single person provided it was understood that they derived from Parliament's own choice. Though the bill did not use the word executive, it did concur with the Instrument in renouncing the combination of law-making and governing that had prevailed in 1649–53. No more than Cromwell did the Parliament want a return to continuous parliamentary sessions. It even added to the Instrument by laying down a maximum length of Parliaments, 240 days. Yet the belief in parliamentary sovereignty which had animated Parliament in the 1640s survived. In the debates, the famous judge Matthew Hale, whom Blackstone would cite as an authority on parliamentary history, established Parliament's position in a statement which would endure in public memory: 'the government should be in a parliament and a single person limited and restrained as the parliament should think fit'.[35] At one point, MPs provocatively proposed to decide what powers to 'give' the protector, though the verb was prudently altered to 'declare'.[36]

Until November, the agreement between the protector and Parliament was more conspicuous than the conflict. Thereafter, consensus fell apart, though a large minority of MPs were anxious to restore it. As usual, quarrels within Parliament destabilized public opinion. In anger and anxiety,

34 *Burton* (n 12) iii 107.
35 Worden (n 18) 28.
36 *Burton* (n 12) i, lxvii.

Cromwell dissolved the Parliament at the earliest possible moment after deciding that five months, the minimum period for which any of the triennial Parliaments was to sit, could mean five lunar months. The dissolution was a critical moment of the Interregnum. Now he had to rule not with the prospect of parliamentary endorsement but in its absence. He kept public order through the rule of the Major-Generals, who commanded a standing force in each region. The Parliament passed none of the ordinances which he had introduced in the first nine months of the protectorate and which the Instrument had obliged him to submit to the assembly. Yet he continued to enforce them after the dissolution. The trial of the merchant George Cony for refusing taxation, which lacked non-parliamentary consent, recalled Hampden's case under Charles I.

Yet the more illegally he ruled, the stronger the case for a legal settlement, along the lines of the Instrument, became. In 1656, in financial straits, he called another Parliament a year earlier than the Instrument required. It proved much more cooperative, though it, too, first had to be purged. Now the constitutional initiative came not from Cromwell but from the Parliament itself, whose members had thought again. The Humble Petition and Advice, an amended version of the Instrument, was designed to civilianize Cromwell's rule, to separate it from the army, and to make him a king, limited by restrictions looser than those of the Instrument but still akin to them and still compatible with the parliamentary demands made of Charles I. The Parliament was careful not to attack the Instrument, even when it was claimed that the text had 'at one breath' repealed all statutes against heresy.[37] Attacks were unnecessary because the failure of the previous Parliament had ended Cromwell's own confidence in the Instrument, which dissolved into the air without even the formality of a repeal. He now blamed the army officers for its adoption in 1653 and welcomed Parliament's offer to replace it. He particularly welcomed Parliament's proposal for the return of a second chamber, whose initial members he would nominate for Parliament's approval. MPs favoured the proposal as a step towards the restoration of the pre-war constitution, but with a Cromwellian rather than the Stuart dynasty and with formal limitations on royal powers. Cromwell favoured it as a check on the Commons. What destroyed the Humble Petition was Cromwell's refusal of the offer of the Crown, which fatally deflated the party that had worked for the Humble Petition. In 1654, army officers had provoked the Parliament by resolving to 'live and die with Instrument', which the assembly was revising.[38] Now they reacted against the civilianization of Cromwell's rule as an affront to its authority. The Humble Petition went ahead, and in July 1657, he was re-installed under its terms but still with the title of protector. In a second session of the Parliament, early in 1658, he allowed back the members who had been excluded

37 *Burton* (n 12) i, 49–50.
38 CH Firth (ed), *The Clarke Papers*, 4 vols (Royal Historical Society 1891–1901) iii, 10–11.

from the first one. They assailed the Humble Petition as, in 1654, they had assailed the Instrument. The constitution survived Cromwell's death but collapsed with the army's overthrow of the protectorate in 1659.

Gardiner maintained that the Instrument and the Humble Petition, for all their pioneering virtue, were 'academical exercises', because no constitution devised after the regicide, when the revolution lurched from sense and moderation, could have secured the basis in national support 'without which the best Constitutions are but castles in the air'.[39] It is true that, as the aftermath of the Revolution of 1688 would show, any alternative to Stuart rule would have encountered lasting hostility and insecurity. Yet the degree of parliamentary acceptance of the Instrument and the parliamentary support for the Humble Petition call Gardiner's assessment into question. The Instrument, after all, pulled back from the hated unicameral rule that had produced and followed the regicide. It may be that the document was defeated not by innate unacceptability but by political contingencies, by Cromwell's volatility, or by miscalculations by the MPs who bargained with him. Though the Instrument of Government could never have survived without parliamentary sanction, who is to say that it could not have become, in amended and statutory form, the basis of the limited monarchy for which the Parliament that fought Charles I would gladly have settled?

Bibliography

Firth CH (ed), *The Clarke Papers*, 4 vols (Royal Historical Society 1891–1901)

Gardiner SR (ed), *The Constitutional Documents of the Puritan Revolution, 1625–1660* (Clarendon Press 1889)

Gough JW, *Fundamental Law in English Constitutional History* (Clarendon Press, Oxford 1961)

Hallam H, *The Constitutional History of England*, 3 vols (J. Murray 1884)

Hume D, *The History of England*, 6 vols (Philadelphia 1795–1796)

Jenks E, *The Constitutional Experiments of the Interregnum* (Cambridge University Press 1890)

Morrill J (ed), *The Letters, Writings, and Speeches of Oliver Cromwell*, 3 vols (Oxford University Press 2023)

Nickolls J (ed), *Original Letters and Papers of State* (London 1743)

Rutt JT (ed), *Diary of Thomas Burton*, 4 vols (London 1828)

Vile MJC, *Constitutionalism and the Separation of Powers* (Oxford University Press 1967)

Whitelocke B, *Memorials of the English Affairs* (London 1682)

Worden B, *The Rump Parliament* (Cambridge University Press 1974)

Worden B, 'Oliver Cromwell and the Instrument of Government' in S Taylor and G Tapsell (eds), *The Nature of the English Revolution Revisited* (Boydell Press 2013)

39 Gardiner (n 7) liii–lxiv. He also judged that the Instrument had an inherent flaw, in failing to make provision for its own amendment. Yet that omission was immaterial once Cromwell had accepted Parliament's intention to turn the document into a statute.

Worden B, 'Checks and Balances: The Cromwellian Origins of the Presidency' in B Lowe (ed), *Political Thought and the Origins of the American Presidency* (University Press of Florida 2021)
Worden B, 'Checks and Balances; The Birth of a Vocabulary' in P Hammond and A Hadfield (eds), *Words at War. The Contested Language of the English Civil War* (Oxford University Press 2024)
Worden B, *God's Instruments. Political Conduct in the England of Oliver Cromwell* (Oxford University Press 2012)

6 The Toleration Act and the confessional state[1]

Mark Goldie

6.1 The Toleration Act and the virtues of intolerance

Passed a few months after the English Revolution of 1688, the Act of Toleration (1 W & M c. 18) marked a caesura in the historical relationship between religion and civil society. Hitherto, the Church of England had perpetuated the medieval Catholic concept of the unity of the Christian faith and the duty of temporal rulers to enforce religious uniformity. Accordingly, England before 1689 was a persecuting society. True enough, religious repression was intermittent and depended upon the zeal of monarchs, parliaments, clergy, magistrates, and juries. But until the 1680s, Roman Catholics were put to death for their religion: the first had been Thomas More in 1535, and the last, Oliver Plunkett, martyred in 1681. And Protestant Nonconformists (or 'Dissenters'), the heirs to the Puritan tradition, were fined and jailed. Earlier in the century, bishops had disciplined Puritan clergy who refused to conform to a Church judged to be 'but halfly reformed'.[2] In despair, some Puritans emigrated from 'prelatical' England and sought to create a godly Zion in America. After the Civil Wars, under the restored monarchy, the Elizabethan laws against 'recusancy' were augmented by new laws against nonconformity, the so-called Clarendon Code, which renewed the legal requirement to attend the worship of the national Church and made alternative worship, in 'conventicles', a crime.[3]

1 A note on terminology. Although some historians are hesitant, and although it did not become common usage until the nineteenth century, the term 'Anglican' may be used interchangeably with the 'Church of England', at least from the time of the re-establishment of the Church in 1660. The term 'Established Church' was also not routine before the nineteenth century; earlier, the terms 'National Church' or simply 'Church of England' prevailed. After 1660, the terms 'Dissenter' and 'Nonconformist' can be used interchangeably. During the eighteenth century, 'Dissenter' was more common, thereafter 'Nonconformist'. The principal Dissenting groups were the Presbyterians, Congregationalists (or Independents), Baptists, Quakers, and, later, Methodists and Unitarians.

2 This was William Fuller's famous and forthright rebuke, in 1585, to Queen Elizabeth for backsliding.

3 The Code comprised the Corporation Act 1661, Act of Uniformity 1662, Quaker Act 1662, Five Mile Act 1665, and two Conventicle Acts 1664 and 1670.

DOI: 10.4324/9781032658698-7

The Conventicle Acts emboldened informers, who feigned being Baptists or Quakers, Presbyterians or Congregationalists, in order to infiltrate clandestine congregations and took financial rewards from fines exacted by magistrates. Some targets of these laws achieved fame through victimhood, their literature of righteous suffering reinforcing the Nonconforming tradition. The Baptist John Bunyan, repining in Bedford Gaol, produced a great spiritual classic, *The Pilgrim's Progress* (1678). The Quaker William Penn prompted a landmark legal precedent when, in 1670, in *Bushel's Case*, the right of a jury to reach an independent judgment without coercion by a judge was established, a judge having jailed Bushel and his fellow jurymen for failing to find Penn guilty of conventicling. Neither Catholics nor Dissenters could open schools or graduate from universities. Gentry Catholic children were sent to colleges on the Continent, while clandestine Dissenting academies led a fugitive existence in England. Neither Catholics nor Dissenters could lawfully be married or buried except in a parish church.

It is difficult for the secular mind to grasp the ideology behind coercive religious uniformity. That ideology had three components. The first was political: religious dissent was held to be anarchic and twin of, or cloak for, political rebellion. In the case of 'papists', sedition seemed manifest: Catholics refused the oaths of allegiance and of royal supremacy, were presumed to owe obedience to a foreign power, and, in the Gunpowder Plot (1605), had attempted a terrorist atrocity. Radical Puritans, it was argued, had provoked the catastrophes of civil war, regicide, and Cromwellian dictatorship. The second argument was ecclesiological: Christ's Church, as the creed has it, is 'one, holy, catholic' – 'catholic' in the sense of universal and encompassing. To breach the unity of the Church was the sin of 'schism'. The denigration of 'schismatics' was visceral. It was the duty of the 'Godly prince' to purge schism and to use the secular sword to enforce liturgical and ecclesiastical conformity. The third argument was theological and philosophical. It was held that while coercion could not, by itself, convince the mind of the truth of the Church's teaching, it could indirectly do so by compelling the wayward to come and hear the truth. Coercion was propaedeutic. Here, the argument of St Augustine (who has been called the patron saint of religious persecution) rang down the ages: *compelle intrare*, 'compel them to come in', echoing Christ's injunction, 'go into the highways and hedges and compel them to come in, that my house may be filled' (Luke 14:23).

One consequence of these ideas was that, in the seventeenth century, 'toleration' was often pejorative, denoting unwarranted laxness. The heresiographer Thomas Edwards instanced 'express scriptures, proving the sinfulness and wickedness of tolerations, and the magistrate's duty . . . to suppress blasphemies, errors, heresies, schisms'.[4] John Locke published his celebrated *Letter*

4 Thomas Edwards, *The Casting Down of the Last and Strongest Hold of Satan, or, a Treatise Against Toleration* (1647) 2. Edwards was a Presbyterian. In the 1640s Presbyterians shared

Concerning Toleration in 1689, but his rejection of religious coercion and his separation of church from state was far from the accepted view. The tract was immediately critiqued by two Anglican clergy. Thomas Long assumed that the anonymous author was a seditious Puritan 'sectary', while Jonas Proast repeated Augustine's case for pastoral coercion. Even among those inclined towards latitude, the ideal was not toleration (a promiscuous plurality of sects), but 'comprehension', a broadening of the Church of England's requirements so that the Church could once again embrace everybody.

The Act of Toleration was limited and grudging, and most of this chapter is about what it did *not* tolerate. The Act was a reluctant compromise: the Church made an historic concession to Dissenters as the price for achieving Protestant solidarity in bringing down England's last 'popish' monarch, James II, in the Revolution of 1688. Nowhere in the Act does the word 'toleration' appear. Its proper title is 'An Act for Exempting their Majesties Protestant Subjects Dissenting from the Church of England from the Penalties of Certain Laws'.[5] In form, it was an act of indemnity, repealing the punishments but not the crimes. It enabled the opening of Nonconformist chapels, so long as they were licenced and unlocked during services. Their ministers were obliged to accept most of the Thirty-Nine Articles of the Church, exempting only infant baptism and those articles which stipulated government by bishops and worship according to the rituals and ceremonies of the Established Church. The Act did not exempt anyone from paying tithes (taxes which supported the Church), nor from the jurisdiction of the ecclesiastical courts, although the latter were in decline. The Act did not exempt subjects from the obligation to attend *a* church each Sunday, although in practice, there was no means of enforcing this.

In the following discussion, several implications of the Toleration Act will be explored, the survey extending to the present day, in order to use the Act both to explore the evolution of church-state relations in modern Britain and to show how the Act's ambiguities are still reflected in the indeterminate place of religion in contemporary British civil society.

6.2 Catholics, Quakers, and the Protestant state

The Toleration Act did not extend to Catholics and reiterated the existing obligation to forswear the authority of the 'see of Rome'. Technically, it remained a crime (capital until 1700, thereafter 'perpetual imprisonment') for a priest to say Mass, although in practice, discrete worship in private chapels went

---

with their 'prelatical' enemies commitment to intolerance; a generation later, themselves now victims of the Clarendon Code, they adopted toleration.

5 Most statutes cited in this chapter may be read online at legislation.gov.uk. Of several printed compilations the most useful is WC Costin and JS Watson (eds), *The Law and Working of the Constitution*, 2 vols (Adam and Charles Black 1952).

unmolested. Against Catholics, new legislation was enacted, the anti-popish instincts of the English being deeply ingrained for two further centuries, exacerbated by the role of Catholics in the Jacobite rebellions of 1715 and 1745 in support of the continuing royal claims of the deposed House of Stuart. An Act for the Further Preventing the Growth of Popery 1700 (11 W & M c. 4) prevented Catholics from inheriting or purchasing land. The Security of the Sovereign Act 1714 (1 Geo. 1 c. 13) obliged Catholics to register their names and estates. Catholics liable to the land tax were made to pay double.

The persisting Protestant character of the English state lent Catholicism a special trajectory. Priests died in jails as late as the 1750s if guilty of involvement in the Jacobite rebellion. Not until 1766 did the papacy finally recognise Britain's Protestant monarchy. There were interminable negotiations throughout the century to devise a form of allegiance oath acceptable to both Catholics and the British state. Until the nineteenth century, oath formularies required renunciation of the 'papal deposing power', the pope's historical claim to authorise nations to depose their heretical monarchs. Of great importance along the road toward amelioration of anti-Catholicism was the Quebec Act 1774 (14 Geo. 3 c. 83), which, after the seizure of French Canada, appeased Quebec's Catholics by granting the first general civil as well as religious emancipation of Catholics within British dominions. It outraged Protestants in both Britain and Revolutionary America. The British state's need to raise troops to put down American rebels promoted moves in England to relax anti-Catholic laws. (Across early modern Europe, the need for troops was a driver of pragmatic religious toleration.) Astutely, Scottish Catholic bishops, recently pastors to Jacobite rebels, now offered the Protestant state fighting men in exchange for toleration. The Catholic Relief Act 1778 (18 Geo. 3 c. 60) allowed Catholics to join the army and purchase and inherit land. But it provoked a violent backlash. In London, the Gordon Riots of 1780 saw several days of destruction of Catholic chapels and the homes of liberal Protestants. However, a drastic shift of sensibility occurred just a decade later, in the wake of the French Revolution, when Christianity *tout court* seemed at risk, and thousands of Catholic clergy and exilic Catholic schools fled to England. The Catholic Relief Act 1791 (31 Geo. 3 c. 32) legalised Catholic chapels so long as they did not have steeples or bells, a prohibition lifted in 1829. It permitted Catholics to be lawyers and to open schools. Full emancipation (the removal of civil disabilities) was delayed by George III's refusal, on the ground that it would breach his coronation oath, and by Catholics' own objection to allowing the state any role in the appointment of bishops. The Catholic Emancipation Act (10 Geo. 4 c. 7) was finally passed in 1829. But Protestant pushback continued. When a Catholic diocesan hierarchy was restored by the pope in 1850, a backlash prompted the Ecclesiastical Titles Act 1851 (14 & 15 Vict. c. 60), which forbad Catholic use of territorial titles (e.g., 'bishop of Southwark') – but it was never enforced. Local politics in such cities as Liverpool and Glasgow would continue to be fuelled by Protestant anti-popery until after the Second World War.

The Toleration Act did not exempt Quakers, who refused to swear oaths and pay tithes. They achieved exemption from the former in the Quaker Relief Act 1696 (7 & 8 Will. 3 c. 34), but not from the latter, as a Quaker Tithes Bill failed in 1736. Resistance to tithes by Dissenters persisted until the nineteenth century: a series of Acts from 1836 eroded the remnants of the tithe system. After 1689, Nonconformist education remained restricted. The Dissenting Academies suffered a short-lived proscription under the Schism Act 1714 (13 Ann. c. 7), repealed in 1719. The Toleration Act did not end the Anglican monopoly of the two universities. Not until the Universities Tests Act 1871 (34 & 35 Vict. c. 26), after prolonged controversy, were Oxford and Cambridge required to admit Nonconformists and Catholics to academic posts. Only then did the old universities cease to be the seminaries of the Anglican Church. And not until the twentieth century did attendance at college chapel cease to be expected. The prospectus for the new London University in 1827 gave as its first aim the breaking of the Anglican monopoly on higher education, earning it the sobriquet 'the godless institute of Gower Street'.

6.3 Public office and the consequences of Establishment

Crucially, the Toleration Act extended only to worship and not to public office. The Corporation and Test Acts (1661, 1673, 1678) remained in place. To hold national or local office, a person had to acquire a certificate demonstrating that, at least annually, they had received the sacrament of Holy Communion (the Lord's Supper) according to Anglican rites. It was evaded: Dissenters would obtain their annual certificate and attend their own chapels regardless. In 1697, the Mayor of London outraged Anglican sensibilities by processing from church to chapel in official regalia. There ensued the Occasional Conformity controversy, which led to the Occasional Conformity Act 1711 (10 Ann. c. 6), banning this subterfuge. But this was repealed in 1719, and after 1727, Acts of Indemnity routinely exonerated breaches of the Test Act (1 Geo. 2 c. 23). Restricting offices, such as shrievalties, which controlled parliamentary elections, to Anglicans could damage the pro-Dissenter Whig vote. Not until the Test and Corporation Repeal Act 1828 (9 Geo. 4 c. 17) were most public offices formally opened to Dissenters. The Catholic Emancipation Act likewise freed Catholics to enter most areas of public life. Today, one public office remains restricted to Protestants: the monarchy. The Act of Settlement 1701 (12 & 13 W. 3 c. 2) excluded Catholics from inheriting the crown, ensuring that it passed to the House of Hanover in 1714.

It is possible to describe the Toleration Act as an act of semi-disestablishment in so far as it made alternative religious affiliations partially lawful. Yet, it is a peculiar characteristic of modern Britain that there has been no formal separation of church and state on the American or French models. There remains a Church *of* England (whereas Catholics speak of their Church *in* England). In the Victorian era, Prime Minister William Gladstone pressed Liberalism in a separationist direction, promoting legislation to disestablish the (Protestant

Episcopal) Church of Ireland (1869: 32 & 33 Vict. c. 42), conscious that the Irish majority was Catholic. A later Liberal government enacted the Welsh Church Act 1914 (4 & 5 Geo. 5 c. 91), which disestablished the Church in Wales, with effect from 1920, for in Wales, the majority was Nonconformist. Today, a conspicuous constitutional remnant of the Establishment survives in the form of Anglican bishops sitting in the House of Lords. (Only the UK and Iran have clerics sitting in their legislatures *ex officio.*) Other remnants have been eroded. Anglican bishops are still appointed by the crown on the Prime Minister's advice, but nominations have, since 1977, been devolved to a Church commission. (In episcopal churches beyond Britain, bishops are elected by churchgoers.) Church of England schools are still funded by the state – but so, too, are Catholic, Jewish, and Muslim schools. Nonconformist anger against the Conservative Education Act 1902 (2 Edw. 7 c. 42), which favoured Anglican and Catholic schools, contributed to the Liberal landslide of 1906, the last general election to be significantly impacted by religious allegiances. The Butler Education Act 1944 (7 & 8 Geo. 6 c. 31), which set the scene for post-War schooling, marked a success for the combined forces of the Christian churches. Notionally, the Act still requires a daily act of worship in schools, as does the School Standards and Framework Act 1998 (c. 31).[6] The Education Act 2002 (c. 32) requires schools to promote the 'spiritual' development of pupils. In this sense, there are no secular schools, and Muslims, among others, stress this fact.[7]

6.4 The geography of religion

The Toleration Act had a long legacy in which the socio-economic landscape of England became entwined with the religio-political. By 1700, especially once the geography of Dissenting chapel licences became visible, it was apparent that Dissent was strong in urban and mercantile/artisanal communities, while Anglicanism was predominant in agrarian shires. The Whig party and its nineteenth-century heir, the Liberal party, became the protector of Dissent, guardian of the Toleration Act, and advocate of the mitigation or abolition of the Test Acts. In the eighteenth century, the Tory party was often called 'the Church party', and it denounced Whigs as patrons of 'schismatics'. The Church of England became, in a famous epithet, the Tory party at prayer. After the 1710 Tory electoral landslide, galvanised by the slogan of the 'Church in Danger', there were fears that the Toleration Act itself would be repealed. It was this administration that passed the Occasional Conformity and Schism Acts.

During the era of industrialisation and urbanisation, the Church of England progressively failed demographically and pastorally in the growing cities

6 Since 1963, statutes have been designated by calendar rather than regnal year.

7 'There are no such things as secular schools in England': www.muslimparents.org.uk/collective-worship.

while remaining burdened with the medieval legacy of 9,000 mainly rural churches. In contrast, by the mid-nineteenth century, the new cities were rich in Dissenting and Catholic chapels and churches. The Established Church made two conspicuous legislative efforts to remedy this crisis. The Fifty New Churches Act 1710 (9 Ann. c. 17) aimed to create new urban churches in London. Only 12 were built, and these tended to be more successful architecturally than pastorally. Nicholas Hawksmoor's Christ Church, Spitalfields, is magnificent, yet from the sixteenth to the twenty-first centuries, Spitalfields is testimony to religious pluralism, drawing successive waves of textile-working immigrants, Huguenots, Jews, and Bangladeshis. The Church Building Act of 1818 (58 Geo. 3 c. 45) had a greater impact, promoting a wave of building of urban 'Commissioners' Churches'.

6.5 The Erastian tradition

The Toleration Act was not 'separationist'. It built no wall between church and state and was far from reducing churches to private associations. England continued to be an Erastian state, one in which the external governance and even the doctrines of the national church belonged to the remit of the civil state. Notions of the 'Godly Prince' or 'Godly Parliament' did not wholly dissipate. This was a legacy of the Henrician 'magisterial' Reformation, executed by royal fiat and parliamentary statute. Erastianism was an active ideology which, by the eighteenth century, might be called a 'civil religion'. Antipathy to the pretensions of ecclesiastics and recollections of both clerical persecution by hierarchies and pulpit-inspired fanaticism by Puritan sects encouraged a belief in the necessity of state power to check overmighty clergies. If religion was to be made safe, its governance must belong to the laity and not to priests. In the eighteenth century, the state came to be seen as an agent of education in civic values that would temper the antisocial zeal of religion. The cult of 'politeness', and a new theology that accented ethics over doctrine and civility over creeds were conscious counterpoints to the persecutions and wars of religion of previous centuries. This was the sensibility we summarise with the term 'Enlightenment'. Whigs *defended* an Established Church because that meant secular control, a legacy of old hostility to 'prelatical' rule, and to the pretensions of 'divine right episcopacy'. And it certainly suited Whigs to have appointee bishops in the House of Lords. This Erastian consensus was underwritten by the theological doctrine of 'adiaphora', deriving from sixteenth-century Protestant thought. The word means 'things indifferent' to salvation, as opposed to 'things necessary'. Many doctrines, rituals, and hierarchies were, it was argued, not stipulated by Christ in scripture; rather, they were human, historical artifices, and hence at the disposal of earthly governments to settle.

Until the seventeenth century, church hierarchies sought to enforce both Christ's injunctions and 'adiaphora' by ecclesiastical law, inherited from medieval canon law and augmented by canons passed in the Church's assembly, Convocation. The church courts exercised authority over morality, marriage, and testamentary inheritance. But, the conflicts of that century provoked resistance to the autonomous legislative and judicial power of the Church. The common lawyers gradually eroded the jurisdiction of ecclesiastical courts, although it was not until a series of Ecclesiastical Courts Acts in the 1850s that the courts' powers over the laity were finally terminated.

However, Erastian moves to cancel the apartness of spiritual from temporal jurisdiction could, paradoxically, lead to an increase in clerical intrusion into civil society. After 1664, clergy relinquished their right to tax themselves independently in Convocation. This now entitled them to the franchise in parliamentary elections and created a phalanx of 10,000 mostly Tory voters. If, in the eighteenth century, the ecclesiastical courts declined, nonetheless, clergy increasingly sat in secular magistrates' courts as justices of the peace, by 1830 accounting for one-quarter of the total. The 'squarson' (squire-parson) had indeed become a kind of civil servant and scarcely distinguishable from the lay elite. A strand of Erastianism had always supported a civic role for the clergy: it was clerical pretensions to *autonomous* ecclesiastical authority that rankled.

The need for parliamentary legislation often frustrated initiatives for pastoral and ecclesiastical reform, and the structures of the Church remained largely unchanged during the eighteenth century. The distorted economics of episcopal and clerical incomes, by which some dioceses and benefices were rich and others poor, required legislation to amend. The Queen Anne's Bounty Act 1703 (2 & 3 Ann. c. 20) took steps to augment poor benefices (funded in part by proceeds of the slave trade). It was not until the Ecclesiastical Commissioners Act 1836 (6 & 7 Will. 4. c. 77) that equity was brought to the wildly unequal wealth of bishoprics.

Erastianism provoked in opposite wings of the Church of England, Anglo-Catholic and evangelical, resistance to secular domination. After 1689, a 'Nonjuror' movement formed a breakaway church, which lasted a century. It was born of outrage that bishops who repudiated the Revolution were sacked by parliamentary fiat. Bishops were, Nonjurors insisted, Christ's anointed and not pawns of secular powers. When, in the early 1700s, a 'High Church' movement (the term now came into use) used Convocation to denounce Dissent and heresy, the Whig government, in 1717, closed it down, destroying it for over a century. (It was revived in the mid-nineteenth century and then replaced by the Church Assembly in 1919 and by the present Synod in 1970.) In the mid-eighteenth century, a sense of Anglican spiritual stasis and capture of the Church by a complacent secular power prompted the Methodist movement, an evangelical renewal that, in due course, broke from the Church. In the nineteenth century, decisions by the secular courts could profoundly shake the Church. The Gorham Judgment of 1850, in which the Privy Council ruled on a matter of doctrine,[8] caused a cohort of 'Oxford Movement' Anglicans to convert to Roman Catholicism. In 1928, the House of Commons refused to

8 https://vlex.co.uk/vid/gorham-v-the-bishop-803812737.

pass an amended Book of Common Prayer that was seen as Anglo-Catholic in tendency. On the other hand, the Church itself had earlier resorted to statute to attempt to arrest the popularity of Anglo-Catholic ritualism in the Public Worship Regulation Act 1874 (37 & 38 Vict. c. 85).

6.6 Asymmetric unions: Scotland and Ireland

The Act of Toleration was an English Act. Scotland and England were independent polities until the Treaty of Union of 1707. The Revolution settlement in Scotland in 1689 took an entirely different form. It abolished episcopacy, a largely alien English imposition, and established a Presbyterian church, the Kirk. This settlement has persisted until the present day, producing the strange cohabitation of two different Established religions within the same polity. The independence of the Kirk (and of Scots law) was guaranteed by the Union. This set a constitutional conundrum: if the Westminster Parliament is sovereign, why may it not dissolve the Scottish Presbyterian establishment? (Notoriously, A. V. Dicey pronounced that the Act of Union had no more authority than the Dentists Act 1878; that is to say, both are repealable.)[9] This is one reason why Scottish nationalists insist that the Union was a 'treaty' between two independent states with binding obligations and repudiate the English misnomer of the 'Act' of Union, for an English Act of Parliament could have no jurisdiction over a foreign state. The conundrum was far from theoretical in 1705–7 when hundreds of Scottish communities petitioned against the Union because they could see no means of guaranteeing their religion in a Union Parliament in which Scots would have minority representation. As early as 1711, the Church Patronage Act (10 Ann. c. 21), passed despite the votes of a majority of Scottish MPs, breached one aspect of the Kirk settlement by re-establishing lay patronage, abolished in 1690: the entitlement of the laity, typically gentry, to impose their choices of ministers on parishes. This would have grievous consequences within Scotland. Many Presbyterians resented lay patronage: congregations wished to select their own ministers. This provoked schisms that fragmented the Presbyterian tradition, most prominently in the Disruption of 1843, when 450 ministers broke from the Church of Scotland to form the Free Church. The Scottish settlement of 1689 diverged from England in another way. Initially, there was no Toleration Act. Episcopalians were ejected in a wholesale purge of parishes. Episcopalians, established and dominant in England, were criminal sectarians in Scotland. This deeply rankled. A Toleration Act was passed for Scotland in 1711 (10 Ann. c. 10).

Ireland was likewise a distinct kingdom with its own Parliament, albeit under the control of the English crown. While King William III was able to acquire the English crown in 1688–9 without a civil war, he acquired his Irish crown on the battlefield. At the Battle of the Boyne, he crushed James II, who had

9 AV Dicey, *Introduction to the Study of the Law of the Constitution* (Liberty Fund 1982) 78.

sought to recover his lost crowns via Ireland. James's short-lived Irish Catholic kingdom was suppressed, and the Protestant Ascendancy ensued, secure for more than a century thereafter. A series of anti-popish Acts in the Dublin Parliament was more savage than those in England. The Ascendancy could itself be truculent about English rule, notwithstanding that it depended on English force to maintain it, for Protestants represented only one-tenth of the population. When a Protestant Irish patriot, William Molyneux, in *The Case of Ireland* (1698), argued in Lockean fashion that Ireland had never consented to English rule, a Jacobite critic, Charles Leslie, retorted that most of the Irish people had never consented to Protestant rule. Not until 1793 were Irish Catholics formally granted freedom of worship, but in advance of England, they were also admitted to most public offices (33 Geo. 3 c. 21 Ir). So deeply entangled was the Ascendancy with the socio-economic character of Ireland that, in the nineteenth century, 'toleration' must be construed in relation to land reform. The largest expropriation of land to have occurred in the history of the British Isles was the seventeenth-century reduction of Irish Catholic landholding from 60 to 15 per cent. Anglo-Irish politics after the Union of the two Parliaments in 1800 was embittered and embattled by campaigns to alleviate the position of the impoverished Catholic tenantry, there now being a large cohort of Irish MPs sitting in the Parliament of the United Kingdom.

6.7 Doctrine, heresy, and unbelief

The English Toleration Act was almost entirely ecclesiastical, not doctrinal. It concerned liturgy and church governance. Anglicans and Dissenters generally shared the theology of the Nicene Creed, and, in so far as there were differences as regards soteriology (the theology of salvation), these differences cut across the divide between Anglicans and Dissenters. Both parties were increasingly riven between Calvinist predestinarians, who accented the act of faith and the unconditionality of divine grace, and 'Arminians', who leaned toward the possibility of salvation for all believers and accented the role of human action in cooperation with divine grace. Because the sixteenth-century Church had been Calvinist in theology, the 17th of the Thirty-Nine Articles (never yet repealed) is predestinarian, yet, since the eighteenth century, that doctrine has been almost entirely abandoned. (Notwithstanding, Anglican clergy are still required to assent to the Articles today.)

The Toleration Act did not address such matters. It took up a single doctrinal question, in excluding 'Socinians' from toleration, those who denied the doctrine of the Trinity: that God the Father, Son, and Holy Ghost are three and one. Socinians would soon be called Unitarians (the word arrived in the 1680s). Socinianism was felt to be especially threatening, for if the godhead of Christ were doubted, then the authority and sacraments of the Church he created seemed undermined. Socinianism generally remained covert. John Locke and Isaac Newton were probably Socinians but remained practising members of the Church of England. In the 1770s, there grew a movement for the legislative abolition, or modification, of subscription to the Articles. The Dissenters' Relief Act 1779 (19 Geo. 3 c. 44) relieved Dissenters of subscription and henceforth required them only to declare that they were 'Christian and Protestant', but the campaign on behalf of Anglican doubters failed, and a number of them left and formed Unitarian churches. The formal remedy came with the Doctrine of the Trinity (or Unitarian Relief) Act 1813 (53 Geo. 3 c. 160), which lifted the Toleration Act's exclusion of non-Trinitarians from the right to worship.

Socinianism aside, the Toleration Act did not amend the laws of heresy. The last burning of a heretic in England had occurred in 1612, and the death penalty for heresy had been annulled in 1678 (29 Car. II c. 9) for fear that a Catholic monarch might revive the 'Fires of Smithfield' – the burnings exacted by 'Bloody Mary' in the 1550s. As late as the 1660s, the philosopher Thomas Hobbes feared prosecution for heresy and devoted considerable intellectual energy to investigating heresy's legal history. In Scotland, an Edinburgh University student, Thomas Aikenhead, was hanged for 'atheism' in 1697. John Locke anxiously gathered documents about the case.

Varieties of unbelief surfaced during the eighteenth century. Anticlericalism took hold in Whig culture, and a new word, 'priestcraft', entered regular usage in the 1690s, which would resonate throughout the Anglophone Enlightenment. Commonplace anticlericalism was entirely consistent with orthodoxy and devout piety. But, radicals were apt to claim that church creeds had historically been manufactured by devious clerics to serve their own interests. For 'deists', the teachings of 'natural religion' were few and simple, and the fabric of formal religion was spurious. Too much of Christianity was 'priestianity', and a truer Christianity was scarcely more than the morality that reason could demonstrate and that pagan philosophers had taught. Such talk found remarkable tolerance in England, at least in elite circles. Voltaire, visiting in the 1720s, was impressed.

There were periodic attempts to stem the tide. Conspicuous was the Blasphemy Act 1698 (9 Will. 3 c. 35), in fact, a heresy act, for it outlawed denial of the Trinity and of the divine authority of the Bible, as well as the profaning of Christianity. It was rarely used but not repealed until 1967. A handful of eighteenth-century imprisonments for heresy depended upon the common law crime of heresy. A late prosecution for the offence of blasphemous libel, in 1977, was of the magazine *Gay News* for a poem which depicted Christ as homosexual.[10] Such offences were abolished in 2008. Meanwhile, the last witch execution in England took place in 1716 and in Scotland in 1727, but, in England, the offence was not entirely abolished by the Witchcraft Act 1735 (9 Geo. 2 c. 5), and the jailing of a spiritualist medium as late as 1944 led to its final repeal.

10 *Whitehouse v Lemon* [1979] 1 AC 617.

Blasphemy laws have arguably been resurrected in a new form. The contemporary British state has pluralised blasphemy beyond Christianity. Under the Racial and Religious Hatred Act 2006 (c. 1), religious hate speech is criminalised. The Hate Crime and Public Order (Scotland) Act, effective from 2024, simultaneously decriminalised the historic crime of blasphemy and replaced it with a new offence, no longer confined to protecting Christianity.

6.8 The reformation of manners

The Toleration Act of 1689 did not address morality. It remained a presumption that the state was obliged to enforce public morals. Many supporters of toleration of worship indeed backed campaigns for a state-sponsored 'Reformation of Manners'. They saw the Revolution as an opportunity for a righteous reorientation of the priorities of English society. Whereas church and state had hitherto exerted themselves to punish conscientious worshippers for trivial liturgical deviations, they had, it was held, turned a blind eye to libertinism. Those priorities should now be reversed. Campaigns for the Reformation of Manners, ebbing and flowing during the ensuing centuries, invoked statute and common law to crack down on fornication, prostitution, drunkenness, swearing, and sabbath-breaking. (Sociologists use the term 'moral panic' to denote periodic upsurges in societal anxiety about moral collapse.) The disentanglement of the state from Christian morality did not occur wholesale until the 1960s, in enactments liberalising homosexuality, divorce, abortion, suicide, and censorship of the arts. The Sunday Trading Act 1994 (c. 20) breached the Christian sabbath, although Christians salvaged Easter Sunday. In jurisprudence, a classic debate occurred in the 1960s between Lord Devlin and Herbert Hart, speaking respectively for the state's persisting (Christian) moral character and for secular liberalism.[11]

In recent decades, the courts have adjudicated boundaries between Christian orthodoxy and secular morality. In *Lee v Ashers Baking Company Ltd*, a Christian baker in Northern Ireland was alleged to have breached the Equality Act 2010 by refusing to bake a cake celebrating gay marriage. In *Eweida v United Kingdom*, the case before the European Court of Human Rights concerned British Airways' ban on stewards wearing religious jewellery (in this case, a crucifix). In both cases, the final decisions upheld individuals' rights to manifest their religion.[12] Arguably and ironically, today, a further step is being taken within civil society: a new Reformation of Manners in the shape of a movement to enforce acceptance of moral positions alien to traditional

11 Patrick Devlin, *The Enforcement of Morals* (Oxford University Press 1965); HLA Hart, *Law, Liberty, and Morality* (Oxford University Press 1963).

12 Respectively, [2018] UKSC 9; (2013) (Application nos. 48420/10, 59842/10, 51671/10, and 36516/10.

Christianity. Those who publicly oppose abortion or gay rights can face ostracism and exclusion.

Public bodies are also called upon to adjudicate what counts as a religion. At stake are tax concessions and protections under the Equality Act 2010. In 1999, the Charity Commission ruled that Scientology was not a religion, qua charity, but in 2013, the Supreme Court ruled that it was, qua worship.[13] Both judgments stand.

The idea of the state as the instrument of Christian moral purpose manifested in another way between the mid-nineteenth and mid-twentieth centuries in Christian socialist movements for public welfare and social reform, a tradition culminating in Archbishop William Temple's bestselling *Christianity and the Social Order* (1944). In earlier centuries, it was already understood that the peculiarly English system of statutory parish poor relief was (despite its reputation for harshness) a state-sanctioned fulfilment of the Christian duty of charity. The Welfare State was heir to the Poor Law.

6.9 Evangelism, empire, and slavery

The Toleration Act did not preclude a continuing role for the state in Christian evangelizing. A small example is the Parochial Libraries Act 1708 (7 Ann. c. 14), which encouraged the provision of religious libraries to better equip parish ministers in their role as preachers and defenders of the faith.

Today, we think of toleration as a secular liberal value, but at that time, from a theological point of view, toleration was a pastoral strategy. Locke's *Letter Concerning Toleration,* now readily called a manifesto of 'liberalism', is an evangelical tract, for it begins with the premise that 'we' all wish that people would embrace Christ and only differ as to whether coercion or persuasion is the legitimate or effective method. When Locke served in government on the Board of Trade and Plantations, he used instruments of the state, such as instructions to colonial governors, to promote such organisations as the New England Company, which proselytised among Native Americans; the newly founded Society for the Propagation of the Gospel in Foreign Parts, which was given a royal charter in 1701; and Thomas Bray's project for religious libraries in England and America. The College of William and Mary was created in Williamsburg, Virginia, by royal charter in 1693, intended to propagate Anglicanism. The Toleration Act did not retard the creation of *new* Anglican Church Establishments. The Church of England became the Established Church in Maryland in 1700, a colony previously strongly Catholic. Nor did those who, in England, were regarded as 'Dissenters' let go of the ideal of establishment, since, in Massachusetts, Puritan Congregationalism continued to be established until 1833, its charter modified in 1691 to provide toleration, although not for Catholics. Church Establishment remained an American norm. The

13 *Marriages* [2013] UKSC 77.

episcopal church was established in New York in 1693, with accommodations for the Dutch Reformed Church, and William III established the Trinity (Church of England) Church in New York by royal charter in 1697. The much-vaunted American 'separation' of church and state was a late flowering and never unambiguous.

Evangelisers were particularly anxious to bring enslaved African people to the Christian faith. The conversion of the enslaved was resisted by slave-owners, fearing it would encourage demands for free time for worship and schooling, but particularly because of a tradition that held that embracing Christianity entailed manumission, release from slavery. The era of the Toleration Act coincided with a growing insistence that conversion did *not* entail manumission. Accordingly, Acts of the Assemblies of Virginia in 1667, South Carolina in 1712, and Maryland in 1715 expressly stipulated that baptism did not confer freedom. These provisions allowed slavery and evangelisation to thrive alongside each other.

6.10 Non-Christians and migrant communities

The Toleration Act presumed a Christian society. Locke asserted that Jews and Muslims were entitled to toleration (although he excluded Catholics and atheists as incapable of trustworthy citizenship). Yet, there was no separate legislation for non-Christians until 1753. Jews had, after their medieval expulsion, been re-admitted by Oliver Cromwell in the 1650s – not from pluralistic instincts but from the millenarian belief that the conversion of the Jews was a staging post on the path to Christ's Second Coming. Thereafter, the monarchy protected the small Jewish presence through the royal prerogative. It was prerogative, rather than statute, that also protected Protestant Huguenot immigrants, some of whom preserved independent chapels, while others integrated into the Church of England. An attempt was made in the 'Jew Bill' of 1753 to allow Jews to become naturalised, but, although pushed through by the Whigs, it was repealed the following year amid a wave of antisemitism (26 Geo. 2 c. 26). From the 1830s onward a struggle ensued to remove civil disabilities from Jews, in a series of failed bills. Eventually, the Jews Relief Act 1858 (21 & 22 Vict. c. 49) allowed them to sit in Parliament, while the Oaths Act 1858 (21 & 22 Vict. c. 48) exempted them from the Christian affirmation. More generally, non-religious affirmations for courts of law were authorised in 1869–70 and for MPs in 1888. Charles Bradlaugh, an atheist, had been elected to Parliament in 1880 and, for several years, was refused his seat.

Historically, the admission of refugee Christian groups was as controversial as the admission of non-Christians. After the Revolution, the Whigs championed immigration with mixed motives of pan-Protestant solidarity and acquiring human capital for economic growth. (Arguments for toleration regularly included an economic case.) The Foreign Protestant Naturalization Act 1708 (7 Ann. c. 9) naturalised thousands of Huguenots (whose arrival had recently put the word 'refugee' into the English language) and was followed by an influx of 'Poor Palatines', Germans fleeing persecution and war. The Tories repealed the Act in 1711 (10 Ann. c. 9). However, this left intact a long-established procedure of denization, by which individuals could acquire residency status (neither citizen nor alien) by royal prerogative. A private Act of Parliament could naturalise a named individual, but general legislation to enable naturalisation was not achieved until the nineteenth century.

Jews aside, non-Christian groups found toleration on the coattails of legislation not originally intended for them. A side-effect of the Unitarian Relief Act 1813 was the freeing of Muslim worship. Much later, a small but landmark statutory toleration for non-Christians, passed in 1976 with surprisingly little objection, exempted turban-wearing Sikhs from laws requiring the wearing of crash helmets (1976 c. 62).

6.11 The multi-confessional state

The coronation of King Charles III in 2023 nicely encapsulated the peculiar historic settlement of 1689: toleration plus the privileged status of the Protestant Church of England. Charles was arrayed with representatives of many religions, but he swore the oath he was obliged to take, to 'maintain the Protestant Reformed Religion established by law' and 'maintain and preserve inviolably the settlement of the Church of England, and the doctrine, worship, discipline, and government thereof'. In earlier years, he had spoken of wishing to be a defender of all faiths – a reference to the antique royal title still visible on British coins: 'F.D.', Fidei Defensor, Defender of the Faith.

Oddly, the existence of an Established Church and of tax-funded religious schools are scarcely live political issues in contemporary Britain, in contrast, for example, with French *laicité*. Rather, it is the boundaries of toleration in what many now call a post-secular society that are in contention. Arguably, religion *tout court* has gained increasing legal and social protection in recent decades. It is probably harder now than a generation ago for agnostics and atheists to be vocally critical of religion. The tendency to treat religion as a species of ethnicity – rather than a set of philosophically contestable propositions – lends to religion the protection of laws against racism and of ethical injunctions to show respect. The confessional state no longer gives way to secularity but rather to a multi-confessional state.

A small example of the transition from mid-twentieth-century secularism to twenty-first-century post-secularism is visible on the campus of the University of Sussex. When the university was created in the 1960s, Christians were prevented from designating a 'chapel', and the building they used was obliged to be called the 'Meeting House'. But, today, a few yards away, there is a Muslim Prayer Room explicitly designated as such.

The Toleration Act of 1689 marked a pragmatic truce in an internecine war among Protestant Christians. In *A Letter Concerning Toleration* of the same year, John Locke set toleration on its path towards becoming a cardinal doctrine of modern secular liberalism. He (or, rather, the translator from his

Latin) famously remarked that churches should be treated like 'clubs for claret': that is to say, like any other private association, to be accepted in a free society so long as they accord with civil peace.[14] Today, post-liberal and post-secular theorists accuse classical liberalism of presuming an anaemic conception of religion as if it were merely the private penchant of individuals. Secular liberalism, they argue, fails to acknowledge religion's communal and necessarily public character as an identity demanding affirmation so that religion has special claims to a privileged position in civil society. If this view prevails, Britain will move further along a path toward a post-secular, multi-confessional social order. In January 2024, Baroness D'Souza argued that, instead of 26 Anglican bishops with protected seats in the House of Lords, 'to have different faiths and denominations statutorily appointed would be a good idea'.[15,16]

Bibliography

Catterall P, 'Religion and the Constitution Since the Glorious Revolution' in P Cane and H Kumarasingham (eds), *The Cambridge Constitutional History of the United Kingdom*, 2 vols (Cambridge University Press 2023), vol 2

Costin WC and Watson JS (eds), *The Law and Working of the Constitution*, 2 vols (Adam and Charles Black 1952)

Devlin P, *The Enforcement of Morals* (Oxford University Press 1965)

Hart HLA, *Law, Liberty, and Morality* (Oxford University Press 1963)

Locke J, '*Second Treatise of Government and A Letter Concerning Toleration*' in M Goldie (ed), (Oxford University Press 2016)

14 John Locke, *Second Treatise of Government* and *A Letter Concerning Toleration* (M Goldie, ed, Oxford University Press 2016) 161.

15 Evidence to the Public Administration and Constitutional Affairs Committee, 9 January 2024. https://committees.parliament.uk/oralevidence/14056/html.

16 For approaches complementary to this chapter, see P Catterall, 'Religion and the Constitution Since the Glorious Revolution' in P Cane and H Kumarasingham (eds), *The Cambridge Constitutional History of the United Kingdom*, 2 vols (Cambridge University Press 2023), ii, 140–67. For commenting on a draft of this chapter I am grateful to Esther Counsell.

7 The Act of Settlement 1701

*Chris Monaghan**

7.1 Introduction

For those concerned with the law and legal profession, the Act of Settlement 1701 may be best known for establishing security of tenure for judges and thus ensuring that senior judges could not be dismissed simply because they had earnt the displeasure of the monarch. Whilst the statutory protection of judicial independence is and remains significant and was, of course, an important issue for those drafting the legislation, it was the succession to the English Crown that was the chief concern in the final years of William III's reign. This chapter will consider why and how Parliament sought to legislate to amend the order of succession, to exclude Catholics from the throne, and to disinherit the natural successor to James II, his son Prince James Edward. Significantly, the Act of Settlement assured a Protestant monarchy, the Hanoverian accession, and, in turn, led to the creation of the office of Prime Minister, the development of cabinet government, and the constitutional monarchy. It is an Act that continues to discriminate against Catholics, as a Catholic still cannot become monarch. Nonetheless, despite its clear discriminatory language, it is apparent that the Act of Settlement has played a pivotal role in securing judicial independence and ensuring meaningful security of tenure for judges and the development of the rule of law. Thus, it is a 'leading work' in British constitutional history.

7.2 James II, England's Catholic king

It is important to appreciate the origins of the need for the Act of Settlement. In 1685, James II succeeded his brother Charles II. James' accession was never certain, given the attempts to exclude him from the succession to the Crown during the reign of his brother Charles II[1] (such as the Rye House plot of

* Principal Lecturer in Law, University of Worcester. I am grateful to my colleague, Dr Michael Lane, for reading a draft version of this chapter.

1 See the exclusion crisis of 1678–81. Mark Knights 'The grievances that underpinned the crisis can be summed up by the deceptively simple slogan of "popery and arbitrary government"'. (Mark Knights, *Politics and Opinion in Crisis: 1678–81* (Cambridge University Press 1994) 17). See also Elizabeth Clarke, 'Re-reading the Exclusion Crisis' (2006) 27(1) The Seventeenth Century 141.

DOI: 10.4324/9781032658698-8

1683). Openly Catholic, James' religious faith was at odds with the majority of his English subjects. There had not been a Catholic monarch in England since the death of Mary I in 1558 (even if Charles II had been suspected of converting to Catholicism on his deathbed),[2] and Catholics faced statutory discrimination, such as the Test Act 1673 and Test Act 1678. The parliamentary justification for the Test Acts was Charles II's willingness to allow individuals to be exempt by using the prerogative to dispense with prior legal restrictions and his controversial 1672 Declaration of Indulgence. Catholics were very much the other, regarded as a threat to the state, and viewed with suspicion and hostility, which manifested in Titus Oates' alleged Popish plot in 1677. This discrimination even applied to James, who, as Duke of York, had to resign as Lord High Admiral.[3] The Test Acts served a clear purpose – to weaken the position of James as king.[4] The irony was that the legislation helped James to become king, as Dennis Dixon argues that '[w]ithout the Test Acts reassuring Anglican-royalist opinion, it is doubtful if James II would have retained his rights as successor to the throne after the Exclusion Crisis of 1678–81.'[5]

When James ascended the throne, his heirs were his daughters Mary and Anne, who were both Protestants. Mary was married to a leading Protestant figure, her cousin Prince William of Orange. Thus, it seemed likely that James would be succeeded by a Protestant. As Enid Campbell argues, James himself had 'made no secret of the fact that it was his intention to fill all offices of public trust at his disposal with persons who professed the Roman Catholic faith . . . contrary to the Test Act 1673.'[6] James' policy was arguably (at least to his supporters) justifiable, as he 'wanted a toleration and more for his Catholic Subjects' and sought Parliamentary support in repealing the Test Act 1673.[7] The failure to gain this support resulted in James' use of his purported power to dispense with a statute.[8] An example of this was James' appointment of the Catholic Sir Edward Hales as a colonel in violation of the Test Act 1673,

2 See Patricia Gael, 'Kingship and Catholicism in Posthumous Representations of Charles II, 1685–1714' (2014) 29(2) The Seventeenth Century 173. Gael is clear that Charles' rumoured conversion impacted his posthumous reputation. However, Gael is clear that 'News of Charles's deathbed conversion to Catholicism probably was not widespread–at least not in published form–until 1686' (178). Therefore, news of the conversion took some time to become well-known.

3 Enid Campbell, 'Oaths and Affirmations of Public Office under English Law: An Historical Retrospect' (2000) 21(3) The Journal of Legal History 1, 10.

4 Dennis Dixon, 'Godden v Hales Revisited – James II and the Dispensing Power' (2006) 27(2) The Journal of Legal History 129, 137 (fn. 53). Dixon 'The belief was that, whatever the views of the king, Catholicism could never be in the political ascendancy if Catholics could not serve as ministers, advisers or officials' (137).

5 Ibid 137.

6 Campbell (n 3) 12.

7 Carolyn A Edie, 'Tactics and Strategies: Parliament's Attack Upon the Royal Dispensing Power 1597–1689' (1985) 29(3) The American Journal of Legal History 197, 226.

8 Ibid 226.

an appointment which was challenged in the courts. In *Godden v Hales*,[9] the court found for the king. As a consequence of the decision, James used his prerogative power to suspend the Test Acts.[10] James' approach was viewed as a justification for the revolutionary settlement.[11] Coupled with the birth of his son, James Edward, in 1688, James' policy was a decisive factor in bringing about the Glorious Revolution.[12]

7.3 The revolutionary settlement of 1688–89

The events of late 1688 and 1689 saw James deposed and the Crown offered to Mary and William. The Bill of Rights was presented to William and Mary as a pre-condition to their accession to the English Crown.[13] It represented James' departure from the throne as an abdication, although this was ambiguous as it could mean two things: being deposed or voluntarily giving up the throne.[14] This was deliberate. Those who had advocated for William prior to his military invasion of England 'presented the Dutch invasion as continuation of God's reformation of England,' because under James, 'a righteous protestantism had been undermined by a vicious and catholic court.'[15] James' conduct has been depicted as inevitably deserving his removal from the throne; an example of this is that '[he] had pushed his power beyond what custom and perhaps beyond what law allowed.'[16] Furthermore, James, whose religion made him a rarity in his own kingdom, was described as '[t]he Catholic king [who] had granted dispensations freely, setting aside statutes to bring Catholics into

9 See the critique of the decision by Dixon 'was wrongly decided' and James did not have the 'stated justification for his frequent use of the dispensing power' (Dixon (n 4) 152).

10 Campbell (n 3) 12. See also Dixon (n 4) 130.

11 Carolyn A Edie, 'Revolution and the Rule of Law: The End of the Dispensing Power, 1689' (1977) 10(4) Eighteenth-Century Studies 434, 440.

12 See Michael Muffett, *James II and English Politics 1678–1688* (Routledge 2008) 72 and John Mctague, 'Anti-Catholicism, Incorrigibility and Credulity in the Warming-Pan Scandal of 1688–9' (2013) 36(3) Journal for Eighteenth-Century Studies 433. As Mctague notes, '[James Edwards] birth conjured the possibility of extended Catholic rule in England.' Mctague argues, 'While I can concede that the birth may not have been essential to the revolution, I will not concede that it did not shape it. It had an effect.' (435). This is at odds with Steve Pincus' secular account of the revolution, see Steve Pincus, *1688: The First Modern Revolution* (Yale University Press 2009) 327).

13 The Convention Parliament (which had not been legally assembled), took the perhaps dubious, but certainly, from their perspective, a necessary step, of interpreting James II's (permitted) flight to France to be proof that the English throne was vacant. See Lucinda Maer and Oonagh Gay, 'The Bill of Rights 1689' (House of Commons Library, 5 October 2009) <https://commonslibrary.parliament.uk/research-briefings/sn00293/>

14 See, in particular, Thomas P Slaughter, '"Abdicate" and "Contract" in the Glorious Revolution' (1981) 24(2) The Historical Journal 323, 335–36 for a discussion about the significance of the ambiguity.

15 Tony Claydon, 'William III's Declaration of Reasons and the Glorious Revolution' (1996) 39(1) The History Journal 87, 107.

16 Edie (n 7) 230.

his service and, presumably, into his designs for absolutism.'[17] James' misuse of his powers was regarded as 'intolerable' and contrary to the rule of law.[18]

The Bill of Rights was entitled 'an Act of Parliament was made, intituled, An Act for declaring the Rights and Liberties of the Subject, and for settling the Succession of the Crown.' A similar statute, the Claim of Right, was enacted by the Scottish Parliament. Both pieces of legislation were attempts to limit the power of the Crown (after perceived abuses by James II and to protect the liberties of the Crown's subjects). The Bill of Rights had been intended to provide a clear line of succession (thereby seeking to remove the problem of James II and his heirs from being restored) and was based upon the assumption that William and Mary, who were to rule jointly produced an heir (which was not unlikely), and failing that the Crown would be succeeded by Mary's sister, Princess Anne, and eventually her heirs.

The impact of the Glorious Revolution and the Bill of Rights is significant, not least that the Act of Settlement which followed it, sought to reject James II and his heir, James Edward, and his transformative constitutional agenda. As Lord Norton argued, despite its significance in shaping the development of Britain, there is an unwillingness to celebrate it (unlike the Magna Carta) because 'the Glorious Revolution produced a state of affairs that became taken for granted and one that consequently was not deemed worthy of extended study.'[19] A similar point was made by HT Dickinson, who viewed the reluctance to celebrate as partly being down to embarrassment because it marked 'the political triumph of Protestantism over Catholicism' and the legacy it has had in Ireland.[20] Furthermore, HT Dickinson argued that

> [t]he 1688 Revolution is seen, at worst, as a rather squalid palace coup or the political triumph of a narrow aristocratic oligarchy. At best it is regarded as an unheroic, if sensible and pragmatic, arrangement which made minor changes in the succession to the throne.[21]

7.4 The need for the Act of Settlement 1701

The Act of Settlement 1701 was a product of the final years of William III's reign. The king had seen the election of 1698 result in a House of Commons that was hostile to his policy and his Whig allies (the Whig Junto). The army was reduced in size, a nationality requirement was introduced to remove foreign soldiers, and a resolution passed on 10 April 1700 to force the removal

17 Edie (n 11) 434.

18 Ibid 440.

19 Philip Norton, 'The Glorious Revolution of 1688: Its Continuing Relevance' (1989) 42(2) Parliamentary Affairs 135, 136 and 146.

20 HT Dickinson, 'How Revolutionary Was the "Glorious Revolution" of 1688?' (1988) 11(2) Journal for Eighteenth-Century Studies 125.

21 Ibid.

of William's non-English advisors in the Council.[22] It is unsurprising that William contemplated abdication. The subsequent election of 1701 resulted in a Tory ministry replacing the Whig Junto. Robert Harvey (the future 1st Earl of Oxford) was appointed speaker of the House of Commons and played a key role with his ministerial colleagues in setting out the agenda of the new ministry. This was done in consultation with William. Harvey's influence was critical, as according to DW Hayton:

> Harley had several private audiences with William, in which he proposed a bill to declare the succession to the crown in the Hanoverian line. He warned the King that the opposition to the settlement would be indirect, through the addition of various 'limitations', but hoped to be able to postpone their operation until the Hanoverian succession, a ploy which would bring in the Tories, and leave only the 'Commonwealth's people' outside.[23]

These limitations offer the prospect of seeing a path not chosen in English constitutional history, whereby there would be a separation of powers between those in the House of Commons and those who worked for the king within the executive. The prohibition of those who held a position from Crown from being an MP was significant. Had this not been repealed in 1706, before it had even come into effect with the death of Anne, then we would have seen a very different political system develop from the British Westminster system, and one that would do more to create a genuine separation of powers in the British constitution. As Naamani Tarkow observes, this provision amounted to a

> Critical phase in the constitutional history of England. As in the case of the . . . the responsibility of the Privy Councillors, had [this] . . . not been repealed, the present English system of Cabinet government would have been impossible. The Commons would have never attained the desired control over the ministers that they now hold. There would have resulted a practical separation of powers – separation of executive and legislative personnel. The king would have chosen his ministers from the Upper House, and the power of the Lower House would have materially diminished. Its virtual repeal in 1707, however, permitted the retention of those individuals with seats in the Commons who filled ministerial offices created before 1705 and who were deemed desirable

22 Barry Coward, *The Stuart Age: England 1603–1714* (2nd edn, Longman 1994) 388.

23 DW Hayton, 'Harley, Robert (1661–1724), of Brampton Bryan, Herefs' in DW Hayton, E Cruickshanks and S Handley (eds), *The History of Parliament: The House of Commons 1690–1715* (History of Parliament Trust 2002). This is available at <https://www.historyofparliamentonline.org/volume/1690-1715/member/harley-robert-1661-1724>

> by reelection. Furthermore, new ministerial offices have been put in the same category by the acts creating them.[24]

This was a view echoed by Robert Stevens, who regarded the repeal of the key provisions in the Act of Settlement as a rejection of what would be viewed as the separation of powers in preference to the balance of powers:

> Historically, the Act of Settlement marks the crossroads of the English Constitution. The provisions of the Act, both with respect to placemen and judges, represented an inarticulate effort to have the kind of separation of powers spelled out with much greater clarity at the Constitutional Convention in Philadelphia 75 years later. The effort to keep the executive out of the legislature and to offer a measure of protection to the judiciary could have led to a concept of the separation of powers along the American model. Almost at once the English decided that they preferred a balance of powers rather than the separation of powers.[25]

Members of the government could not be MPs, and, therefore, this would prevent, in part, the fusion between the Commons and the government, which is underscored by the need for the government to retain the confidence of the Commons. The provision restricting placemen would have limited the monarch's and ministry's patronage, as MPs could not be offered lucrative positions. According to Gary Cox:

> The Act of Settlement contained a new legal defense against royal vote buying. Reacting to William's vigorous attempts to influence the House of Commons, [it] . . . declared that anyone who held an office under, or received a pension from, the Crown was ineligible to sit in Parliament. Statutes passed in 1705–1707 weakened this prohibition, allowing members to accept various offices from the king, so long as they resigned their seat in the Commons and stood for reelection.[26]

Clayton Roberts saw the Act of Settlement as one of a series of inroads into the monarch's prerogative powers, although he noted that it was '[t]he most apparent diminution, but the least important.'[27] Even the provision that

24 I Naamani Tarkow, 'The Significance of the Act of Settlement in the Evolution of English Democracy' (1943) 58(4) Political Science Quarterly 537, 554–55.

25 Robert Stevens, 'The Act of Settlement and the Questionable History of Judicial Independence' (2001) 1(2) Oxford University Commonwealth Law Journal 252, 261.

26 Gary W Cox, 'Was the Glorious Revolution a Constitutional Watershed?' (2012) 72(3) The Journal of Economic History 567, 570–71.

27 Clayton Roberts, *The Growth of Responsible Government in Stuart England* (Cambridge University Press 1966) 326.

would force ministers to claim responsibility for the advice that they offered the monarch would be repealed in 1706. As Roberts observes, 'Englishmen now have the sophistication to know that secrecy was necessary to the good government of the realm.'[28] The requirement that the monarch must seek advice from his Privy Councillors and that this advice must be in writing and signed was 'impracticable,' contrary to the need for cabinet confidentiality, and would deter people from serving the king.[29] This provision was intended to remove the monarch's usage of the cabinet as a form of government, and give precedence to governance through the Privy Council. As Naamani Tarkow argues:

> For a long time the Cabinet Council was viewed with grave concern, especially by Parliament . . . . Finally Parliament decided to put an end to the Cabinet "menace" and inserted the provision in the Act of Settlement to revive the old system . . . . Parliament, however, soon realized its folly. The restrictions on the councillors and ministers were too severe. Many would refrain from offering any advice at all to the king.[30]

The significance of the provision would have proved fatal to the evolution of cabinet government, as this provision attempted

> to stop the natural development of one of the greatest political institutions of all time, and to go contrary to the spirit of English common law, that soon made the sagacious English parliamentarians aware of their grave mistake and led them to rectify it early in the reign of Queen Anne by repealing the measure.[31]

The British constitution would have developed in a very different manner. This difference may have proved to have had long-term benefits or might have led to a more challenging path to Britain becoming a parliamentary democracy. For those who teach the nuances of the British constitution, the debates about Montesquieu and the separation of powers and the fusion between the legislature and the executive within the Westminster system would be somewhat altered.

Also significant was the inclusion of a prohibition on monarchs from pardoning ministers who were impeached. This meant that the monarch could intervene to prevent a minister (or someone else) from being found guilty at trial by the House of Lords. This would not prevent the monarch, if an individual was found to be guilty, from using their prerogative powers to pardon

28 Ibid 398.
29 Ibid 438.
30 Naamani Tarkow (n 24) 549–50.
31 Ibid 550–51.

the individual.[32] Mark Goldie regards the probation of a pardon as 'the most comprehensive statutory restriction of royal prerogative in the early modern period.'[33] The inclusion of this prohibition was in response to Charles II's controversial decision to pardon his minister, the Early of Danby, and prevent him from being impeached by the Commons.[34] The problem was that Danby was being impeached for acting under instruction from the king; clearly, Charles could not be proceeded against as 'the King could do no wrong,' but his minister was culpable.[35] Noting the significance of the Act of Settlement, Robin Eagles observes that 'The Revolution of 1688–1689 had transformed the political landscape of Britain. The 1701 Act of Settlement provided explicitly for preventing future monarchs from protecting failed ministers who had been impeached by the Commons.'[36]

7.4.1 Securing the Protestant monarchy

The Act of Settlement was formally entitled 'An Act for the further Limitation of the Crown, and the better securing of Rights and Liberties of the Subject.' The Act of Settlement was intended to be a successor to the Bill of Rights 1689. Therefore, it is within this context that the Act of Settlement can be seen as safeguarding the success of the Palace coup or the *status quo*, or as George Harrison saw the revolution, to safeguard the counter-revolution against James II's far more significant revolution in the reformation of government and religion. George Harrison regarded James II's rule as a break from the past and an attempt to revolutionise government and the church.[37] Indeed, Harrison argued that James II's policies were 'more genuinely revolutionary' than that of the Glorious Revolution, which could be viewed as 'little more than a successful counter-revolution' by James' opponents, who were worried that he would succeed.[38] It is worth emphasising MA Thomson's observation that '[t]here can be no doubt that the constitutional settlement of 1689 was acceptable to the vast majority of politically conscious Englishmen.'[39]

32 Mark Goldie gives the example of the pardoning of three rebels who had been impeached in 1715 (Mark Goldie, 'Impeachment in Seventeenth-Century England' in C Monaghan and M Flinders (eds), *British Origins and American Practice of Impeachment* (Routledge 2024) 57).
33 Ibid 57.
34 Raoul Berger, *Impeachment: The Constitutional Problems* (Harvard University Press 1973) 55.
35 Roberts (n 27) 435.
36 Robin Eagles, 'British Politics and Impeachment in the Eighteenth Century' in C Monaghan and M Flinders (eds), *British Origins and American Practice of Impeachment* (Routledge 2024) 65.
37 George Harrison, 'Prerogative Revolution and Glorious Revolution: Political Proscription and Parliamentary Undertaking, 1687–88' (1990) 10(1) Parliaments, Estates and Representation 29.
38 Ibid 29.
39 MA Thomson, 'The Safeguarding of the Protestant Succession 1702–18' (1954) 39(135/136) History 39.

The Act of Settlement was an attempt at a longer-term settlement for England as William III and Mary II had failed to produce heirs (Mary had died in 1694). The heir to the Crown, Princess Anne, had recently lost her one surviving child, Prince William, Duke of Gloucester, in July 1700. The Act stated that it was

> a further Provision to be made for the Succession of the Crown in the Protestant Line, for the Happiness of the Nation, and the Security of our Religion; and it being absolutely necessary for the Safety, Peace and Quiet of this Realm, to obviate all Doubts and Contentions in the same, by reason of any pretended Title to the Crown, and to maintain a Certainty in the Succession thereof.

To secure the exclusion of the House of Stuart, the Act designated Anne's successor to be Sophia, the Electress of Hanover, who 'is hereby declared to be the next in Succession, in the Protestant Line, to the Imperial Crown and Dignity of the said realms of England, France and Ireland.' This settlement would not be challenged politically, as the Hanoverian dynasty would produce heirs and become accepted as English monarchs, with George III becoming the first English-born Hanoverian monarch. The settlement was challenged militarily, with Prince James Edward invading Scotland and England in 1715 and his son, Prince Charles Edward, doing the same in 1745. Both attempts were unsuccessful.

7.4.2 The exclusion of the House of Stuart

If England was to have a Protestant succession then the choice was Sophia of Hanover and her issue. But who was Sophia? Sophia of Hanover was the daughter of Elizabeth, Electress of Palatinate, who was the daughter of James I and Anne of Denmark. Sophia had married Ernest Augustus, the Elector of Hanover. Sophia's brothers, Princes Rupert and Maurice, had fought for the royalists during the English Civil Wars. To help Sophia's position as Anne's heir, the Sophia of Hanover Naturalisation Act 1705 was enacted to make her and her family English, and The Princess Sophia's Precedence Act 1711 was designed to acknowledge her place in the court hierarchy as Anne's successor. Despite being heir to the Crown, Sophia was refused permission to visit England. Sophia's relationship with Anne was complicated, which is unsurprising given the fact that the more influence Sophia would have gained in England and with politicians, then this would risk detracting from Anne's own influence (something that would become a problem for the Hanoverian monarchs who had uneasy relationships with their own heirs). On this complicated relationship, AW Ward has noted that

> while Queen Anne from the first professed to favour the succession of that house, her goodwill towards it was shown both fitfully and

> grudgingly; and above all she would never hear of fulfilling the promise of William III, and inviting to England the electress dowager and the electoral prince.[40]

Another important issue was whether Queen Anne supported the exclusion of her brother from the succession. AW Ward noted that Sophia 'feared a secret sympathy on Queen Anne's part with the pretender'.[41] However, as Edward Gregg has argued that '[a]fter Anne's death, of course, most political groups had a vested interest in claiming that she had indeed had been scheming to restore her brother. But historians must treat this propaganda with the greatest caution.'[42] Anne's family circumstances were complicated to say the least, and it is not unreasonable that Anne had some sympathy for the position of her brother. However, as Bennett has commented to those in power, including Anne, the 'Hanoverian succession [was] inevitable.'[43] This did not prevent Robert Harvey from playing James Edward in order to gain his support and raise the prospect (through negotiations with him) of Parliament declaring him the heir to the throne, which in turn would be useful in gaining the votes of those Tories with Jacobite sympathies.[44] This, of course, never happened.[45] Nevertheless, Harley's correspondence with the exiled Stuarts was not uncommon, as Hayton stated, 'a number of prominent political figures . . . made contact with the Jacobites, but generally as a political "insurance policy" [because of the] . . . prospect of a disputed succession to Queen Anne.'[46] The contact with the exiled Stuart court is not surprising given the fractious domestic politics, party rivalries, the realities of having no living child to be the Protestant heir, and wider European diplomacy at play.

Given Sophia's age, it was unlikely that Sophia would herself actually become monarch, and therefore the Act stated that her son, 'the most Noble George Augustus Electoral Prince of Hanover and Duke of Cambridge', would succeed her.

40 AW Ward, 'The Electress Sophia and the Hanoverian Succession' (1886) 1(3) The English Historical Review 470, 493.

41 Ibid 497.

42 Edward Gregg, 'Was Queen Anne a Jacobite' (1972) 57(191) History 358, 358.

43 GV Bennett, 'English Jacobitism, 1710–1715; Myth and Reality' (1982) 32 Transactions of the Royal Historical Society 137, 146. For a discussion of Tory resistance to the succession and the lukewarm opposition, see DW Hayton, 'The Politics of the House' in DW Hayton, E Cruickshanks and S Handley (eds), *The History of Parliament: The House of Commons 1690–1715* (History of Parliament Trust 2002). This is available at: <https://www.historyofparliamentonline.org/volume/1690-1715/survey/politics-house>. Hayton is clear that, 'For all that some back-bench Whigs assumed the existence of a strong Jacobite element within the Tory party in 1701, hard evidence of Jacobite sympathies among Tories at this time is scarce.'

44 GV Bennett, 'English Jacobitism, 1710–1715; Myth and Reality' (1982) 32 Transactions of the Royal Historical Society 137, 144.

45 Hayton (n 23).

46 Hayton (n 43).

In his written evidence to Parliament Robert Blackburn observes that 'Parliament re-routed the prospective succession' and

> [w]ere it not for the Act of Settlement, there would naturally have been a very different line of succession . . . the present monarch of the United Kingdom would have been 'Queen Mary III', an Italian countess. Her son and heir to the throne, in Prince Charles's place, would succeed her as 'King Uberto I', whose actual name is Uberto Omar Gasche; he was born in 1951 and works in Rome as a dog breeder and photographer.[47]

Now, of course, had the House of Stuart continued to rule, then, in the event of a similar transition to constitutional monarchy as did actually occur, in reality, the actual heir would not necessarily have been Uberto Omar Gasche.

7.4.3 The obvious omission: the Crown of Scotland

The Act of Settlement legislated for the English succession.[48] There was no Scottish equivalent, which meant that the Crown of Scotland would pass on Anne's death to her heir, the natural heir being her brother, James Edward. Obviously, the English state would not permit an end to the personal union of Crowns that had been in place since James I and VI's accession to the English Crown in 1603, especially if the new monarch was a Catholic member of the Stuart dynasty. The Claim of Rights 1689 had given the Crown to William and Mary and provided an order of succession identical to the Bill of Rights,

> The said Croune and Royall Dignity of the said Kingdome to be to the heirs of the body of the said Queen which failing to the Princess Ann of Denmark and the airs of her body which also failing to the aires of the Body of the said William King of England.

This presented a problem: How to ensure the Hanoverian succession in Scotland. To solve this, William III and then Anne supported a union between England and Scotland.[49] A union would ensure that Hanoverian succession and the exclusion of the Stuarts. In terms of union, it was apparent that a federal union was not the goal of Anne's English or Scottish ministers and the Court; what was favoured was a personal union and the Hanoverian succession with

47 House of Commons Political and Constitutional Reform Committee, Rules of Succession. 11th Report of Session 2010–12, HC 1615, available at <https://publications.parliament.uk/pa/cm201012/cmselect/cmpolcon/1615/1615.pdf> (written evidence of Professor Robert Blackburn).

48 Karin Bowie, *Scottish Public Opinion and the Anglo- Scottish Union 1699–1707* (Boydell & Brewer Ltd 2007) 73.

49 Ibid 73.

Scotland maintaining its independence from England. Whatley makes clear is that the head of the Scottish ministry, the Marquis of Tweeddale, had the objective 'to secure the Hanoverian succession in an independent Scotland.'[50] The talks between England and Scotland on a union collapsed in 1702.[51] This was significant, as the issue of succession remained unresolved. As Patrick and Whatley argued, this posed real problems, as

> The Hanoverian Protestant succession was still unresolved in Scotland, and from St Germain James Francis Stuart – the 'Old Pretender'– and his energetic supporters posed a real threat to the Revolution settlement. Relations between Scotland and England were in freefall from 1702, although they had begun to degenerate into bouts of mutual hostility earlier.[52]

Although the Scottish Parliament had lost its freedom in determining Scotland's own foreign policy or its own home affairs, it still could resist William and Anne, which it had done since 1689.[53] As Rosalind Mitchison remarked in her assessment of the power dynamics, that although 'Anne was dominated by her English ministry, and through her it could order the Scottish ministers about, and expect them to obey, but there were limits to what these ministers could do when Parliament was insubordinate.'[54] The Scottish Parliament still could play its trump card and enact legislation to declare James Edward to be his sister's heir.[55] Such a move would be to act against the Scottish Crown.[56] According to Mitchison, had such a decision been taken, then it would inevitably have resulted in an independent Scotland, which would suffer financially without trade with England, and there would be the constant threat of war.[57] Things, though, need not have seemed so bleak for Scotland had it pursued such a course, as Mitchison noted that 'there was just a chance of a stretch of peace if the return to the Stewart dynasty was made now, quickly, while the English were deep in war with France.'[58] Rather than doing this, what the Scottish Parliament did was use the matter of Scottish succession to lobby for a union on its own terms. It did this by enacting the Act of Security, which

50 Christopher A Whatley, 'Economic Causes and Consequences of the Union of 1707: A Survey' (1989) LXVIII (186) The Scottish Historical Review 150, 154.

51 Bowie (n 48) 73.

52 Derek J Patrick and Christopher A Whatley, 'Persistence, Principle and Patriotism in the Making of the Union of 1707: The Revolution, Scottish Parliament and the squadrone volante' (2007) 92(306) History 162, 176.

53 Rosalind Mitchison, *A History of Scotland* (3rd edn, Routledge 2002) 235.

54 Ibid.

55 Ibid.

56 Ibid.

57 Ibid.

58 Ibid.

Mitchison regarded as adopting the 'English technique of withholding supply till grievances had been met. The "cess" must wait on the "Act of Security". This proposed legislation was a vigorous demand for independence.'[59] As Karin Bowie explains,

> In 1703 the Court party sought an act of parliament to confirm Sophia of Hanover, the named successor in England, as the heir to the Scottish crown. The opposition countered with overtures for an Act of Security in an attempt to force a renegotiation of the terms of the union of crowns before accepting the Hanoverian successor.[60]

The Act was intended 'to limit the powers of Scotland's future monarch' whilst, '[n]evertheless, their core commitment was to the Protestant succession as established at the Revolution.'[61] The Act of Settlement was explicit that the next Scottish monarch did not have to be Sophia of Hanover:

> unless that in this present Session of Parliament or any other Session of this or any ensuing Parliament during her Majesties reign there be such conditions of Government settled and enacted as may secure the honour and sovereignty of this Crown and Kingdom, the freedom frequency and power of Parliaments, the religion liberty and trade of the Nation from English or any foreigne influence With power to the said Meeting of Estates to add such further conditions of Government as they shall think necessary the same being consistent with and no ways derogatory from those which shall be enacted in this and any other Session of Parliament during her Majesties reign.

Queen Anne gave royal assent to the Act of Security, even if her assent was given reluctantly. The Act of Security prevented any Catholic from becoming the monarch, but did not name Sophia of Hannover as Anne's heir. Relations between Anne's kingdoms were strained, and there was a 'rising level of Anglophobia in Scotland', which culminated in the execution of the English crew of the *Worcester* in 1705.[62] The Act of Security was met with the Aliens Act 1705, which restricted the rights of Scots in England.[63] Crucially, whilst commentators in England might disregard Scotland's right to choose its next monarch, the Scottish regarded the English response to the Act of Security as 'support[ing] the picture of a bullying nation trying to force acceptance of the

59 Ibid 236.
60 Bowie (n 48) 73.
61 Patrick and Whatley (n 52) 177.
62 Ibid 173 fn.45.
63 Mitchison (n 53) 237.

Hanoverian succession on Scotland.'[64] An example of the Scottish response was James Anderson's *An historical essay, shewing that the crown and kingdom of Scotland, is imperial and independent*, which was published in 1705.[65]

The intention of the Act of Security was clear. Bowie noted that the book, *The Act of Security is the only rational method of procuring Scotland a happy constitution, free from the illegal invasions of its liberties and laws, and the base usurpation of its ancient sovereignty* (1704) was typical in arguing that the Act would 'Secure our Indendency from the undue Intermeddling of the English Court' by 'set[ting] us upon such an Equal Foot with the English, that they will be obliged to Grant us Concessions. . . Thus an happy and lasting Union might be Established without Civil Dissention.'[66]

The Act of Security resulted in the fact 'that pressures for incorporating (as opposed to federal) union came almost exclusively from the English side, following Queen Anne's "grudging" acceptance of the Scots Act of Security in 1704.'[67] This should not ignore that the need for union was felt in Scotland, given Scotland's weakening financial position.[68] Faced with pressures from England that would restrict access to English trade markets, 'the Scottish parliament had little option but to surrender to what was in effect economic blackmail.'[69] Whatley has argued that caution is needed when concluding that financial considerations made the union inevitable.[70] However, despite the attempt to gain a beneficial position for Scotland by using the succession issue, it did not work, as ultimately, England achieved the union because it could threaten economic consequences.[71]

7.4.4 The modern problem – discriminating against Catholics

The Act of Settlement may have been viewed as justifiable in 1701; however, it is a 'nakedly discriminatory' Act of Parliament that remains a reminder of the discrimination faced by Catholics as a consequence of England's turbulent history in the sixteenth and seventeenth centuries.[72] Discrimination against Catholics and their religion was justified 'because, in people's minds, they represented a threat to both the security of the nation and its religion.'[73] As *The*

64 Bowie (n 48) 89.
65 Ibid 89.
66 Ibid 74.
67 Whatley (n 50) 156.
68 Ibid 157.
69 Ibid 157.
70 Ibid 165.
71 Bowie (n 48) 169.
72 Stephen Bates, 'Act of Settlement: A Nakedly Discriminatory Law' (*The Guardian*, 27 March 2009) <https://www.theguardian.com/uk/2009/mar/27/act-of-settlement-monarchy-catholic>
73 Lucinda Maer, 'The Act of Settlement and the Protestant Succession' (House of Commons Library, 24 January 2011) <https://researchbriefings.files.parliament.uk/documents/SN00683/SN00683.pdf>

Guardian noted, 'It has been a long time since any but the most conservative of churchmen has defended the equitability of the legislation.'[74] Equally, *The Telegraph's* view was that 'It is condemned by many today as "Britain's grubby little secret", a piece of institutionalised discrimination against Roman Catholics.'[75] In 2003, the Fabian Society pondered whether in 'a modern democracy. In the context of increasing cultural diversity, and an expectation of civil and social equality, can institutionalised gender and religious discrimination any longer be acceptable?'[76] Robert Blackburn is clear that the exclusion of a Catholic from becoming monarch (which remains the case despite the enactment of the 2013 Act) is discriminatory. As Blackburn points out, there was a cross-party consensus that the Act of Settlement was discriminatory to Catholics, which critics, including

> Michael Howard ('it is an anachronism that Catholicism should be singled out') and Michael Forsyth ('the British constitution's grubby secret and nobody wants to tackle it') . . . and John Reid ('as a Roman Catholic myself, I am only too well aware of the very deep feelings and passions which surround this issue').[77]

Blackburn was clear that a solution could be to disestablish the Church of England and amend the coronation oath, as 'Disestablishment of the Church of England would automatically bring to an end the religious requirements and Catholic disqualification applicable to a British monarch.'[78] He noted that this would not have the support of the then monarch, Queen Elizabeth II.[79] In 2005, Lord Dubs, who escaped the Holocaust as a child through the Kindertransport, introduced a (unsuccessful) private members bill to remove his discrimination. In parliamentary debates, Dubs had argued,

> Such discrimination against Catholics is surely unacceptable in this day and age. What must many people in Commonwealth countries such as Canada and Australia think, given that they have large Catholic

74 Bates (n 72).

75 Martin Beckford, 'The Act of Settlement: 300 Years of Discrimination Against Roman Catholic' (*The Telegraph*, 26 March 2009) <https://www.telegraph.co.uk/news/5056680/The-Act-of-Settlement-300-years-of-discrimination-against-Roman-Catholics.html>

76 Maer (n 73).

77 House of Commons Political and Constitutional Reform Committee, Rules of Succession. 11th Report of Session 2010–12, HC 1615 <https://publications.parliament.uk/pa/cm201012/cmselect/cmpolcon/1615/1615.pdf> (written evidence of Professor Robert Blackburn).

78 Ibid.

79 Ibid.

> populations? Indeed, coming nearer home, how must this be seen by the Catholic population of Northern Ireland?[80]

In response, the Lord Chancellor, Lord Falconer of Thoroton, set out the constitutional justification for the Act of Settlement, 'The critical ongoing relevance of the Act, as both right reverend Prelates identified, is that the English Established Church is the Church of England, of which the sovereign is supreme governor.'[81]

The Succession to the Crown Act 2013 was intended to remove many of the discriminatory elements within the rules of succession. Whilst the Act did amend the anti-Catholic discriminatory provisions relating to a Catholic marrying the heir to the throne or removing the requirement that those members of the royal family who married a Catholic would lose their place in the order of succession, it did remove the exclusion of a Catholic from becoming monarch. Section 1 of the Succession to the Crown Act 2013 removed primogeniture, which had given preference to male son over that of an older female sibling.[82] This applies to those individuals born after 28 October 2011 and, therefore, would not affect the current line of succession (i.e., giving Princess Anne, the Princess Royal, a position above both her younger brothers). The change necessitated consultation and the agreement of the other realms where Elizabeth II was Queen. Section 2 of the Succession to the Crown Act 2013 states that 'A person is not disqualified from succeeding to the Crown or from possessing it as a result of marrying a person of the Roman Catholic faith.' This amended both the Bill of Rights and Act of Settlement by virtue of Section 3 of the Succession to the Crown Act 2013. Therefore, a monarch would be permitted to marry a Catholic but would not be permitted to convert to Catholicism.[83] Nor would their eldest child, if they decided to become a Catholic, would be able to succeed to the Crown. Arguably, this remains absurd in the twenty-first century and is a reminder of England's troubled history. This incomplete reform, which still prevents a Catholic from becoming

80 HL Deb 14 January 2005 vol 668 cc495–515, 496.

81 HL Deb 14 January 2005 vol 668 cc 495–515, 510.

82 The legislation was motivated to ensure the first-born child, regardless of gender, would succeed Prince William. See Caroline Davies, 'Royal Baby Girl's Right of Succession Would Face Commonwealth Obstacles' (*The Guardian*, 22 July 2013) <https://www.theguardian.com/uk-news/2013/jul/22/royal-baby-succession-commonwealth-primogeniture>

83 As Parpworth observes, 'The cumulative effect of the Bill of Rights 1688, the Act of Settlement 1700, the Act of Union 1707 and the Accession Declaration Act 1910, is that a monarch cannot be a Roman Catholic.' The Coronation Oath states, 'I [here insert the name of the Sovereign] do solemnly and sincerely in the presence of God profess, testify, and declare that I am a faithful Protestant, and that I will, according to the true intent of the enactments which secure the Protestant succession to the Throne of my Realm, uphold and maintain the said enactments to the best of my powers according to law.' (Neil Parpworth, 'The Succession to the Crown Act 2013: Modernising the Monarchy' (2013) 76(6) Modern Law Review 1070, 1091).

monarch, has been criticised, notably by Parpworth: '[R]emoving one piece of religious discrimination whilst leaving another in place betrays an inconsistent approach.'[84]

The bottom line is that many people view the Act as discriminatory, and the justification for excluding Catholics from the throne and the line of succession is no longer relevant, as they are not 'viewed as a threat to the political security of the state, as it was at the time three centuries ago when the Bill of Rights and Act of Settlement were passed.'[85] It is discriminatory and harks back to a time when Catholicism was regarded as at odds with loyalty to the Crown and country, priest holes, the gunpowder plot, the Test Acts, and the exclusion of Catholics from public life. Thus, it is a relic and not something that should consigned, like other forms of discrimination, to the past. Is there any real democratic or constitutional (bar the Established Church of England) impediment to a Catholic monarch? The answer to modern Britain is surely no, as the temporal circumstances have changed, just as it makes no difference as to whether the Prime Minister is Protestant, Catholic, or Hindu. The absurdity of this restriction was emphasised by the Earl of Mar and Kellie in 2005, 'the Act of Settlement should be off the statute book, not just because of its discrimination against Roman Catholics, but also because Prince James Francis Edward no longer poses any threat.'[86]

7.5 Judicial independence and the constitution

The Act of Settlement ensured judicial independence by restricting the monarch's ability to dismiss judges. Never again would monarchs enjoy the discretion exercised by the Stuart monarchs (especially Charles II and James II) to sack those judges who fell out of favour. As Sir John Baker has written, '[t]he independence of the judiciary from political control is now regarded as one of the pillars of the constitution, but it was built on an unsure foundation.'[87] This is a key tenant of the rule of law, and the independence of the judiciary has been regarded as a major factor in the development of the modern UK constitutional system and the common law's ability to protect the rights of the subject. It is questionable to some extent, given the mixed record of the judiciary in the seventeenth century, whether without this statutory protection Lord Camden would have felt secure enough to find for John Entick in the seminal decision on *Entick v Carrington*.[88] Equally, the propositions of independence

84 Ibid 1091.

85 House of Commons Political and Constitutional Reform Committee (n 77).

86 HL Deb 14 January 2005 vol 668 cc 495–515, 505.

87 Sir John Baker, *An Introduction to English Legal History* (5th edn, Oxford University Press 2019) 177.

88 (1765) 19 Howell's State Trials 1029.

from Lord Mansfield in the decision of *R v Wilkes*,[89] demonstrate the significance of justice being achieved despite political considerations.

Mansfield had commented on how the press had sought to influence his decision:

> Reasons of policy are urged, from danger to the kingdom, by commotions and general confusion. Give me leave to take the opportunity of this great and respectable audience, to let the whole world know, all such attempts are vain. Unless we have been able to find an error which will bear us out, to reverse the outlawry; it must be affirmed. The constitution does not allow reasons of State to influence our judgments: God forbid it should! We must not regard political consequences; how[soever] formidable soever they might be: if rebellion was the certain consequence, we are bound to say 'fiat justitia, ruat cælum.' . . . We are to say what we take the law to be: if we do not speak our real opinions, we prevaricate with God and our own consciences.

The former President of the International Criminal Court Chile Eboe-Osuji, has argued that '[i]n those words, written in 1764, Lord Mansfield spoke a cardinal creed for all judges and for all time.'[90] Mansfield gave judgment in another controversial decision, *Somerset v Stewart*,[91] which involved the status of slavery within England. The decision had big implications for the approximately 15,000 enslaved individuals living in England, the financial interests of the state and the enslavers, and the wider metropolitan and colonial economy.[92] Nonetheless, it is important to question the assumption of an independent judiciary in the eighteenth century, as David Lemmings argues that

> The judges who made the crucial decisions were clearly acting in the interests of government, rather than justice, and there are good evidential grounds for doubting the famed independence of the eighteenth-century

89 *R v Wilkes* (1768) 4 Burr 2527 at pp 2561–62.

90 Chile Eboe-Osuji, 'Struggles of Justice in a Highly Political Context' (*International Criminal Court*, 17 January 2020) <https://www.icc-cpi.int/sites/default/files/iccdocs/presidency/200116-hague-academy-pres-speech.pdf> 4.

91 (1772) 98 ER 499, (1772) Lofft 1. Mansfield had declared 'let justice be done whatever be the consequence' (509).

92 See Paul Finkelman, 'Let Justice Be Done, Though the Heavens May Fall: The Law of Freedom' (1994) 70(2) Chicago-Kent Law Review 325. As Finkelman noted, 'if Lord Mansfield declared Somerset to be free there would be vast economic consequences. The Chief Justice estimated there were about 15,000 slaves in England at the time, each worth at least £50. Thus, "a loss follows to the proprietors of above £700,000 sterling. How would the law stand with respect to their settlement; their wages?"' (325). See also William M Wiecek, 'Somerset: Lord Mansfield and the Legitimacy of Slavery in the Anglo-American World' (1974) 42(1) The University of Chicago Law Review 86, 87–88.

judiciary, because many judges were effectively lawyer-politicians, and some of the most senior ones behaved liked ministers.[93]

7.5.1 *The road to* de jure *independence*

During the Middle Ages, the king was poor, and the payment of judges was irregular and supported by religious benefices, as judges were formally members of the clergy.[94] The problem was that '[t]his feature of judicial life led to the judges being heavily dependent on other sources of income,' such as bribes.[95] There was also the problem of judges becoming associated with court politics. As Sir Henry Brooke noted, during the reign of Edward III, the king's dismissal (and subsequent reappointment) of four judges 'illustrated the problems that were likely to arise if judges were treated as if they were politicians.'[96] In response, judges themselves started to see themselves not as politicians.[97] However, things were to take a turn for the worse during the reign of Richard II, which continued to see England in turmoil, not least caused by the failure in the war against France and the financial difficulties faced by the state, but also the king's weak position.[98] The development of impeachment in the Good Parliament of 1376, in which the Commons impeached key royal officials, meant that Richard II had inherited a kingdom where Parliament had started to attack royal officials.[99] To prevent impeachment from being used against his officials, Richard, who had seen his Lord Chancellor, Michael de la Pole, impeached in 1386, asked his judges ten questions to determine the legality of this device.[100] The judges answered in favour of the king. Subsequently,

> The judges who gave this advice (who included the two Chief Justices and the Chief Baron of the Exchequer) were all impeached, convicted and sentenced to death. In the event only Tresillian CJ was hanged, and the rest were banished to various parts of Ireland.[101]

93 David Lemmings, *Law and Government in England During the Long Eighteenth Century: From Consent to Command* (Palgrave Macmillan 2015) 182.

94 Henry Brooke, 'The History of Judicial Independence in England and Wales' (2015) 5 European Human Rights Law Review 446, 448.

95 Ibid 448.

96 Ibid 448.

97 Ibid 448.

98 See CC Bayley, 'The Campaign of 1375 and the Good Parliament' (1940) 55 (219) The English Historical Review 370.

99 See TFT Plucknett, 'The Impeachments of 1376' (1951) 1 Transactions of the Royal Historical Society 153.

100 For the background see, JS Roskell, *The Impeachment of Michael de la Pole Earl of Suffolk in 1386 in the Context of the Reign of Richard II* (Manchester University Press 1984) and TFT Plucknett, 'State Trials under Richard II' (1952) Fifth Series 2 Transactions of the Royal Historical Society 159.

101 Brooke (n 94) 448.

As a consequence, the judiciary and the courts were distanced from politics, and therefore, the judges 'enjoyed a high degree of practical independence from political interference.'[102] This long period of *defacto* independence was broken by Mary I, who removed three judges because of the controversy surrounding her accession to the throne.[103] Sir Edward Montagu was removed in 1553 as Chief Justice of the Court of Common Pleas because of his half-hearted support to change the succession to favour Lady Jane Grey.[104] Another judge, Sir James Hales, was reappointed by Mary I, but in 1553, was then imprisoned on the orders of Bishop Stephen Gardiner, the Lord Chancellor, and subsequently died by suicide.[105]

The reason why Mary could dismiss her judges was that prior to the Act of Settlement 1701, the monarch had typically appointed judges to serve at their pleasure, which permitted the monarch to dismiss judges at their discretion.[106] This power of dismissal meant that the seventeenth century proved particularly challenging for the judiciary. Sir Edward Coke was perhaps the most famous

102 Stephen F Black, 'The Courts and Judges of Westminster Hall During the Great Rebellion, 1640–1660' (1986) 7(1) Journal of Legal History 23, 23. For commentary on what this meant see Baker (n 87) 177–78.

103 'Overview of the Judiciary' (Courts and Tribunals Judiciary) <https://www.judiciary.uk/about-the-judiciary/history-of-the-judiciary-in-england-and-wales/history-of-the-judiciary/>. See also Brooke (n 94) 446.

104 Sir John Baker, *The Oxford History of the Laws of England: Volume VI 1483–1558* (Oxford University Press 2003) 61.

105 Edward Foss, *The Judges of England, From the Time of the Conquest*, vol V (Longman, Brown, Green, Longmans and Roberts 1857) 372–73. See Baker (n 104) 419. Baker regarded Sir James Hales' position as 'an individual and rather hopeless stand against a new regime.' This, however, did not prevent other judges from resisting orders from the government. Baker is clear that 'independence was unquestionably hailed throughout the period as a virtue and as an attainable ideal.'

106 See, for example, the attempt by Charles I to dismiss Sir John Walter in 1628, who had been appointed to serve during his good behaviour). For a discussion see Sam J Ervin, 'Separation of Powers: Judicial Independence' (1970) 35(1) Law and Contemporary Problems 108 (particularly 109–12), Lord Burnett of Maldon, 'Institutional Independence and Accountability of the Judiciary' (The Lionel Cohen Lecture 2022, Hebrew University of Jerusalem, 30 May 2022) <https://www.judiciary.uk/wp-content/uploads/2022/07/Cohen-Lecture-300522-1.pdf>, and CH McIlwain, 'The Tenure of English Judges' (1913) 7(2) The American Political Science Review 217. In terms of the historic distinction between 'during good behaviour' and at the monarch's pleasure, see R Rowberry, 'The Origins and Development of Judicial Tenure "During Good Behaviour" to 1485' in TR Baker (ed), *Law and Society in Later Medieval England and Ireland: Essays in Honour of Paul Brand* (Routledge 2018). As Rowberry argued 'tenure "during good behaviour" held real value and meaning . . . [as judges] with tenure "during good behaviour" enjoyed increased security in office over those with tenure "during pleasure", particularly against arbitrary or deliberate royal replacement.' (185) Indeed, Rowberry takes the view that, '[t]he true innovation of the seventeenth-century judicial reformers, it seems, lies not in creating judicial tenure "during good behaviour" but rather in extending this form of tenure to all judges on appointment to office' (186).

example of a judge being dismissed by the king, as a result of displeasing his sovereign.[107] As Henry Brooke has written, 'judges held office at the good pleasure of the Crown (*durante bene placito*), and it was the good pleasure of the Stuart Kings to sack their judges if they disapproved of their judgments.'[108] According to Stephen Black, the realities of this challenge meant that: 'the Stuart monarchs came more and more to look upon and treat the courts and judges as instruments of political policy . . . the judges of the ancient courts of common law and equity – King's Bench, Common Pleas, Exchequer, and Chancery – gradually succumbed to pressure to identify with the King's party and policy.'[109] The consequences of this were that when Parliament sat in 1640, those judges who had supported the *illegal* use of ship money to raise taxation were impeached.[110]

Charles I, who had dismissed judges who challenged his policies, was forced in 1641 by the Long Parliament to agree that judges held their office 'during good behaviour.'[111] As Black noted, 'The change was significant: no judge holding office under the altered form of tenure could be removed unless the king could show good cause for dismissal in proceedings upon a writ of scire facias.'[112] Cromwell continued with this change of tenure, only dismissing judges where the judges opposed his policy. Smith observes an example of this, such as when, in 1655, the judges refused to accept the legality of Cromwell's ordinances after he had dismissed Parliament, 'Five Cromwellian judges had been removed from office essentially because they would not recognize certain promulgations or ordinances passed by a government which they felt still had no legally constituted basis in law.'[113] Nonetheless, three judges were later reappointed to key positions by Cromwell.[114] Following the restoration of the monarchy, the judiciary was initially appointed subject to their good behaviour. This changed when Charles II reverted to appointing judges at his pleasure in 1668. The justification was that 'greater obedience among the judges was thought desirable.'[115] In response, the Parliament of 1673 sought

107 See Sir John Baker, *The Reinvention of Magna Carta 1216–1616* (Cambridge University Press 2017) 435–41.

108 Brooke (n 94) 449.

109 Black (n 102) 23.

110 The Long Parliament impeached seven of the judges for their role in upholding the legality of Ship Money (Black (n 102) 24).

111 Lord Neuberger, 'Magna Carta: The Bible of the English Constitution or a Disgrace to the English Nation' (*Guildford Cathedral*, 18 June 2015) <https://www.supremecourt.uk/docs/speech-150618.pdf> [48].

112 Black (n 102) 24.

113 Cornelia D Smith, 'A Seventeenth-Century Judge Views the Law: Oliver St. John's Introduction to His Charge at the Thetford in 1658' (1986) 130(1) Proceedings of the American Philosophical Society 37, 39.

114 Black (n 102) 45.

115 Ibid fn.7 24.

to introduce legislation that judges 'held office during good behaviour rather than at the King's pleasure.'[116] The consequence of the 1668 change to judicial tenure is stark; as Henry Brooke observes, 'in the last 11 years of his reign Charles II sacked 11 of his judges. Not to be outdone, his brother James II sacked 12 in three years.'[117] From 1689, William and Mary II held that judges held their office on the condition of their good behaviour.[118]

7.5.2 Security of tenure

The Act of Settlement 1701 provided that:

> That after the said limitation shall take effect as aforesaid, judges commissions be made quamdiu se bene gesserint, and their salaries ascertained and established; but upon the address of both Houses of Parliament it may be lawful to remove them.

The Act did not prevent a monarch from dismissing judges 'in the 6 month-period after his or her accession.'[119] This six-month period was abolished in 1760 by an Act that 'established the principle that judges were entitled to tenure for life.'[120]

This provision is now contained in Section 11 of the Senior Courts Act 1981. Subsection (3) states that 'A person appointed to an office to which this section applies shall hold that office during good behaviour, subject to a power of removal by Her Majesty on an address presented to Her by both Houses of Parliament.' Section 1 defined senior courts as the 'Court of Appeal, the High Court of Justice and the Crown Court.' Section 14 of the Appellate Jurisdiction Act 1876 had provided for the security of tenure of Lords of Appeal in Ordinary,[121] and now Section 33 of the Constitutional Reform Act 2005 provides security of tenure for a judge of the Supreme Court.

As Lord Neuberger has observed,

> Judicial security of tenure was finally enshrined in law in the Act of Settlement . . . [because] Parliament had become sufficiently powerful and

116 Mark Knights, *Politics and Opinion in Crisis: 1678–81* (Cambridge University Press 1994) 31–32.

117 Brooke (n 94) 450.

118 Sir Stephen Sibler, 'Presumed Guilty? Judge Jeffreys, Fair Trial and the Bloody Assizes' (*The Kalisher Lecture*, 17 January 2022) <https://www.thekalishertrust.org/wp-content/uploads/2021/11/KALISHER-LECTURE-2022.pdf> 8–9.

119 Ibid 9.

120 Ibid 9 and Baker (n 87) 179.

121 This was provided for on the same terms as section 9 of the Supreme Court of Judicature Act 1873.

> confident to recognise the fundamental importance of the point that a judge cannot be removed at the government's will.[122]

This statutory protection of judicial tenure had originally been intended to be part of the Bill of Rights but had been rejected by William of Orange.[123] The clear benefit of the security of tenure enjoyed by judges was the scope for greater independence. As Trevelyan wrote,

> Justice and humanity, divorced from all party considerations, gained greatly from the signal overthrow of James and Jeffreys. The Judges ceased to be removable at the will of the Crown. Trials were conducted with decency and on the whole with fairness.[124]

But what had made the judges stooges to the Crown? As Sir Stephen Sibler reflected,

> The puzzling issue is why these experienced judges like Jeffreys . . . behaved in this way and were so keen to obtain convictions by any means. I believe that there is strong evidence that these judges behaved in this way because they did not have any form of security of tenure and . . . would be dismissed without any form of redress if they did not comply with the wishes of the Monarch.[125]

7.6 The positive legacy of the Act of Settlement

So, what did the Act of Settlement achieve, and does it deserve to be regarded over three centuries later as a leading work of the constitution? Barry Coward was candid in his assessment: '[a]part from settling the Protestant succession the Act of Settlement settled very little.'[126] To Coward, the repeal in 1706 of the provisions that would have prevented royal officers from being members of the House of Commons detracts from the importance of the Act of Settlement, as he notes that this repeal

> considerably reduces the significance of the Act of Settlement in the long-term development of the English (later British) constitution. The Act is much more significant as a reflection of majority opinion among MPs and their constituents and their disenchantment with William's war and its effects on the country.[127]

122 Neuberger (n 111) [50].
123 Tom Bingham, *The Rule of Law* (Allen Lane 2010).
124 George Macaulay Trevelyan, *History of England*, vol 2 (Doubleday Anchor Books 1954) 274.
125 Sibler (n 118) 8.
126 Coward (n 22) 388.
127 Coward (n 22) 388.

The impact of the Act of Settlement on the judiciary is perhaps the Act's greatest legacy, and one, in light of the discriminatory nature of the legislation can be seen as positive today. Understandably, judicial independence is valued by senior judges. Lord Steyn believed that the fact that British judges could act as '[a] neutral arbiter on disputes between citizens, and between citizens and the state, is essential to the working of a democratic system. An independent and impartial judiciary is therefore an indispensable part of our system.'[128] As Sir Stephen Sedley argues, '[t]he security of tenure accorded by the Act of Settlement set the scene of a more confident constitutional jurisprudence than had been feasible under the post-Restoration Stuart dynasty.'[129] This ensured the evolution of the peculiar form of separation of powers that exists in the United Kingdom.[130] Taking a similar view, Lady Hale observes that '[s]ince the Act of Settlement of 1701, the senior judiciary have held office [during good behaviour] . . . Far from being a threat, it is a guarantee of their independence from the government.'[131] Lord Hailsham has remarked that '[t]he Act of Settlement, which requires the resolution of each House of Parliament before a judge is removed, has worked well for over three hundred years.'[132] Nonetheless, it is important to consider the relative power imbalance of the judiciary to Parliament. Unlike the US Supreme Court, neither the Appellate Committee of the House of Lords nor its successor, the Supreme Court, has had the right to challenge the validity of Acts of Parliament.[133] This was a point noted by Dicey, who remarked that:

> Our judges are independent, in the sense of holding their office by a permanent tenure, and of being raised above the direct influence of the Crown or the Ministry; but the judicial department does not pretend to stand on a level with Parliament; its functions might be modified at any time by an Act of Parliament; and such a statute would be no violation of the law.[134]

Whilst the Act removed the ability of the Crown to sack judges at the monarch's pleasure, there is debate as to whether the Act of Settlement excluded

128 Johan Steyn, 'The Weakest and Least Dangerous Department of Government' in in *Democracy Through Law: Selected Speeches and Judgments* (Routledge 2004) 97.

129 Stephen Sedley, *Lions Under the Throne: Essays on the History of English Public Law* (Cambridge University Press 2015) 71.

130 Ibid 188.

131 Lady Hale, *Spider Woman* (Vintage 2021) 179.

132 Lord Hailsham, *On the Constitution* (Harper Collins 1992) 61.

133 See *Marbury v Madison* 5 U.S. (1 Cranch) 137 (1803). For commentary, see Larry D Kramer, 'Marbury and the Retreat from Judicial Supremacy' (2003) 20 Constitutional Commentary 205. As Kramer argues, 'the process of upholding the British constitution against the claims of Parliamentary sovereignty had deepened Americans' commitment to a constitution's basis in popular sovereignty' (208).

134 AV Dicey, *Introduction to the Study of the Law of the Constitution* (8th edn, Macmillan 1915).

the other pre-existing methods of removing judges. Shetreet and Turenne argue that the Act of Settlement did not exclude the pre-existing methods under the common law to remove judges.[135] As Shetreet and Turenne observe, 'At common law, prior to the Act of Settlement 1700, judicial office held during good behaviour could be terminated by impeachment, by judicial proceeding commenced by a write of scire facias to repeal the letters patent or upon conviction.'[136] The use of impeachment still technically exists as a way for Parliament to remove a senior judge.[137] The rationale for the continued recourse to impeachment was clear,

> it would be unsound to believe that at a time of struggle for power between Parliament and the Crown, Parliament would give up a strong and efficient power over judges . . . merely in order to assume the milder power of removal by address.[138]

Furthermore, the Act gives parliamentarians the freedom to define good behaviour and, therefore, have the freedom to remove a judge at their discretion.[139] Importantly, Shetreet and Turenne note that 'in exercising the power of removal by address, Parliament is not limited to considerations of "good behaviour" in its technical sense.'[140] As Raoul Berger has observed, that had the Act of Settlement become the only way to remove a judge, then Parliament would have no recourse where a monarch was 'to refuse to remove a corrupt judge upon an Address.'[141]

As discussed previously, a judge could still be removed by way of impeachment.[142] In 1805, there were calls to impeach Mr Justice Luke Fox, an Irish judge, who had fallen foul of his political opponents. During the debate in the House of Lords, Lord Hawkesbury remarked that

> this is the first case of the kind, I believe, which has happened since the passing of the law, that renders the judges independent of the crown. I am extremely sorry that it should have ever been found necessary to

135 Shimon Shetreet and Sophie Turenne, *Judges on Trial: The Independence and Accountability of the English Judiciary* (Cambridge University Press 2013) 313.
136 Ibid 313.
137 Ibid 310–12.
138 Ibid 314–15.
139 Ibid 324–25.
140 Ibid 317.
141 Berger (n 34) 151–52.
142 There were unsuccessful attempts to use the Act of Settlement 1701 or in the alternative, impeachment, to dismiss judges during the nineteenth and twentieth century. See C Monaghan, 'The Nineteenth Century and Beyond: The Existence of the Threat of Impeachment' in C Monaghan and M Flinders (eds), *British Origins and American Practice of Impeachment* (Routledge 2024).

> take a business of this very important and peculiar nature into your consideration, and that such a case should have ever occurred.[143]

The question before the House of Lords was whether to continue to investigate Fox's conduct or to turn the matter over to the House of Commons to allow them to bring impeachment proceedings and thus allow the Lords to judge the trial. During the debate, the Lords considered the different methods of removal under impeachment and an address under the terms of the Act of Settlement 1701.

In any event, since 1701, just one senior judge, Sir Jonah Barrington, has been removed, and this was by an address. That is not to say there have not been attempts to remove judges, such as when Sir John Donaldson faced an attempt in the 1970s by a considerable number of Labour MPs to remove him as a result of his leadership of the Industrial Relations Court.[144] There are, of course, limits to the protection accorded by the Act of Settlement. For example, Shetreet and Turenne highlight the case of the elderly Mr Justice Lawrence being appointed the Lord Chief Justice. His appointment was on the basis 'that he would retire when called upon to do so.'[145] The Lord Chancellor, Lord Birkenhead, complained to the Prime Minister, David Lloyd George, that this

> violates the letter of [The Act of Settlement]. . . . and defeats the object for which the enactment was passed. That object was to secure that the judges should hold office independently of any political or other influence and should be removable only for the most serious judicial misbehaviour and then in the most public and open manner.[146]

The Act of Settlement has achieved in safeguarding judicial independence and permitting a degree of separation between the judicial and the other branches of government. This did not mean there was a clear separation, as judges continued to play a role within the executive branch. An example of this was Lord Ellenborough, who, as Lord Chief Justice, was a member of the coalition ministry in 1806.[147]

143 HL Deb 15 January 1805, Lord Hawkesbury, vol 3 cols 22–24.

144 Robert Stevens, *Law and Politics: The House of Lords as a Judicial Body, 1800–1976* (The University of North Carolina Press 1978) 413–14.

145 Shetreet and Turenne (n 135) 319.

146 Ibid 319.

147 Lord Thomas LCJ, 'Judicial Leader' (Conference on the Paradox of Judicial Independence, UCL Constitution Unit, 22 June 2015) <https://www.judiciary.uk/wp-content/uploads/2015/06/ucl-judicial-independence-speech-june-2015.pdf> [11].

In terms of the impact of the Act of Settlement on the judiciary, McIlwain offered a cautious assessment in the early twentieth century. To McIlwain,

> the procedure by address has proved to be very unsatisfactory in operation. Actually applied only once, and that away back in 1830, failing of operation several times, rendered ineffectual and uncertain because it involves the most unsettled point in the English system – the line between the law of parliament and the law of the land.[148]

That said, the ineffectiveness of the procedure must be balanced against the security that it gave the judges in light of the turmoil of British politics during the eighteenth century. Looking beyond the early 1700s, Robert Stevens is clear that the Act has had a global significance: '[i]ts importance was profound if not immediately so. Yet we can see it was setting the standard for the whole common law world.'[149]

The importance of the Act of Settlement was clear to Naamani Tarkow:

> the Act, either by challenge or assertion, crystallized most of the cardinal tenets of future English political democracy: the Cabinet system, ministerial responsibility, parliamentary supremacy, and the independence of judges. If one is given to making sweeping statements, one may say that, save the Magna Carta (more truly, its implications), the Act of Settlement is probably the most significant statute in English history.[150]

To those concerned with the modern British Constitution, the Act of Settlement has played a pivotal role in securing the independence of the judiciary and brought to an end a turbulent century where judges had been dismissed by monarchs, impeached by Parliament, or seen as the creatures of an absolute monarch. This is the Act's substantial legacy.

Bibliography

Baker J, *The Oxford History of the Laws of England: Volume VI 1483–1558* (Oxford University Press 2003)

Baker J, *The Reinvention of Magna Carta 1216–1616* (Cambridge University Press 2017)

Baker J, *An Introduction to English Legal History* (5th edn, Oxford University Press 2019)

148 CH McIlwain, 'The Tenure of English Judges' (1913) 7(2) The American Political Science Association 217, 228.

149 Robert Stevens, 'The Act of Settlement and the Questionable History of Judicial Independence' (2001) 1(2) Oxford University Commonwealth Law Journal 252, 267.

150 Naamani Tarkow (n 24) 561.

Bates S, 'Act of Settlement: A Nakedly Discriminatory Law' *The Guardian* (27 March 2009) <https://www.theguardian.com/uk/2009/mar/27/act-of-settlement-monarchy-catholic>

Bayley CC, 'The Campaign of 1375 and the Good Parliament' (1940) 55(219) The English Historical Review 370

Beckford M, 'The Act of Settlement: 300 Years of Discrimination Against Roman Catholic' *The Telegraph* (26 March 2009) <https://www.telegraph.co.uk/news/5056680/The-Act-of-Settlement-300-years-of-discrimination-against-Roman-Catholics.html>

Bennett GV, 'English Jacobitism, 1710–1715; Myth and Reality' (1982) 32 Transactions of the Royal Historical Society 137

Berger R, *Impeachment: The Constitutional Problems* (Harvard University Press 1973)

Bingham T, *The Rule of Law* (Allen Lane 2010)

Black SF, 'The Courts and Judges of Westminster Hall During the Great Rebellion, 1640–1660' (1986) 7(1) Journal of Legal History 23

Bowie K, *Scottish Public Opinion and the Anglo- Scottish Union 1699–1707* (Boydell & Brewer Ltd 2007)

Brooke H, 'The History of Judicial Independence in England and Wales' (2015) 5 European Human Rights Law Review 446

Burnett (Lord Burnett of Maldon), 'Institutional Independence and Accountability of the Judiciary' *The Lionel Cohen Lecture* 2022, Hebrew University of Jerusalem (30 May 2022) <https://www.judiciary.uk/wp-content/uploads/2022/07/Cohen->

Campbell E, 'Oaths and Affirmations of Public Office Under English Law: An Historical Retrospect' (2000) 21(3) The Journal of Legal History 1

Clarke E, 'Re-Reading the Exclusion Crisis' (2006) 27(1) The Seventeenth Century 141

Claydon T, 'William III's Declaration of Reasons and the Glorious Revolution' (1996) 39(1) The History Journal 87

Coward B, *The Stuart Age: England 1603–1714* (2nd edn, Longman 1994)

Cox GW, 'Was the Glorious Revolution a Constitutional Watershed?' (2012) 72(3) The Journal of Economic History 567

Davies C, 'Royal Baby Girl's Right of Succession Would Face Commonwealth Obstacles' *The Guardian* (22 July 2013) <https://www.theguardian.com/uk-news/2013/jul/22/royal-baby-succession-commonwealth-primogeniture>

Dicey AV, *Introduction to the Study of the Law of the Constitution* (8th edn, Macmillan 1915)

Dickinson HT, 'How Revolutionary Was the "Glorious Revolution" of 1688?' (1988) 11(2) Journal for Eighteenth-Century Studies 125

Dixon D, 'Godden v Hales Revisited – James II and the Dispensing Power' (2006) 27(2) The Journal of Legal History 129

Eagles R, 'British Politics and Impeachment in the Eighteenth Century' in C Monaghan and M Flinders (eds), *British Origins and American Practice of Impeachment* (Routledge 2024)

Eboe-Osuji C, 'Struggles of Justice in a Highly Political Context' *International Criminal Court* (17 January 2020) <https://www.icc-cpi.int/sites/default/files/iccdocs/presidency/200116-hague-academy-pres-speech.pdf>

Edie CA, 'Revolution and the Rule of Law: The End of the Dispensing Power, 1689' (1977) 10(4) Eighteenth-Century Studies 434

Edie CA, 'Tactics and Strategies: Parliament's Attack upon the Royal Dispensing Power 1597–1689' (1985) 29(3) The American Journal of Legal History 197

Ervin SJ, 'Separation of Powers: Judicial Independence' (1970) 35(1) Law and Contemporary Problems 108

Foss E, *The Judges of England, from the Time of the Conquest*, vol V (Longman, Brown, Green, Longmans and Roberts 1857)

Gael P, 'Kingship and Catholicism in Posthumous Representations of Charles II, 1685–1714' (2014) 29(2) The Seventeenth Century 173

Goldie M, 'Impeachment in Seventeenth-Century England' in C Monaghan and M Flinders (eds), *British Origins and American Practice of Impeachment* (Routledge 2024)

Gregg E, 'Was Queen Anne a Jacobite' (1972) 57(191) History 358

Hale B, *Spider Woman* (Vintage 2021)

Harrison G, 'Prerogative Revolution and Glorious Revolution: Political Proscription and Parliamentary Undertaking, 1687–88' (1990) 10(1) Parliaments, Estates and Representation 29

Hayton DW, 'Harley, Robert (1661–1724), of Brampton Bryan, Herefs' in DW Hayton, E Cruickshanks and S Handley (eds), *The History of Parliament: The House of Commons 1690–1715* (History of Parliament Trust 2002a)

Hayton DW, The Politics of the House' in DW Hayton, E Cruickshanks and S Handley (eds), *The History of Parliament: The House of Commons 1690–1715* (History of Parliament Trust 2002b) <https://www.historyofparliamentonline.org/volume/1690-1715/survey/politics-house>

House of Commons Political and Constitutional Reform Committee, Rules of Succession. 11th Report of Session 2010–12, HC 1615 <https://publications.parliament.uk/pa/cm201012/cmselect/cmpolcon/1615/1615.pdf> (written evidence of Professor Robert Blackburn)

Knights M, *Politics and Opinion in Crisis: 1678–81* (Cambridge University Press 1994)

Kramer LD, 'Marbury and the Retreat from Judicial Supremacy' (2003) 20 Constitutional Commentary 205

Lemmings D, *Law and Government in England During the Long Eighteenth Century: From Consent to Command* (Palgrave Macmillan 2015)

Macaulay Trevelyan G, *History of England, Volume 2* (Doubleday Anchor Books 1954)

Maer L, 'The Act of Settlement and the Protestant Succession' *House of Commons Library* (24 January 2011) <https://researchbriefings.files.parliament.uk/documents/SN00683/SN00683.pdf>

Maer L and Gay O, 'The Bill of Rights 1689' *House of Commons Library* (5 October 2009) <https://commonslibrary.parliament.uk/research-briefings/sn00293/>

McIlwain CH, 'The Tenure of English Judges' (1913) 7(2) The American Political Science Review 217

Mctague J, 'Anti-Catholicism, Incorrigibility and Credulity in the Warming-Pan Scandal of 1688–9' (2013) 36(3) Journal for Eighteenth-Century Studies 433

Mitchison R, *A History of Scotland* (3rd edn, Routledge 2002)

Monaghan C, 'The Nineteenth Century and Beyond: The Existence of the Threat of Impeachment' in C Monaghan and M Flinders (eds), *British Origins and American Practice of Impeachment* (Routledge 2024)

Muffett M, *James II and English Politics 1678–1688* (Routledge 2008)

Naamani Tarkow I, 'The Significance of the Act of Settlement in the Evolution of English Democracy' (1943) 58(4) Political Science Quarterly 537

Neuberger D, 'Magna Carta: The Bible of the English Constitution or a Disgrace to the English Nation' *Guildford Cathedral* (18 June 2015) <https://www.supremecourt.uk/docs/speech-150618.pdf>

Norton P, 'The Glorious Revolution of 1688: Its Continuing Relevance' (1989) 42(2) Parliamentary Affairs 135

Parpworth N, 'The Succession to the Crown Act 2013: Modernising the Monarchy' (2013) 76(6) Modern Law Review 1070

Patrick DJ and Whatley CA, 'Persistence, Principle and Patriotism in the Making of the Union of 1707: The Revolution, Scottish Parliament and the Squadrone Volante' (2007) 92(306) History 162

Pincus S, *1688: The First Modern Revolution* (Yale University Press 2009)

Plucknett TFT, 'The Impeachments of 1376' (1951) 1 Transactions of the Royal Historical Society 153

Plucknett TFT, 'State Trials under Richard II' (1952) Fifth Series 2 Transactions of the Royal Historical Society 159

Roberts C, *The Growth of Responsible Government in Stuart England* (Cambridge University Press 1966)

Roskell JS, *The Impeachment of Michael de la Pole Earl of Suffolk in 1386 in the Context of the Reign of Richard II* (Manchester University Press 1984)

Rowberry R, 'The Origins and Development of Judicial Tenure "During Good Behaviour" to 1485' in TR Baker (ed), *Law and Society in Later Medieval England and Ireland: Essays in Honour of Paul Brand* (Routledge 2018)

Sedley S, *Lions under the Throne: Essays on the History of English Public Law* (Cambridge University Press 2015)

Shetreet S and Turenne S, *Judges on Trial: The Independence and Accountability of the English Judiciary* (Cambridge University Press 2013)

Sibler S, 'Presumed Guilty? Judge Jeffreys, Fair Trial and the Bloody Assizes' *The Kalisher Lecture* (17 January 2022) <https://www.thekalishertrust.org/wp-content/uploads/2021/11/KALISHER-LECTURE-2022.pdf-300522-1.pdf>

Slaughter TP, '"Abdicate" and "Contract" in the Glorious Revolution' (1981) 24(2) The Historical Journal 323

Smith CD, 'A Seventeenth-Century Judge Views the Law: Oliver St. John's Introduction to His Charge at the Thetford in 1658' (1986) 130(1) Proceedings of the American Philosophical Society 37

Stevens R, *Law and Politics: The House of Lords as a Judicial Body, 1800–1976* (The University of North Carolina Press 1978)

Stevens R, 'The Act of Settlement and the Questionable History of Judicial Independence' (2001) 1(2) Oxford University Commonwealth Law Journal 252

Steyn J, 'The Weakest and Least Dangerous Department of Government' in *Democracy Through Law: Selected Speeches and Judgments* (Routledge 2004)

Thomas J, 'Judicial Leader' (Conference on the Paradox of Judicial Independence, UCL Constitution Unit, 22 June 2015) <https://www.judiciary.uk/wp-content/uploads/2015/06/ucl-judicial-independence-speech-june-2015.pdf>

Thomson MA, 'The Safeguarding of the Protestant Succession 1702–18' (1954) 39(135/136) History 39

Ward AW, 'The Electress Sophia and the Hanoverian Succession' (1886) 1(3) The English Historical Review 470

Whatley CA, 'Economic Causes and Consequences of the Union of 1707: A Survey' (1989) LXVIII (186) The Scottish Historical Review 150

Wiecek WM, 'Somerset: Lord Mansfield and the Legitimacy of Slavery in the Anglo-American World' (1974) 42(1) The University of Chicago Law Review 86

8 1707 union between England and Scotland

Elizabeth Wicks

8.1 Introduction

In this chapter, I will explore the constitutional consequences of the 1707 union between England and Scotland. It is hard to overestimate the significance of this event, for it created not only a new sovereign state, but also a new Parliament for that state. I will first briefly discuss the union agreement and then outline the main constitutional impacts of the new state and new parliament before reflecting on whether the 1707 Articles of Union amount to a Constitution. Finally, I will offer some thoughts on Scotland's position within the union and the sovereign interests and rights of the Scottish people in the context of the United Kingdom's evolving Constitution.

8.2 The union

The union between England and Scotland of 1707 is based upon a complex series of documents, including multiple Acts of two different national Parliaments and, arguably, an international treaty. It is noteworthy and highlights the constitutional uniqueness of the events of 1707 that the parties who created these documents ceased to exist by virtue of them.

The terms of the union were negotiated by Commissioners representing the Parliaments of England and Scotland. It is commonly asserted that the pressure for union rested upon concerns of security south of the border and finances north of the border, although an alternative perception is that the union negotiations 'formed part of a process of post-Stuart centralization'[1] based on a core state located in the southeast of England and linked to other centralising manoeuvres such as the final suspension of the Council of Wales in 1694 and active repression of the majority opinion in Ireland.[2] Certainly, England was the dominant party through the negotiations, and it was at its insistence that the union finally agreed to be an incorporating one, in which

1 Murray Pittock, 'Scottish Sovereignty and the Union of 1707: Then and Now' (2012) 14 National Identities 11, 12.
2 Ibid.

DOI: 10.4324/9781032658698-9

a new state was born. Scottish commissioners did propose an alternative federal union, but the proposal was rejected, as they knew it would be, by the English.[3]

The 'Articles of Union' were signed and sealed at Westminster on 22 July 1706 and have been described by Smith as 'more in the nature of a record of negotiations' than an international treaty.[4] They were then debated in the Scottish Estates, amendments were made, and an Act for securing the Scottish church was passed before the Articles of Union were passed as the Union with England Act 1707. The significance of this Act was apparently recognised at the time, with MacCormick describing how, within the debate in the Scottish Parliament, the 'sense of betrayal of a long independent history appears to have been palpable.'[5] The focus then shifted to England, where the English Parliament passed the Union with Scotland Act 1706, accepting the Scottish additions and adding provisions to safeguard the Church of England. Somewhere within these legislative steps, a new state is created, and a constitution is transformed. Some writers regard the whole agreement, namely the Articles as amended by the Scottish estates, the additional Acts to secure the churches, and the final Act passed by the English Parliament to amount to a 'treaty.'[6] Even if this were true, crucially, the state parties who negotiated and agreed to the treaty ceased to exist soon afterwards, and, thus, it is the substance of the Articles of Union – the terms on which the two states combined – that had the transformational impact upon the British Constitution, most notably by creating this state for the first time.

There are 25 Articles of Union and they range from fundamental high principles to specific (even grubby) details. The first three articles bear some resemblance to a modern constitution. They are constitutive and create the new state of Great Britain, its name and flag (Article 1); set out the executive power, including rules of succession for the monarchy (Article 2); and the legislative power, creating a new Parliament for the new state (Article 3). The arcane language cannot obscure the (constitutional) revolutionary tone of concepts such as 'for ever after, be united into one kingdom' or 'be represented by one and the same parliament.' The next 14 articles comprise the free trade provisions, which (with some added protection for Scottish interests) created by far the largest customs union in the world at the time, complete with a common market and single currency. The third branch of government – the judiciary – is the focus of Articles 18–19, with the Scottish legal system preserved, with the Scottish courts to remain 'in all time coming' as now constituted (Article 19), and the laws of Scotland (with some exceptions) to remain in force and, if concerning 'private right' only to be alterable by the

3 Neil MacCormick, *Questioning Sovereignty* (OUP 1999) 57.
4 TB Smith, 'The Union of 1707 as Fundamental Law' [1957] PL 99, 104.
5 MacCormick (n 3) 50.
6 Smith (n 4) 105.

new Parliament if for 'evident utility' of the Scottish subjects (Article 18). Notably, there is no comparable protection for English laws or the English legal system. Articles 20–23 are concerned with the composition of the new Parliament created, while Article 24 deals with the seal. Finally, Article 25 sets out the hierarchy of laws in the new state of Great Britain, making clear the superiority of the Articles of Union over all other laws and statutes in either kingdom. It neglects to explain the status of Acts of the new British Parliament and whether that body can supersede the provisions of the Union. It is an omission that has led to much fascinating constitutional debate in the last century. Beyond the 25 Articles of Union, it is also important to note the two Acts for securing the Established Churches in Scotland and England. They, too, are vital elements of the complex negotiations that led to the union, and are expressed as being 'fundamental and essential conditions' of union[7] and to be 'observed in all time coming . . . without any altering thereof, or derogation thereto in any sort for ever.'[8]

The concept of a union 'for ever after' runs through the Articles seemingly as a foundational concept for the new state, but it is worth noting that a period of disillusionment soon followed, during which a number of proposals were made for its repeal.[9] It had been a voluntary union, but one agreed upon 'such a tide of mutual suspicion and resentment'[10] that its endurance forever after seemed less than likely. That it has endured, and crucially *evolved*, is a testament to the odd *rigid flexibility* of the British Constitution, in which nothing is unchangeable but what works can endure. The new state of Great Britain evidently worked.

8.3 Creating a new state

The main significance of the events of 1707 was the creation of a new state in the United Kingdom of Great Britain. It is hard to overestimate the impact of this change in both constitutional and international law terms. Great Britain did not exist as an entity before 1707, and the United Kingdom of today, although it was changed by the terms of the Union with Ireland in 1800, Republic of Ireland independence, and more recent devolutionary settlements, remains a union state comprised of the unions, voluntary or otherwise, of previously independent sovereign nations located on these Isles.

7 Act for securing the church of England, Article XI.
8 Act for securing the Protestant religion and presbyterian church government in Scotland, Article V.
9 Lord Sumption, 'The Disunited Kingdom: England, Ireland and Scotland' (2014) 3 CJICL 139, 147.
10 Ibid.

In international law terms, the creation of Great Britain is extremely interesting (and I have grappled with these issues previously).[11] Great Britain was a sovereign state created by means of cession – the transfer of sovereignty by agreement, usually by means of an international treaty. From some perspectives, the 1707 union was unique because the merging of two states into one new state, and thereby the erasure of those pre-existing states (in legal terms, if not political or sentimental ones), seems not to have many comparators. An obvious one is Germany's reunification in 1990, whereby the German Democratic Republic (GDR) and Federal Republic of Germany (FRG) ceased to exist when (re-)united by agreement into one state. However, there are clear distinctions with this situation given that it was a reunification and the two states that ceased to exist were artificial and recent constructs. The ending of the ancient kingdoms of England and Scotland would have a much more substantial affect. While it has been argued that the 1707 union is not unique and that most modern-day states are 'composites, built out of territories that were once autonomous'[12] (with examples such as Italy, Germany, and India), such examples might also be distinguished on the basis that they, while composite states, were created by gradual merging into a larger existing state, and often through violent means rather than cession. Thus, it is hard to find an exact replica of the situation in 1707 when two long-established sovereign states voluntarily gave up their existence in favour of a new state that did not yet exist.

A curiosity in legal terms is that the new state of Great Britain was not a party to the 'Treaty of Union' by which it was created. As discussed later, it may well be bound in constitutional terms by its constitutive documents, but in international law terms, it could not be bound by the terms of a treaty to which it was not a party.[13] Nor could either the English nor Scottish Acts of Union have legal status within the new state. This might suggest conditional renunciations of title by England and Scotland, and in previous work, I have insisted that the 1707 Union comprised the dissolution of both England and Scotland and the creation of Great Britain.[14] The second stage is undeniable, but in this chapter, I now wish to query whether the two pre-existing kingdoms were inevitably dissolved or whether it is possible that they simply continued in merged form. One aspect that might support such a claim is that, despite the constituting of a new state with a new name, 'the underlying assumption was that the larger partner was a continuing entity.'[15] As will be seen further on, the new legislature for the new state bore a great

11 Elizabeth Wicks, 'A New Constitution for a New State? The 1707 Union of England and Scotland' (2001) 117 LQR 109.
12 Sumption (n 9) 140.
13 Smith (n 4) 106.
14 Wicks (n 11) 112.
15 MacCormick (n 3) 57.

resemblance to the previous English Parliament, even down to membership and location, and little changed on the ground for English citizens. (Indeed, it is not uncommon, even today, for England to be confused by both those living inside and outside of it, with the state of which is only one part, the United Kingdom.) Perhaps of greater significance, however, are arguments around the continuation of the smaller entity: Scotland. As Pittock has pointed out, the Union documentation seems to explicitly retain the Kingdom of Scotland, for example, through the continuation of the crown, sceptre, sword of state, and records of Scotland in Article 24 and through the protection of the Scottish church.[16] He argues that this 'ambiguity between a continuing Scottish and a new united kingdom has continued to the present day.'[17] It might also be argued that the Scottish devolution settlement suggests that Scotland survived 1707 to re-emerge later. This possibility will be discussed further later on, but it is important to note here the pertinent distinctions between a sovereign state at international law, a concept of national sovereignty, and a concept of popular sovereignty or self-determination of a people. There can be no doubt that the Scottish people remain, nor that the Scottish nation endures, but in international law terms, the independent state of Scotland did dissolve itself in 1707 by agreeing to merge with England into a brand-new state. One thing that this new state needed was a new Parliament to make laws for it.

8.4 Establishing a new parliament

Article III of the Articles of Union constitutes a new legislature. It clearly states that the new state 'be represented by one and the same parliament, to be styled *The Parliament of Great Britain*.' As MacCormick has succinctly stated, 'it was a new Parliament with a new name, a new territorial jurisdiction, and a new membership.'[18] The latter point is worth expansion for, at first glance, it might be assumed that the English Parliament continued post-Union with the addition of a few Scottish members. This is because the Parliament continued to sit in the same building and with the same privileges and procedures, and most notably, the same English members as the previous English Parliament. Elections for the new British Parliament were not held until 1708, meaning that, in reality, Scottish members joined an ongoing legislative body. These factors lend some support to arguments that the new Parliament was merely a continuation of the old English one. However, of crucial importance is the fact that the English Parliament had no authority to legislate for the new state of Great Britain (nor indeed for the old state

16 Pittock (n 1) 13.

17 Ibid.

18 Neil MacCormick, 'Does the United Kingdom have a Constitution? Reflections on MacCormick v Lord Advocate' (1978) 29 NILQ 1, 2.

of Scotland). Furthermore, the similarities are due entirely to the Articles of Union themselves, which in Article XXII permits the members of the English Parliament to remain and requires that the new Parliament continue only until such time as that English Parliament might have continued. It was, therefore, the Union agreement itself which required the new Parliament to look superficially so much like a continuation of the English Parliament. This perception was also helped by the limited number of Scottish members – 16 Scottish peers and 45 Scottish MPs – permitted to join the new Parliament.[19] However, while this was an under-representation in terms of population, it was, in fact, an over-representation for Scotland in terms of the method of calculating representation at the time, namely according to value for land-tax.[20]

Thus, despite superficial appearances, the Parliament created by the Articles of Union was a new body and indeed a creature of statute. This is a point rarely recognised in today's constitution with the towering shadow of a Diceyian sovereign body so well established. But some writers have argued that Parliament, being a creature of statute, is, like any other statutory body, 'bound by its constituent charters.'[21] This is sometimes expressed as Parliament being 'born unfree',[22] and it is a direct challenge to the unlimited, and indeed illimitable, conception of parliamentary sovereignty that has grown to be accepted within the British Constitution. While there have been other challenges to this conception, not least the acceptance of European legal supremacy during the lengthy period of UK membership of the European Union, it has nonetheless become a trite principle of British constitutional law, recognised by all three branches of government, including a recent reconfirmation by the Supreme Court.[23] Few undergraduate constitutional law modules would ignore the infamous 'make or unmake any law' aspect of the Diceyian parliamentary sovereignty doctrine.[24] And yet, if Parliament was indeed 'born unfree' and a 'creature of statute' bound by its 1707 constituent document, it cannot be sovereign in such a legally unlimited manner. It could not 'unmake' the Union.

It is clear that the Articles of Union seem intended to be a higher law and binding upon the new Parliament which it creates. This is evidenced by the

19 Article XXII.

20 MacCormick (n 3) 51.

21 Michael Upton, 'Marriage Vows of the Elephant: The Constitution of 1707' (1989) 105 LQR 79, 79.

22 The phrase is that of JDB Mitchell, *Constitutional Law* (2nd edn, W Green & Son 1968) 69). See also Smith (n 4); MacCormick (n 18); Upton (n 21); and A O'Neill, 'A Tale of Two Constitutions' (1997) 26 SLT 205.

23 *R (on the application of Miller and another) v Secretary of State for Exiting the European Union* [2017] UKSC 5.

24 AV Dicey, *An Introduction to the Study of the Law of the Constitution* (10th edn, Macmillan 1959) 39–40.

language used, such as the Union lasting 'for ever after' (Article I). While this was not unusual language for the time, it is widely acknowledged that the 1707 legislators were seeking to entrench the Union agreement. For example, even Dicey, the leading proponent of the lack of limits on Parliament's legislative competence, acknowledges that those drafting the Articles of Union 'assuredly intended to give to certain provisions of them more than the ordinary effect of statutes.'[25] In a later work, he further noted that the 1707 legislators 'though giving full sovereign power to the Parliament of Great Britain, clearly believed in the possibility of creating an absolutely sovereign Legislature which should yet be bound by unalterable laws.'[26] The idea of the Union legislation being unalterable was also recognised during the eighteenth century. Daniel Defoe, writing in 1786, regarded it as self-evident that Parliament could not alter the Treaty which formed it 'since all constituted power is subordinate, and inferior to the power constituting it.'[27] Later, in the twentieth century, Smith (one of the proponents of Parliament being 'born unfree') argued that the Union legislation is fundamental law, with the force of a constituent document, and that it has been treated as such. He argues the Acts of Union have not been, in practice, treated 'as of no greater sanctity than ordinary legislative Acts.'[28] The case of *MacCormick v Lord Advocate*[29] is notorious for hinting at some judicial acceptance of this position as well. Of particular pertinence, the Lord Advocate conceded that the British Parliament 'could not' repeal or alter those provisions expressed as unalterable.[30] Lord Cooper (with whom Lord Carmont agreed) also seemed to acknowledge that certain aspects of the Union are fundamental and unalterable and explicitly doubted that Parliament can be regarded as 'absolutely sovereign' in the sense of being free to alter the Treaty of Union at will.[31]

However, Lord Cooper also raised the problematic issue of the powers of the courts in respect of upholding the Articles of Union, noting that 'it is of little avail to ask whether the Parliament of Great Britain "can" do this thing or that, without going on to inquire who can stop them if they do.'[32] Ultimately, Lord Cooper was not convinced that there was either precedent or authority for the courts of either Scotland or England to determine whether an Act of the British Parliament conforms to a Treaty.[33] But arguably, if the

25 Ibid 65.
26 AV Dicey and Robert S Rait, *Thoughts on the Union between England and Scotland* (Macmillan 1920) 252.
27 Daniel Defoe, *The History of the Union between England and Scotland* (1786) 246, quoted by P Scott, *1707: The Union of England and Scotland* (Chambers 1979) 62.
28 Smith (n 4) 111.
29 1953 S.C. 396.
30 Ibid 409.
31 Ibid 412.
32 Ibid 412.
33 Ibid 413.

'Treaty' is a fundamental constitutive document, Parliament acts *ultra vires* by purporting to breach them, and the courts' role under the rule of law would necessitate judicial intervention. This is exactly the point raised by Baroness Hale in another context in *Jackson v Attorney-General* when she noted that certain types of Acts (such as those abolishing judicial review) may entail a particular response by the courts, meaning they would 'treat with particular suspicion (and might even reject) any attempt to subvert the rule of law.'[34] Although this was a very different context, and the courts are always likely to be particularly sensitive to threats to their judicial competence, it was an argument based upon the courts' inherent constitutional role under the rule of law, and it might be argued that such a role would empower intervention if a constitutive, fundamental, unalterable document were to be ignored by a legislative body created under it. A similar point was evident in *Marbury v Madison* in the United States when the US Supreme Court recognised that if there are limits to the legislative power written into the Constitution, the courts must be able to enforce them.[35] It is really not such a big leap from this to judicial enforcement of the 1707 Union *if* the Articles of that Union are regarded as fundamental and constitutive. Whether they are or not remains debatable, and it is an issue often obscured by the narrower question of whether the Articles of Union amount to a Constitution in their own right.

8.5 Are the Articles of Union a constitution?

While there is no doubt that the British Parliament was created by the Articles of Union, and thus the Articles are constitutive of both a new state and a new legal order with a Parliament at its apex, that does not suffice in order for them to be unambiguously viewed as a Constitution. This would require that they also play a legitimising role in relation to the new order and that they have ongoing significance because they continue to bind the organs of government.[36] In short, the Articles of Union have the potential to be regarded as a Constitution of the new state of Great Britain, but only if they amount to fundamental law above the laws of Parliament. Admittedly, this is, in a sense, a circular argument: the Articles are a Constitution if they are higher law, and, of course, they are higher law if they are a Constitution. We have seen that the Articles were certainly intended to be higher law, and hints of acceptance of that by some judges, but also a reluctance to accept a judicial role in enforcing the terms of the Union against a purportedly sovereign Parliament. On this point, Dicey's position is once more worth quoting. While defending

34 [2005] UKHL 56, [2005] 4 All ER 1253.
35 5 U.S. (1 Cranch) 137 (1803).
36 See Wicks (n 11) 117.

the absolute law-making competence of Parliament, he nonetheless concluded that a sovereign Parliament

> though it cannot be logically bound to abstain from changing any given law, may, by the fact that an Act when it was passed had been declared to be unchangeable, receive a warning that it cannot be changed without grave danger to the Constitution of the country.[37]

This idea of a tangible impact upon the Constitution from undermining the terms of the Union is an important one. It fits well with the recognition of the British Constitution as an evolving but nonetheless binding constitution.[38] The benefit from a Diceyian perspective, of course, is in avoiding the need for the courts to directly challenge Parliament's sovereign law-making powers by setting aside legislation. But, it also highlights that the 1707 Union legislation is not the same as other pieces of primary legislation; it is a (foundational) part of the British Constitution, and there will be constitutional consequences for breaching it. This was recognised even in the eighteenth century by Daniel Defoe, who wrote that it is plain that the Articles and Treaty of Union 'cannot be touched by the Parliament of Britain; and that the moment they attempt it, they dissolve their own Constitution.'[39] Two centuries later, Smith argued that the entrenched provisions of the Treaty of Union 'could only be superseded by revolution – in the sense of a fundamental reconstruction of the British Constitution.'[40] This approach has much to support it, for it proves the contemporary constitutional significance of the 1707 Union. It is a Union that cannot be guaranteed to last 'for ever after,' but if it ends, the Constitution will be completely reconstructed.

8.6 Scotland, sovereignty, and self-determination

MacCormick has identified what he terms a 'Scottish anomaly' at the heart of the British state.[41] This is because, despite being an incorporating Union, the 1707 agreement provides special dispensation for Scotland, including its laws, courts, and church, and thus there is a continuing, protected existence of a strong civic identity for Scotland.[42] In MacCormick's words, 'Scotland was

37 Dicey and Rait (n 26) 252.

38 See Elizabeth Wicks, *The Evolution of a Constitution: Eight Key Moments in British Constitutional History* (Hart 2006) for an argument that the British Constitution is an evolving one, sufficiently flexible to incorporate new principles and practices but not without strength and standards that endure.

39 Defoe (n 27) 246.

40 Smith (n 4) 113.

41 MacCormick (n 3) 60.

42 Ibid.

incorporated, but Scotland stayed different.'[43] Indeed, this might imply that the Union was less incorporating than it might have been. The two parliaments were united, but the churches, the legal systems, and the *nations* were not. This meant that Scotland retained a clear and distinct national identity in a way that facilitated a later revival of Scottish nationalism in the twentieth century and beyond.[44]

It is clear within the Articles of Union that, alongside a theme of incorporation and common shared elements, there is a recognition and protection for what was to remain distinct in the formerly separate parts of Great Britain. In the former can be found elements such as the Crown, Parliament, flag, currency, and free trade – many of the main elements of a new state – while in the latter are civic institutions such as the courts and common law, churches, systems of local government and of education.[45] As Smith has noted, an incorporating Union 'maintaining complete severalty of administration of justice, may well be unique.'[46] This has led MacCormick to note that the distinctive, protected features of Scotland 'has made an ostensibly unitary state . . . function internally in a markedly federal way.'[47] Of course, the United Kingdom today is not a federal state, even with the devolution of recent decades, but it is correct to say that neither is it a typically unitary state. There remain different nations within the UK and, arguably, at least some of those nations retain a degree of sovereignty.

Sovereignty is a complex notion, or more accurately, notions, and it is worth unpacking its varied meanings. First, within international law, state sovereignty is both an indicator of and a consequence of the existence of an independent state. I have argued elsewhere that state sovereignty requires a defined territory and permanent population, together with a social organisation and political structure, an internal body with authority to rule, and a degree of freedom of action and decision on the international place.[48] There is no doubt that the United Kingdom of Great Britain, formed in 1707 and still in existence in revised form today, is an independent state possessing state sovereignty at international law. The same cannot be said of either England or Scotland, who both relinquished their state sovereignty alongside their independent statehood when agreeing to the Treaty of Union. However, it is conceivable that they both retain an element of national sovereignty. This second form of sovereignty can be contrasted with state sovereignty in that it attaches not to a state entity but to a people, recognising close ties of

43 Ibid.

44 TC Smout, 'The Road to Union' in G Holmes (ed), *Britain After the Glorious Revolution 1689–1714* (Macmillan 1969) 178.

45 MacCormick (n 3) 52.

46 Smith (n 4) 99.

47 MacCormick (n 3) 60.

48 Elizabeth Wicks, 'State Sovereignty – Towards a Refined Legal Conceptualisation' (2000) 29 Anglo Am L Rev 282.

nationhood and distinctive national identity and culture. Although Scotland and England surrendered their state sovereignty when uniting in 1707, there is no reason to suppose they also surrendered their national sovereignty, and indeed, it might be doubted whether commissioners from the national Parliaments were in a position to do so, even if they had so desired. The protection for Scottish national interests, which formed so core a part of the Union ensured the preservation of a degree of national sovereignty for that ancient kingdom. As Pittock has explained, despite the creation of a new kingdom of Great Britain, the Scottish kingdom continued to have political existence and rights within the new kingdom.[49] He argues that both kingdoms – British and Scottish – simultaneously exist, and 'in respect of certain Scottish sovereign rights one is not extinguished by the other.'[50] This idea of one sovereign state containing two nations with (national) sovereignty rights is a helpful way of explaining the unique constitutional settlement of 1707. Until recent decades, Scotland had no internal governing body to act for it, and the elements of national sovereignty that endured laid dormant, but with the rise in nationalist sentiment during the latter half of the twentieth century and the concept of devolved government for Scotland from 1998, the true meaning of Scotland as a continuing nation, enjoying a degree of national sovereignty, has become apparent. Of course, for many Scottish nationalists, devolution is not enough and only an independent state of Scotland will suffice. If such a state were to emerge in the future, Scotland might regain state sovereignty, but short of that state of affairs, and within the union state first created in 1707, it is Scottish national sovereignty that endures.

While I have chosen to describe the sovereignty of Scotland post-1707 as 'national sovereignty,' for some writers, it is better viewed as a third form of sovereignty: the popular sovereignty of the Scottish people.[51] This approach would sidestep the question of whether a Scottish nation survives within the union state (although here it is argued that it does) and would instead attach the sovereignty of Scotland directly to its people rather than to a nation or kingdom. Popular sovereignty is an important concept in international law. It recognises the rights of people to a say in their future, and it is closely linked to the concept of self-determination of peoples, which is protected as a right in UN human rights treaties.[52] In a recent case about whether the devolved Scottish Parliament had the competence to enact legislation to hold a second referendum on Scottish independence, the Scottish National Party (SNP) intervened to argue that UK law should be interpreted in a way

49 Pittock (n 1) 14.
50 Ibid.
51 See, for example, Pittock (n 1): 'the Scottish sovereignty left intact at the union was one which would come to be understood in terms of popular sovereignty.'
52 Joint Article 1 of International Covenant on Civil and Political Rights (ICCPR) and International Covenant on Economic, Social and Cultural Rights (ICESCR).

consistent with this right to self-determination protected at international law.[53] This was a novel attempt to rely upon a right to self-determination to bolster the concept of Scottish sovereignty. However, the Supreme Court held that the right to self-determination was 'not in play here' and that the UK was not in breach of international law, not least because devolution to Scotland (and other nations and regions) is founded upon a principle of subsidiarity.[54] The approach of the Supreme Court drew upon that of the Supreme Court of Canada, which, in the case of *Reference re Secession of Quebec,* had sought to limit the self-determination of a people to situations such as colonialism or subjugation.[55] In adopting this approach, the UK Supreme Court failed to engage with fundamental issues such as whether the Scottish are a 'people' in international law and to what extent their popular sovereignty endures within the union state. In discussing this case, Sanger and Young note that the right to self-determination in international law offers support to a people to choose their own political form in only 'very limited circumstances, and in exceptional and clear-cut cases,' and that outside of such situations, it 'leaves political and democratic questions about the relationship of a "people" within a unified constitutional entity to be worked through at the national level.'[56] They do note, however, that the international right of self-determination might, in such cases, strengthen the need for negotiation on both sides.[57] If correct, this is likely to be of future relevance to the Scottish people and the pro-independence movement because neither the Union agreement nor the devolution settlement leaves Scotland's future entirely within the hands of the Scottish people.

Finally, it is worth reflecting upon the voluntary nature of the Union. While ostensibly a voluntary union with negotiated terms between equal parties, England's dominance (in military and economic terms, as well as the size of its population) overshadowed the agreement. Scotland saw clear economic advantages in joining with its more prosperous southern neighbour, and the terms of the final Union secure extensive protections for core Scottish interests, as we have seen, but it has even been claimed that 'in the last analysis it was not a choice between Union and independence for Scotland but between the treaty and an English conquest.'[58] While this may overstate the issue, it reminds us of the uneven bargaining positions of the two parties to the Union, as well as the protection for Scottish interests, given that

53 *Reference by the Lord Advocate of devolution issues under para 34 of Sch 6 to the Scotland Act 1998* [2022] UKSC 31; [2022] All ER 64.

54 ibid, and see Andrew Sanger and Alison L Young, 'An Involuntary Union? Supreme Court rejects Scotland's Claim for Unilateral Referendum on Independence' (2023) 82 CLJ 1.

55 [1998] 2 SCR 217.

56 Sanger and Young (n 54) 8.

57 Ibid.

58 WA Speck, *The Birth of Britain – A New Nation 1700–1710* (Blackwell 1994) 20.

no such protection was perceived as being necessary for the more dominant partner of England. When this historical context is added to the concerns of the pro-independence movement in the twenty-first century that even asking the Scottish people the question about withdrawal from the Union is not in the hands of Scotland itself, it might raise issues about the extent of popular sovereignty that exists in Scotland and the right of the Scottish people to determine their own political future. However, a Union that went against the interests of Scotland would not have endured for over 300 years and, as Lord Sumption has noted, the 'generally co-operative character' of the Union over this long period suggests that it 'has always been closer to an alliance than a merger of nations.'[59]

This alliance is between two nations that continue to have a distinctive national character and, importantly, it is an alliance that has evolved greatly in the last few decades as Scotland has gained devolutionary powers, including extensive legislative powers for a Scottish Parliament. That the ongoing relationship between Scotland and England, and the rest of the United Kingdom, has been able to change illustrates the strengths of the evolving Constitution, which typically has managed to secure core constitutional principles such as the union state and the legislative sovereignty of the Westminster Parliament, while enabling new political settlements, such as Scottish devolution to ensure the Constitution remains broadly acceptable to the people it governs. The existence of a Scottish nation within the United Kingdom is recognised in today's Constitution, by both the terms of the 1707 Union, which ensured Scotland would continue as a distinct entity from England in many core respects, and in more recent devolution legislation, which recognises the need for subsidiarity and self-government for the people of Scotland. Should those twin protections not be felt to suffice in the future to ensure respect for the sovereignty of the Scottish people, and should Scotland make a democratic choice to end its union with England, the UK Constitution will be required to adapt to accommodate the necessary changes in territory and jurisdiction. Such a change might be viewed by some as a constitutional revolution – a break in continuity in the UK Constitution; by others as proof that the UK has no binding constitution capable of stopping such fundamental changes; but a better view is that it would merely demonstrate the ongoing evolutionary nature of the UK Constitution which adapts to changing political circumstances but nonetheless is a source of higher law at any moment in time. Since 1707, that Constitution has had, as a core part, a voluntary union of states, a British Parliament, and protection for Scottish legal and religious interests. For as long as the Union continues, those core constitutional principles will remain central to the UK Constitution and unchangeable under it.

59 Sumption (n 9) 158.

8.7 Conclusion

In this chapter, I have sought to emphasise the importance of the 1707 Union for the British Constitution, both at the time and today. The significance of the Union has not always been fully appreciated, with some writers downplaying the two Acts of Union as merely normal Acts of Parliament, and as changeable as any other. Such an approach makes no logical sense when the most basic fact of 1707 is that two previously sovereign, independent states joined together to create a new sovereign state that had not previously existed and that required a new legislature to make laws for it. Neither the English nor Scottish Parliaments had the legislative authority to make laws for the new United Kingdom of Great Britain, and the new British Parliament could hardly have passed a law before it came into existence, nor could it create itself. It is also interesting to note, however, that at times other writers may have overstated the 1707 Articles of Union by classifying them as a Constitution in their own right and emphasising the limited nature of the Parliament 'born unfree' because of it. A better view is that the Articles of Union have constitutional status within a broader, evolutionary, but still binding British Constitution. It is not always easy to accept that a constitution can be both flexible in its evolutionary nature and binding in higher law form from day to day, but this is, in my long-held view,[60] the only way to explain the UK's unusual Constitution. It is a viewpoint strengthened by the story of the UK's development into a union state and by the centuries of constitutional history evident throughout this book, during which the constitutional rules of the state have evolved but had meaning. The union state, the new British Parliament, and the preservation of the Scottish nation and its sovereign rights have remained firmly protected in the British Constitution since 1707 until the present day.

Bibliography

Defoe D, *The History of the Union Between England and Scotland* (1786)

Dicey AV, *An Introduction to the Study of the Law of the Constitution* (10th edn, Macmillan 1959)

Dicey AV and Rait RS, *Thoughts on the Union Between England and Scotland* (Macmillan 1920)

MacCormick N, 'Does the United Kingdom Have a Constitution? Reflections on MacCormick v Lord Advocate' (1978) 29 NILQ 1

MacCormick N, *Questioning Sovereignty* (OUP 1999)

Mitchell JDB, *Constitutional Law* (2nd edn, W Green & Son 1968)

O'Neill A, 'A Tale of Two Constitutions' (1997) 26 SLT 205

Pittock M, 'Scottish Sovereignty and the Union of 1707: Then and Now' (2012) 14 National Identities

Sanger A and Young AL, 'An Involuntary Union? Supreme Court Rejects Scotland's Claim for Unilateral Referendum on Independence' (2023) 82 CLJ 1

Scott P, *1707: The Union of England and Scotland* (Chambers 1979)

60 Wicks (n 38).

Smith TB, 'The Union of 1707 as Fundamental Law' [1957] PL 99
Smout TC, 'The Road to Union' in G Holmes (ed), *Britain After the Glorious Revolution 1689–1714* (Macmillan 1969)
Speck WA, *The Birth of Britain – A New Nation 1700–1710* (Blackwell 1994)
Sumption (Lord), 'The Disunited Kingdom: England, Ireland and Scotland' (2014) 3 CJICL 139
Upton M, 'Marriage Vows of the Elephant: The Constitution of 1707' (1989) 105 LQR 79
Wicks E, 'State Sovereignty – Towards a Refined Legal Conceptualisation' (2000) 29 Anglo-Am L Rev 282
Wicks E, 'A New Constitution for a New State? The 1707 Union of England and Scotland' (2001) 117 LQR 109
Wicks E, *The Evolution of a Constitution: Eight Key Moments in British Constitutional History* (Hart 2006)

9 Bolingbroke's *Remarks on the History of England* and *Dissertation upon Parties*

*Max Skjönsberg**

Henry St John, 1st Viscount Bolingbroke (1678–1751), was a prominent Tory parliamentarian in 1701–1708 and 1710–1715.[1] In his early parliamentary career, he was closely allied with the moderate Country Tory Robert Harley, with whom he served in the mixed ministry in 1704–1708 as Secretary at War. But his friendship with Harley deteriorated and turned into rivalry during the Tory administration of 1710–1714, as Bolingbroke aimed for leadership of the High-Church Tories, which is ironic considering his later anticlericalism. The pinnacle of his political career was the Treaty of Utrecht, which he negotiated as Secretary of State in 1713. This made him an enemy of the Hanoverian court and the Whigs. Shortly after the death of Queen Anne and the Hanoverian Succession, he fled to France. Bolingbroke's decision to take up a position at the exiled court of James, the Stuart Pretender, whom he served for less than a year, prevented him from returning to Britain until he was pardoned in 1723. During his exile, Bolingbroke studied philosophy and history and befriended men of letters, such as Voltaire and Montesquieu.[2] While living abroad, Bolingbroke moderated his one-time tribal Toryism. In August 1723, he wrote to his friend Jonathan Swift: 'I forget I was ever of any Party myself; nay . . . I am ready to imagine that there never was any such Monster as Party.'[3]

Though Bolingbroke's property was restored to him in 1725, he remained barred from taking up his seat in the House of Lords. Deprived of a voice in Parliament, he launched the *Craftsman* journal with the opposition Whig William Pulteney in 1726. The *Craftsman* was part of a wider intellectual opposition to Robert Walpole's Court Whig administration and the concomitant culture of finance and (alleged) corruption ('Robinocracy'). It was to

* The Hamilton School of Classical and Civic Education, University of Florida.

1 See esp. HT Dickinson, *Bolingbroke* (Constable & Company 1970).

2 Nick Childs, *Political Academy in Paris, 1724–1731: The Entresol and Its Members* (Voltaire Foundation 2000).

3 George Sherburn (ed), *The Correspondence of Alexander Pope*, 5 vols (Oxford University Press 1956), II, 187. For Bolingbroke and party politics, see Max Skjönsberg, *The Persistence of Party: Ideas of Harmonious Discord in Eighteenth-Century Britain* (Cambridge University Press 2021) ch. 3.

DOI: 10.4324/9781032658698-10

become the best-selling publication in the country for many years and won the respect even of its fiercest opponents, with Lord Hervey remarking that it was 'a much better written paper than any of that sort that were published on the side of the Court.'[4] The literary part of this opposition comprised such luminaries as Swift, Alexander Pope, John Gay, Dr Arbuthnot, and, at a later stage, James Thomson, Samuel Johnson, and Henry Fielding.[5] Bolingbroke had known many of these wits since his time in government, as he was a supporter and member of what would later be known as the Scriblerus Club. As a political writer, Bolingbroke became central to what Jürgen Habermas termed the first 'public sphere' (*Öffentlichkeit*), a new environment in which members of the public could participate in discussions of political, cultural, and social issues in a relatively open and critical manner.[6] Two of Bolingbroke's most famous political works were serialised in the *Craftsman*: *Remarks on the History of England* in 1730–1731 and the *Dissertation upon Parties* in 1733–1734.

A polemic against Walpole's ministry and the writers in the government-sponsored newspapers, the *Remarks* took the form of chronologically organised reflections on the British constitution, and in particular, the significance of the 'spirit of liberty' for its flourishing and the 'spirit of faction' for its disintegration. Covering English history until the civil war in the work, the key political move made by Bolingbroke was to associate opposition to the court with the spirit of liberty. He began the *Remarks* by setting out that 'liberty cannot be long secure, in any country, unless a perpetual jealousy watches over it.' This jealousy has to be 'permanent and equal'.[7] Since Bolingbroke viewed the love of power as natural and insatiable, he believed that liberty was always to some extent under threat in every government. Accordingly, 'perpetual jealousy' in the shape of political opposition 'may have the good effect of destroying a wicked minister, of checking a bad, or of reclaiming a misguided prince.'[8]

In the process of justifying opposition to Walpole through his historical commentary and parallels, Bolingbroke dissected the British constitution. Referring to Britain as a 'limited monarchy', he differentiated it from continental absolutist states, the democracy of Athens, and the mixed government

4 John Hervey, *Some Materials Towards Memoirs of the Reign of King George II*, 3 vols (Romney Sedgwick ed, Eyre and Spottiswoode 1931) I, 263.

5 See esp. Christine Gerrard, *The Patriot Opposition to Walpole: Politics, Poetry, and National Myth, 1725–1742* (Oxford University Press 1994); JGA Pocock, *The Machiavellian Moment: Florentine Political Thought and the Atlantic Republican Tradition* (first published 1975, Princeton University Press 2003) 477–86; Isaac Kramnick, *Bolingbroke and His Circle* (first published 1968, Cornell University Press 1992) 205–35; Bernard A Goldgar, *Walpole and the Wits: The Relation of Politics to Literature, 1722–42* (University of Nebraska Press 1976).

6 Max Skjönsberg, 'The Communication of Fame' in Brian Cowan (ed), *A Cultural History of Fame in the Age of Enlightenment* (Bloomsbury Publishing 2025) 23–42.

7 Bolingbroke, *Historical Writings* (Isaac Kramnick ed, University of Chicago Press 1972) 157.

8 Ibid 164.

of Rome.[9] Still, the Roman state offered instruction because it declined after the people had lost the spirit of liberty through luxury and corruption, even though the state preserved the outward form of its constitution.[10] By contrast, British freedom had survived for much longer. 'I feel a secret pride in thinking that I was born a Briton', wrote Bolingbroke, 'when I consider that the Romans, those masters of the world, maintained their liberty little more than seven centuries; and that Britain, which was a free nation above seventeenth hundred years ago, is so at this hour.' This did not mean that it had been a straightforward journey. Indeed, Bolingbroke argued that '[f]ew nations have gone through more revolutions, few governments have appeared more unsteady, or fluctuated more between prerogative and privilege, than this of Great Britain.'[11]

Bolingbroke traced the spirit of liberty to 'the original freedom of the British and Saxon constitutions'.[12] The Romans had portrayed the ancient Britons as savage, but even Julius Caesar had acknowledged that they had fought for their liberties. Moreover, Bolingbroke maintained that 'there is good reason to believe, from his [Caesar's] manner of writing, and abrupt way of leaving this island, that they gave him a warmer reception than he is willing to own.' The Saxons would later provide the institutional support of the spirit of liberty. Among them, 'supreme power centered in the micklemote, or wittagenmote, composed of the king, the lords, and the Saxon freemen, that original sketch of a British parliament.'[13] Though William the Conqueror imposed new laws and customs after the Norman Conquest in 1066, Bolingbroke was convinced that 'neither he nor they could destroy the old constitution; because neither he nor they could extinguish the old spirit of liberty.'[14] In short, despite Bolingbroke's historical scepticism expressed in his more rigorous and detached works, as a political writer in the *Craftsman* he was a thorough ancient constitutionalist.[15]

Bolingbroke's most sustained discussion of the British constitution occurs in Letter 7 of the *Remarks*, where he describes it as a system of different functions that are characterised by both 'independency' and 'dependency', that

9 Ibid 158.
10 Ibid 166–67.
11 Ibid 177.
12 Ibid.
13 Ibid 178.
14 Ibid 179.
15 See also Bolingbroke, *Political Writings* (David Armitage ed, University of Cambridge 1997) 111–21, 152–55. For the classic study of ancient constitutionalism, see JGA Pocock, *The Ancient Constitution and the Feudal Law: A Study of English Historical Thought in the Seventeenth Century. A Reissue with a Retrospect* (first published 1957, Cambridge University Press 1987). For Bolingbroke's contribution to historiography, see David Womersley, 'Lord Bolingbroke and Eighteenth-Century Historiography' (1987) 28 The Eighteenth-Century 217–34, but for a more political reading, see also Philip Hicks, 'Bolingbroke, Clarendon, and the Role of Classical Historian' (1987) 20 Eighteenth-Century Studies 445–71.

is to say, by the separation of powers as well as checks and balances.[16] His description is worth quoting at length because it is arguably unmatched in its sophisticated blending of the principles of the separation of powers and checks and balances in eighteenth-century constitutional thought prior to the *Federalist Papers* in 1787–88:

> A king of Great Britain is that supreme magistrate who has a negative voice in the legislature. He is entrusted with the executive power, and several other powers and privileges, which we call prerogatives, are annexed to this trust. The two houses of parliament have their rights and privileges; some of which are common to both, others particular to each. They prepare, they pass bills, or they refuse to pass such as are sent to them. They address, represent, advise, remonstrate. The supreme judicature resides in the lords. The commons are the grand inquest of the nation, and to them it belongs likewise to judge of national expences, and to give supplies accordingly.
>
> If the legislative as well as the executive power, was wholly in the king, as in some countries, he would be absolute; if in the lords, our government would be an aristocracy; if in the commons, a democracy. It is this division of power, these distinct privileges attributed to the king, to the lords, and to the commons, which constitute a limited monarchy.
>
> Again: as they constitute a limited monarchy, so the wisdom of our government has provided, as far as human wisdom can provide for the preservation of it, by this division of power, and by these distinct privileges. If any one part of the three which compose our government, should at any time usurp more power than law gives, or make an ill use of a legal power, the other two parts may, by uniting their strength, reduce this power into its proper bounds, or correct the abuse of it; nay, if at any time two of these parts should concur in usurping, or abusing power, the weight of the third may, at least, retard the mischief, and give time and chance for preventing it.
>
> . . .
>
> Since this division of power, and these distinct privileges constitute and maintain our government, it follows that the confusion of them tends to destroy it. This proposition is therefore true; that, in a constitution like ours, the safety of the whole depends on the balance of the parts. Let us see whether it be true, that the balance of the parts consists in their mutual independency.

16 See JH Burns, 'Bolingbroke and the Concept of Constitutional Government' (1962) 10 Political Studies 264–76; Robert Shackleton, 'Montesquieu, Bolingbroke, and the Separation of Powers' (1949) 3 French Studies 25–38; CH McIlwain, *Constitutionalism Ancient and Modern* (Cornell University Press 1940) 5–9.

> To speak again without any metaphor, the power, which the several parts of our government have of controlling and checking one another, may be called a dependency on one another, and may be argued for by those who want to throw darkness round them, as the dependency opposed to the independency mentioned in the proposition. But the fallacy is gross. We have shown that this power of control in each, which results from the division of power amongst all the parts of our government, is necessary to the preservation of it: and thus a sort of constitutional dependency . . . is created among them; but this mutual dependency cannot be opposed to the independency pleaded for. On the contrary, this mutual dependency cannot subsist without such an independency . . . The constitutional dependency . . . consists in this; that the proceedings of each part of the government, when they come forth into action and affect the whole, are liable to be examined and controlled by the other parts. The independency pleaded for consists in this; that the resolutions of each part, which direct these proceedings, be taken independently and without any influence, direct or indirect, on the others. Without the first, each part would be at liberty to attempt destroying the balance, by usurping or abusing power; but without the last, there can be no balance at all.[17]

After years of fluctuation and turbulence, Bolingbroke contended that the constitution finally regained its balance during Elizabeth I's reign. The government was then brought back to the condition of the Saxons. The increase in trade and the diminution of the clergy and nobility under the Tudors made the commons richer and the lower house of parliament more powerful. In this way, Bolingbroke's social history – in some ways the most original part of his historical writings – explained constitutional developments. But he was not blind to the influence of 'great men' in history. Instead, he wrote at length about how James I squandered the marvellous legacy of Elizabeth I, partly by misinterpreting the English Crown as hereditary and absolute,[18] and paved the way for the civil war in his son's reign.

The civil war was a disastrous outcome of the Stuarts's misguided monarchical interpretation of the constitution. With a nod to his own struggle against Walpole's ministry, Bolingbroke argued that the appropriate response was reform by way of constitutional renewal. The most effective 'means of reformation' was what Machiavelli had recommended in the *Discourses on Livy*: renewing the state by drawing it back to its 'first principles'.[19] For Bolingbroke,

17 *The Works of the Late Right Honorable Henry St. John, Lord Viscount Bolingbroke*, 5 vols (David Mallet ed, London 1754) I, 339–41 (the spelling has been updated to reflect modern usage).

18 Ibid 299–302.

19 Ibid 165, referring to Machiavelli, *Discourses on Livy* (The University of Chicago Press 1998) 209.

the first principles of any state had to be sound, because otherwise the state would not have subsisted, let alone made progress. But like everything else, the state was subject to degeneration: 'governments, like other mixed bodies, tend to dissolution by the changes which are wrought in the several parts, and by the unaptness and disproportion, which results from hence throughout the whole composition.'[20]

Reform by way of restoration remained a principal theme in Bolingbroke's second major work in the *Craftsman,* the *Dissertation upon Parties.* The *Dissertation* was serialised in 19 editorial letters between October 1733 and December 1734. A politico-historical work, it picks up where the *Remarks* had left off, with the political struggle of the first half of the seventeenth century, but it moves rapidly forward to the Restoration, the Glorious Revolution, and beyond into Walpolean Britain. Bolingbroke's explicit intention was to make 'an enquiry into the rise and progress of our late parties; or a short history of Toryism and Whiggism from their cradle to their grave, with an introductory account of their genealogy and descent.'[21] The kernel of his argument was that Tory and Whig had become redundant as political parties since there was no longer any disagreement about the fundamentals of the British constitution among honest people. When the parties had come into being during the Exclusion Crisis, there had been real differences at stake, with the Tories espousing divine-right monarchy, lineal succession, and passive obedience and the Whigs seeking to exclude the Catholic Duke of York from the succession to the throne. Bolingbroke described the Glorious Revolution, which was carried out by a coalition of the two parties, as 'a fire, which purged off the dross of both parties; and the dross being purged off, they appeared to be the same metal, and answered the same standard.'[22] After the Revolution, the Whigs and Tories had no need to fear each other, as they both had rid themselves of their extreme doctrines: republicanism and divine right of kings, respectively. While the real essence of the parties had disappeared, the names had survived for factious purposes and continued to haunt and divide the political nation like ghosts. More specifically, he accused the Court Whigs in power of having turned into a faction that sought to keep alive artificial party distinctions for their own benefit.

This was a time when Bolingbroke sought to create a Country party alliance between Tories and discontented Whigs as a stable force in opposition to Walpole. The Country party had a distinct ideology that emphasised the importance of the independence of parliament from Court influence, support of the landed and traded interests in opposition to the moneyed interest, and a

20 Ibid.
21 Ibid 12.
22 Ibid 65.

preference for a citizen militia and a strong navy rather than a standing army.[23] Both the Whig and Tory parties had had Country elements since the Glorious Revolution, but they had usually only collaborated on specific issues, for example, the standing army question in 1697–98. From the reign of Queen Anne onwards, Country sentiments were more dominant among Tories than Whigs, with the former becoming known as the 'country gentlemen'.[24] Bolingbroke wanted to turn the occasional Country coalition into a permanent political force, and this was the aspiration of his joint enterprise with Pulteney.

To this end, in the *Dissertation,* he defined three political camps: first, those who were enemies of the government but friends of the constitution (the Country party); second, the enemies of both (the Jacobites); and finally, those who were attached to the government but not to the constitution (Walpole and the Court Whigs).[25] Distinguishing the Tories from the Jacobites and showing the latter to be insignificant were crucial for his purposes, as he needed to distance himself from the Stuart cause as well as make the Tories palatable collaborators for opposition Whigs.[26] But the key conceptual distinction made by Bolingbroke was the one between 'government' and 'constitution', describing the former as an administrative activity undertaken by magistrates, whereas the latter meant 'that assemblage of laws, institutions and customs, derived from certain fixed principles of reason, directed to certain fixed objects of public good, that compose the general system, according to which the community hath agreed to be governed.'[27] For Bolingbroke, any government that was 'unconstitutional' – a term he may have coined[28] – could

23 Max Skjönsberg, 'Patriots and the Country Party Tradition in the Eighteenth Century: The Critics of Britain's Fiscal-Military State from Robert Harley to Catharine Macaulay' (2023) 33 Intellectual History Review 83–100; HT Dickinson, *Liberty and Property: Political Ideology in Eighteenth-century Britain* (Weidenfeld & Nicholson 1977) 163–92; Quentin Skinner, 'The Principles and Practice of Opposition: The Case of Bolingbroke versus Walpole' in Neil McKendrick (ed), *Historical Perspectives: Studies in English Thought and Society in Honour of J.H. Plumb* (Europa 1974) 93–128; JGA Pocock, 'Machiavelli, Harrington and English Political Ideologies in the Eighteenth Century' (1965) 3rd series 22 William and Mary Quarterly 549–83; Caroline Robbins, *Eighteenth-Century Commonwealthman* (Harvard University Press 1959).

24 David Hayton, 'The "Country" Interest and the Party System' in Clyve Jones (ed), *Party and Management in Parliament, 1660–1784* (Palgrave Macmillan 1984) 40–44.

25 Bolingbroke, *Political Writings*, 85, 177.

26 It should be noted, however, that although many Jacobites distrusted him after his short and inglorious stint as the Pretenders's Secretary, Bolingbroke appears to have been periodically and opportunistically involved in Jacobite plotting later in his career; see Eveline Cruickshanks, 'Lord Cornbury, Bolingbroke and a Plan to Restore the Stuarts 1731–1735' (1986) 27 Royal Stuart Papers 1–12. For the continued relevance of Jacobitism as an alternative for several British Tories, see Eveline Cruickshanks, *Political Untouchables: The Tories and the '45* (Duckworth 1979).

27 Bolingbroke, *Political Writings*, 88.

28 Ibid xvi. No earlier entries can be found in Eighteenth-Century Collections Online (ECCO), though its data is not complete and word searches are not entirely reliable.

legitimately be opposed by those he dubbed 'constitutionists'. But what did it specifically mean to act unconstitutionally?

In Bolingbroke's view, all monarchs since William III had ruled according to 'original contracts' between the prince and the people, which made the institution of monarchy 'plainly conditional'.[29] This contract was protected by constitutional safeguards in the shape of several pieces of legislation passed between 1689 and 1701 that collectively became known as the Revolution Settlement. As he wrote: 'the settlement then made is looked upon by the whole Country party as a new Magna Carta'.[30] These comprised the Bill of Rights 1689, the Triennial Act 1694, and the Act of Settlement 1701, which together secured 'the rights and privileges of the people.'[31] But he also referred to the legacy of the Glorious Revolution in more general terms, a legacy he believed had been squandered during the Whig Supremacy, for instance, through the repeal of the Triennial Act in 1716.[32] For Bolingbroke, it was essential to return at least to triennial, and perhaps even annual, parliamentary elections. Annual sessions were necessary but not sufficient.[33] The call for annual parliaments, common among Hanoverian Tories, would become a key part of the reformist platform – often known as 'radicalism' – in the late eighteenth and early nineteenth centuries.

Central to Bolingbroke's politics was the contention that the Glorious Revolution did not introduce anything new but rather restored the ancient constitution.[34] During the seventeenth century, the British government had been misinterpreted by the Stuarts as inflexibly hereditary and absolute, and this remained true of Jacobites and some High Church Tories in the eighteenth century. Bolingbroke criticised non-juror George Harbin's divine-right pamphlet, *The Hereditary Right of the Crown of England Asserted*, which had been published in 1713 when Bolingbroke was the parliamentary leader of the High Church Tories.[35] As a writer in the *Craftsman* and a promoter of the Country party, Bolingbroke was convinced that the Stuart and 'Tory' interpretation of the British government was 'modern' and almost by extension a mere 'illusion'. According to Bolingbroke, British kings ruled by parliamentary right, which was confirmed not only by 1688–89 but also by the Act of Recognition of 1603, and a plethora of other examples cited in the *Dissertation* and the *Remarks*.[36] In a word, the Glorious Revolution did not alter the constitution

29 Ibid 83.
30 Ibid 9.
31 Ibid 84.
32 Max Skjönsberg, 'Ancient Constitutionalism, Fundamental Law, and Eighteenth-Century Toryism in the Septennial Act (1716) Debates' (2019) 40 History of Political Thought 270–301.
33 Bolingbroke, *Political Writings*, 98–110.
34 Ibid 65.
35 Ibid 73–74, 78–79.
36 Ibid 79–81.

but 'renewed it, and brought it back to the first principles, and nearer to the primitive institution'.[37] For Bolingbroke, it represented a continuation of Saxon liberty and the maintenance of 'our Gothic institution of government'.[38]

However, the Glorious Revolution was incomplete and unable to prevent future abuses of power.[39] Bolingbroke was convinced that Walpole – the 'grand corrupter'[40] – had undermined the workings of the balanced constitution through the practice of parliamentary corruption. By using the influence and funds of the Crown to build majorities in the House of Commons through bribes and sinecures, he believed that the independence of the legislature was threatened by executive overreach.[41] This kind of technical corruption, or influence, was defended by the Walpole press in the 1730s and David Hume more famously in 1741.[42] For Bolingbroke, placemen in the House of Commons were anathema because they compromised the balanced constitution. In this way, Bolingbroke's politics once again looked back to the Country party ideology of his one-time mentor Harley,[43] as well as forward to later reformers such as Catharine Macaulay and Richard Price in the later eighteenth century and William Cobbett and Francis Burdett in the early nineteenth. Bolingbroke was one of the constitutional authorities singled out by the Society for Constitutional Information at its inception in the spring of 1780, and in January 1783, it added extracts from the *Dissertation* and his other political works to its books.[44]

The question of parliamentary corruption, or executive influence over the legislature, went to the heart of Bolingbroke's understanding of the constitution as allowing the three powers in the state (king, lords, and commons) to act independently, yet check and balance one another. Each part had specific rights, powers, and privileges, and their independence 'consists properly and truly in the free, unbiassed, uninfluenced and independent exercise of these rights, powers, and privileges, by each part, in as ample extent as the constitution allows'. Beyond that point, 'the constitutional dependency of each part of the others commences.'[45] Explicitly arguing against the Walpole-sponsored *London Journal*, Bolingbroke held that though no one

37 Ibid 82.
38 Ibid 83.
39 Ibid 92.
40 Ibid 4.
41 Ibid 93–97. See also ibid 160–61.
42 Kramnick, *Bolingbroke and His Circle*, 123–24; David Hume, 'Of the Independency of Parliament' in *Essays: Moral, Political, and Literary* (first published 1741, Liberty Fund 1985) 42–46.
43 Angus McInnes, 'The Political Ideas of Robert Harley' (1965) 50 History 309–22.
44 Minute books of the Society of Constitutional Information, the National Archives, Kew Gardens, TS 11/1133, ff. 5, 132, 138.
45 Bolingbroke, *Political Writings*, 120.

disputed that the Crown was the source of all public employments, it did not follow that

> the constitutional independency of the king would be lost, because the House of Commons give the supplies, if he [the king] had not the power of giving part of this money, in places and pensions, back again to the members of this house.[46]

On the contrary, the balance of the constitution would be lost if the Crown was able to exert its influence in the legislature in such a way.

In the *Dissertation,* Bolingbroke calls the British constitution a 'mixed government', combining democracy, aristocracy, and monarchy.[47] Interestingly, he refers to it as a mixture of three 'estates'. His usage of the term 'estate' represented a change in the English language that can be traced to the 1640s and Charles I's *Answer to the Nineteen Propositions* (1642), drafted by Sir John Colepeper and Lucius Cary, Viscount Falkland. The term *estate* is derived from *status* in Latin and originally meant social or juridical position. It was applied to representative institutions in the Middle Ages when rights were enjoyed by corporate bodies rather than individuals.[48] Originally, the estates of the realm in medieval and early-modern Europe did not include the monarch, who was above them, but rather referred to society's division into those who pray (the clergy), those who fight (the nobility), and those who labour (burghers), with peasants occasionally comprising a fourth estate.[49] But in the 1640s, the concept of estates merged with classical terminology, referring to the one, the few, and the many. Viewing the monarch as one of the three estates rather than above them was essential for Bolingbroke's notion of patriot kingship, which he would fully elaborate on in *The Idea of a Patriot King* (1738), but which he anticipated in the *Dissertation.*[50] '[A]s our government is now constituted', wrote Bolingbroke, 'the three estates have not only one common interest, which they always had; but they have, considered as estates, no separate, contradictory interest.'[51]

Crucially, though Bolingbroke believed that the king-in-parliament was in one sense 'supreme', he agreed with John Locke that it was not arbitrary

46 Ibid 121.

47 Ibid 125, 163.

48 Wim Blockmans, 'Representation (Since the Thirteenth Century)' in CT Allmand (ed), *The New Cambridge Medieval History. Volume VII, c.1415–c.1500* (Cambridge University Press 1999) 29–64, at 33.

49 Michael Mendle, *Dangerous Positions: Mixed Government, the Estates of the Realm, and the Answer to the XIX Propositions* (University of Alabama Press 1985) ch. 2.

50 'A popular King of Great Britain will be always not only easy and secure, but in effect absolute. He will be, what the British constitution alone can make any prince, the absolute monarch of a free people'. See Bolingbroke, *Political Writings*, 162.

51 Ibid 163.

but 'limited to the public good of society.'[52] While citing Locke's argument that the force of natural law did not cease in civil society, he put his own case in constitutional terms: '[T]here is something which a Parliament cannot do. A Parliament cannot annul the constitution.'[53] In Bolingbroke's view, any attempt to subvert the constitution would legitimise the nation's resistance, return the people to their natural rights, and allow them to create a new constitution. But the much-preferred option was to reform the state, or rather, bring it back to its first principles. In the *Dissertation,* Bolingbroke hinted that this should entail reforming Britain's highly irregular system of parliamentary elections and representation to make the 'rule of property' more uniform:

> [F]or the Revolution was, in many instances, and it ought to have been so in all, one of those renewals of our constitution that we have often mentioned. If it had been such, with respect to the elections of members to serve in Parliament, these elections might have been drawn back to the ancient principle on which they had been established; and the rule of property, which was followed anciently, and was perverted by innumerable changes that length of time produced, might have been restored; by which the communities to whom the right of electing was trusted, as well as the qualifications of the electors and the elected, might have been settled in proportion to the present state of things. Such a remedy might have wrought a radical cure of the evil that threatens our constitution.[54]

In the *Dissertation,* Bolingbroke repeatedly refers to the 'constitution in Church and state'.[55] For the Country party – 'the nation, speaking and acting in the discourse and conduct of particular men' – to be united, Churchmen and Protestant Dissenters had to tolerate one another.[56] It was vital for Bolingbroke to show that the Tories, under the banner of the Country party, were no longer hostile to Protestant Nonconformity. It is indeed remarkable how sympathetic the *Dissertation* is to the plight of the Protestant Dissenters, a sentiment that was far from shared by his Tory friends in parliament. We have to remember that Bolingbroke was already at this stage anticlerical, which was hinted at in the *Remarks,* but would not become fully evident until after the posthumous publication of his philosophical writings in the 1750s. In the *Dissertation,* however, Bolingbroke indicated his support of the status of the Established Church combined with extensive toleration of Protestant Nonconformity. Though his religious opinions would later become scandalous, his

52 Ibid 165, citing John Locke, *Two Treatises of Government* (Peter Laslett ed, Cambridge University Press 1960) 357–58 (§135).

53 Ibid 165.

54 Ibid 172.

55 Ibid 18, 22, 40, 44, 47, 62, 119.

56 Ibid 37, 40.

political position with respect to religion was, in fact, fairly mainstream and closer to Walpole and the Court Whigs than to the extremes of either party.

Bibliography

Blockmans W, 'Representation (Since the Thirteenth Century)' in CT Allmand (ed), *The New Cambridge Medieval History. Volume VII, c.1415–c.1500* (Cambridge University Press 1999)

Bolingbroke, Henry St John, Viscount, *Historical Writings* (Isaac Kramnick ed., University of Chicago Press, 1972)

Bolingbroke, Henry St John, Viscount, *Political Writings* (David Armitage ed., Cambridge University Press 1997)

Burns JH, 'Bolingbroke and the Concept of Constitutional Government' (1962) 10 Political Studies 264–76

Childs N, *Political Academy in Paris, 1724–1731: The Entresol and Its Members* (Voltaire Foundation 2000)

Cruickshanks E, 'Lord Cornbury, Bolingbroke and a Plan to Restore the Stuarts 1731–1735' (1986) 27 Royal Stuart Papers 1–12

Cruickshanks E, *Political Untouchables: The Tories and the '45* (Duckworth 1979)

Dickinson HT, *Bolingbroke* (Constable & Company 1970)

Dickinson HT, *Liberty and Property: Political Ideology in Eighteenth-Century Britain* (Weidenfeld & Nicholson 1977)

Gerrard C, *The Patriot Opposition to Walpole: Politics, Poetry, and National Myth, 1725–1742* (Oxford University Press 1994)

Goldgar BA, *Walpole and the Wits: The Relation of Politics to Literature, 1722–42* (University of Nebraska Press 1976)

Hayton D, 'The "Country" Interest and the Party System' in C Jones (ed), *Party and Management in Parliament, 1660–1784* (Palgrave Macmillan 1984)

Hervey J, *Some Materials Towards Memoirs of the Reign of King George II*, 3 vols (Romney Sedgwick ed, Eyre and Spottiswoode 1931)

Hicks P, 'Bolingbroke, Clarendon, and the Role of Classical Historian' (1987) 20 Eighteenth-Century Studies 445–71

Hume D, 'Of the Independency of Parliament' (1741) in *Essays: Moral, Political, and Literary* (Liberty Fund 1985)

Kramnick I (ed), Bolingbroke *Historical Writings* (University of Chicago Press 1972)

Kramnick I, *Bolingbroke and His Circle* (first published 1968, Cornell University Press 1992)

Locke J, *Two Treatises of Government* (Peter Laslett ed, Cambridge University Press 1960)

Machiavelli N, *Discourses on Livy* (The University of Chicago Press 1998)

Mallet D (ed), *The Works of the Late Right Honorable Henry St. John, Lord Viscount Bolingbroke*, 5 vols (London 1754), vol 1

McIlwain CH, *Constitutionalism Ancient and Modern* (Cornell University Press 1940)

McInnes A, 'The Political Ideas of Robert Harley' (1965) 50 History 309–22

Mendle M, *Dangerous Positions: Mixed Government, the Estates of the Realm, and the Answer to the XIX Propositions* (University of Alabama Press 1985)

Pocock JGA, 'Machiavelli, Harrington and English Political Ideologies in the Eighteenth Century' (1965) 3rd series 22 William and Mary Quarterly 549–83

Pocock JGA, *The Ancient Constitution and the Feudal Law: A Study of English Historical Thought in the Seventeenth Century. A Reissue with a Retrospect* (first published 1957, Cambridge University Press 1987)

Pocock JGA, *The Machiavellian Moment: Florentine Political Thought and the Atlantic Republican Tradition* (Princeton University Press 2003)

Robbins C, *Eighteenth-Century Commonwealthman* (Harvard University Press 1959)

Shackleton R, 'Montesquieu, Bolingbroke, and the Separation of Powers' (1949) 3 French Studies 25–38

Sherburn G (ed), *The Correspondence of Alexander Pope*, 5 vols (Oxford University Press 1956)

Skinner Q, 'The Principles and Practice of Opposition: The Case of Bolingbroke Versus Walpole' in N McKendrick (ed), *Historical Perspectives: Studies in English Thought and Society in Honour of J.H. Plumb* (Europa 1974)

Skjönsberg M, 'Ancient Constitutionalism, Fundamental Law, and Eighteenth-Century Toryism in the Septennial Act (1716) Debates' (2019) 40 History of Political Thought 270–301

Skjönsberg M, *The Persistence of Party: Ideas of Harmonious Discord in Eighteenth-Century Britain* (Cambridge University Press 2021)

Skjönsberg M, 'Patriots and the Country Party Tradition in the Eighteenth Century: The Critics of Britain's Fiscal-Military State from Robert Harley to Catharine Macaulay' (2023) 33 Intellectual History Review 83–100

Skjönsberg M, 'The Communication of Fame' in *A Cultural History of Fame in the Age of Enlightenment* (Brian Cowan ed, Bloomsbury Publishing 2025)

Womersley D, 'Lord Bolingbroke and Eighteenth-Century Historiography' (1987) 28 The Eighteenth-Century 217–34

10 Entick v Carrington

Rt Hon the Baroness Hale of Richmond DBE

> These are in His Majesty's name to authorise and require you (taking a Constable to your assistance) to make strict and diligent search for the Authors, Printers and Publishers of a Seditious and Treasonable paper intitled the North Briton, Number XLV, Saturday April 23rd 1763 printed for G Kearsley, in Ludgate Street London, and them, or any of them having found to Apprehend and Seize, together with their Papers and to bring in Safe Custody, before me, to be Examined concerning the Premises and further dealt with according to Law. In the due Execution thereof all Mayors Sheriffs Justices of the Peace Constable and all other His Majesty's Officers Civil and Military and loving Subjects to whom it may Concern are to be aiding and assisting to you as there shall be Occasion and for so doing This shall be your Warrant. Given at St James the twenty sixth day of April 1763 in the third year of His Majesty's reign.
>
> Dunk Halifax
>
> To Nathan Carrington, John Money, James Waters and Robert Blackmore, four of His Majesty's messengers in ordinary

To modern eyes, this is a truly remarkable document. It is signed not by an independent Judge or a Justice of the Peace but by Lord Halifax, one of the principal Secretaries of State to His Majesty King George III. It is addressed not to a Constable, but to the King's Messengers, whose principal role was to carry messages between the King and his officials. It is in entirely general terms, not naming either the persons to be arrested or the premises to be entered and searched, only the publication which is alleged to be 'seditious and treasonable'. It is not supported by sworn evidence, either of the publication and its seditious content or of the people believed to be associated with it.

DOI: 10.4324/9781032658698-11

10.1 Executing the warrant

What happened in consequence of the warrant was even more remarkable.[1] On 28 April 1763, five days later, a printer called Dryden Leach and his household were ordered out of their beds. Leach, his servants, and journeymen were all arrested, and his papers were carried away for inspection, even though Leach had nothing to do with Number 45 (he had printed an earlier number some months before). Rather more plausibly, the bookshop of George Kearsley, publisher of *The North Briton*, was raided at dawn, he was arrested, and his papers seized. The actual printer of Number 45, Richard Balfe, suffered the same fate. Kearsley was interrogated by the two Secretaries of State, Lord Egremont and Lord Halifax. He revealed, and Balfe confirmed, that the actual author of Number 45 was John Wilkes, Member of Parliament for Aylesbury and a well-known opponent of the government.

There are some farcical elements to this story. The Messengers turned up at Wilkes' house in Great George Street that night to arrest him, but they decided not to do so because he was so drunk. He had, in fact, been partying with his old friend Dryden Leach, who was under arrest at Messenger Blackmore's house. But they were waiting outside his house the following morning. Even so, he persuaded Blackmore to let him 'visit a friend in the Temple', promising to be back by nine o'clock. In fact, he was off to Balfe's printing house to see what had happened to Number 46 of *The North Briton*, which he had been trying to rush out in answer to the arrests. But it had already been raided. Returning to his house at mid-morning, he politely asked the messengers into his house for breakfast and equally politely declared the warrant to be 'nothing to me' and refused to be arrested. In his view, the warrant was clearly unlawful. Eventually, however, having been 'threatened with immediate violence and a regiment of guards if necessary', he surrendered his sword and was solemnly carried by sedan chair to Lord Halifax's house, which was a few yards away in Great George Street. But he still refused to answer their questions, and so he was committed to the Tower of London under close guard.

Meanwhile, his patron, Lord Temple, had secured a Writ of Habeas Corpus from the Court of Common Pleas. But it was addressed to the Messengers who had detained Wilkes in his home, and he had since passed from their custody to the Secretaries of State and then to the constables who were taking him to the Tower, so, shockingly, the Secretaries of State felt able to ignore it. His home was ransacked, papers pulled out of drawers and carried away in sealed bags, locks picked, and cabinets broken open. Lord Temple, who was there, described the scene as 'too barbarous an act for any human eye to witness'. Wilkes remained in prison until 7 May, when he appeared before the Chief Justice of the Court of Common Pleas in Westminster Hall. He made

1 The account which follows is largely taken from Peter Moore, *Life, Liberty and the Pursuit of Happiness, Britain and the American Dream 1740–1776* (Chatto & Windus 2023).

a rousing speech, invoking Magna Carta and complaining of Star Chamber tyranny:

> The Liberty of all Peers and Gentlemen, and what touches me more sensibly, that of all the middling and inferior Classes of People, who stand most in Need of Protection, is in my Case this Day to be finally decided upon: a Question of such Importance as to determine at once whether English Liberty be a Reality or a Shadow.

Well, not quite. Chief Justice Pratt ruled that his arrest had violated his Parliamentary privilege, so he was released. On his short walk back to Great George Street, he was joined by a large crowd of ordinary people shouting 'Wilkes and Liberty'. There followed a remarkable series of lawsuits as a result of which, eventually, the reality of English liberty was established.

10.2 Why the warrant was issued

But what was all the fuss about? Why were the authorities so cross with *The North Briton* and Number 45 in particular? George III had acceded to the throne in 1760 and was determined to rule as well as to reign (the previous Hanoverians were not fluent in English and were obliged to leave many things to their Ministers). Britain had been at war with France since 1756, mainly over its territories in North America. The government led by the Duke of Newcastle and William Pitt (the elder) was anxious to pursue the war. The new King and his 'Favourite', the Earl of Bute, were anxious to make peace. The resignation of Pitt in 1761 and Newcastle in 1762 made way for Bute to take their place.

Both factions were supported by weekly periodicals containing short essays or pretend letters by anonymous authors. *The Monitor: or British Freeholder*, pro-Pitt and anti-Bute, had been going since 1755, edited by Arthur Beardmore, an attorney, and sometimes written by John Entick, a prolific author and schoolmaster. Bute responded by funding *The Briton*, edited by Tobias Smollett, the popular Scottish novelist. A week after *The Briton* first appeared, another anti-Bute weekly, *The North Briton*, funded by Lord Temple, was launched. Its anonymous authors were John Wilkes and Charles Churchill. The first number began with the assertion that 'The liberty of the press is the birth-right of a Briton, and is justly esteemed the firmest bulwark of the liberties of this country. It has been the terror of all bad ministers'. Its title was a deliberate dig at Bute, a Scotsman. Week after week, it entertained its growing number of readers with irreverent attacks on Bute and his supporters. It also led the opposition to the peace treaty being negotiated with France, which was eventually concluded in February 1763. Nevertheless, Bute was so unpopular that he resigned. But the King's speech at the prorogation of Parliament on 19 April 1763 (then, as now, written by his Ministers) praised the treaty as 'so honourable to My Crown' and 'so beneficial to My People' and pleaded for 'that spirit of concord, and that obedience to the laws, which is essential to good order'.

This prompted Wilkes to respond with *The North Briton*, Number 45, published on 23 April 1763. He attacked the speech as the 'most abandoned piece of ministerial effrontery ever attempted to be imposed upon mankind', 'not to be paralleled in the annals of this country', containing 'an infamous fallacy', that prostituted 'the honour of the Crown'. The 'spirit of concord' was not to be expected from people who were being made subject to arbitrary searches and seizures. Rather, the 'spirit of liberty' should rise up in proportion to the grievance they felt – 'freedom is the English subject's prerogative'. The King and his Ministers were outraged. The general warrant was issued on 26 April. A warrant to the same effect had been issued against earlier issues of *The North Briton* in November 1762 but was used to intimidate the printers into refusing to print it rather than to arrest the author.

10.3 How the practice grew up

As Tom Hickman has observed,

> By the eighteenth century, it had become established practice for Secretaries of State to issue warrants for the arrest of persons suspected of certain crimes against the state, namely, treason, coming out of France without leave and seditious libel, and for their committal to prison pending trial.[2]

The power of the Secretaries of State to issue such warrants was upheld by the Court of King's Bench, led by Chief Justice Holt, in *R v Kendal and Row*,[3] a case about assisting a person charged with treason to escape. It was expressly applied to cases of seditious libel in *R v Derby*[4] and in *R v Erbury*.[5] Hickman points out that once the Star Chamber had been abolished in 1641 and the Licensing Act had lapsed in 1695, the law of seditious libel became the only effective means of suppressing dissent which challenged the authority of the government. The Judges sympathised with the objective and developed the law to support it. As Lord Chief Justice Holt put it in *R v Tutchin*, 'If men should not be called to account for possessing the people with an ill opinion of the Government, no Government can subsist; for it is very necessary for every Government, that the people should have a good opinion of it'.[6] The legality

2 Tom Hickman, 'Revisiting *Entick v Carrington*: Seditious Libel and State Security Laws in Eighteenth-Century England' in A Tomkins and P Scott (eds), *Entick v Carrington – 250 Years of the Rule of Law* (Hart 2015) 51.

3 (1700), 1 Ld Raym 65, 91 ER 304.

4 (1711), Fort 140, 92 ER 794.

5 (1722), 8 Mod 177, 88 ER 130.

6 (1704), Holt 424, 90 ER 1133.

of also authorising the search and seizure of documents had never been tested, but it was the logical concomitant of authorising arrest, bringing the arrested person before the Secretaries of State for examination, and committal. In the light of all this, it was reasonable for the Secretaries of State and those acting under their warrants to assume that the courts would uphold their actions. But it was not to be.

10.4 How the general warrant fared in the courts

Wilkes himself issued claims for false imprisonment and trespass against the Messengers, the Under-Secretary of State Robert Wood, the Treasury Solicitor Phillip Webb, and Lord Halifax himself. He also organised the printers and apprentices who had been arrested under the general warrant to bring claims against the Messengers. Claims by such ordinary persons were unheard of. The first two came on remarkably quickly in July 1763. One was brought by a journeyman printer who had worked for Dryden Leach. The jury returned a verdict of guilty and awarded him £300 plus costs. The next case, brought by another printer, resulted in an award of £200. After this, the messengers agreed to verdicts in the other cases for £200 each, subject to challenging the level of damages as excessive. But Chief Justice Pratt refused the motion for a new trial: the jury had been entitled to award exemplary damages, having been struck by the Secretary of State 'exercising arbitrary power, violating Magna Carta, and attempting to destroy the liberty of the kingdom, by insisting on the legality of this general warrant'. Neither side was anxious to put the question of the legality of the general warrant to the test – the Wilkes side wanted the facts to be put before the jury for maximum effect upon public opinion, and the government may have been deterred by the clearly expressed views of Chief Justice Pratt. Sufficient unto the day.

In December 1763, Wilkes himself achieved a verdict of £1000 against Under-Secretary of State Robert Wood, who had been present at the search and seizure of Wilkes' papers, although he had not been named in the warrant or seized the papers himself. The jury heard evidence of how the messengers had piled all Wilkes' private papers that they could find into a sack without an inventory and brought in a smith to open locked drawers and bureaus. Lord Halifax had to admit that he had issued the warrant three days before he had the information that Wilkes was involved.

Also in December 1763, Dryden Leach obtained a verdict against the Messengers for £400 damages and costs. This time, the verdict was challenged, thus raising the question of the legality of general warrants. But the government eventually dropped the challenge, ostensibly because the Messengers could not have been acting in obedience to the warrant because Leach was not the printer of Number 45 of *The North Briton*. But the real reason was probably the clear view expressed by Lord Mansfield, Lord Chief Justice of the Court of King's Bench, and the other Judges that general warrants were unlawful – because they left it to the Messengers to decide whom to arrest. This, coupled with the risk of picking on the wrong person, made general warrants pretty impracticable. No more were issued, although their legality was never formally decided. But the case of *Leach v Money, Watson and Blackmore*[7] is referred to in *Entick v Carrington*[8] as 'the case of General Warrants'.

10.5 Entick v Carrington

So what was *Entick v Carrington* all about? It was not about a general warrant of the sort used against *The North Briton*, but a more specific warrant, issued on 6 November 1762, by Lord Halifax, targeting the *Monitor: or British Freeholder*:

> These are in His Majesty's name to authorise and require you, taking a constable to your assistance, to make strict and diligent search for John Entick, the author, or one concerned in writing of several weekly very seditious papers, intitled the Monitor, or British Freeholder, No. 357, 358, 360, 373, 376, 378, 379 and 380, printed for J. Wilson and J. Fell in Pater Noster Row, which contains gross and scandalous reflections and invectives upon his majesty's government, and upon both houses of parliament; and him, having found you are to seize and apprehend, and to bring, together with his books and papers, in safe custody before me to be examined concerning the premisses and further dealt with according to law.

Halifax also issued warrants against Arthur Beardmore and his clerk, David Meredith, the publishers Isaac Wilson and John Fell, a printer, John Medley, and a former editor, Jonathan Scott (who was never arrested). Entick's and Beardmore's premises were searched, and papers seized. They and Meredith were bailed after six days, and the others a few days later. They were released from their recognisances in June 1763 and never prosecuted. The aim of this – and other similar warrants – was to intimidate and suppress publication rather than to bring prosecutions.

John Entick, Arthur Beardmore, and the others all brought claims. Beardmore's claim against the messengers for false imprisonment and trespass to goods was tried in May 1764. The jury was told to assess damages on the basis that 'the trespass and imprisonment committed under the warrant could not be justified by any plea whatsoever' and awarded £1000. In the same month, a motion for a new trial on the ground that the damages were excessive was rejected by the full court of the Court of Common Pleas, presided over by Chief Justice Pratt: see *Beardmore v Carrington, Watson, Ardran and*

7 (1765), 19 St Tr 1001, 1 Blk W 555, 96 ER 320.
8 (1765), 19 St Tr 1029, 2 Wils KB 274, 95 ER 807.

Blackmore.[9] The liability of the Messengers and Lord Halifax was joint and several:

> [S]o the Court must consider these damages as given against Lord Halifax: and can we say that £1000 are monstrous damages as against him who has granted an illegal warrant to a messenger who enters into a man's house, and prys into all his secret and private affairs, and carries him from his house and business, and imprisons him for six days. It is an unlawful power assumed by a great minister of State. Can any body say that a guinea per diem is sufficient damages in this extraordinary case, which concerns the liberty of every one of the King's subjects? We cannot say that the damages of £1000 are enormous.

Wilson and Fell's claims against the Messengers were heard in June 1764, and they were awarded £600. Entick's claim against the Messengers was heard in July 1764, and he was awarded £300. Claims by Entick, Beardmore, Meredith, Fall, and Wilson against Lord Halifax were heard in December 1764, and they were awarded £20, £500, £200, £40, and £10, respectively (taking account of the sums already recovered in the actions against the Messengers to avoid double recovery). Beardmore may have achieved more than the others because of the interference with his practice as a lawyer and the seizure of privileged documents. Meredith may have achieved more because he had not sued the Messengers.

Strikingly, in none of these cases was the legality of the warrant and its execution put in issue by the parties. But in *Entick v Carrington*, the jury itself did so by returning a special verdict. This set out the facts they had found in great detail but explained that they were 'altogether ignorant' of whether the defendants were guilty of trespass and the plaintiff ought to maintain his action against them and prayed 'the advice of the Court thereupon'. If they were guilty and the plaintiff ought to maintain his action, they assessed the damages as £300; if they were not guilty, or the plaintiff ought not to maintain his action, then the defendants were not guilty. This time, Chief Justice Pratt, who was elevated to the peerage as Lord Camden in 1765, insisted that the case be thoroughly argued – as he said when giving the judgment of the court 'the public, as well as the parties, have a right to our opinion'. So it was argued before the court twice in 1765 before judegment was given in November.

10.6 The judgment in *Entick v Carrington*

The judgment of the Court, given by Lord Camden, does indeed deserve to be regarded as a 'leading work in the history of the Constitution'. It is both

9 (1764), 2 Wils KB 244, 95 ER 790.

erudite and forceful. The report in Serjeant Wilson's reports,[10] readily accessible to subscribers to the English Reports,[11] gives a full account of the jury's verdict and the arguments of counsel but contains an abbreviated account of the judgment. A fuller account, taken from the judge's own notes, appears in State Trials.[12]

The Messengers had raised two defences. The first was section 6 of the Constables Protection Act 1750, which is still in force today, and protects 'any constable, headborough or other officer' or 'any person or persons acting by his order or in his aid' from liability for 'anything done in obedience to any warrant under the hand and seal of any Justice of the Peace' even if it turns out that the Justice did not have the power to issue it. The defence argued that a Justice of the Peace was the equivalent of the ancient office of conservator of the peace and the Secretary of State was a conservator. The second defence was that the warrant was lawful in any event.

Lord Camden, therefore, begins by setting out the four questions which arose upon the special verdict:

(1) Whether, as Secretary of State or privy counsellor, or on any other basis, Lord Halifax counted as a 'conservator of the peace'.
(2) If he did, whether he was 'within the equity' of Section 6 of the Constables Protection Act 1750.
(3) Whether the defendants acted in obedience to the warrant.
(4) The 'great question' of whether the warrant to seize and carry away the plaintiff's papers is lawful.

He makes it clear at the outset, and later, that the court is in no position to overrule the judgments of the King's Bench in *Kendal and Row*, *Derby* and *Earbury* confirming the power of a Secretary of State to commit for some crimes, 'even though we are persuaded that the commencement of it was erroneous'. However, when answering question (1), he comprehensively demolishes the argument for the existence of such a power prior to those judgments, either as a Secretary of State or as a privy counsellor. He points out, among other matters, that if it had existed, it would have been mentioned by Lord Chief Justice Coke when giving his account of the office of secretary in the Petition of Right of 1628, in the Habeas Corpus Act 1641, and in the case of the Seven Bishops tried for seditious libel in 1688.[13] Somehow or other, the Secretary of State had assumed the power as a transfer from the power of the King. As Secretary of State or privy counsellor he was clearly not a conservator at common law. If

10 (1765), 2 Wils KB 274.
11 95 ER 807.
12 19 St Tr 1029.
13 12 St Tr 183.

he had borrowed the right of conservatorship from the King himself, so great a person could not be within the meaning of the Constables Protection Act.

But, for the sake of argument, he assumes the Secretary of State to be a conservator for the purpose of answering question (2). Obviously, he is not within the express words of the statute, for he is not a Justice of the Peace. Nor is he within its meaning by analogy because the conservator does nothing that Justices of the Peace do. Nor is he within the policy of the Act because he did not need its protection. Thus, neither the Secretary of State nor the Messengers are within the meaning of the Act.

Question (3) is dealt with very quickly. In any event, the messengers were only protected by the Act if they had acted in obedience to the warrant. And they had not. They had not taken a constable with them. And they had taken the plaintiff to be examined, not by Lord Halifax himself, but by Mr Lovell Stanhope, his assistant. If Lord Halifax were a magistrate, he would not be able to delegate his powers to his clerk. The Judge is clearly upset that, having established the practice of issuing such warrants, the Secretary of State had delegated its execution to his minions. Question (3) would, of course, have been a complete answer to the defence based on the Constables Protection Act, but the Court chose to answer questions (1) and (2) at considerable length as well.

Question (4) 'though it is not the most difficult, it is the most interesting'. Lord Camden emphasises the breadth of the claimed power. It is 'an execution on all his papers'.

> His house is rifled; his most valuable secrets are taken out of his possession, before the paper for which he is charged is found to be criminal before any competent jurisdiction, and before he is convicted of either writing, publishing or being concerned in the paper.

And if he turns out to be innocent, he is 'as destitute of remedy' as the guilty. Such a power 'is not supported by one single citation from any law book extant'.

Instead, it is argued that such warrants had been issued frequently since the Revolution of 1688; that they are like warrants to search for stolen goods; that they have been executed without resistance upon many printers, booksellers, and authors; and that 'this power is essential to government and the only means of quieting clamors and sedition'.

He demolishes each of these arguments in turn.

'If it is the law, it will be found in our books. If it is not to be found there, it is not law'. This might be thought of as a very conservative approach to the incremental development of the common law – after all, if arrest and committal are allowed, why not a search for and seizure of the offending material? But this warrant allowed much more than that.

'By the laws of England, every invasion of private property, be it ever so minute, is a trespass. No man can set his foot upon my ground without my licence, but he is liable to an action, though the damage be nothing'. If he cannot show a legal justification, in statute or the common law, the plaintiff must have judgment.

Furthermore, the invasion of privacy makes it worse:

> Papers are the owner's goods and chattels: they are his dearest property, and are so far from enduring a seizure, that they will hardly bear an inspection; and though the eye cannot by the law of England be guilty of a trespass, yet where private papers are removed and carried away, the secret nature of those goods will be an aggravation of the trespass, and demand more considerable damages in that respect.

This case is nothing like a warrant to search and seize stolen goods. There are many procedural safeguards. The owner is entitled to his goods back but only after the thief has been convicted. Inventing similar safeguards for these warrants 'would be, not judgment, but legislation' – another interesting comment on the limits of judicial law-making.

As to practice since the Revolution, if it began then, it began too late to be law now (another reference to the ancient law books). As an aside, the Revolution was not the source of our liberties. It 'restored this constitution to its first principles. It did no more. It did not enlarge the liberty of the subject; but gave it a better security. It neither widened nor contracted the foundation, but repaired, and perhaps added a buttress or two to the fabric'.

The fact that no one until now had resisted such warrants is no answer:

> There has been a submission of guilt and poverty to power and the terror of punishment. But it would be strange doctrine to assert that all the people of this land are bound to acknowledge that to be universal law, which a few criminal booksellers have been afraid to dispute.

The Star Chamber had issued warrants, and the Licensing Act had provided for them. He strongly suspected that the present warrants were modelled on those permitted by the Licensing Act, but that had lapsed, and he could find no authority that such a power could be justified by the common law.

As to the argument that such a power was necessary, then if the legislature thought it necessary, they would revive the Licensing Act, but they had not done so.

> And with respect to the argument of state necessity, or a distinction that has been aimed at between state offences and others, the common law does not understand that kind of reasoning, nor do our books take notice of any such distinctions.

The Ship Money judges[14] were impeached for holding that state necessity would justify the raising of money without the consent of Parliament and that the King was the judge of that necessity. If the King could not do it, then surely the Judges could not do so either.

As to the argument that such a power was useful as a means of detecting offenders by discovering evidence, 'it is very certain, that the law obligeth no man to accuse himself; because the necessary means of compelling self-accusation, falling upon the innocent as well as the guilty, would be both cruel and unjust; and it would seem that the search for evidence is disallowed upon the same principle. And even if there were such a power, this crime ought to be an exception, because the search is unnecessary. It is committed in open day-light, and in the face of the world; every act of publication makes new proof'.

Having disposed of all the arguments, the Court were all agreed that the warrant to seize and carry away the party's papers in the case of a seditious libel was illegal and void.

This did not mean that he was an advocate of libels.

> All civilised governments have punished calumny with severity; and with reason; for these compositions debauch the manners of the people; they excite a spirit of disobedience; and enervate the authority of government; they provoke and excite the passions of the people against their rulers, and rulers oftentimes against the people.

10.7 Aftermath

The immediate aftermath for Number 45 of *The North Briton* and its author was not auspicious. The King and his ministers were out for vengeance, although Wilkes enjoyed the vociferous support of the public. Number 45 was condemned in Parliament as 'a false, scandalous and seditious libel' and sentenced to a symbolic burning outside the Royal Exchange. But the attempt to do this provoked a riot. Parliament voted to deprive Wilkes of his seat. He fled to Paris before his trial for seditious libel, at which he was inevitably found guilty. He was summoned to appear before the Court of King's Bench, and when he did not appear, the Court pronounced him an outlaw. It was some years before he was able to redeem his fortunes.

So, it is hard to see the saga as a triumph for freedom of speech. But it certainly did much to alert not only the British public but also the people of the American colonies to the importance of free speech among the liberties of the subject. The furore raised by Number 45 and Wilkes' resistance caught the imagination of the American public. It may be no accident that the First

14 The seven Judges who had found for the King in the case of *R v Hampden* (1637), 3 St Tr 825.

Amendment to the Constitution of the United States of America provides that 'Congress shall make no law . . . abridging the freedom of speech, or of the press'.

More plausibly, it was a triumph for freedom from improper search and seizure. The Fourth Amendment accurately responds to the concerns raised in *Leach v Money* and *Entick v Carrington*:

> The right of the people to be secure in their persons, houses, papers, and effects, against unreasonable searches and seizures, shall not be violated, and no warrants shall issue, but upon probably cause, supported by oath or affirmation, and particularly describing the place to be searched, and the persons or things to be seized.

The same concerns are reflected in article 8(1) of the European Convention on Human Rights:[15]

> Everyone has the right to respect for his private and family life, his home and his correspondence.

Until the Human Rights Act 1998 turned the Convention rights into rights in UK law, the common law had not developed a tort of invasion of privacy. But it is clear from Lord Camden's judgment that where another tort was committed, the invasion of privacy involved was a seriously aggravating factor.

But above all, the saga showed that the government and its ministers were not above the law. There was no defence of state necessity unless Parliament legislated for it. No-one argued that Lord Halifax, and those acting at his command, enjoyed the immunity from legal action that the King himself enjoyed. Until the Crown Proceedings Act 1947 made it possible to sue the Crown, an individual public servant would be put up as defendant to a claim.

As Sir Stephen Sedley has put it, 'the conflict and settlement of the 17th century had resolved into Parliament's authority to speak the final word on what the law was to be'. The events of the 1760s recognised the 'judges' authority to speak the final word on what the law was'.[16] They made it clear, as it may not have been before, that there are two fundamental principles in the British Constitution: the sovereignty of Parliament, yes, but also the rule of law. Parliament and the Judges are sovereign in their different spheres.

15 Article 12 of the Universal Declaration of Human Rights 1948 and article 17 of the International Covenant on Civil and Political Rights 1966.

16 Sir Stephen Sedley, The Denning Lecture, *New Corn from Old Fields: Ministerial Government, History and the Law* (Lincoln's Inn, November 2012).

Bibliography

Hickman T, 'Revisiting *Entick v Carrington*: Seditious Libel and State Security Laws in Eighteenth-Century England' in A Tomkins and P Scott (eds), *Entick v Carrington – 250 Years of the Rule of Law* (Hart 2015)

Moore P, *Life, Liberty and the Pursuit of Happiness, Britain and the American Dream 1740–1776* (Chatto & Windus 2023)

Sedley S, 'The Denning Lecture' in *New Corn From Old Fields: Ministerial Government, History and the Law* (Lincoln's Inn, November 2012)

11 William Blackstone's *Commentaries on the Laws of England*

*Max Skjönsberg**

William Blackstone (1723–1780) has become synonymous with Whiggery,[1] which is curious since it is indisputable that he absorbed and contributed to the Toryism that dominated the University of Oxford in the eighteenth century. As a longstanding Fellow of All Souls, he was heavily involved in Tory electoral politics as it concerned Oxford, both at the university and parliamentary levels.[2] One of his early publications, *The Pantheon: A Vision* (1747), was a defence of High Anglicanism and associated Protestant Dissent with the 'good old cause', or civil-war republicanism, much as he would do in his *Commentaries on the Laws of England* (4 vols., 1765–1769). There is no evidence of Blackstone ever espousing Jacobite sympathies, even though he had friends who did, as sympathy for the Stuarts was rife at Oxford as late as the 1750s and even beyond. Edward Gibbon, a student at the university in the 1750s wrote in his autobiography that the 'constitutional toasts [at Magdalen College] were not expressive of the most lively loyalty for the house of Hanover'.[3] The country gentleman Sir Roger Newdigate was Blackstone's closest political friend. Both Newdigate and Blackstone were fiercely anti-Whig and intimately involved in the political networks of the oppositional Tory party in the middle decades of the eighteenth century. Blackstone was part of the group of Tories who chose Newdigate as a new MP for Oxford University after Lord Cornbury – Clarendon's grandson, to whom Bolingbroke addressed his *Letter on the Spirit of Patriotism* (1736) – was elevated to the House of Lords in 1750, and it was indeed Blackstone who approached Newdigate about the prospect.[4]

After the accession of George III in 1760, the proscription of the Tories was ended, and Oxford became loyalist. In 1761, Blackstone sought to

* The Hamilton School of Classical and Civic Education, University of Florida.

1 David Lieberman, *The Province of Legislation Determined: Legal Theory in Eighteenth-Century Britain* (Cambridge University Press 1989) 58.

2 Wilfrid Prest, *William Blackstone: Law and Letters in the Eighteenth Century* (Oxford University Press 2008) ch. 6; RJ Robson, *The Oxfordshire Election of 1754: A Study in the Interplay of City, County and University Politics* (Oxford University Press 1949).

3 Edward Gibbon, *Memoirs of My Life* (Betty Radice ed, Penguin 1990) 80, 90–91.

4 Ian Dolittle, *William Blackstone: An Autobiography* (Self-published 2001) 16.

DOI: 10.4324/9781032658698-12

convince his former pupil William Petty Fitzmaurice, 2nd Earl of Shelburne, that their friend William King, the diehard Jacobite of St Mary Hall, Oxford, had become completely reconciled to the Hanoverian regime under the new king.[5] Blackstone was himself eager to take advantage of the opportunities the new reign had to offer to Tories such as himself. In fact, he had been gifted £200, equalling his annual professorial salary, by George III when he was Prince of Wales for sending his lectures to his tutor and mentor, John Stuart, 3rd Earl of Bute.[6] Blackstone was more of a careerist than his friend Newdigate, which was not surprising since he unlike Newdigate did not possess a country estate. In 1761, Blackstone became a member of Parliament for the rotten borough Hindon in Wiltshire, entirely thanks to his acquaintance with Shelburne. The government, via Bute, spent £2,000 on having Blackstone elected. Upon taking his seat in the House of Commons, Blackstone wrote to Newdigate and thanked him for 'approving the Steps I have lately made into public Life', assuring him that he would retain his independence in parliament and 'follow his own Sentiments in such Matters as shall come before Him'.[7]

Blackstone's career in Parliament was relatively short and mediocre. When speaking against the Rockingham administration's repeal of the Stamp Act in 1766, he denied the link between taxation and representation since the Commons did not raise taxes alone but in conjunction with the monarch and the Lords. He told the House that he 'had rather preserve our old constitution than have a new one of their [modern political architects'] erection'.[8] In February 1768, he joined Newdigate in support of William Beckford's bill against bribery and corruption at elections. But his independent temperament, what he had viewed as the central principle of the opposition to establishment Whiggery, made him unsuitable for the partisan climate of the 1760s, during which the Tories, who had long been a dwindling force, became an irrelevant one in parliamentary terms. Blackstone left Parliament in 1770 and devoted himself to what became a more distinguished career as a judge.

It is as a scholar and the author of the *Commentaries on the Laws of England* that Blackstone was primarily known in his lifetime, and his fame today rests entirely on this work. The first professor to teach English law as an academic subject at university as opposed to as a professional one in the Inns of Court in London, Blackstone's magnum opus was based on a lecture course he delivered at Oxford from 1753, as Vinerian Professor of Law from 1758. By his death in 1780, the work had seen eight English, six Irish, and three American

5 David Greenwood, *William King: Tory and Jacobite* (Oxford University Press 1969) 301.
6 Prest (n 2) 162–63.
7 Blackstone to Newdigate, 1 May 1761. Warwickshire County Record Office, Newdigate MSS CR 136/B. 1497.
8 *Parliamentary Diaries of Nathaniel Ryder, 1764–7* (PDG Thomas ed), in *Volume 7: Camden Miscellany*, vol XXIII (Cambridge University Press 1969) 268.

editions, and many more would follow. The *Commentaries* seemed to provide justification for the emerging 'Whig' ideology of parliamentary sovereignty, which was surprising considering Blackstone's background as an Oxford Tory.[9] Already in his *Analysis of the Laws of England* (1756), Blackstone had formulated his well-known theory of parliamentary sovereignty: 'In all States there is an absolute SUPREME Power, to which the right of Legislation belongs; and which, by the singular Constitution of these Kingdoms, is vested in the King, Lords, and Commons'.[10] The purpose of statute law, made by King, Lords, and Commons in Parliament, was 'to supply the Defects, or amend what is amiss, of the Unwritten Law [i.e. the common law]'.[11] In the *Commentaries*, Blackstone wrote notoriously that the King-in-Parliament was indeed 'the place where that absolute despotic power, which must in all governments reside somewhere, is entrusted by the constitution of these kingdoms'. According to Blackstone, Parliament could 'change and create afresh even the constitution of the kingdom and of parliaments themselves', as illustrated by the Septennial Act (1716). In short, Parliament could 'do every thing that is not naturally impossible'.[12]

In his discussion of parliamentary sovereignty, Blackstone referred to the authority of Edward Coke, who at least in one place held that 'the power and jurisdiction of the Parliament, for making laws in proceeding by Bill, it is so transcendent and absolute, as it cannot be confined either for causes or persons within any bounds'.[13] Blackstone noted that it would be 'too bold' to speak of 'the omnipotence of parliament' as Coke had done, presumably because of its religious connotation, but the key point was that no authority *on earth* could undo what Parliament had done. In this context, he went on to discuss John Locke's theory of underlying popular sovereignty, and more specifically, the idea that the people retained the power to alter the legislature if it acted contrary to its trust that ultimately tied them to the voters. Although this notion may be just in theory, Blackstone thought that it would be impossible to adopt in practice. If the people took back the power they had transmitted to the government it would entail the entire dissolution of the state and a return to the 'original state of equality', that is to say, to the state of nature.[14] Since no human law could presuppose the annihilation of all positive law, if the people took back their power from Parliament, it would mean the destruction of the entire constitution. The Glorious Revolution could only

9 See JCD Clark, *English Society, 1660–1832: Religion, Ideology and Politics during the Ancien Régime* (first published 1985, 2nd edn, Cambridge University Press 2000) esp. 241–49.

10 William Blackstone, *An Analysis of the Laws of England* (Oxford University Press 1756) 2.

11 Ibid 4.

12 William Blackstone, *Commentaries on the Laws of England*, 4 vols (Wilfrid Prest gen. ed, Oxford University Press 2017) I, 107. See also ibid 41.

13 Edward Coke, *The Fourth Part of the Institutes of the Lawes of England* (London 1669) 36.

14 Blackstone *Commentaries* I (n 12) 108. This was only a theoretical move by Blackstone as he did not think that there had ever been a time when there was no society. See ibid 38.

be justified because of the compromise fiction that James II had abdicated the throne, which became vacant.[15] But the event did not amount to a return to a Lockean state of nature as the Convention Parliament emphasised that James II had only ***endeavoured*** to subvert the constitution and abdicated before succeeding.

Yet Blackstone's theory of sovereignty was not unitary in the Hobbesian sense; indeed, for him, liberty was ensured by the independence of the judiciary, the separation of the legislative and executive powers, and the equilibrium among the different branches of the legislature (i.e., King, Lords, and Commons). 'In all tyrannical governments', wrote Blackstone in a deliberate echo of Montesquieu,

> the supreme magistracy, or the right both of *making* and of *enforcing* the laws, is vested in one and the same man, or one and the same body of men; and wherever these two powers are united together, there can be no public liberty.[16]

Thanks to its mixed constitution, both the idea and practice of political liberty flourished in Britain.[17] Moreover, the 'true excellence of the English constitution' consisted in its system of mutual checks:

> In the legislature, the people are a check upon the nobility, and the nobility a check upon the people; by the mutual privileges of rejecting what the other has resolved: while the king is a check upon both [via the royal veto], which preserves the executive power from encroachments. And this very executive power is again checked, and kept within due bounds by the two houses, through the privilege they have of enquiring into, impeaching, and punishing the conduct (not indeed of the king, which would destroy his constitutional independence; but, which is more beneficial to the public) of his evil and pernicious counsellors.[18]

Despite Blackstone's reputation for 'conservatism', reformers had high expectations on his work. As Catharine Macaulay wrote in the first volume of her *History of England*, published in 1763: 'I take this opportunity of mentioning the late excellent institution in the university of Oxford; of a profession of the common law of England; which, if carried on with the same ability and spirit

15 Ibid 101.

16 Ibid 98; Montesquieu, *The Spirit of the Laws* (Anne M Cohler, Basia C Miller and Harold S Stone eds, Cambridge University Press 1989) 157. See also Howard L Lubert, 'Sovereignty and Liberty in William Blackstone's *Commentaries on the Laws of the England*' (2010) 72 The Review of Politics 271–97, esp. 287–91.

17 Blackstone, *Commentaries* I (n 12) 86.

18 Ibid 103. See also ibid 40–41.

that Dr. Blackstone has begun it, must be productive of the greatest public utility'.[19] Would she have been disappointed considering Blackstone's theory of parliamentary sovereignty and his dismissal of Lockean popular sovereignty? Most likely, both yes and no. Macaulay's expectations may have been based on *A Discourse on the Study of the Law; Being an Introductory Lecture* (1758). In this work, Blackstone approvingly cited Montesquieu's singling out of Britain as the only country where 'political or civil liberty is the very scope and end of the constitution'.[20] Crucially, the *Discourse* included critical reflections on the state of politics: 'The mischiefs that have been arisen to the public from inconsiderate alterations in our laws, are too obvious to be called into question'. The problem was that uneducated legislators mistreated the common law with 'all the rage of modern improvement'.[21]

The *Discourse* was incorporated into the introduction to the *Commentaries*, and there and elsewhere, Blackstone amplified his critical reflections on recent politics. He referred to the commonplace that Britain's liberties 'can only be lost or destroyed by the folly or demerits of its owner: the legislature'.[22] In a classic Country Tory manner, he went on to express his concerns about the growth of crown patronage and what he perceived as the Crown's increasing influence over Parliament, the expansion of the national debt, and the maintenance of the standing army in peacetime. Fortunately and crucially, however, the people had five rights to defend their liberties against defective legislation passed by Parliament: political representation, restrictions on the royal prerogative, the right to justice, the right to petition the monarch and Parliament, and the right to bear arms for self-defence and to resist oppression.[23] Furthermore, even though Blackstone represented a small borough, he was critical of great men having 'a larger share in elections than is consistent with general liberty'. Most significantly, he suggested that 'if any alteration might be wished or suggested in the present frame of parliaments, it should be in favour of a more complete representation of the people'.[24] By studying the available student notes of Blackstone's lectures, Wilfrid Prest has shown that his oral delivery was more outspoken than the printed version of the *Commentaries*. Though this should not come as a surprise, it is interesting to note that his 1761 lecture reflected critically on the 'prodigious influence' of the crown since the Glorious Revolution, whereas the *Commentaries* distinguished between the crown and the 'corrupt and servile influence from those who are intrusted with its

19 Catharine Macaulay, *Political Writings* (Max Skjönsberg ed, Cambridge University Press 2023) 11.

20 William Blackstone, *A Discourse on the Study of the Law; Being an Introductory Lecture* (Oxford University Press 1758) 4; Montesquieu (n 16) 156.

21 Blackstone (n 20) 10.

22 Blackstone, *Commentaries* I (n 12) 86. See also ibid 107.

23 Ibid 96–97. See also Stephen Skinner, 'Blackstone's Support for the Militia' (2000) 44 American Journal of Legal History 1–18.

24 Blackstone, *Commentaries* I (n 12) 113.

authority', and added a note of confidence in George III's 'veneration for the free constitution of Britain'.[25]

As David Lieberman has aptly noted, what looks like panegyrics in the *Commentaries* often carries a critical edge.[26] We may add that the reason why Blackstone argued that the English law had reached its 'theoretical perfection' after the Restoration and during the reign of Charles II – the time when 'the true balance between liberty and prerogative was happily established by *law*' – rather than after the Glorious Revolution, was doubtless because he was unhappy with the drift of parliamentary legislation in Hanoverian Britain.[27] Alongside the Habeas Corpus Act (1679) – 'that second *magna carta*' – Blackstone listed the Triennial Act (1664) as great achievements of the Restoration. In agreement with Bolingbroke and in anticipation of Burke, Blackstone argued that although the Glorious Revolution 'in appearance and nominally, reduced the strength of the executive power . . . the crown has, gradually and imperceptibly, gained almost as much in influence, as it has apparently lost in prerogative'.[28] This would only surprise us if we forget that his ideological background was oppositional Toryism rather than establishment Whiggism.

Jeremy Bentham was wide of the mark, then, when he derided the author of the *Commentaries* as 'everything as it should be' Blackstone, even if he used Blackstone's own words against him.[29] We have seen that Blackstone wanted a more complete representation of the people, and he remarked that it was a 'misfortune' that so many abandoned villages remained represented.[30] But his central objective was to improve the quality of parliamentary legislation by educating British legislators, especially about the common law and the rights of the people.[31] Rather than pitching his work to future lawyers exclusively, he specifically addressed those 'ambitious of representing their country in parliament', and sought to give them a sense of their responsibility.[32] The conclusion to the entire work summarises the spirit of the *Commentaries*:

> The Protection of THE LIBERTY OF BRITAIN is a Duty which they (such Gentleman of the Kingdom as are delegated by their Country to

25 Ibid 216; Prest (n 2) 218–19.

26 Lieberman (n 1) 58–60.

27 Blackstone, *Commentaries* IV (n 12) 282–83. See also Robert Willman, 'Blackstone and the "Theoretical Perfection" of English Law in the Reign of Charles I' (1983) 26 Historical Journal 39–70.

28 Blackstone, *Commentaries* IV (n 12) 284.

29 Bentham, *A Fragment on Government* (London 1776) xxxviii–xxix. See also Philip Schofield, 'The "Least Repulsive" Work on a "Repulsive Subject": Jeremy Bentham on William Blackstone's *Commentaries on the Laws of England*' in Anthony Page and Wilfrid Prest (eds), *Blackstone and His Critics* (Oxford University Press 2018) 23–40.

30 Blackstone, *Commentaries* I (n 12) 114.

31 See John F Stinneford, 'The Original Meaning of "Unusual": The Eighth Amendment as a Bar to Cruel Innovation' (2008) 102 Northwestern University Law Review 1739–825, 1790–92.

32 Blackstone, *Commentaries* I (n 12) 12.

> Parliament) owe to themselves, who enjoy it; to their Ancestors, who transmitted it down; and to Posterity, who will claim at their Hands this, the best Birth-Right, and noblest Inheritance, of Mankind.[33]

A key part of Blackstone's intention was thus to remind future legislators of the antiquity of England's laws and liberties. His introductory lecture highlighted that parliaments in some shape had existed since Saxon times and in its present form for at least 500 years.[34] Like the *Commentaries,* the lecture was replete with references to 'our Alfred and Edward', 'our immemorial customs', and 'the free constitution of Britain'.[35] In 1759, Blackstone had published an edition of Magna Carta (1215), along with the Charter of the Forest (1217), 'the two great charters of liberties'.[36] In his introductory discourse, he wrote that

> it is agreed by all our historians that the great charter of king John was for the most part compiled from the antient [sic] customs of the realm, or the laws of Edward the Confessor; by which they usually mean the old common law, which was established under our Saxon princes, before the rigors of feodal [sic] tenure and other hardships were imported from the continent by the kings of the norman line.[37]

The language of ancient constitutionalism remained at the heart of the *Commentaries.* The reign of Charles II represented the restoration of the 'ancient constitution' as well as 'the complete restitution of English liberty, for the first time, since its total abolition at the [Norman] conquest'.[38] For Blackstone, common law was composed of ancient customs, 'used time out of mind', collected by Alfred and consolidated by Edgar and Edward the Confessor. Accordingly:

> the liberties of Englishmen are not (as some arbitrary writers would represent them) mere infringements of the king's prerogative, extorted from our princes by taking advantage of their weakness; but a restoration of that antient constitution, of which our ancestors had been defrauded by the art and finesse of the Norman lawyers, rather than deprived by the force of the Norman arms.[39]

33 Ibid IV, 285.
34 Blackstone (n 20) 9. See also idem, *Commentaries* I (n 12) 99.
35 Blackstone (n 20) 2.
36 Blackstone, *The Great Charter and Charter of the Forest, with Other Authentic Instruments* (Oxford University Press1759) lxxvi.
37 Ibid vii.
38 Blackstone, *Commentaries* IV (n 12) 282.
39 Ibid II (n 12) 34.

It is unclear which 'arbitrary writers' he referred to, but it is plausible that he had the royalist historian Robert Brady (1627–1700) in mind, which underlines the differences between seventeenth-century and eighteenth-century Toryism. Blackstone's own favourite Restoration historian was William Prynne (1600–1669), whose works he collected.[40] Blackstone's ancient constitutionalism would be radicalised by his second successor as Vinerian law professor at Oxford, Richard Wooddeson, who told his students in the 1770s that the ancient Britons had had legislative assemblies 'of the democratical kind'.[41] In any event, Blackstone's ancient constitutionalism was exactly the kind of language Bentham would find absurd and criticise in his early *Comment on the Commentaries*, published posthumously in 1928, and *A Fragment on Government* (1776). But we should note that Blackstone highlighted, like his predecessors John Selden and Matthew Hale, whom he greatly admired, that the common law had been continuously improved and, therefore, changed.

Blackstone did not justify English law solely on the basis of history but also of natural law. In a word, Blackstone agreed with Edward Coke and other early-modern English common lawyers that law must conform to rationality and the natural order, but rather than equating reason with universal, abstract principles, the common lawyers 'identified it with a specific set of historically and culturally situated legal rules, the common law of England'.[42] Long usage was thus the most dependable basis for evaluating the law, and the same applied to constitutional procedures. Blackstone maintained, for instance, that if a tenant of a farm had continually crossed someone else's land by 'immemorial usage', the tenant developed a *right* of way across that land.[43]

Yet the natural law element remains a contested aspect of Blackstone's thought, and parliamentary sovereignty plays a more decisive role in the parts of the *Commentaries* that deal with the mixed and balanced constitution. His emphasis on parliamentary sovereignty would put Blackstone on a collision course with reformers and Patriots on both sides of the Atlantic as the imperial crisis intensified in the 1760s and 1770s. As we have seen, Blackstone had cited Coke to support his argument in favour of parliamentary sovereignty, but this appeared to contradict Coke's notion that the common law could overrule statute, as famously expressed in *Dr Bonham's Case*,[44] cited by protesting colonists.[45] This became a central issue in the third quarter of the

40 For Prynne, see esp. CC Weston and JR Greenberg, *Subjects and Sovereigns: The Grand Controversy Over Legal Sovereignty in Stuart England* (Cambridge University Press 1981) ch. 5.

41 Richard Wooddeson, *A Systematical View of the Laws of England; As Treated of in a Course of Vinerian Lectures, Read at Oxford, During a Series of Years, Commencing in Michaelmas Term, 1777*, 3 vols (London 1792–93) I, 6.

42 Stinneford (n 31) 1770.

43 Ibid 1774.

44 (1610) 8 Co. Rep. 107a, 118a.

45 Lieberman (n 1) ch. 1. See also John Phillip Reid, *Constitutional History of the American Revolution*, 4 vols (University of Wisconsin Press 1986–95).

eighteenth century, especially as the Americans in the 1760s objected to the British Parliament's right to tax them and were supported by English merchants, Whigs, and reformers (often called 'radicals').[46] The American question put Blackstone firmly on the side of authority: he belonged to the minority in Parliament who voted against the Rockingham ministry's repeal of the Stamp Act in 1766, and we have already seen that he spoke against repeal.[47] In the same year, a pamphlet that argued for Parliament's right to legislate for and tax the Americans supported its case with quotations from the first volume of the *Commentaries*.[48]

J. C. D. Clark has argued that Blackstone's American reception focused on him as 'restructuring [the law] in the interest of the monarchy and the Established Church'.[49] But Blackstone was, in fact, an authority cited by both sides. Indeed, at least 16 subscribers to the first American edition of the *Commentaries* (1772) would later sign the Declaration of Independence.[50] In Britain, a 1766 pamphlet arguing not only for more equal representation in Britain but also for the inclusion of America quoted Blackstone in support of the notion that it had formerly been the practice to admit towns into a share in the legislature as they grew richer and more populous by trade.[51] In the 1780s, Blackstone became one of the main constitutional authorities for the reformist Society of Constitutional Information (SCI).[52] The most important publication coming out of the SCI was Thomas Hinton Burley Oldfield's *Entire and Complete History, Political and Personal, of the Boroughs of Great Britain* (3 vols., 1792). Attached to the first volume was an essay of nearly 200 pages presenting 'An original sketch of constitutional rights', in which Oldfield repeatedly cited Blackstone as an authority while attacking Sir Martin Wright as a 'friend to feudal oppression'.[53]

46 See esp. Colin Bonwick, *English Radicals and the American Revolution* (University of North Carolina Press 1977).

47 *A List of the Minority in the House of Commons Who Voted Against the Bill to Repeal the American Stamp Act* (1766) 3, 6.

48 *Some Strictures on the Late Occurrences in North America* (London 1766) 12–13.

49 JCD Clark, *The Language of Liberty: Political Discourse and Social Dynamics in the Anglo-American World, 1660–1832* (Cambridge University Press 1994) 84.

50 David Lemmings, 'Editor's Introduction to Book I' in Blackstone (ed), *Commentaries* I, xxxix.

51 *Reflexions on Representation in Parliament* (London 1766) 5, citing Blackstone, *Commentaries* I (n 12) 114: 'But as trade is of a fluctuating nature, and seldom long fixed in a place, it was formerly left to the crown to summon, *pro re nata* [according to circumstances], the most flourishing towns to send representatives to parliament. So that as towns encreased in trade, and grew populous, they were admitted to a share in the legislature'.

52 Minute books of the Society of Constitutional Information, the National Archives, Kew Gardens, TS 11/1133, f. 5.

53 THB Oldfield, *Entire and Complete History, Political and Personal, of the Boroughs of Great Britain*, 3 vols (London 1792) I, 67, 75, 85, 88, 91, 96, 98, 138. Wright, a judge of the King's Bench between 1740 and 1755, had written *An Introduction to the Law of Tenures,* first published in 1729 and reprinted twice in 1792.

One aspect of Blackstone's *Commentaries* which chimed with eighteenth-century Toryism was his defence of the Church of England and his critical stance on Protestant Dissenters. In a nutshell, he argued that the seventeenth-century statutes directed against religious nonconformity, the Test and Corporation Acts, were still technically in place, though some of them were suspended by the Toleration Act 1689. This stance was especially notable in the fourth book of the *Commentaries*, published in 1769, which attracted critical commentary from Protestant Dissenters such as Joseph Priestley and Philip Furneaux.[54] The same Priestley had previously cited Blackstone approvingly in 1765, when only the first volume had been published.[55] Blackstone respected Priestley and moderated his portrayal of religious nonconformity in subsequent editions, insisting that his portrayal of the penal laws and the limitations of the Toleration Act was simply descriptive and not prescriptive. Blackstone and Newdigate began to diverge on this question in the 1770s, with the former moderating his stance and the latter sticking to High Church Anglicanism.[56] As Blackstone's modern editor has shown, however, Blackstone continued to blame Dissenters for the civil wars and the regicide, and many, though not all, of his pejorative references to religious nonconformists remained in later editions.[57]

Oxford Toryism for Blackstone entailed defence of the Established Church, independence from corruption, respect for the ancient constitution, and above all, opposition to the Whig oligarchy, in short, 'true constitutional independency' and 'the genuine Principles of Christian Religion' to cite Newdigate's description of the virtues of Oxford University as a constituency.[58] In the late 1750s and especially after 1760, when the Whig supremacy was broken, Toryism became less oppositional than it had been earlier in Hanoverian Britain. This is amply illustrated by Blackstone's career, but it did not necessarily make him a 'convert' from eighteenth-century Toryism.[59] Times simply changed after George III's accession when oppositional Toryism began to assimilate into the British state. As a critic of recent politics, Blackstone was well-positioned

54 Joseph Priestley, *Remarks on Some Paragraphs in the Fourth Volume of Dr. Blackstone's Commentaries on the Laws of England, Relating to the Dissenters* (London 1769); Philip Furneaux, *Letters to the Honourable Mr. Justice Blackstone Concerning His Exposition of the Act of Toleration, and Some Positions Relative to Religious Liberty in His Celebrated Commentaries on the Laws of England* (London 1769); William Blackstone, *A Reply to Dr. Priestley's Remarks on the Fourth Volume of the* Commentaries (London 1769). See also *Remarks on Several Late Publications Relative to the Dissenters; In a Letter to Dr. Priestley. By a Dissenter* (London 1770).

55 Joseph Priestley, *An Essay on a Course of Liberal Education for Civil and Active Life* (London 1765) 89, 113.

56 Prest (n 2) 277–78.

57 Ruth Paley, 'Editor's Introduction to Book IV' in *Commentaries* xxi. See also Anthony Page, 'Rational Dissent and Blackstone's *Commentaries*' in Anthony Page and Wilfrid Prest (eds), *Blackstone and His Critics* (Oxford University Press 2018) 77–96.

58 From Newdigate's resignation letter on 1 June 1779, Newdigate MSS CR 136/B. 2012.

59 Cf. Clark (n 49) 87.

to analyse both the history and the workings of the British constitution in the eighteenth century. Similarly to Montesquieu's *Spirit of the Laws*, Blackstone's *Commentaries* became a constitutional and legal encyclopaedia that different people used for various purposes.

Bibliography

Anon, *A List of the Minority in the House of Commons Who Voted Against the Bill to Repeal the American Stamp Act* (Paris 1766a)
Anon, *Reflexions on Representation in Parliament* (London 1766b)
Anon, *Some Strictures on the Late Occurrences in North America* (London 1766c)
Anon, *Remarks on Several Late Publications Relative to the Dissenters; In a Letter to Dr. Priestley. By a Dissenter* (London 1770)
Bentham J, *A Fragment on Government* (London 1776)
Blackstone W, *An Analysis of the Laws of England* (Oxford University Press 1756)
Blackstone W, *A Discourse on the Study of the Law; Being an Introductory Lecture* (Oxford University Press 1758)
Blackstone W, *The Great Charter and Charter of the Forest, with Other Authentic Instruments* (Oxford University Press 1759)
Blackstone W, *A Reply to Dr. Priestley's Remarks on the Fourth Volume of the Commentaries* (London 1769)
Blackstone W, *Commentaries on the Laws of England* 4 vols (Wilfrid Prest gen. ed, Oxford University Press 2017)
Bonwick C, *English Radicals and the American Revolution* (University of North Carolina Press 1977)
Clark JCD, *The Language of Liberty: Political Discourse and Social Dynamics in the Anglo-American World, 1660–1832* (Cambridge University Press 1994)
Clark JCD, *English Society, 1660–1832: Religion, Ideology and Politics During the Ancien Régime* (2nd edn, first published 1985, Cambridge University Press 2000)
Coke E, *The Fourth Part of the Institutes of the Lawes of England* (London 1669)
Dolittle I, *William Blackstone: An Autobiography* (Self-published 2001)
Furneaux P, *Letters to the Honourable Mr. Justice Blackstone Concerning His Exposition of the Act of Toleration, and Some Positions Relative to Religious Liberty in His Celebrated Commentaries on the Laws of England* (London 1769)
Gibbon E, *Memoirs of My Life* (Betty Radice ed, Penguin 1990)
Greenwood D, *William King: Tory and Jacobite* (Oxford University Press 1969)
Lieberman D, *The Province of Legislation Determined: Legal Theory in Eighteenth-Century Britain* (Cambridge University Press 1989)
Lubert HL, 'Sovereignty and Liberty in William Blackstone's *Commentaries on the Laws of the England*' (2010) 72 The Review of Politics 271–97
Macaulay C, *Political Writings* (Max Skjönsberg ed, Cambridge University Press 2023)
Minute Books of the Society of Constitutional Information, the National Archives, Kew Gardens, TS 11/1133
Montesquieu, *The Spirit of the Laws* (Anne M Cohler, Basia C Miller and Harold S Stone eds, Cambridge University Press 1989)
Newdigate MSS, Warwickshire County Record Office
Oldfield THB, *Entire and Complete History, Political and Personal, of the Boroughs of Great Britain*, 3 vols (London 1792)
Phillip Reid J, *Constitutional History of the American Revolution*, 4 vols (University of Wisconsin Press 1986–1995)
Prest W, *William Blackstone: Law and Letters in the Eighteenth Century* (Oxford University Press 2008)

Priestley J, *An Essay on a Course of Liberal Education for Civil and Active Life* (London 1765)

Priestley J, *Remarks on Some Paragraphs in the Fourth Volume of Dr. Blackstone's* Commentaries on the Laws of England, *Relating to the Dissenters* (London 1769)

Robson RJ, *The Oxfordshire Election of 1754: A Study in the Interplay of City, County and University Politics* (Oxford University Press 1949)

Schofield P, 'The "Least Repulsive" Work on a "Repulsive Subject": Jeremy Bentham on William Blackstone's *Commentaries on the Laws of England*' in A Page and W Prest (eds), *Blackstone and His Critics* (Oxford University Press 2018) 23–40

Skinner S, 'Blackstone's Support for the Militia' (2000) 44 American Journal of Legal History 1–18

Stinneford JF, 'The Original Meaning of "Unusual": The Eighth Amendment as a Bar to Cruel Innovation' (2008) 102 Northwestern University Law Review 1739–1825

Thomas PDG (ed), 'Parliamentary Diaries of Nathaniel Ryder, 1764–7' in *Volume 7: Camden Miscellany Vol. XXIII* (Cambridge University Press 1969)

Weston, CC and Greenberg JR, *Subjects and Sovereigns: The Grand Controversy over Legal Sovereignty in Stuart England* (Cambridge University Press 1981)

Willman R, 'Blackstone and the "Theoretical Perfection" of English Law in the Reign of Charles I' (1983) 26 Historical Journal 39–70

Wooddeson R, *A Systematical View of the Laws of England; As Treated of in a Course of Vinerian Lectures, Read at Oxford, During a Series of Years, Commencing in Michaelmas Term, 1777*, 3 vols (London 1792–93)

12 Jean-Louis de Lolme, *The Constitution of England*

Angus Harwood Brown

12.1 Introduction

Since at least the seventeenth century, Parliament has enjoyed near-universal esteem as the font and guardian of British liberty. Legally, 'Parliamentary Sovereignty' is a property of the Crown in Parliament and the triune exercise of power by the monarch, Lords, and Commons. In practice, the United Kingdom has long enjoyed a system of *de facto* legislative dominance, in which the House of Commons enjoys effectively unlimited power, a system which has been widely praised as the source of a long tradition of political liberty. For constitutional writers from Edward Coke to A.V. Dicey, parliamentary sovereignty was both a fact of constitutional life and the foundation of our system's remarkable durability and freedom.[1] This account of the much-lauded 'English Constitution', as it was then generally known, was common to many eighteenth-century thinkers, who deeply admired the gentlemanly class who composed the Parliaments of the eighteenth century, 'the guardians of the English Constitution; the makers, interpreters, and repealers of the English laws', as Blackstone put it.[2] If, unlike us, they saw the balance between three co-equal branches of government as the essential principle of the constitution, they nonetheless shared our view that Parliament was the lynchpin of that Constitution and that it was the Commons which had won our freedom. Thus, for Montesquieu, the independence of Parliament was the crux of Britain's remarkable government, whose corruption would lead to the downfall of the nation's freedom.[3] Britain was free, her eighteenth-century defenders and admirers argued, because her

1 Edward Coke, *The Second Part of the Institutes of the Laws of England* (E. and R. Brooke 1797) and AV Dicey, *Introduction to the Study of the Law of the Constitution* (8th edn, Macmillan 1915).

2 William Blackstone, *Commentaries on the Laws of England*, vol 1 (J.B. Lippincott 1893) 8. See on eighteenth century ideas about the Constitution, Mark Goldie, 'The English System of Liberty' in Mark Goldie and Robert Wokler (eds), *The Cambridge History of Eighteenth-Century Political Thought* (CUP 2006) 40, *passim*.

3 Charles-Louis de Secondat and Baron de Montesquieu, *The Spirit of the Laws* (Anne M Cohler, Basia Carolyn Miller and Harold Stone ed and tr, CUP 1989) 156–66.

DOI: 10.4324/9781032658698-13

most important magistrates were elected and because the executive power, though hereditary, was subordinated to the people's representatives. In effect, the British enjoyed liberty whilst the other peoples of Europe did not because their state was a republic with a balanced constitution, dressed in the hand-me-down clothes of vanished monarchical authority. But Jean-Louis de Lolme thought differently.

For de Lolme,[4] who was born in Geneva in 1741 and arrived in Britain as a political exile in 1767, the true source of 'English liberty' was neither the power of Parliament to check the executive nor the extension of power to the rising commercial gentry. Instead, in his 1771 book *La Constitution de l'Angleterre* (published as *The Constitution of England: Or, An Account of the English Government* in 1775), de Lolme contended that the British political culture so inspiring to his contemporaries had its origins in the unusual strength of the executive branch. For those of us raised on the myth of our ancient 'Anglo-Saxon' or 'Gothic' constitution, won back from the tyrannising Norman Yoke in the seventeenth century, de Lolme's account is at once ludicrous and intriguing, a contrarian inversion of established values and a bracing challenge to stultifying historical convention.[5] For de Lolme, the liberties of the English were a product of the security, stability, and unity afforded by a monarchy which had established its absolute power early in its history and which existed in dynamic tension with the representatives of the nation to the people's benefit. It was this arrangement of institutions which provided a lasting bulwark against the tyranny of an aristocratic minority, whether of feudal lords or the rising commercial elite, and Parliament, far from the guardian of liberty, in fact, contained the seeds of its destruction.

This chapter does not seek to vindicate or disprove de Lolme's theory of the British Constitution as a historical account but rather to offer it up as a clarifying alternative to our prevailing Parliamentarian mythology. In taking de Lolme's monarchical theory of British liberty seriously, we can uncover issues with our own constitutional architecture about which eighteenth-century thinkers knew, but we have forgotten, even if we do not accept de Lolme's particular constitutional prescriptions. To that end, this chapter is divided into two parts. The first recounts de Lolme's description of the British Constitution in greater detail and provides critical historical context for understanding the origins and aims of *The Constitution of England*. The second then reconstructs a more abstract constitutional theory from the basic principles of political analysis laid down by de Lolme, which I follow him here in referring to as 'metapolitics'.

4 Sometimes incorrectly rendered as 'Delolme'. It would also be improper to omit the particle 'de', following general Francophone convention about its proper usage before monosyllabic surnames.

5 On the 'Gothic' and 'Norman' theories of the Constitution, see Martin Loughlin, *The British Constitution: A Very Short Introduction* (OUP 2013) 24–28.

The chapter then briefly concludes with an outline of what de Lolme's work can offer to politicians, constitutional theorists, and lawyers today.

12.2 An account of the English government

As de Lolme observed in the introduction to the English edition of *The Constitution of England*, the British Constitution is quite commonly treated as 'a system which is supposed to be so complicated as not to be understood or developed, but by those who have been initiated in the mysteries of it from their infancy'.[6] This constitutional mysticism is almost as common in our day as it was in de Lolme's. But, de Lolme argued, British reverence for the mysteries of a time-honoured constitution blinded those who were familiar with it to the relative simplicity of the constitutional principles upon which the country's unique freedom lay. What had made England, and later Britain, different from other free states was that she enjoyed a powerful monarchy and, therefore, a history of political unity under uniform and strictly enforced laws.[7] This was not to say that a strong executive alone was enough to make a country free. France, with her strong absolute monarchy established under Louis XIV, was, after all, not a free country like Britain. But the peculiar historical circumstances from which English feudalism – and later the British state – had emerged had served to make executive power a salutary force in the nation's history.

'It is at the era of the Conquest', de Lolme argued, 'that we are to look for the real foundation of the English Constitution'.[8] With William I's conquest of England in 1066, he argued, a new form of government had been established, which rendered appeals to 'German liberty' and the ancient 'Saxon' Constitution irrelevant.[9] Whereas the rest of Europe had borne witness to the rise of feudal states characterised by an independent nobility with the resources and the independence to enjoy *de facto* sovereignty in their demesne, in England, the conquest had transformed the whole Kingdom into a fief of the King, at least in law, and generated an unprecedented centralisation of executive and judicial power.[10] It was this rupture which had set England on the road to

6 Jean-Louis de Lolme, *The Constitution of England, or an Account of the English Government* (G.G.J. and J. Robinson and J. Murray 1788) 2. Having first published the book in French in 1771 and in English in 1775, de Lolme republished *The Constitution of England* in revised form on several occasions and made particularly extensive changes to the fourth edition in 1784. Here I have used the last English edition printed during his lifetime. For an extensive survey of the different versions of this text, see David Lieberman, 'Introduction' in Jean-Louis de Lolme (ed), *The Constitution of England; or, an Account of the English Government* (Liberty Fund 2007) 7–16.

7 de Lolme (n 6) xii–xiii.

8 Ibid 7. De Lolme even doubted that trial by jury was Saxon rather than Norman, see ibid 357–58.

9 Ibid 6–7.

10 Ibid 14–17.

freedom because the common subjection of Lords and Commoners alike ensured that 'the principle of primaeval equality became everywhere diffused and established'.[11] In other words, de Lolme argued, 'It was the excessive power of the King which made England free, because it was this very excess that gave rise to the spirit of union, and of concerted resistance'.[12] Because the King possessed all power, the local oppressions, struggles between feudal lords, and conflicts between the peasants and nobility which plagued other European monarchies were sublimated into a single struggle between the King and his subjects. The earliest fruit of this struggle was 'the Great Charter' (Magna Carta) in the reign of King John, and by the time of Henry III, it had led to the emergence of a Parliament in 1295 composed of both Lords and Commons, united in a cross-class alliance to limit the power of the King.[13] At the same time, the unusual strength of the English King meant that England 'possess[ed] the immense advantage of being one undivided state', from the conquest on, and enjoyed standardised laws, barrier-free commerce, and a uniformity of political organisation far earlier than other European states. It was a testament to the importance he placed on this latter process that de Lolme ranked the standardisation of weights and measures promised by Magna Carta alongside its supposed guarantees of equality before the law and a right to trial by jury.[14]

Put differently, England's freedom was an accident of history which arose because 'circumstances . . . concurred . . . to strengthen the Regal power to such a degree that no Men in the State could entertain a hope of succeeding in any other design than that of setting bounds to it'.[15] In consequence, an unprecedented unity of resistance by the people gave rise to a single, national, Parliament representing the interest of all classes, rather than the regional 'Estates' (parliaments) of France which could never actively resist the King or the aristocratic parliaments of Sweden and pre-union Scotland which excluded the people.[16] As early as the thirteenth century, Parliament had won the right to approve all taxes under Edward I and, with it, eventually, the supreme legislative power.[17] In turn, the Commons quickly became the sole body able to initiate legislation and the font of taxation upon which the monarchy depended. Legislative authority was now shared between the Commons, the Lords, and the monarch, who still wielded a veto but was no longer able to

11 Ibid 22–23.
12 Ibid 21.
13 Ibid 32–35.
14 Ibid 27. On Magna Carta, see Chapter 1. On its distorted eighteenth century reputation, see also Alexander Lock, 'Reform, Radicalism and Revolution: Magna Carta in Eighteenth- and Nineteenth-century Britain' in Lawrence Goldman (ed) *Magna Carta: History, Context, and Influence* (University of London Press 2018) 101–16.
15 de Lolme (n 6) 338.
16 Ibid 44–45 and 235–36.
17 Ibid 77.

make laws as they wished. With these innovations, the struggle between King and people eventually produced a novel constitutional settlement: a free state with a powerful monarch, where all executive authority and all administration of justice flowed from the hands of a single person, but in which that august official was entirely dependent for their ability to act upon the consent of the people's representatives. The English were free under uniform laws, over which the common people exercised considerable influence because their common subjection had united the whole people, from the most powerful Lord down to the lowliest peasant, in a common struggle against an overwhelming royal power, a struggle which they had, ultimately, won.

The strong monarchy established by the Normans had thus, inadvertently, allowed Britain to win her freedom – but, in quite a different manner, de Lolme also believed that the strength of the monarchy *kept* Britain free. This was the consequence of the other remarkable aspect of Britain's constitutional history: that, despite a brief interregnum, she had not 'exterminated' or 'destroyed' her Kings and their kin, as had all other free states who had liberated themselves from kingly power.[18] Instead, after overthrowing Charles I and briefly governing themselves as a republic, the English had invited his son to return to become their King. Likewise, after their 'second revolution' (the Glorious Revolution of 1688), the English had not overthrown monarchy as such but simply removed one monarch to save a monarchical constitution.[19] If the history of struggle against monarchy had made England free, it was monarchy's persistence, and not the presence of elections or of a popular legislative power, which kept it that way: 'the immediate cause of English liberty', de Lolme contended, lay in 'having placed all the executive authority in the State out of the hands of those in whom the people trust'.[20]

If this might seem a strange contention even to those convinced by de Lolme's historical account of the origins of Britain's tripartite constitution, it should be put in the context of what de Lolme was trying to do in his book. Whilst the book's title page promises a comparison 'both with the REPUBLICAN Form of GOVERNMENT, and the other MONARCHIES in EUROPE', in truth de Lolme's work is much more concerned with republicanism and free government than it is with unfree monarchies.[21] As the historian Richard Whatmore has argued, de Lolme's writings on England were influenced, above all, by his own experience of the failures of republicanism in his native Geneva and his desire to find a new model for free government in the modern world, as de Lolme himself admitted in the preface to the book.[22] In Geneva,

18 Ibid 388.
19 Ibid 53–58.
20 Ibid 393.
21 Ibid, title page.
22 Richard Whatmore, *Against War and Empire: Geneva, Britain, and France in the Eighteenth Century* (Yale University Press 2012) 97, 112–14. In de Lolme (n 6) i–ii.

de Lolme had been a radical agitator against the aristocratic government of the ruling 'Council of Twenty Five', and he had come to England because he had been expelled for his subversive political activities in defence of democracy against the 'aristocratic' republic of his homeland.[23] But, after coming to England, de Lolme modified his account of the nature of free government. Now he argued that Geneva, and the other republics of the eighteenth century, had ceased to be free because they had become imbalanced: popular government had given way to the rule of the few, oscillating between demagoguery – and in some cases even popular tyranny – and aristocracy. Whatmore argues that de Lolme saw Britain as a truly republican state, and a model for republican stability.[24] In fact, however, de Lolme made quite clear that Britain was free precisely because she was *not* a republic at all but a free state with a balanced constitution and a *King*.[25]

In Britain, unlike the republics of Europe, liberty could be guaranteed because the monarchy was 'able to counterbalance the excessive and unrestrained freedom of the People',[26] and, perhaps more importantly, to prevent the elite, whether aristocrats or powerful commoners, from becoming the people's masters.[27] However, if the monarch was the guardian of the people's liberties, it was not because they were a 'Caesarist' or 'Bonapartist' champion of the people against the nobility, or, as Bolingbroke had termed it, a 'Patriot King', who would overawe the people's oppressors.[28] In France, de Lolme believed, the common people really had elevated the King to the position of 'one common uncontrouled master' equally able to oppress their noble oppressors during the reign of Louis XIV.[29] But, it had not made them any freer, only transferred their oppression from a thousand aristocratic masters to a single, royal sovereign. In fact, de Lolme recognised that English monarchs continued to be potential enemies of liberty, as the Stuarts had proven – though he did not appear to believe the ruling house of Hannover was as active in subverting the Constitution.[30]

Instead, what had made the monarch the 'ballast' of a free constitution was that the structure of monarchy neutralised and muted the competition for

23 Ibid 91 and 96.
24 Ibid 113.
25 de Lolme (n 6) 232, 271, 393–94.
26 Ibid 471.
27 This is discussed in more detail later.
28 Henry Bolingbroke, 'The Idea of a Patriot King' in Richard Armitage (ed), *Political Writings* (CUP 1997) 217.
29 de Lolme (n 6) 37.
30 For example, de Lolme believed that James II's 30,000-strong standing army had been created to better combat his Parliamentary enemies, although this ultimately failed. See, ibid 468–69.

power, which had marred all prior free governments. 'The first peculiarity of the English Government, as a free Government', de Lolme explained:

> [I]s its having a King, its having thrown into one place the whole mass, if I may use the expression, of the Executive Power, and having invariably and for ever fixed it there. By this very circumstance also has the depositum of it been rendered sacred and inexpungable; by making, one great, very great Man, in the State, has an effectual check been put to the pretentions of those who other wise would strive to become such, and disorders have been prevented, which, in all Republics, ever brought on the ruin of liberty, and, before it was lost, obstructed the enjoyment of it.[31]

In every republic which the world had ever known, the lust for power by the 'great men' of the state had spelled ruin for free government, either because their conflict had brought about its end, as in Rome, or because a formally free constitution had given way to a 'state masquerade' in which a republican constitution was but a mask for the rule of oligarchs, as in de Lolme's native Geneva.[32] Soon, either aristocrats would seize the state, or the people would select a favourite to be their protector, 'and the protector becomes a Tyrant'. What was more, 'the same causes which have given a Master to the State give it two, give it three. All those rival powers endeavour to swallow each other; the State becomes a scene of endless quarrels' and, eventually, civil war.[33] Either way, the result would be the same, and the formal liberty of a free constitution would give way to some species of despotism.

This did not mean that de Lolme rejected the role of Parliament in safeguarding the liberties of the nation – on the contrary, he regarded England's beneficent balance of institutions as a more than salutary defence against tyranny and particularly admired the House of Commons as a median between aristocratic rule and direct democracy. But, it was the presence of a monarchy which made England unique. In contrast to all other free states, the presence of an inviolable monarchy in England meant that no matter what acclaim a demagogue or party leader won, he could never hope but to be the first minister to a King reigning for life, and whose successor was chosen automatically upon the birth of the heir to the throne. As de Lolme put it:

> [T]he remarkable liberty enjoyed by the English Nation, is essentially owing to the impossibility under which their Leaders, or in general all Men of power among them, are placed, of invading and transferring

31 Ibid 196.
32 Ibid 197–202 and 264.
33 Ibid 200.

> to themselves any branch of the Governing Executive authority; which authority is exclusively vested, and firmly secured, in the Crown.[34]

Retaining the monarchy even after she became a free state meant that Britain had avoided all the maladies of republics, in which ceaseless competition for executive power had brought about anarchy and despotism. As de Lolme noted, the Romans lived under Consuls, Dictators, Patricians, Nobles, and even finally, an empire, and suffered all manner of despotisms that they might be ruled under 'any appellation than that horrid one *Rex*'.[35] By contrast, the English had embraced that horrid appellation and, as a consequence, could enjoy liberty under not 'the capricious power of the Man, but . . . the lawful authority of the Head of the State'.[36] It was as though the English had declared, '[L]et us choose ourselves one Master, that we may not have fifty'.[37] Or, as his fellow Genevan, the republican writer Jean-Jacques Rousseau once put it, they had chosen a prince so as not to have a master.[38] Although a King's reign lasted a lifetime, moreover, it provided for a definitive and peaceful transfer of power, which marked a moment of reformation as any encroachments made upon the constitution by the previous monarch were reset by his successor's oath to uphold the laws of the Kingdom and, more cynically, by their need to curry favour with Parliament to ensure the reauthorisation of the Civil List.[39]

Under a King, even the most terrible of ambitions were limited, and, furthermore, they turned to the service of liberty, for they would be naturally opposed to the authority of the monarch, which limited their ambition. So, too, would the monarch's ambition to increase their power only strengthen the alliance of Lords and Commons upon which liberty depended. And it was for this reason that de Lolme believed that the English alone had realised:

> A Constitution the more likely to produce all the effects we have mentioned, and to procure in general the happiness of the People, in that it has taken Mankind as they are, . . . I shall add, the more difficult to discover, because its form was complicated, while its principles were natural and simple, Hence it is that the Politicians of Antiquity, sensible of the inconveniences of the Governments they had opportunities of knowing, wished for the establishment of such a Government, without much hopes of ever seeing it effected.[40]

34 Ibid 387.
35 Ibid 241.
36 Ibid 418.
37 Ibid 491.
38 Jean-Jacques Rousseau, 'Discourse on the Origin and the Foundations of Inequality Among Men' in Victor Gourevitch (ed and tr), *The Discourses and Other Early Political Writings* (CUP 1997) 115, 180.
39 de Lolme (n 6) 80–81.
40 Ibid 537.

By the eighteenth century, the British had done nothing less than solve the mystery of human government and realised on Earth the cherished and ancient dream of a balanced constitution in which '[a]ll the political passions of Mankind . . . are satisfied and provided for'.[41] And this discovery, however accidental, had revealed with it the true principles upon which all political and constitutional thought could be recast.

12.3 Metapolitics and the 'material constitution'

Politics, de Lolme believed, could be reduced to essential principles which were true in all contexts, derived from the essential character of human beings, and society itself understood through rational inquiry. The extension of the critical, sceptical, and rationalist method of thinking we now associate with 'the Enlightenment' to the study of politics could thus reveal the essential principles of political organisation common in all places and all times.[42] As we have seen, de Lolme believed that, although disguised under layers of custom and tradition, at its heart, the English Constitution owed its success to its ability to satisfy essential human passions and because it operated on the principle that 'we will not seek to counteract nature, but rather to follow it'.[43] Indeed, the passions which ruled in English politics were a product of an essential and immutable human nature and informed the construction of all states. 'It is upon the passions of Mankind, that is upon causes which are unalterable', de Lolme claimed, 'that the various parts of a State depends. The machine may vary as to its dimensions, but its movement and acting springs still remain intrinsically the same'.[44] As the historian Iain McDaniel has argued, it was on this basis that de Lolme produced a conceptually innovative 'science of politics', oriented towards understanding how liberty might be preserved in an era of intense international competition and imperial expansion.[45] De Lolme himself conceptualised this new political science as 'the science of *Metapolitics*', which bore the same relation to politics as metaphysics to the physical sciences. If metaphysics represented 'the Science of those things which lie beyond physical, or substantial things', metapolitics represented the study of the essential and timeless elements which lay behind day-to-day politics.[46]

What were the essential principles of this new science of politics? Although de Lolme left this answer vague in *The Constitution of England*, as McDaniel argues its insights can be found throughout that work as well as in another of de Lolme's books, the 1772 treatise *A parallel between the English constitution*

41 Ibid 388.
42 Ibid 1–2.
43 Ibid 494.
44 Ibid 31.
45 Iain McDaniel, 'Jean-Louis de Lolme and the Political Science of the English Empire' (2012) 55 The Historical Journal 21.
46 de Lolme (n 6) 419.

and the former government of Sweden.[47] For de Lolme, the science of politics consisted of three essential subjects: 1) the outward form taken by the state, subject to sceptical scrutiny, 2) an analysis of the nature of mankind itself, and finally, 3) the analysis of the relations of 'real power' which undergirded the outward form of the 'state masquerade', and lay at the intersection of institutional forms and the passions and behaviours of mankind. In the *Parallel*, de Lolme presented the most precise definition of his metapolitical theory, writing that:

> In our disquisitions on the liberty of a Nation, we must indeed pay a great attention to the description of the outward form of its Government: but it is at the distribution of real power that has been introduced, we must chiefly look. Governments are the work of force: like the treaties between Princes, they only subsist by the continued effect and weight of force; and it may be laid down as a maxim, that, in any shape of Government, whatever may be got on the side of form, never can compensate what is lost in point of real strength.[48]

As we have already seen, de Lolme regarded the outward forms of constitutions as, at best, deceptive. A state, like Geneva, which possessed a free constitution, could be just as easily ruled by tyrants as a formal monarchy like France, whilst a state like England could enjoy free government under the trappings of a quite absolute monarchy. The theory of metapolitics and the analysis of 'real power', could penetrate below this surface level and reveal the true principles by which a state operated and the interplay of social forces which undergirded its institutions. De Lolmean metapolitics was thus quite close to the modern jurisprudential study of 'material constitutionalism', which concerns itself with the 'real' operation of power which partly intersects with and is partly occluded by the outward appearance of formal political rules.[49]

Of particular importance to de Lolme was the role of 'aristocracy' or of what we tend to call 'elites', though de Lolme did not use this quite modern term. '[G]reat, or wealthy Men in the Nation', de Lolme believed, will always rise to the top in politics and dominate the government, either because of talent, force of personality, or wealth.[50] This could even be a force for good,

47 Jean-Louis de Lolme, *A Parallel between the English Constitution and the Former Government of Sweden* (J. Almon 1772). In McDaniel (n 45) see 'de Lolme and the Political Science of the English Empire' 26–30.

48 Quoted in McDaniel (n 45) 'de Lolme and the Political Science of the English Empire' 29.

49 Marco Goldoni and Michael A Wilkinson, 'Introduction: The Return of the Material Constitution' in Marco Goldoni and Michael A Wilkinson (eds), *The Cambridge Handbook on the Material Constitution* (CUP 2023) 1, and for a more explicitly 'anti-elitist' account see Camila Vergara, *Systemic Corruption: Constitutional Ideas for an Anti-Oligarchic Republic* (Princeton University Press 2020) 102–21.

50 de Lolme (n 6) 368–69.

as it was in England, where the most 'notable' of commoners formed the vanguard of opposition to an overweening executive and aristocracy. But it could also spell ruin if not properly contained, with the elite coming to form 'a single overgrown head', a dominating class which ruled for its own purposes and oppressed the people.[51] Such a dynamic was particularly likely in republics, where elites competed for power in the name of the people but used the positions popular politics won them to their own advantage, as de Lolme believed the Tribunes of the Plebs had at Rome, leading to the 'continued desertion of the cause of the People' common to the demagogic politicians of republican states.[52] Elite rule without limit would soon subvert the state, leaving behind only a mirage of freedom, hiding the rule of the few in the name of the people.

The people were certainly not powerless: in fact, de Lolme believed that it was 'the People, who, whatever may be the force of the Government, always possess . . . the reality of power'.[53] Such power, however, was largely inert:

> Forming . . . as it were, 'one' body, the People, at every instant, have it in their power to strike the decisive blow which is to level everything. Like those mechanical powers the greatest efficiency of which exists at the instant which precedes their entering into action, it has an immense force, just because it does not yet exert any; and in this state of stillness, but of attention, consists its true *momentum*.[54]

As long as this force could keep their rulers 'in awe', the people's rights would be safe. The problem arose when the people decided to create a new order after levelling the state. Then they tended to seek out leaders, and these popular champions soon sought power for themselves and its own sake, 'and the Protector becomes a Tyrant'.[55] Consequently, although the people possessed a far greater 'real power', they could easily be reduced to the peons of the great men of the state, whose talents enabled them to rise at the head of a people to become their master. This could take both the overt form of the tyranny of a single master or the rule of a clique of oligarchs cloaked in the language of constitutionalism. Without sufficient counterweights, de Lolme believed that this was the inevitable fate of all free societies, relegating all of humanity to oppression either under the despotic regimes of the 'Eastern monarchs' who ruled by force or of demagogues and aristocrats who ruled nominally free states through the manipulation of public opinion and the abuse of constitutional powers.

51 Ibid 278.
52 Ibid 356.
53 Ibid 197.
54 Ibid 322.
55 Ibid 199.

12.4 Conclusion: the asylum of liberty?

It was that she had avoided this fate which made England so remarkable, 'the most singular Government upon Earth, . . . which has carried farthest the liberty of the individual',[56] in which, at last, 'Liberty has at length disclosed her secret to Mankind and secured an Asylum to herself'.[57] Nor, de Lolme argued, did Britain face the collapse into tyranny to which all free states had previously been doomed. In his own celebrated account of the British Constitution, Montesquieu had predicted that 'Since all human things have an end, the state of which we are speaking will lose its liberty; it will perish . . . when legislative power is more corrupt than executive power'.[58] Whilst de Lolme acknowledged the fragility of all human things, he felt he had good reason to believe that 'When the World shall have been again laid waste by Conquerors, [England] will still continue to show Mankind, . . . the form under which they ought to be united', under a free and durable government.[59] But de Lolme did not end his account without a warning. Montesquieu, he suggested, had supplied 'defective arguments' about the character of the English regime, driven by a fanciful account of 'luxury', 'corruption', and Parliamentary virtue, and had missed the uniqueness of Britain's balanced constitution under a vigorous monarchy.[60] On the contrary, de Lolme argued, it was not the legislative power upon whose security the Constitution depended. Instead, he claimed, 'The English Government will be no more, either when the Crown shall become independent of the Nation for its supplies, or when the Representatives of the People shall begin to share in the Executive Authority'.[61] In other words, the end of the ancient and hallowed English Constitution would come about the moment either monarch or people triumphed in their age-old battle and replaced the elegant balance of forces with the domination of one power over the others.

We live in the world which de Lolme feared. In the United Kingdom today, the representatives of the people do not share in the executive power but dominate it entirely, leaving only a vestigial and largely 'ceremonial' monarchy in the place of the constitutional Kingship which de Lolme admired. As Walter Bagehot put it in a quite different book titled *The English Constitution*, written in the nineteenth century, beyond the dignified residue of the old English Constitution, an entirely new constitutional order had begun to operate, dominated by the House of Commons.[62] We are accustomed to seeing this as an entirely positive, even 'progressive' historical trajectory. There

56 Ibid 487–88.
57 Ibid 540.
58 Montesquieu (n 3) 166.
59 de Lolme (n 6) 539–40.
60 Ibid 497–98.
61 Ibid 498.
62 Walter Bagehot, *The English Constitution* (Chapman and Hall 1867) 4–5.

are, indeed, good reasons for thinking this way. It cannot be denied that the democratisation of the British government has been a positive development, nor that the executive power could not legitimately have been left in the hands of an essentially arbitrary institution and wielded, if not wholly at the discretion of, at least relatively unaccountably by, a lone individual selected only for their birth.

Yet one cannot ignore the extent to which the outcome which de Lolme feared has come to pass: Britain, like all states, has succumbed to the power of the 'great men of the republic' in the absence of any significant counterweight to them. The history of modern free states, whether crowned or not, clearly vindicates de Lolme's 'metapolitical' analysis of the tendency of all states towards oligarchy and elite rule in the absence of a sufficiently effective 'counter-power'. Both our own recent history and the histories of those nations most like Britain have also, to some extent, vindicated de Lolme's thesis that a free state without institutions to balance against elite power will oscillate between the rule of an aristocratic minority and the domination of popular demagogues. It may also be true that the vestiges of monarchy in this country have been the only guardrail against the rise of demagogues who identify their own will with the state and seek to place themselves above the law. Whatever the case, trust in both Parliament and the Cabinet seems particularly weak today and not entirely without good reason: it would not be unfair to wonder today whether the will to power has not entirely eclipsed the common good. Jean-Louis de Lolme did not believe that politicians would ever labour for the freedom of the people or the security of the state unless institutional incentives aligned to induce an alliance between the elite and the people, and that Parliament's status as the guarantor of British liberty depended upon its alliance with the people against the King. Whilst we may not agree with the means by which de Lolme believed that alliance could be guaranteed, we might yet take his diagnosis into account when trying to correct the ills of our own constitutional settlement. As we turn anew to question whether or not Britain can remain the asylum of liberty so admired by a politically exiled Genevan in the eighteenth century, we must also wonder what we might do to correct for the errors of our time without sacrificing the advantages we have won by bitter experience. For de Lolme, it was clear that just 'as a sick Man trusts to his Physician . . . so the great number of the Citizens must trust to those who have more abilities than themselves' and grant their government to representatives.[63] But what happens when the interests of the representative no longer align with those of the represented? To whom can a sick polity turn? Who, to coin a phrase from Burke, could possibly be the physician of the state?[64]

63 de Lolme (n 6) 249.
64 Edmund Burke, *Reflections on the Revolution in France* (JGA Pocock ed, Hackett 1987) 150.

Bibliography

Bagehot W, *The English Constitution* (Chapman and Hall 1867)

Blackstone W, *Commentaries on the Laws of England*, vol 1 (J.B. Lippincott 1893)

Bolingbroke H, 'The Idea of a Patriot King' in R Armitage (ed), *Political Writings* (CUP 1997)

Burke E, *Reflections on the Revolution in France* (JGA Pocock ed, Hackett 1987)

Coke E, *The Second Part of the Institutes of the Laws of England* (E. and R. Brooke 1797)

de Lolme JL, *A Parallel Between the English Constitution and the Former Government of Sweden* (J. Almon 1772)

de Lolme JL, *The Constitution of England, or an Account of the English Government* (G.G.J. and J. Robinson and J. Murray 1788)

de Lolme JL, *The Constitution of England; Or, an Account of the English Government* (Liberty Fund 2007)

Dicey AV, *Introduction to the Study of the Law of the Constitution* (8th edn, Macmillan 1915)

Goldie M, 'The English System of Liberty' in M Goldie and R Wokler (eds), *The Cambridge History of Eighteenth-Century Political Thought* (CUP 2006)

Goldoni M and Wilkinson MA, 'Introduction: The Return of the Material Constitution' in M Goldoni and M A Wilkinson (eds), *The Cambridge Handbook on the Material Constitution* (CUP 2023)

Lock A, 'Reform, Radicalism and Revolution: Magna Carta in Eighteenth- and Nineteenth-Century Britain' in L Goldman (ed), *Magna Carta: History, Context, and Influence* (University of London Press 2018)

Loughlin M, *The British Constitution: A Very Short Introduction* (OUP 2013)

McDaniel I, 'Jean-Louis de Lolme and the Political Science of the English Empire' (2012) 55 The Historical Journal 21

Montesquieu (Baron de), *The Spirit of the Laws* (Anne M Cohler, Basia Carolyn Miller and Harold Stone ed and trans, CUP 1989)

Rousseau JJ, 'Discourse on the Origin and the Foundations of Inequality Among Men' in Victor Gourevitch (ed and trans), *The Discourses and Other Early Political Writings* (CUP 1997)

Vergara C, *Systemic Corruption: Constitutional Ideas for an Anti-Oligarchic Republic* (Princeton University Press 2020)

Whatmore R, *Against War and Empire: Geneva, Britain, and France in the Eighteenth Century* (Yale University Press 2012)

13 Mary Wollstonecraft on the constitution

Sylvana Tomaselli

Mary Wollstonecraft (1759–1797) cannot be said to have produced a leading work on constitutions or, indeed, even to have made a significant contribution to constitutional debates. Her first overtly political work, *A Vindication of the Rights of Men, in a Letter to the Right Honourable Edmund Burke; Occasioned by His Reflections on the Revolution in France* (1790), was principally a diatribe against what she took to be Edmund Burke's irrational reverence for the English constitution.* And yet, she merits a place in a volume such as this, not as a token female political commentator, but because she raised a simple but nonetheless crucial question about the legitimacy of this constitution in the first *Vindication*. Her unforgiving critique of Burke's *Reflections on the Revolution in France, and on the Proceedings in Certain Societies in London Relative to that Event: in a Letter intended to have been sent to a gentleman in Paris* (1790) makes her subsequent pronouncements on the English constitution from within revolutionary France all the more poignant and revelatory about both authors' political understanding, as this chapter endeavours to show. To be sure, Wollstonecraft was by no means alone in her line of questioning of Burke's constitutional interpretation. The once famous and now rediscovered historian and political theorist Catherine Macaulay (1731–1791), for instance, engaged him in a comparably rigorous manner and indeed put forward her own ideal of a mixed constitution.[1] The debate which Burke's *Reflections* generated was itself largely provoked by a sermon delivered by Richard Price, which appeared in print as *A Discourse on the Love of Our Country, delivered on Nov. 4, 1789, at the Meeting-House in the Old Jewry, to the Society for Commemorating the Revolution in Britain* (1789), it is well to consider it in what follows, for it shows how the question of the nature of the feelings that

* I am grateful to Samuel Harrison for his invaluable contributions on this chapter.

1 See, for instance, Lynne E Withey, 'Catharine Macaulay and the Uses of History: Ancient Rights, Perfectionism, and Propaganda' (1976) 16(1) Journal of British Studies 59–83; Max Skjönsberg, 'Patriots and the Country Party Tradition in the Eighteenth Century: The Critics of Britain's Fiscal-Military State from Robert Harley to Catharine Macaulay' (2023) 33(1) Intellectual History Review 83–100.

DOI: 10.4324/9781032658698-14

constitutions should elicit was set from the very start of the dispute and would form an integral part of it.

It was her publisher and patron, Joseph Johnson (1728–1809), who encouraged Wollstonecraft to respond to Burke's *Reflections.* Wollstonecraft did so in great haste and, despite a momentary loss of confidence, produced her pamphlet within the month of November of *Reflections*' publication. The first of possibly as many as 70 replies the work received, it appeared anonymously on 29 November and under Wollstonecraft's name on 18 December. Like many others, Burke's reaction to the events in France took Wollstonecraft by surprise.[2] He had long been known to be sympathetic to the American cause and highly critical in Parliament of the government's intransigence over its punitive taxation in several speeches, most explicitly in those concerning the tea duty in 1774. He called for conciliation with the Americans, insisted on their being treated as Englishmen with the right of representation, especially concerning taxation, and seemed to have conceived of the empire as a family whose younger members should be granted increasing independence over time.[3] That such a Member of Parliament should then condemn what was generally seen in the early stage of the Revolution as justified demands by the French people for reforms and political representation was nothing short of astonishing to many within as well as outside the Houses of Parliament.[4] It would have seemed extraordinary, especially as Burke had not criticised the American Constitution, which might arguably have been considered an instance of pure political artifice, an invention without historical precedent. However, Burke, who supported the Federalists, thought the Federal Constitution an achievement as it was well-suited to the reality of American society and its political culture. As things were, following the war of independence, it was evident that in the absence of recognised social ranks, the authors of the Constitution could not have created a mixed constitution based on social estates; theirs was a piece of pure constitutionalism, and they had done the best they could in America's specific situation. Moreover, as his *Appeal from the New to the Old Whigs* was to make clear in August 1791, he thought the American Constitution was within the English constitutional tradition, with its separation of powers, bicameralism, and individual liberty as its core.

Responding to *Reflections* in the wake of its publication, Wollstonecraft was not concerned with being a fair reader of Burke's corpus of speeches and could

2 Sylvana Tomaselli, *Wollstonecraft: Philosophy, Passion, and Politics* (Princeton University Press 2020) 142.

3 'Burke, Edmund (1729–97), of Beaconsfield, Bucks' in L Namier and J Brooke (eds), *The History of Parliament: The House of Commons 1754–1790*, 3 vols, vol 2 (Boydell & Brewer 1964). Online version <https://www.historyofparliamentonline.org/volume/1754-1790/member/burke-edmund-1729-97>

4 However, Richard Bourke makes a strong case for Burke's consistency in his treatment of these two revolutions: see his *Empire and Revolution: The Political Life of Edmund Burke* (Princeton University Press 2015) 748.

not foresee what he would feel necessary to clarify in subsequent years. For her, the work was not merely revelatory of Burke's true opinions and political opportunism; it was, as we shall see further on, a most disrespectful attack on a highly esteemed leader of the Dissenting community, Dr Richard Price (1723–1791), a community in which she had many friends, not least her loyal publisher. A member of the Society for Constitutional Information founded by Major John Cartwright (1740–1824), Price delivered a sermon to the London Revolution Society on 4 November 1789 for the commemoration of the anniversary of the Glorious Revolution in 1688, published, as we said previously, as *A Discourse on The Love of our Country*. The events of 1688 freed the people of Great Britain from the dangers of popery and arbitrary government, Price began. He then explained that a country was not defined by its geography but by its 'community of which we are members; or that body of companions and friends and kindred who are associated with us under the same constitution of government, protected by the same laws, and bound together by the same civil polity.'[5] Next, he stressed that our love of our country need not be exclusive, nor should it imply superiority over people of other countries or any other form of competition. True love of one's country entailed the duty to enlighten it: 'for by endeavouring to liberalize and enlighten it, to discourage vice and to promote virtue in it, and to assert and support its liberties, we shall endeavour to do all that is necessary to make it great and happy.'[6] Price added that this required 'us to obey its laws, and to respect its magistrates.'[7] Such obedience and respect were absolutely essential as:

> [C]ivil government . . . is an institution of human prudence for guarding our persons, our property, and our good name, against invasion; and for securing to the members of a community that liberty to which all have an equal right, as far as they do not, by any overt act, use it to injure the liberty of others. Civil laws are regulations agreed upon by the community for gaining these ends; and civil magistrates are officers appointed by the community for executing these laws.[8]

Thus, Price highlighted the necessity for obedience to the law and respect for those who enforced them. However, respect was one thing; adulation was quite another, Price warned. Civil authorities were the servants of the public,

> and a King is no more than the first servant of the public, created by it, maintained by it, and responsible to it: and all the homage paid him, is due to him on no other account than his relation to the public.[9]

5 Richard Price, *A Discourse on the Love of Our Country* (T. Cadell 1789) 3. Reproduced by Liberty Fund: <https://oll.libertyfund.org/titles/price-a-discourse-on-the-love-of-our-country>
6 Ibid 21.
7 Ibid.
8 Ibid.
9 Ibid.

But he also deplored what he saw as the other extreme:

> [T]hat is, a disdainful pride, derived from a consciousness of equality, or, perhaps, superiority, in respect of all that gives true dignity to men in power, and producing a contempt of them, and a disposition to treat them with rudeness and insult. . . . Persons justly informed on the subject of government, when they see men dazzled by looking up to high stations, and observe loyalty carried to a length that implies ignorance and servility: such persons, in such circumstances, are in danger of spurning at all public authority, and throwing off that respectful demeanor to persons invested with it which the order of society requires. There is undoubtedly a particular deference and homage due to civil magistrates, on account of their stations and offices; nor can that man be either truly wise or truly virtuous, who despises governments, and wantonly speaks evil of his rulers; or who does not, by all the means in his power, endeavour to strengthen their hands, and to give weight to their exertions in the discharge of their duty. – Fear God, says St. Peter. Love the brotherhood. Honour all men. Honour the King. – You must needs, says St. Paul, be subject to rulers, not only for wrath (that is, from the fear of suffering the penalties annexed to the breach of the laws), but for conscience sake. For rulers are ministers of God, and revengers for executing wrath on all that do evil.[10]

Generally overlooked as scholarly analysis understandably tends to focus on the radical political principles voiced by theorists such as Price, the sentiments expressed in this lengthy quotation are not far from what Burke would argue in his *Reflections*. The balance of feelings towards the institutions of government and the laws lay at the heart of the debate from its outset, as it had in resistance theories since the Reformation, if not earlier.

Together with the notion that the King was nothing more than the servant of the people and the apparent implication that government could be generated or changed at will, it was the comparison Price was to draw later in the *Discourse* between the Glorious, the American, and French Revolutions that Burke thought not only false but highly dangerous. What was unfolding in France had nothing in common with the Glorious, or even the American, Revolution, Burke argued. There was nothing to be praised about developments across the Channel, which Burke saw not as the creation of a new constitutional order but as the ignorant dismantling of its civil society and all that government was meant to secure, individual safety, liberty, and property. What was taking place in France was unnatural and unwarranted, without precedent in the American Revolution, let alone 1688. It was an attack on civilisation itself.

10 Ibid 27–28.

For Price, on the contrary, the events marked stages in a constitutional work in progress. While he praised the Glorious Revolution for its achievements and indeed repeatedly noted his gratitude to it, as he thought it had laid the ground for toleration and liberty, he believed much more needed to be done, not least extending political representation. On this alone, Burke might also not have minded Price's Sermon. What he disputed was what Price thought to be drawn from 1688 as principles, namely,

> First; The right to liberty of conscience in religious matters.
> Secondly; The right to resist power when abused. And,
> Thirdly; The right to chuse our own governors; to cashier them for misconduct; and to frame a government for ourselves.

Burke was no enemy of freedom of conscience, but he was to the disestablishment of national Churches and all that undermined the independence of the Church, as well as any endeavour to weaken religious faith, be it Protestantism in England or Catholicism in Ireland, Quebec, or France.[11] As for the right to resist power when abused, he thought that if truly discontented, a people would rebel, as he had foreseen the Americans would, but that was not a right established in law or principle to be deduced from 1688. It could not be a constitutional matter. And thus, he did not think it an established right to choose one's government as if from a shelf, whatever 'metaphysical' credentials were given to it. To be sure, there had been a deviation from the rule in England in 1688. The direct line of royal descent had been broken. But a deviation did not constitute a rule.[12] Reason of state justified the Revolution and the Settlement that followed it, for Burke, though this was perhaps not entirely convincing even to himself. In any event, it was, in his view, undertaken within the spirit of the existing political order. As Richard Bourke has demonstrated, Burke accepted that government was a matter of convenience, but he did not infer from this that its structures could be altered at will. Constitutional governance provided the conditions for careful deliberation over the nature of this convenience. This is the reason for his desire, in *Reflections*, to elaborate on the emotions which underpin continuity in political institutions: namely, those moral and aesthetic sentiments that encourage respect and veneration for the history of the nation and its customs.[13] One had to truly understand the political nature of one's country to truly love it, and both truly understand and love it in order to contemplate reforming it.

11 On Burke and the Quebec Act, see Bourke's excellent discussion in *Empire and Revolution* (n 4) 460–70.

12 Edmund Burke, *Reflections on the Revolution in France: A Critical Edition* (JCD Clark ed, Stanford University Press 2001) 159–72.

13 Bourke (n 4) 678. See also Samuel Harrison, 'The Concept of Dignity in Edmund Burke's Writings on the French Revolution' (2024) 32(3) British Journal for the History of Philosophy 525–46, 531–32.

In the *Vindication of the Rights of Men*, Wollstonecraft poured ridicule on the idea of revering such a constitution, which she saw as nothing more than the haphazard result of generations of conflict, unhappy compromise, and manoeuvring between opposing political elites. She confessed not knowing where to begin in addressing Burke's nonsense: 'I glow with indignation when I attempt, methodically, to unravel your slavish paradoxes, in which I can find no fixed first principle to refute.' 'I shall not, therefore,' she continued, 'condescend to shew where you affirm in one page what you deny in another; and how frequently you draw conclusions without any previous premises.'[14] She thought the *Reflections* showed Burke to have:

> [A] mortal antipathy to reason; but, if there is any thing like an argument, or first principles, in your wild declamation, behold the result: – that we are to reverence the rust of antiquity, and term the unnatural customs, which ignorance and mistaken self-interest have consolidated, the sage fruit of experience: nay, that, if we do discover some errors, our feelings should lead us to excuse, with blind love, or unprincipled filial affection, the venerable vestiges of ancient days. These are gothic notions of beauty – the ivy is beautiful, but, when it insidiously destroys the trunk from which it receives support, who would not grub it up?[15]

As Wollstonecraft interpreted the *Reflections*, it committed Burke to inaction. She believed him to think one should not risk the inconvenience that touching the constitutional order might cause the present generation, even for the sake of a better life for generations to come. Injustice would thus reign perpetual.

Interestingly, she was fully aware of Burke's fear that the revolution in France was far more consequential than it appeared and was, in fact, undermining European civilisation itself. Moreover, she did not deny it or dread it but welcomed its demise, as she derided the idea that modern European society was civilised:

> The civilization which has taken place in Europe has been very partial, and, like every custom that an arbitrary point of honour has established, refines the manners at the expence of morals, by making sentiments and opinions current in conversation that have no root in the heart, or weight in the cooler resolves of the mind.[16]

14 Mary Wollstonecraft, 'A Vindication of the Rights of Men' in Sylvana Tomaselli (ed), *A Vindication of the Rights of Men and a Vindication of the Rights of Woman and Hints* (Cambridge University Press 1995) 7–8.

15 Ibid 8.

16 Ibid 8–9.

It was important to Wollstonecraft's case against Burke to present the state of European emotions as a chaotic sham. Where reason did not prevail, neither could true love nor reverence. Antiquity, tradition, and precedence did not equate to rationality, in her view. In her account, of course, Burke was not only irrational himself but rejected any attempt to subject the *status quo* to rational scrutiny.

The question she posed in her *Vindication* was at which point and through which process had the right to property and liberty that he seemed to value so highly come into being:

> Will Mr. Burke be at the trouble to inform us, how far we are to go back to discover the rights of men, since the light of reason is such a fallacious guide that none but fools trust to its cold investigation?[17]

And answered herself:

> In the infancy of society, confining our view to our own country, customs were established by the lawless power of an ambitious individual, or a weak prince was obliged to comply with every demand of the licentious barbarous insurgents, who disputed his authority with irrefragable arguments at the point of their swords; or the more specious requests of the Parliament, who only allowed him conditional supplies.[18]

Wollstonecraft was pressing a plain and simple, but nonetheless crucial, point: 'Are these the venerable pillars of our constitution?'[19] Could one love a constitution anchored on such things? Revere it? 'And is Magna Charta,' she went on, 'to rest for its chief support on a former grant, which reverts to another, till chaos becomes the base of the mighty structure – or we cannot tell what? – for coherence, without some pervading principle of order, is a solecism.'[20] Wollstonecraft quoted David Hume's *History of England* (1754–1761) on the reign of Edward III: the historian contended that 'he was a prince of great capacity, not governed by favourites, not led astray by any unruly passion, sensible that nothing could be more essential to his interests than to keep on good terms with his people: yet, on the whole, it appears that the government, at best, was only a barbarous monarchy, not regulated by any fixed maxims, or bounded by any certain or undisputed rights, which in practice were regularly observed.'[21] She traced how the Commons arose, acquiring increasing privi-

17 Ibid 9.
18 Ibid.
19 Ibid.
20 Ibid.
21 Ibid 9–10.

leges which they demanded in return for the assistance they provided King Edward to finance his many wars. The Commons 'became a check on both king and nobles.'[22]

The system of government had no illustrious ancestry. There was no wondrous story to tell about its origins, nor of that of the liberty and right to private property it allegedly protected:

> Thus was the foundation of our liberty established, chiefly through the pressing necessities of the king, who was more intent on being supplied for the moment, in order to carry on his wars and ambitious projects, than aware of the blow he gave to kingly power, by thus making a body of men feel their importance, who afterwards might strenuously oppose tyranny and oppression, and effectually guard the subject's property from seizure and confiscation.[23]

As the resemblance between this account of the rise of the English Commons and the contemporary triumph of France's Third Estate is pretty clear, Wollstonecraft's choice of historical moment to illustrate the vicissitudes of constitutional history was likely to have been deliberate. While she mentioned John Wycliffe (c. 1324–1384) and the ray of reason that was briefly cast by him, it led her only to ask: 'Where was the dignity of thinking of the fourteenth century?'[24]

On her account, the history of what passed as the English Constitution was an ignoble one, and this to such a degree that she thought it undeserving of the name:

> The imperfection of all modern government must, without waiting to repeat the trite remark, that all human institutions are unavoidably imperfect, in a great measure have arisen from this simple circumstance, that the constitution, if such a heterogeneous mass deserve that name, was settled in the dark days of ignorance, when the minds of men were shackled by the grossest prejudices and most immoral superstition. And do you, Sir, a sagacious philosopher, recommend night as the fittest time to analyze a ray of light?[25]

For her, Burke's response to Price's *Love of our Country* was an irrational mix of misplaced feelings and sentimentality equal to his absurd reaction to the events in France, kindled by his enduring juvenile infatuation with Queen Marie-Antoinette, a love that prompted Thomas Paine's (1730–1807) famous

22 Ibid 10.
23 Ibid 10–11.
24 Ibid 11.
25 Ibid 11.

quip in his *Rights of* Man (1791) that Burke 'pities the plumage, but forgets the dying bird.'[26]

In this debate, the emotions mattered. Their appropriateness mattered. Their consistency mattered. Wollstonecraft admitted she raked up all she could to undermine Burke, the man, and his politics of feelings. Referring to Burke's parliamentary interventions during the period of George III's so-called madness, she exclaimed:

> I have, Sir, been reading, with a scrutinizing, comparative eye, several of your insensible and profane speeches during the King's illness. . . . what but the odious maxims of Machiavellian policy could have led you to have searched in the very dregs of misery for forcible arguments to support your party? Had not vanity or interest steeled your heart, you would have been shocked at the cold insensibility which could carry a man to those dreadful mansions, where human weakness appears in its most awful form to calculate the chances against the King's recovery. Impressed as you are with respect for royalty, I am astonished that you did not tremble at every step, lest heaven should avenge on your guilty head the insult offered to its viceregent. But the conscience that is under the direction of transient ebullitions of feeling, is not very tender or consistent, when the current runs the other way.[27]

Not only had Burke argued for the gross maltreatment of the King when ill, and 'with unfeeling disrespect, and indecent haste, wished to strip him of all his hereditary honours,' but his passion for Marie-Antoinette stood in sharp contrast to his indifference to the plight of Queen Charlotte during the Regency.[28] Not content to show that even he, the great apologist for monarchy and hereditary rank, was unable to sustain consistent feelings of due reverence for Kings and Queens, Wollstonecraft also stressed Burke's lack of respect for age. He who made so much of longevity in relation to the constitution, thought nothing of the respect due to Price's age:

> In reprobating Dr Price's opinions you might have spared the man; and if you had had but half as much reverence for the grey hairs of virtue as for the accidental distinction of rank, you would not have treated with such indecent familiarity and supercilious contempt, a member of the community whose talents and modest virtues place him high in the scale of moral excellence.[29]

26 Ibid 27. Thomas Paine, *Rights of Man: Being an Answer to Mr. Burke's Attack on the French Revolution* (Cambridge University Press 2012) 26.

27 Wollstonecraft (n 14) 27–28.

28 Ibid.

29 Ibid. Harrison suggests Wollstonecraft's treatment of Burke on this point was not entirely just: see 'Burke's Writings' (n 13) 529.

If Burke himself could not maintain any degree of coherence in the nature and extent of his emotions, what justification could he proffer for continued devotion to a constitutional framework that relied on it, one that she had shown was itself the product of political expediency?

Only reason could legitimise a constitution. Neither Burkean Gothic sentimentalism nor nostalgic hankering for the restoration of the liberty an ancient Anglo-Saxon constitution was said to have once secured were the proper starting point for what she and many others saw as the dawn of a new constitutional age. History, we saw, was a record of much ignorance and injustice in her view. It was now time to clear away the dense thickets of overweening executive power, venality, and moral corruption that had sprouted over it in the modern age. In contrast to Richard Price, who had written in 1778 that had Britain not pursued an aggressive policy towards the Americans, 'The liberty of America might have preserved our liberty, and, under the direction of a patriot king or wise minister, proved the means of restoring to us our almost lost constitution,'[30] Wollstonecraft's views in the first *Vindication* were devoid of any romanticism about an ancient constitution. Such a constitution had no intrinsic claim to political legitimacy, which could be bestowed only by the exercise of reason. To exercise one's reason would, in turn, lead to recognition of the universality of the rights of man and woman, as she was to argue in her second *Vindication* (1792), rights which were themselves derived from a true understanding of God's purpose in creating humanity.

But was it only the exercise of reason? Or even really the exercise of reason? Even if we take into account the dynamics of rhetoric, Wollstonecraft seemed far from excluding feelings, and one feeling in particular, as the source of her conviction in the rights she vindicated:

> I reverence the rights of men. – Sacred rights! For which I acquire a more profound respect, the more I look into my own mind; and, professing these heterodox opinions, I still preserve my bowels; my heart is human, beats quick with human sympathies – and I FEAR God!
>
> I bend with awful reverence when I enquire on what my fear is built. – I fear that sublime power, whose motive for creating me must have been wise and good; and I submit to the moral laws which my reason deduces from this view of my dependence on him. – It is not his power that I fear – it is not to an arbitrary will, but to unerring reason I submit. – Submit – yes; . . .
>
> This fear of God makes me reverence myself. – Yes, Sir, the regard I have for honest fame, and the friendship of the virtuous, falls far short of the respect which I have for myself.[31]

30 Richard Price, 'Two Tracts on Civil Liberty, the War with America, and the Debts and Finances of the Kingdom: With a General Introduction and Supplement (1778)' in DO Thomas (ed), *Political Writings* (Cambridge University Press 1991) 56.

31 Wollstonecraft (n 14) 30.

Wollstonecraft thus firmly anchored the dignity of man in the existence of God. Reason took her to true belief. It was the fear of God, however, that made her revere his laws, from which rights flowed. One might note, given that Price's *Discourse* was about love, love of one's country, and that Burke's *Reflections* also very much spoke of bounds of loyalty, that the emotion that Wollstonecraft evoked was the sublime one of fear.

Rich though her first *Vindication* is in its critique of Burke and social and political inequities was, it does not go beyond this assertion of rights and does not attempt to sketch a constitutional proposal. Moreover, any fair-minded reader of Burke would have to conclude that her portrayal of his ideas does them little justice. Hers was, in part, an *ad hominem* argument, venturing as far as to question his masculinity. However, Wollstonecraft was right to question him as she did about the history whose legacy was the political practice of eighteenth-century Britain and about the extent to which Europe could be said to be civilised. She was also right to challenge him on the terrain on which he stood his ground as had Price, namely, feelings of reverence, respect, and awe.

In contrast to Wollstonecraft and other of his critics, Burke thought rights had been enshrined in the English constitution; not only was there no need for reasoning from first principles, but indeed such efforts risked unravelling the benefits of practices vestigial of former ages. Accordingly, the true test of a constitution, in his view, was not whether it had been formed in a 'legitimate' fashion, whether this was to be measured by the rationality of its framing or by any other extraneous test, but rather whether it served the purpose of upholding liberty in the present day.[32] Pressing questions over the formal validity of a constitution was not merely a distraction from this essential question but a threat to liberty itself. For Burke, to believe that the only good constitution was one ordained by reason would necessarily blind one to all the positive attributes and effects of the existing one. It was also a denial of Providence. Like Wollstonecraft, Burke's views were framed in a firm belief in Creation and God's will for humanity. He did believe that history showed humanity to have made progress and saw the hand of Providence in it.[33] However, his parliamentary record and unpublished work show that he wanted some very important reforms in America, as already mentioned, as well as in the governance of India and Ireland.[34] What mattered was not to risk, as he thought Price

32 See, for example, his comments on the purpose of royal power in Burke (n 12) 179–80.

33 Burke (n 12) 262.

34 See his criticism of legal discrimination against Catholics in Ireland in Edmund Burke, *The Writings and Speeches of Edmund Burke*, 9 vols, vol 4 (Paul Langford et al. eds, Oxford University Press 2015) 437–42; and Frederick Whelan's discussion of his criticisms of the East India Company in 'Burke on India' in Christopher Insole and David Dwan (eds), *The Cambridge Companion to Edmund Burke*, Cambridge Companions to Literature (Cambridge University Press 2012) 168–80.

and others were, destroying what advancement in securing liberty and respect for humanity had already been achieved in the hope of achieving an uncertain future. His was a gradualism with which Wollstonecraft had no truck in 1790.

This makes Wollstonecraft's opening comments in her *An Historical and Moral View of the Origin and Progress of the French Revolution; and the Effect it has produced in Europe* (1794) quite striking. Written partly on the strength of personal observations in Paris, it evinces a shift away from a procedural approach to constitutionalism and towards one, like Burke's, founded on the desirability of its effects. As a practising historian, Wollstonecraft became more attentive to social and political developments over time. Communication between nations, scientific discoveries, and 'the friction of arts and commerce have given to society the transcendently pleasing polish of urbanity; and thus, by a gradual softening of manners, the complexion of social life has been completely changed.'[35] To be sure, Wollstonecraft was quick to note that the 'remains of superstition and the unnatural distinction of privileged classes, which had their origin in barbarous folly, still fettered the opinions of man, and sullied his native dignity.'[36] However, she followed this by writing of the 'several distinguished english [sic] writers' who had begun to discuss political issues and thereby created the thread that would enlighten Europe:

> Locke . . . recommended in a more methodical manner religious toleration, and analyzed the principles of civil liberty; for in his definition of liberty we find the elements of *The Declaration of the Rights of Man*, which, in spite of the fatal errours [sic] of ignorance, and the perverse obstinacy of selfishness, is now converting sublime theories into practical truths.[37]

From the Continent, she could see that despite the corruption that corroded

> [B]ritish freedom. – Still, when the rest of Europe groaned under the weight of the most unjust and cruel laws, the life and property of englishmen [sic] were comparatively safe; and, if an impress-warrant respected the distinction of ranks, when the glory of England was at stake, splendid victories hid this in the best existing constitution; and all exultingly recollected, that the life or liberty of a man never depended on the will of an individual.[38]

35 Mary Wollstonecraft, *The Works of Mary Wollstonecraft*, 7 vols, vol 6 (Janet Todd and Marilyn Butler eds, Emma Rees-Mogg, Assistant ed., William Pickering 1989) 16.

36 ibid.

37 ibid.

38 Ibid.

She went on to excuse the English pride in their constitution:

> Englishmen were then, with reason, proud of their constitution; and, if this noble pride have [sic] degenerated into arrogance, when the cause became less conspicuous, it is only a venial lapse of human nature; to be lamented merely as it stops the progress of civilization, and leads the people to imagine, that their ancestors have done every thing possible to secure the happiness of society, and meliorate the condition of man, because they have done much.[39]

That Wollstonecraft came to think much better of England and its constitution is evident throughout her *An Historical and Moral View of the Origin and Progress of the French Revolution*. The measure she used for its merit was now the extent to which its people enjoyed the benefits of the rule of law. More or less explicitly throughout the work, she gave much credit for the country's improvement to its Reformation: 'With respect to the improvement of society, since the destruction of the roman empire, England seems to have led the way, rendering certain obstinate prejudices almost null, by a gradual change of opinion.'[40] But she also noted, amongst other factors, how, in England, the nobility mixed with the commercial classes, thereby eroding the aristocratic sense of superiority that prevailed in France and elsewhere in Europe.

What was to be a history of the causes of the revolution in France was set against a loosely drawn political history of England. Wollstonecraft's praise or critique of her country was no longer based on the legitimacy of the origins of its political institutions. She repeatedly maintained the superiority of England over Europe and underscored how this led to complacency, but she spoke of liberty having a history:

> But whilst all Europe was enslaved . . . the Britons [sic], in a great degree, preserved the liberty that they first recovered. This singular felicity was not more owing to the insular situation of their country, than to their spirited efforts; and national prosperity was the reward of their exertions. Whilst, therefore, Englishmen were the only free people in existence, they appear to have been not only content, but charmed with their constitution; though perpetually complaining of the abuses of their government.[41]

Whilst the English people complained, they nonetheless were unable to conceive of a simpler system of government, Wollstonecraft claimed. Blinded by

39 Ibid 17.
40 Ibid 70.
41 Ibid 113.

their felicity as well as their sense of their particularity, which she clearly now shared, they were politically unimaginative. It is noticeable that in contending this, she no longer avoided the language and historical markers conspicuously absent in her first *Vindication*. If liberty in England, she argued,

> had no specific basis beside magna charta, till the habeas corpus act passed, or before the revolution of 1688, but the temper of men; it is sufficient demonstration, that it was a government resting on principles emanating from consent, if not from the sense of the nation.[42]

Her view that the government of England was the product of the random chaos of history had given way to a gradualism more readily associated with Burke:

> The revolutions of states ought to be gradual; for during violent or material changes it is not so much the wisdom of measures, as the popularity they acquire by being adapted to the foibles of the great body of the community, which gives them success. – Men are most easily led astray by the ingenious arguments, that dwell on the equality of man, and these are always employed by the different leaders of popular governments.[43]

Her disparaging comments about the members of the National Assembly were also not far from Burke's in the *Reflections*.[44] Weary of the manipulation of the people by artful politicians, she explained that the absence of practical experience led to a profusion of political visions far ahead of the times; that, in turn, led to the wretchedness of the entire population, which a reader of her history might take to imply a preference for the English's lack of political imagination. Where she once drew on Hume's history of England to support her claim that its constitution was no more than the product of contingency and conflict, she now argued that the utopia depicted in his *Idea of a Perfect Commonwealth* (1777)

> would be eligible only when civilization has arrived at a much greater degree of perfection, and knowledge was more generally diffused than at the present period, was nevertheless chosen as the model for [the French] new government, with few exceptions, by the constituent assembly: which choice doubtless proceeded from members not having had the opportunity to acquire a knowledge of practical liberty.[45]

42 Ibid 114.
43 Ibid 166.
44 Ibid 165–66.
45 Ibid 166.

Some members had sought to draw from the American experience, itself derived 'from the english constitution, but the majority, despising experience, were for forming, at once, a system more perfect.'[46] This, she continued, had led to 'dreadful outrages, and attacks, made by the anarchists of that country, on personal liberty, property, and whatever else society holds sacred.'[47]

These sorry reflections made Wollstonecraft conclude that all governments that had the happiness of the people as their object had to 'make the power of altering peaceably a fundamental principle of their constitution.'[48] It was, however, important not to allow the present failures to implement a perfect system of government to open the floodgates of despair and cease to strive for a simpler polity 'which promises more equal freedom, and general happiness to mankind.'[49] Whether a simpler constitution would be revered or indeed needed to be revered, she did not say. Nor did she ever explain why England was such a beacon of liberty, why, for all its faults, it was blessed with liberty unknown in other countries. What we do know from the body of her works is that for a nation to be truly enviable, its citizens had to be the subjects of mutual respect, and for this, they had to be educated to be respectable. Such a people might then be in a position, one might conjecture, to produce a constitution grounded in reason that could be revered. Whether it would need such reverence is another matter.

Bibliography

Bourke R, *Empire and Revolution: The Political Life of Edmund Burke* (Princeton University Press 2015)

Burke E, *Reflections on the Revolution in France: A Critical Edition* (JCD Clark ed, Stanford University Press 2001)

Burke E, *The Writings and Speeches of Edmund Burke*, 9 vols (P Langford et al. eds, Oxford University Press 2015) vol 4

Harrison S, 'The Concept of Dignity in Edmund Burke's Writings on the French Revolution' (2024) 32(3) British Journal for the History of Philosophy 525–46

Namier L and Brooke J (eds), *The History of Parliament: The House of Commons 1754–1790*, 3 vols (Boydell & Brewer 1964) vol 2

Paine T, *Rights of Man: Being an Answer to Mr. Burke's Attack on the French Revolution* (Cambridge University Press 2012)

Price R, *A Discourse on the Love of Our Country* (T. Cadell 1789)

Price R, 'Two Tracts on Civil Liberty, the War with America, and The Debts and Finances of the Kingdom: With A General Introduction and Supplement (1778)' in DO Thomas (ed), *Political Writings* (Cambridge University Press 1991)

Skjönsberg M, 'Patriots and the Country Party Tradition in the Eighteenth Century: The Critics of Britain's Fiscal-Military State from Robert Harley to Catharine Macaulay' (2023) 33(1) Intellectual History Review 83–100

46 Ibid.
47 Ibid.
48 Ibid 167.
49 Ibid.

Tomaselli S, *Wollstonecraft: Philosophy, Passion, and Politics* (Princeton University Press 2020)
Whelan F, 'Burke on India' in C Insole and D Dwan (eds), *The Cambridge Companion to Edmund Burke*, Cambridge Companions to Literature (Cambridge University Press 2012) 168–80
Withey LE, 'Catharine Macaulay and the Uses of History: Ancient Rights, Perfectionism, and Propaganda' (1976) 16(1) Journal of British Studies 59–83
Wollstonecraft M, *The Works of Mary Wollstonecraft*, 7 vols (J Todd and M Butler eds, E Rees-Mogg, Assistant Ed, William Pickering 1989) vol 6, 16
Wollstonecraft M, 'A Vindication of the Rights of Men' in S Tomaselli (ed), *A Vindication of the Rights of Men and A Vindication of the Rights of Woman and Hints* (Cambridge University Press 1995)

14 Edmund Burke's *Thoughts on the Cause of the Present Discontents*

*Max Skjönsberg**

Thoughts on the Cause of the Present Discontents (1770) is the most notable among Edmund Burke's early political pamphlets, and perhaps his most famous overall alongside the *Reflections on the Revolution in France* (1790).[1] The *Present Discontents* must be understood in the context of party politics after the accession of George III in 1760. The new king had one major objective: to break the Whig oligarchy's grip on power and abolish parties by welcoming the Tories back into the fold. His formation was, in that sense, 'Bolingbrokean'; a document related to his education from around 1755–56 states clearly that his great grandfather, George I, had been captured by the Whigs and became 'their instrument for the good of their faction'.[2] At the beginning of 1762, the king reflected that 'Government has now an advantage from the House of Commons having now no party distinctions.'[3] This was not entirely true, but the Whigs had indeed lost their status as the natural party of government, whereas the Tories, now welcome at court, lost much of their cohesion and identity as an oppositional party. Instead of Whig-Tory or Court-Country, parliamentary competition morphed into a struggle between different Whig factions. In this way, George III completed a reconfiguration of politics that could be traced to the rise of the 'patriot minister' William Pitt the Elder during the Seven Years War (1756–1763). Pitt had been supported by Tories in Parliament, though they were still *personae non gratae* at court until George III's accession.

Burke's *Present Discontents* was written in support of the Rockingham Whig parliamentary connection, a party which had grown out of the 'Old Corps of Whigs' under the leadership of the Duke of Newcastle. After Newcastle's fall from office in 1762 and the dismissal of many of his followers, the

* The Hamilton School of Classical and Civic Education, University of Florida.

1 For Burke's political thought, see esp. Richard Bourke, *Empire and Revolution: The Political Life of Edmund Burke* (Princeton University Press 2015).

2 Cited in James Lee McKelvey, *George III and Lord Bute: The Leicester House Years* (Duke University Press 1973) 85.

3 *Letters from George III to Lord Bute, 1756–66* (Romney Sedgewick ed, Macmillan and Co 1939) 83.

DOI: 10.4324/9781032658698-15

leadership of the remnants of the 'Old Corps' gradually shifted to a younger generation, chiefly Charles Watson-Wentworth, 2nd Marquess of Rockingham.[4] In opposition in the early 1760s, they attracted former Country party Tories, such as William Dowdeswell, as they opposed the cider tax and general warrants. The Rockingham party formed the mainstay of a short-lived government in 1765–66, and among its achievements was the repeal of the Stamp Act alongside the passing of the Declaratory Act, which affirmed parliamentary sovereignty over the colonies.[5] Burke had been Rockingham's private secretary since 1765, and he was elected to Parliament for a pocket borough at the end of the year. Alongside Dowdeswell, Burke emerged as a leading spokesman for the Rockingham Whigs in the House of Commons, and, in due course, also their chief publicist. The Rockingham Whigs' identity as a party hardened in opposition in the late 1760s. Rockingham said: 'I think we, and we only, of all the party in opposition, are so on system and principles.'[6] The emphasis on party unity became even more important after the resignation of the elder Pitt (now the Earl of Chatham) and Lord Shelburne in 1769, who together became a rival locus of the Whig opposition but essentially on a non-party platform and the principle of 'Not men, but measures.'

The 'present discontents' in the pamphlet's title refer to the Middlesex election dispute, which had given the Whig opposition a great cause to rally around. John Wilkes had become a hero for the London crowd as a 'populist' critic of George III and his favourite Lord Bute in the early 1760s, but he was forced into exile in 1763 after government prosecution. Because of his indebtedness, Wilkes returned to England permanently in 1768, and he sought a seat in Parliament as a member for Middlesex in order to obtain immunity. As he was an indebted outlaw, however, Wilkes was sent to prison, which only increased his popularity. The House of Commons expelled Wilkes, though the electors continued to vote for him in a series of by-elections in 1769.[7] The crowd rioted in response to the treatment of Wilkes, and for the parliamentary opposition, expelling Wilkes was not only an overstep by the ministry but a plainly unconstitutional act. In April 1769, Burke said in Parliament: 'There is a contest going on between the freeholders of England and the House of Commons.'[8] The *Present Discontents* includes both direct and indirect references

4 Warren Elofson, *The Rockingham Connection and the Second Founding of the Whig Party* (McGill-Queen's University Press 1996); Frank O'Gorman, *The Rise of Party in England: The Rockingham Whigs, 1760–82* (Allen and Unwin 1975).

5 Paul Langford, *The First Rockingham Administration, 1765–66* (Oxford University Press 1973).

6 *Sir Henry Cavendish's Debates of the House of Commons*, 2 vols (J Wright ed, Longman 1841) I, 585.

7 See esp. Robin Eagles, *Champion of English Freedom: The Life of John Wilkes, MP and Lord Mayor of London* (Amberley Publishing 2024) chs. 4–8.

8 *Cavendish's Debates* (n 6) 378.

to 'Wilkes and Liberty'. But Burke's main focus was on the *cause* of the present discontents, which he identified as the Crown's 'secret influence'. Explaining what this was and why it was pernicious meant that Burke could not confine his discussion to contemporary politics but had to embark on constitutional theorising.

The greatest part of the *Present Discontents* is made up of an analysis of the corrupt court system and exposure of the 'double cabinet', according to which government policy was allegedly made by the king in collusion with an informal group of advisers, known as the 'king's friends', as opposed to the appointed ministers. Though the 'double cabinet' has been referred to as a conspiracy theory that misled many generations of scholars,[9] it should not surprise us that George III's accession produced such a reaction. The Rockinghams were convinced that George III and Bute had resuscitated Toryism not only by patronising Tories but also by increasing the powers of the Crown.[10] Bute had at first been appointed as leader of the government on the basis of his personal relationship with the king rather than his standing among the wider political class. After his resignation in 1763, it was claimed that he continued to pull the strings behind the scenes as the king's consigliere. The 'double cabinet' was viewed as nefarious because of its unaccountability and potential to increase the power of the Crown at the expense of the other parts of the mixed and balanced constitution. Protection of the constitution was key for Burke, who understood it as delicately and precariously balanced: 'Our constitution stands on a nice equipoise, with steep precipices, and deep waters upon all sides of it.'[11]

For Burke, the threat was systematic and went beyond the bogeyman of Bute. Some members of the party disagreed with his approach; the Duke of Portland, for instance, wanted a more head-on attack on Bute: 'for surely at the time you are declaring war and irreconcilable enmity to the whole party of *Kingsmen,* it must appear very strange to show any tenderness to their chief.'[12] Burke's pamphlet certainly referred to Bute,[13] but its chief spotlight was on what Burke described as 'a cabal of the closet and back-stairs', which had been 'substituted in the place of a national administration'.[14] He pre-empted criticism that he did not spend more time on attacking Bute by arguing that '[w]here there is a regular scheme of operation carried on,

9 John Brewer, 'Party and the Double Cabinet: Two Facets of Burke's *Thoughts*' (1971) 14 Historical Journal 479–501.

10 John Brewer, 'The Misfortunes of Lord Bute: A Case-Study in Eighteenth-Century Political Argument and Public Opinion' (1973) 16 Historical Journal 3–43, at 39.

11 Edmund Burke, *Pre-Revolutionary Writings* (Ian Harris ed, Cambridge University Press 1993) 180.

12 Portland to Rockingham, 3 December 1769, in *Memoirs of Rockingham and His Contemporaries*, 2 vols (George Keppel ed, 6th Earl of Albemarle, Richard Bentley 1852) II, 146.

13 Burke (n 11) 125, 142, 146.

14 Ibid 127.

it is the system, and not any individual person who acts in it, that is truly dangerous.'[15]

Although Burke's attack on the 'double cabinet' as a conspiracy against the constitution was naturally exaggerated, it represented a genuine attempt to grapple with the meaning of George III's accession and Britain's uncodified constitution. For Burke, the system of Court 'favouritism' and 'influence' meant that 'neither office, nor authority, nor property, nor ability, eloquence, council, skill, or union, are of the least importance.'[16] All that mattered was subservience to the Court. The 'double cabinet' – the separation between the administration and an '*interior cabinet*' – had created a confused and feeble government which had sullied Britain's reputation abroad, created discontent at home, and not even benefited the monarch himself. What was worse, the system seriously risked disturbing the balance of the constitution, which Burke believed had been protected by the Whigs since the Glorious Revolution.

Though Burke is known as a critic of Bolingbroke – one of his earliest publications being a satire of Bolingbroke's Deistic philosophy[17] – his key contention in the *Present Discontents* that the power of the Crown was dead as prerogative but had been revived as influence was drawing on the Bolingbrokean tradition.[18] For Burke as for Bolingbroke, it was key to distinguish the spirit from the form of the constitution. If the former was violated, the outward form of the constitution could remain intact but yet be a dead letter. According to the literal reading of the constitution, the king had the right to appoint his own ministers. But if he appointed ministers without paying attention to parliamentary clout, the government would become divorced from the people. Ambitious men would see court favour as the safe road to preferment and would not care to cultivate popularity and public confidence. In this way, Burke inspired an interpretation of the constitution that would be celebrated in nineteenth-century 'Whig' historiography, and contested by Lewis Namier and 'Tory' historiography in the twentieth century, emphasising the personal power of the monarch.[19] In Burke's view, Wilkes's expulsion demonstrated that the 'King's friends' intended to separate the Commons from the will of the people. As he put it, the House of Commons was meant to be a control *for* the people, not *on* the people.[20] But what he viewed as the Court system risked undermining this principle by making the Commons obsequious. If everyone depended on Court favour, no independence could be expected, and 'indiscriminate support to all Ministers' would become the rule.[21]

15 Ibid 142.
16 Ibid 139.
17 Edmund Burke, *A Vindication of Natural Society* (London 1756).
18 Burke (n 11) 124, 162.
19 For discussion, see John Brewer, *Party Ideology and Popular Politics at the Accession of George III* (Cambridge University Press 1976) 26–35.
20 Burke (n 11) 160.
21 Ibid 161.

According to Burke, all parts of the constitution, including King, Lords, and Commons, held office as trustees for the people and represented them. But it was only the House of Commons that was 'the express image of the feelings of the nation'.[22] As such, it was meant to be a body that would check and control the government. But Burke agreed with Bolingbroke that Parliament had, since the Glorious Revolution, increasingly become an instrument of government rather than an assembly holding the executive to account. Bolingbroke's 'Country party' had offered more frequent elections and placed bills to restore the lower house to its 'original' function. Burke agreed that 'the unfrequency of elections' since the Septennial Act 1716 had contributed to turning the lower house into something resembling 'a standing Senate'.[23] This was not at all to his liking:

> A vigilant and jealous eye over executory and judicial magistracy, an anxious care of public money, an openness approaching towards facility to public complaint; these seem to be the true characteristicks of an house of commons; but an addressing house of commons and a petitioning nation; an house of commons full of confidence when the nation is plunged in despair; in the utmost harmony with ministers whom the people regard with the utmost abhorrence; who vote thanks, when the public call upon them for impeachments; who are eager to grant, when the general voice demands account; who in all disputes between the people and administration presume against the people; who punish their disorders, but refuse to inquire into the provocations to them: this is an unnatural, a monstrous state of things in this constitution; such an assembly may be a great, wise, and awful senate, but it is not to any popular purpose an house of commons.[24]

Burke ultimately believed that the 'horrible disorders among the people attending frequent elections' were too high a price to pay for shortening the duration of Parliaments. But his more substantial objection was that more frequent elections with their expenses would impoverish the country gentlemen before it drained the court, and thus contribute to reducing their strength and independence vis-à-vis the Crown.[25] His opposition to parliamentary reform must thus be understood as part of his concern for the Whig party as an effective check on the power of the Crown. Though he was not against excluding certain office-holders in principle, Burke was also against a comprehensive place bill. The official, professional, military, and naval interests 'must be let into a share of representation, else possibly they may be inclined to destroy those institutions of which they are not permitted to partake.' Thanks to its

22 Ibid 160.
23 Ibid 161.
24 Ibid 160–61.
25 Ibid 178.

transparency, the influence of officeholders was less pernicious than 'clandestine corruption'.[26]

Burke's panacea was the return to power of the Rockingham Whigs, held together and able to challenge the monarch on the basis of the principle of party, which he influentially defined as 'a body of men united, for promoting by their joint endeavours the national interest, upon some particular principle in which they are all agreed.'[27] Burke was convinced that party connection was necessary for the fulfilment of public duty. Without concert and bonds of friendship, political action would lack 'uniformity, perseverance, [and] efficacy.' 'When bad men combine, the good must associate', Burke famously wrote, 'else they will fall, one by one, an unpitied sacrifice in a contemptible struggle.'[28] Politics was not about having a clean conscience but making a difference.

The genius of the *Present Discontents* was to explain the necessity of political parties to the workings of Britain's mixed and balanced constitution. This was far from being the established wisdom at the time. As we have seen, George III came to the throne in 1760 with the intention to break the parties, and he was cheered on by large parts of the political nation. For Burke, however, destroying party was a way for the Court to control Parliament and effectively the aristocratic and democratic branches of the constitution. Burke argued that the British political system allowed two safeguards against royal supremacy: 'power arising from popularity, and power arising from connexion.'[29] The former was associated with Chatham, and the latter with Rockingham. Out of the two, Burke saw party connection as much preferable since it was more deeply 'rooted in the country', whereas popularity was 'personal, and therefore transient.'[30] Burke claimed that George III and the Court faction had struck at the first power by getting rid of Pitt and the second power by dismissing Newcastle and then proscribing the Whigs.

The Court cabal wanted to do away with party entirely by propagating the doctrine that 'all political connexions are in their nature factious, and as such ought to be dissipated and destroyed; and that the rule for forming Administrations is mere personal ability, rated by the judgements of this Cabal upon it.'[31] Burke's most significant intervention in the *Present Discontents* was to argue that party connection was required for effective politics and that it could restore the balance of the constitution. For him, what was needed was an administration 'composed of those who recommend themselves to their Sovereign through the opinion of their country', in other words, through their parliamentary strength. Such men would strengthen the executive power

26 Ibid 180.

27 Ibid 187. See also Max Skjönsberg, *The Persistence of Party: Ideas of Harmonious Discord in Eighteenth-Century Britain* (Cambridge University Press 2021) ch. 11.

28 Burke (n 11) 184.

29 Ibid 130.

30 Ibid 129.

31 Ibid 183.

'because they will add the weight of the country to [its] force'.[32] Public principle separated party connections from cabals, with the latter coming together only 'in order to sell their conjunct iniquity at the higher rate'.[33] For this reason, it was vital for Burke that the Rockinghams would be 'attached in office to every principle they had maintained in opposition'.[34]

Burke's defence of party relied on the notion of the importance of intermediary powers in a constitutional system. In mid-eighteenth-century Britain, the French aristocrat Montesquieu was widely conceived as the greatest political genius of the age and an authority on the British constitution. George Grenville cited *De l'esprit des lois* (1748) in Parliament in the context of Wilkes, and even the young George III had studied Montesquieu before his accession.[35] Both as a man of letters and a politician, Burke would have studied Montesquieu carefully, and the brother of his father-in-law is believed to have translated Montesquieu's magnum opus into English in 1750.[36] As William Selinger has argued, however, Burke departed from Montesquieu on fundamental constitutional questions: in advocating stricter separation between the executive and legislative powers, Montesquieu had been inspired by Bolingbroke, whereas Burke recognised the need for cooperation between the executive and legislature.[37] In any case, one of the most influential arguments in Montesquieu's book was his point about intermediate powers as a bulwark against despotism – royal, aristocratic, or democratic.[38] In the *Present Discontents,* Burke wrote that '[i]t is in the nature of despotism to abhor power held by any means but its own momentary pleasure; and to annihilate all intermediate situations.'[39] Under the first two Georges, Burke argued, the Whig party had been an intermediate power between the people and the Court.

By celebrating the legacy of the Whig supremacy – bemoaned by a host of writers on both ends of the political spectrum in the 1760s and 1770s – Burke has sometimes been accused of behaving obsequiously towards aristocracy. In a classic treatment, Alfred Cobban called Burke's conception of government 'oligarchic'.[40] The core of Burke's party was indeed made up of major Whig aris-

32 Ibid 192.
33 Ibid 147.
34 Ibid 142.
35 CP Courtney, *Montesquieu and Burke* (first published 1963, Greenwood Press 1975) 79; GEO/ADD/32/1044-1047, Royal Archives, Windsor Castle.
36 Bourke (n 1) esp. introduction; Iain McBride, 'Burke and Ireland' in David Dwan and Christopher Insole (ed), *The Cambridge Companion to Edmund Burke* (Cambridge University Press 2012) 189.
37 William Selinger, *Parliamentarism: From Burke to Weber* (Cambridge University Press 2019) 68–69.
38 Montesquieu, *The Spirit of the Laws* (first published 1748, Anne M Cohler et al. eds, Cambridge University Press 1989) 17–19, 78.
39 Burke (n 11) 125.
40 Alfred Cobban, *Burke and the Revolt Against the Eighteenth Century* (first published 1929, George Allen 1960) 69. More recently, see FP Lock, *Edmund Burke*, 2 vols (Oxford University Press 1998–2006) I, 282.

tocratic families such as the Cavendishes and the Devonshires. In the *Present Discontents,* however, he pre-empted criticisms on this score by stating that he was 'no friend to aristocracy, in the sense at least in which that word is usually understood', that is to say, as 'austere and insolent domination'.[41] But the Whig aristocrats possessed property, rank, and quality, which gave them independence and, in turn, the ability to stand up to the Court. The Whig cause (the preservation of the Revolution Settlement) had united them in defence of the common good rather than any specific branch of the constitution. In this sense, Burke's conception of party was indeed aristocratic, but it was not aristocracy for its own benefit but for the sake of the whole. Moreover, the idea of party enabled the aristocracy to make common cause with the people's representatives, among whom he numbered. The usual way of analysing the British constitution was, of course, as consisting of King, Lords, and Commons. But in a parliamentary debate in May 1768, Burke described the British constitution as consisting of King, Parliament, and people, with parliamentary members (both Lords and Commoners) as a 'middle class' that would mediate between popular turmoil and royal domination.[42] This middle class played the role of an intermediate power capable of keeping despotism at bay in the way that Montesquieu had theorised. This was only possible, however, if it was sufficiently independent from the Court and the people alike. Party loyalty enabled such independence.

Burke's second solution to the problem of the influence of the Crown centred on what he called '*the interposition of the body of the people itself*', by which he meant a more politically active citizenry and especially electorate.[43] This is a complicated area in Burke's constitutional thought, and it has been much less discussed than his defence of party.[44] It might come as a surprise to some of his readers since he has, ever since his famous speech in Bristol in 1774 in opposition to constituency instructions, become known as the chief representative of the trustee theory of representation.[45] Importantly, he opined on the matter much earlier, before writing the *Present Discontents.* On 10 February 1769, at a meeting of the citizens of London, a set of instructions was agreed to, including: 'That, if any demand should come before parliament, for payments of the debts of the Civil List, you will diligently inquire how those debts have been incurred, to the prejudice of the subject, and the dignity of the Crown.' William Beckford declared in the House of Commons: 'Gentlemen may think, that instructions are not to be regarded; I do think it is the law and custom of parliament.'[46] Though speaking on the same side as Beckford in the broader

41 Burke (n 11) 134–35.

42 Cited in Bourke (n 1) 255.

43 Burke (n 11) 181 (original emphasis).

44 But see David Craig, 'Burke and the Constitution' in David Dwan and Christopher Insole (eds), *The Cambridge Companion to Edmund Burke* (Cambridge University Press 2012) 112–13.

45 Hannah Pitkin, *The Concept of Representation* (University of California Press 1967) 128–29.

46 *Cavendish's Debates* (n 6) 280.

debate on the Civil List, and in general taking a popular line at the time, Burke retorted: 'As to the doctrine of instruction to representatives, it is unfounded in reason; if not put down, it will destroy the constitution.'[47]

It must be emphasised, however, that Burke did not want representatives to be inattentive to the concerns of their constituents. In his *Speech on Enforcement of the Stamp Act* (1766), he said that 'Nothing can hurt a popular assembly so much as being unconnected with its constituents.'[48] In 1769, he told Parliament: 'When they [constituents] come to us upon constitutional ground, the sense of the people without doors is to be listened to with great attention, with great care.'[49] The *Present Discontents* laid out Burke's vision for how the relationship between MPs and constituents could be strengthened by organisational means. He stressed the responsibility of voters to pay attention to the conduct of their representatives. To this end, they should arrange meetings and establish '[s]tandards, for judging more systematically upon their [MPs'] conduct'.[50] Crucially, in order to be able to do this properly, the public needed access to division lists to see how their MPs voted. In a word, Burke believed that the relationship between voters and representatives should be a close one and that politics needed to be transparent for this to be possible. Burke's public letter to the Stewards of the Bell Club in Bristol of 1 November 1777, published in the *Bristol Gazette*, serves as a useful summary of his view of the political role of ordinary citizens in the earlier part of this career:

> You will therefore not listen to those who tell you, that these matters are above you and ought to be left entirely to those into whose hands the King has put them. The publick interest is more your Business than theirs . . . For in this very thing lies the difference between free men, and those that are not free. In a free Country, every man thinks he has a concern in all publick matters; that he has a right to form, and a right to deliver an opinion upon them. They sift, examine, and discuss them. They are curious, eager, attentive, and jealous . . . And this it is, that fills free Countries with men of ability in all Stations . . . In free countries there is often found more real publick wisdom and sagacity in Shops and manufacturers than in the Cabinets of Princes, in Countries, where none dares to have an opinion until he comes into them. Your whole importance therefore depends upon a constant discreet use of your own reason. Otherwise you and your Country sink to nothing.[51]

47 Ibid 287.

48 *The Writings and Speeches of Edmund Burke*, 9 vols (Paul Langford et al. eds, Oxford University Press 1970–2015) II, 52.

49 *Cavendish's Debates* (n 6) 287.

50 Burke (n 11) 181.

51 Burke to Richard Champion, 25 Sep 1777, in *The Correspondence of Edmund Burke*, 10 vols (Thomas W Copeland et al. eds, University of Chicago Press 1958–1978) III, 397–98.

Bibliography

6th Earl of Albemarle, George Keppel (ed), *Memoirs of Rockingham and His Contemporaries*, 2 vols (Richard Bentley 1852)

Bourke R, *Empire and Revolution: The Political Life of Edmund Burke* (Princeton University Press 2015)

Brewer J, 'Party and the Double Cabinet: Two Facets of Burke's Thoughts' (1971) 14 Historical Journal 479–501

Brewer J, 'The Misfortunes of Lord Bute: A Case-Study in Eighteenth-Century Political Argument and Public Opinion' (1973) 16 Historical Journal 3–43

Brewer J, *Party Ideology and Popular Politics at the Accession of George III* (Cambridge University Press 1976)

Burke E, *A Vindication of Natural Society* (London 1756)

Burke E, *Pre-Revolutionary Writings* (Ian Harris ed, Cambridge University Press 1993)

Burke E, *The Writings and Speeches of Edmund Burke*, 9 vols (P Langford et al. eds, Oxford University Press 1970–2015)

Cobban A, *Burke and the Revolt Against the Eighteenth Century* (first published 1929, George Allen 1960)

Copeland TW, et al (eds), *The Correspondence of Edmund Burke*, 10 vols (University of Chicago Press 1958–1978)

Courtney CP, *Montesquieu and Burke* (first published 1963, Greenwood Press 1975)

Craig D, 'Burke and the Constitution' in D Dwan and C Insole (eds), *The Cambridge Companion to Edmund Burke* (Cambridge University Press 2012)

Eagles R, *Champion of English Freedom: The Life of John Wilkes, MP and Lord Mayor of London* (Amberley Publishing 2024)

Elofson W, *The Rockingham Connection and the Second Founding of the Whig Party* (McGill-Queen's University Press 1996)

GEO/ADD/32/1044–1047, Royal Archives, Windsor Castle

Langford P, *The First Rockingham Administration, 1765–66* (Oxford University Press 1973)

Lock FP, *Edmund Burke*, 2 vols (Oxford University Press 1998–2006)

McBride I, 'Burke and Ireland' in D Dwan and C Insole (eds), *The Cambridge Companion to Edmund Burke* (Cambridge University Press 2012)

McKelvey JL, *George III and Lord Bute: The Leicester House Years* (Duke University Press 1973)

Montesquieu, *The Spirit of the Laws* (first published 1748, Anne M Cohler et al eds, Cambridge University Press 1989)

O'Gorman F, *The Rise of Party in England: The Rockingham Whigs, 1760–82* (Allen and Unwin 1975)

Pitkin H, *The Concept of Representation* (University of California Press 1967)

Sedgewick R, *Letters from George III to Lord Bute, 1756–66* (Macmillan and Co 1939)

Selinger W, *Parliamentarism: From Burke to Weber* (Cambridge University Press 2019)

Skjönsberg M, *The Persistence of Party: Ideas of Harmonious Discord in Eighteenth-Century Britain* (Cambridge University Press 2021)

Wright J, *Sir Henry Cavendish's Debates of the House of Commons*, 2 vols (Longman 1841)

15 The depiction of the British constitution in caricature, 1784–1819

*Chris Monaghan and Robert Thomas**

15.1 Introduction

There is a different, important but underexplored source of British constitutional meaning and history: visual, satirical caricature, that is, pictures – prints – that give us an account of the past. They allow those with an interest in the constitution and political machinations to see how these events were depicted by witnesses to what was then breaking news.[1] The caricatures were never a truly accurate representation. They were intended to convey particular viewpoints, often satirical and humourous. Such prints often reflected the views of those who paid for them to be created and published or the artist's own political views. Alternatively, the prints were produced because the artist believed they would sell well. A print critical of Charles James Fox might sell more copies than one depicting William Pitt the Younger. Irrespective, such caricatures embody important constitutional meaning and deserve to be revisited.

To this end, this chapter takes five prints published between 1784 and 1819 during the reign of George III and examines them as leading works of the constitution, which provide considerable insight into the constitution. The caricatures represent how the population may have engaged with and understood the representation of contemporary constitutional events. Today, these prints, and many others, remain a visible legacy of the past and are still easily recognisable, and the most famous are often imitated by contemporary cartoonists to make a point.

Each picture deals with contemporary concerns about what was happening at the time. They also reflect a perennial theme of the constitution and a narrative and commentary upon it. These themes include the risk of absolute

* We are grateful to Dr Robin Eagles for his feedback on an earlier draft of this chapter.

1 NG Howe observes that there are however difficulties for the modern viewer, as will not fully understand the visual cues, since the 'visual vocabulary and convention' limits the ability of 'historians from viewing them through eighteenth-century eyes' (NG Howe, *Statesmen in Caricature: The Great Rivalry of Fox and Pitt the Younger in the Age of the Political Caricature* (IB Tauris 2019) 10).

DOI: 10.4324/9781032658698-16

power, both royal and prime ministerial; the pivotal role of Parliament in holding power to account (e.g., through impeachment proceedings); the need for constitutional balance and the placing of trust in those in high office; and the need for the public to trust those in power to chart and maintain a steady course. Finally, there is the radical critique and debunking of the constitution, undertaken with the purpose of exposing its falseness and hollowness, thereby discrediting its claims to legitimacy. From this perspective, the constitution is seen as an artifice, a subterfuge which conceals the exploitation of the ordinary people. These narratives are recognisable in contemporary constitutional debate and discussion, thereby highlighting a wider continuity. However, before considering the selected prints, it is necessary first to examine the nature of caricature and its place within the society of the time.

15.2 Caricature and caricaturists

English political caricature had its heyday during the golden age of caricatures, roughly 1780 to 1832.[2] The caricaturists, some of whom are still well-known today, such as James Gillray and Thomas Rowlandson, depicted the social and political events of the times in which they lived. Diana Donald observes that within academe, there is a temptation to regard a caricature as a precise representation of what happened.[3] This is problematic as caricatures were certainly not that, nor are they unbiased and fair accounts of historical events. Nonetheless, as Lord Baker observed, they do offer a 'vivid way' to learn about the past. For us today, caricatures offer 'snapshots capturing a moment in history and say more than columns of newsprint'.[4] The caricaturists give us historical figures as larger-than-life characters, with the Whig politician Charles James Fox depicted in various guises throughout his lifetime – from a literal fox (which followed on from the tradition of depicting his father, Henry Fox, as a fox)[5] to a rotund gentleman with his famous eyebrows.[6] The beauty of

2 For a discussion on what time period constitutes the golden age, see Howe (n 1) 2. A great resource for those interested in caricatures and the British constitution see HT Dickinson, *Caricatures and the Constitution 1760–1832* (Chadwyck-Healey 1986). Dickinson's book provides the reader with a large number of examples of caricatures that offered a critique or reflection on the constitution. See also M Dorothy George, *English Political Caricature: A Study of Opinion and Propaganda to 1792* (Oxford University Press 1959).

3 Diana Donald, *The Age of Caricature: Satirical Prints in the Reign of George III* (Yale University Press 1996) vii.

4 Kenneth Baker, *George III: A Life in Caricature* (Thames and Hudson 2007) 7.

5 For example, see James Gillray's 'There's more ways than one' (Published by Hannah Humphrey, 51 New Bond Street, 18 February 1788), which depicted Fox as a fox climbing a post, from which hangs a tavern sign of the crown, in order to eat a large bunch of grapes.

6 The nickname codeword that Fox's fellow Whigs used for him was 'The Eyebrow' (see Leslie Mitchell, *The Whig World 1760–1837* (Hambledon and London 2005) 25). For example, see James Sayers, 'Vox Populi' (Published by Charles Bretherton, New Bond Street, London, 6 April 1782). Although this example depicts a younger and less rotund Fox.

caricature was its simplicity and ease of conveying a clear message. The caricaturists might be highly talented, such as James Gillray, and capable of creating the most sublime and complex caricatures, or slightly amateurish, but with the ability to inflict maximum damage on the subject being criticised, such as James Sayers (see further on).

The importance of these caricaturists must be emphasised. As Lord Baker pithily put it, '[t]hese cartoons were like the paparazzi of the day', and their legacy is the caricatures that enable us as a modern audience to engage with the past.[7] Those familiar with the caricatures of the golden age will quickly recognise the characters and how their personalities were portrayed. Commenting on why caricatures were so effective in communicating the complexities of political events to the public, Marc Baer is clear that they 'allowed caricaturists to present very complex political issues using visual clichés'.[8] It is hardly surprising that accessible, crude, and lowbrow caricatures were popular; they appealed to a wide audience and were remarkably successful as a form of inclusive communication.[9]

The turnaround time of the caricaturist was quick for the most part.[10] The caricatures had to depict current events and be etched and printed quickly.[11] Caricaturists copied the work of their peers,[12] emulated one another, or, as in the case of Gillray, fashioned a caricature to respond to an earlier one by a competitor such as James Sayers by taking a different position but parodying the style of Sayers. Despite Sayers' earliest work being '[h]is most celebrated work', these caricatures were 'also his worst artistically and was parodied by Gillray who, at times, adopted his signature as a tease'.[13] For example, Sayers produced three caricatures critical of the impeachment of Warren Hastings, which were then parodied by Gillray. The first is 'For the trial of Warren Ha[stings]'[14] which was a parody of the tickets issued by Peter Burrell, the deputy Lord Great Chamberlain (the role had been inherited by Burrell's wife,

7 Lord Baker of Dorking, 'The History of British Cartoons and Caricature' (Gresham College, 4 October 2010) <https://www.gresham.ac.uk/watch-now/history-british-cartoons-and-caricature>.

8 Marc Baer, *The Rise and Fall of Radical Westminster, 1780–1890* (Palgrave Macmillan 2012) 218.

9 For example, James Gillray was especially crude and frequently include excrement, urination, vomiting, sex, and flatulence in his prints.

10 The speed at which Gillray could create an etching was extraordinary. It is recorded by Henry Angelo that Gillray once etched a plate in five hours in order to win a bet (see Alice Loxton, *Uproar! Satire, Scandal and Printmakers in Georgian London* (Icon Books 2024) 115–16).

11 For an account of the production process see Howe (n 1) 18–20, see also Loxton (n 10) 107–19.

12 A notorious example was Charles Williams who was employed by the print seller SW Fores to create copies of Gillray's work (see Jim Sherry, 'Identifying a Gillray' <https://www.jamesgillray.org/catalog_identifying.html>).

13 LH Cust, revised by EA Smith, 'Sayers [Sayer], James' (Oxford Dictionary of National Biography, published 23 September 2004).

14 (Published 5 March 1788).

Figure 15.1 For the trial of Warren Ha[stings] seventh day

Source: © Yale University

Figure 15.2 Impeachment ticket. For the trial of W-RR-NH-ST-NGS Esqr

Source: © Yale University

Lady Priscilla Bertie, Baroness Willoughby de Eresby, the daughter of the Duke of Ancaster),[15] that was followed shortly afterwards by James Gillray's 'Impeachment ticket. For the trial of W-RR-NH-ST-NGS Esqr'.[16]

Sayers' caricature was critical of the impeachment trial and included a female figure depicting justice dropping the scales of justice and a judge weeping, indicating the unfairness of the proceedings. By contrast, Gillray's caricature takes a more nuanced position and shows that there is some justification for the impeachment. As Jim Sherry has observed, '[a]s in many of his prints, Gillray assigns blame to both sides'. Gillray's version shows Lord Thurlow (Hastings' friend) as the judge, and Hastings is on his knees before Thurlow begging for mercy. Words on the bottom of the print read: 'From Bribery & Corruption Good Lord deliver us', and 'From Envy & Malice!!! Good Lord, deliver us'.[17] The other Sayers prints were, 'The princess's bow alias the Bow Begum',[18] parodied by Gillray in 'The bow to the throne,-alias-the begging bow',[19] and 'Galante show "redeunt spectacula mane"',[20] which was parodied by Gillray in 'Camera-obscura'.[21] In the final example, Sayers depicts Edmund Burke as magnifying Hastings' supposed misconduct, whilst Gillray depicts Hastings as minimising his misconduct. Given the contemporary (and to a lesser extent current) debate surrounding Hastings' culpability and the justification of his impeachment, both men's caricatures illustrate the contested nature of the impeachment.[22]

15.3 What motivated the caricaturists?

Caution needs to be taken when interpreting the caricatures. These are not accurate depictions of historical events. The caricaturists had their own subjective biases and views. Some, like James Gillray, were (for some of the time) on the government payroll. Gillray was described by his peers as 'shy, reserved, enigmatic, melancholic, hyper-sensitive, and excitable', and had a 'cynicism about politics and politicians'.[23] It was only in 1797 that he sided with Pitt,

15 For the wider context see Chiara Rolli, *The Trial of Warren Hastings: Classical Oratory and Reception in Eighteenth-Century England* (Bloomsbury 2019) 58–61.
16 (Published February 1788).
17 For a useful discussion on the original ticket and both parodies see <https://www.jamesgillray.org/pop/impeachment-ticket.html>
18 (Published by Thomas Cornell, Bruton Street, London, 1 May 1788).
19 (Published by SW Fores, 3 Piccadilly, London, 6 May 1788).
20 (Published by Thomas Cornell, Bruton Street, London, 6 May 1788).
21 (Published by SW Fores, 3 Piccadilly, London, 9 March 1788).
22 See Alfie Banks, 'The Imperial Afterlife of Warren Hastings, 1818–1947' (2022) 50(3) The Journal of Imperial and Commonwealth History 498 and Zareer Masani, 'Warren Hastings, Governor-General of India' (2017) 67(11) History Today <https://www.historytoday.com/archive/warren-hastings-governor-general-india>.
23 Anita McConnell and Simon Heneage, 'Gillray, James' (Oxford Dictionary of National Biography 14 November 2018).

who 'secured his temporary loyalty with a pension'.[24] It took so long for Gillray to ally with Pitt, in part, because he had 'a keen appreciation of his commercial interest'.[25] As McConnell and Heneage argue, in Gillray's work, there was one consistent theme – a critique of the French Revolution and, subsequently, a sustained critique of Fox and other politicians who supported the revolution.[26]

Gillray formed a working relationship with the politician George Canning, who had co-established a magazine called the *Anti-Jacobin*. Canning commissioned Gillray to illustrate the magazine.[27] This was an important relationship for both Gillray and Canning as it provided Gillray with money and insider information (ever useful for the caricaturist) and Canning with effective propaganda.[28] Even so, M Dorothy George has emphasised that despite being awarded a pension, Gillray 'was scarcely a political partisan, and he was never a mere hireling'.[29] Nonetheless, he was consistently anti-Catholic, anti-French, patriotic, and highly critical of Fox.[30]

Others like Sayers could be rewarded for supporting the government. They were not so much political partisans but men and women (such as Elizabeth d'Achery, who, as a print seller, worked with Gillray)[31] who needed to earn a living and were willing to favour those who rewarded them for their services.[32] Howe warns that we simply do not know 'to what extent caricaturists produced work that they believed would sell, regardless of their politics'.[33] Andrew Roberts gives the example of the satirist John Wolcot (who used the alias Peter Pindar), who cruelly critiqued George III purely because it was commercially

24 Ibid.
25 Ibid.
26 Ibid.
27 Ibid.
28 Ibid.
29 M Dorothy George, *English Political Caricature: A Study of Opinion and Propaganda to 1792* (Oxford University Press 1959) 172.
30 Ibid.
31 Elizabeth d'Achery was described by Tim Clayton as a 'briefly important female print publisher, who ran a shop in St James's Street in the early 1780s'. (Tim Clayton, 'Shells to Satire: The Career of Hannah Humphrey' in Cristina S Martinez and Cynthis E Roman (eds), *Female Printmakers, Printsellers, and Print Publishers in the Eighteenth Century: The Imprint of Women, c. 1700–1830* (Cambridge University Press 2024) 212. Like Hannah Humphrey, d'Achery 'specialised in wildly inventive, frequently biting satires that addressed current political and social subjects'. (Amy Torbert, 'A Changing Industry: Women Publishing and Selling Prints in London, 1740–1800' in Cristina S Martinez and Cynthis E Roman (eds), *Female Printmakers, Printsellers, and Print Publishers in the Eighteenth Century: The Imprint of Women, c. 1700–1830* (Cambridge University Press 2024) 186. Elizabeth d'Achery paid Gillray to produce some of his early caricatures.
32 Contemporaries were unsure of Gillray's true politics. Henry Angelo observed, that '[Gillray] probably never inquired further into motives', and John Landseer believed that his 'heart was always on the side of whiggism and liberty' (Loxton (n 10) 164–65).
33 Howe (n 1) 12.

expedient to do so, even if Wolcot personally respected the king.[34] This again demonstrates that we cannot take caricatures at face value, as Wolcot was selling a product rather than offering a true account of George III.

James Sayers may have lacked the artistic talent of Gillray, but his caricatures were extremely effective in damaging Fox and the Whigs. The irony is that Sayers' legacy is his prints from 1783, which George described as his 'least competent' and which he had drawn before he found the method that worked best for him.[35] Sayers' artistic skills are by no means poor and are enjoyable to study, but as an artist, he could not compete with the likes of Gillray and Rowlandson. Sayers' strength was impact, and unusually for a caricaturist of the period, his natural allegiance was to Pitt and the government rather than the opposition.[36] Whilst we know that Sayers was a partisan of Pitt and his prints were true reflections of his own political allegiances, this is not true of most caricaturists. It was common for caricaturists to be paid to create specific plates, i.e., paid for by the government as a form of propaganda or create plates based on another person's drawing. This means that we simply do not know which plates were paid for by the government and are outright propaganda.[37] There is evidence that the creation of prints was a collaborative process: 'Gillray's letters are packed with him pushing new concepts to publishers, and most caricatures were discussed extensively and given the go-ahead before the final design was signed off'.[38]

Creating political caricatures was not always a matter of choice. Some were forced by financial hardship to do political caricatures. As Lord Baker noted, Thomas Rowlandson's gambling habit forced him to undertake the creation of political caricatures.[39] An accomplished artist, Rowlandson had, in 1777, been awarded a silver medal by the Royal Academy.[40] Even if he was forced by circumstances to capture the political events of the 1780s, he did so 'without Gillray's venom and Partisanship'.[41] George observes that Rowlandson seemed 'indifferent to politics but excelled at illustrating the ideas of other people'.[42]

34 Andrew Roberts, *George III: The Life and Reign of Britain's Most Misunderstood Monarch* (Allen Lane 2021) 545–46.
35 M Dorothy George, *English Political Caricature: A Study of Opinion and Propaganda to 1792* (Oxford University Press 1959) 173.
36 Cust (n 13).
37 Howe (n 1) 11–12.
38 Loxton (n 10) 104.
39 Lord Baker of Dorking, 'The History of British Cartoons and Caricature' (Gresham College, 4 October 2010) <https://www.gresham.ac.uk/watch-now/history-british-cartoons-and-caricature>.
40 John Hayes, 'Rowlandson, Thomas' (Oxford Dictionary of National Biography 3 January 2008).
41 Ibid.
42 M Dorothy George, *English Political Caricature: A Study of Opinion and Propaganda to 1792* (Oxford University Press 1959) 172.

Political prints were just a means to an end – Rowlandson was an artist for hire and a great one at that. His best-known political prints relate to the dismissal of the Fox-North coalition and the Westminster Election of 1784, which saw Charles James Fox narrowly retain his seat as an MP. As John Hayes observes, his work during the election made him known to the press as '"the ingenious Caricaturist" (Morning Herald, 25 Dec 1784)'.[43] Another contemporary of Gillray was Isaac Cruikshank (who would be overshadowed by son, George Cruikshank, who illustrated Charles Dickens' work). Robert Patten observes that Cruikshank's caricatures and the politics that they conveyed were motivated by commercial considerations, and therefore 'Cruikshank was not kind to those with radical tendencies, such as Charles James Fox'.[44] Similar to Sayers, Cruikshank 'was an uneven artist; weak drawing, feeble humour, and convoluted political narratives mar some of his productions'.[45] This is an accurate description, as it is fair to describe Cruikshank's output as hit and miss, and even if he was more artistically talented than James Sayers, it was the latter who had the greater ability to hit his mark.

Caricatures were an effective political tool. Dickinson has observed how caricatures were utilised by the East India Company to argue against government interference in its activities, especially during the Fox-North coalition, with a committee set up to pay for caricatures attacking the coalition and the India Bill.[46] There is still a large number of prints hostile to the coalition, and the India Bill that survive to this day. During the political debates of the 1790s, Dickinson notes that caricatures and 'other publications capable of carrying a political message . . . [were] heavily weighted on the conservative side'.[47] This is reflected in the types of prints that survive, which were more likely to be critical of Fox and the Whigs than Pitt and the government.

As discussed previously, Sayers used caricatures to advance his own political views. He did not need employment and instead used his artistic skills as a propagandist against the Fox-North Coalition. According to Horace Twiss,

> Fox said, that Sayers's caricatures had done him more mischief than the debates in Parliament or the works of the press. – The prints of Carlo Khan, Fox running away with the India House, Fox and Burke quitting

43 Ibid.

44 Robert L Patten, 'Cruikshank [Crookshanks], Isaac' (Oxford Dictionary of National Bibliography, 23 October 2004).

45 Ibid.

46 HT Dickinson, *The Politics of the People in Eighteenth-Century Britain* (Macmillan Press 1994) 62.

47 Ibid 272.

Paradise when turned out of office . . . had certainly a vast effect upon the public mind.[48]

Sayers' caricatures depicting the Fox-North Coalition are still effective at conveying the hostility felt by the artist (and those he supported) towards the government and a dislike of the unnatural alliance between Charles James Fox and Lord North.

Examples of this effective use of caricature by Sayers include 'The Mask',[49] which depicts a mask formed out of the faces of Fox and North, that is accompanied by the declaration 'Fronti Nulla Fides' (which translates to 'no reliance can be placed on appearance'); and the bold depiction of Fox stealing the wealth of the East India Company in 'A transfer of East India stock',[50] which depicts Fox carrying the East India Company's Leadenhall Street Headquarters into the treasury, in the manner of a thief and appearing to keep an eye out for witnesses. This caricature, given the common use of a fox to depict Fox, has something of the fox raiding the chicken coop about it, with India bonds flying everywhere akin to feathers. Finally, perhaps the most recognisable is 'Carlo Khan's triumphal entry into Leadenhall Street',[51] which shows Fox sitting upon an elephant (who has the face of Lord North), with Edmund Burke ahead of him with a trumpet heralding Fox, now known as 'Kings of Kings', arriving to claim the riches of the East India Company. As Cust notes, this particular print was so damaging and resulted in Sayers being given a sinecure by Pitt.[52]

15.4 Risky business

Being a caricaturist and publishing these prints could be risky. Publishers, sellers, and artists were potentially liable for prosecution for seditious libel. Some of the caricatures did not hold back when depicting those in power. One notable, if patriotic, example is James Gillray's 'The French invasion; – or – John Bull, bombarding the bum-boats',[53] where Britain, with the face of George III, is literally defecating on France's face. Andrew Roberts notes that the high point of caricatures disrespecting George III was 1792.[54] Eventually, Gillray was given a £200 a year pension by George Canning not to attack the royal family.[55]

48 Horace Twiss, *The Public and Private Life of Lord Chancellor Eldon, With Selections from His Correspondence*, vol 1 (John Murray 1844) 162.
49 (Published by H Bretherton, New Bond Street, London, 21 May 1783).
50 (Published by Thomas Cornell, Bruton Street, London, 25 November 1783).
51 (Published by Thomas Cornell, Bruton Street, London, 5 December 1783).
52 Cust (n 13).
53 (Published by Hannah Humphrey, 18 Old Bond Street, London, 5 November 1793).
54 Roberts (n 34) 545.
55 Ibid 546.

The ability of publishers to sell material that cruelly mocked the monarch, 'amazed observers from abroad'.[56] But all was not what it seemed. Roberts argues that,

> [a]lthough prints such as these seemed to threaten the dignity of the Crown, in fact the ability to satirize and ridicule the royal family – in a way that was prosecuted in contemporary France – actually strengthened the British monarchy by 'helping to give visual articulation and practical example to the notion of the British nation as a formidable fortress of freedom'.[57]

This tolerance was a good thing as it showed George could laugh at himself.[58] Therefore, it was less likely that George III would face a revolution.[59]

The King, despite being ridiculed, was an avid collector of caricatures, as was the Prince of Wales, to whom the caricaturists were no less mean.[60] According to Roberts, the king 'undoubtably understood their political influence, and when outside London he would have the latest prints by such giants of the genre as Gillray . . . bought surreptitiously and delivered to him'.[61] It was not just for his own private viewing as George 'sent caricatures of himself to the University of Göttingen Library in Hanover'.[62] Clearly, even the subject being mocked saw their artistic and historic significance.

However, the conditions in Britain permitted these types of caricatures to be openly produced, sold, and collected by individuals. As Bob Harris observes, the British press enjoyed a lot more freedom than the press in other European countries.[63] This freedom came from the decision not to renew the Licensing Act and a general tolerance towards satire from across the political spectrum.[64] Following 1695, the government, having lost the right to censor works before they were published, had to resort to prosecutions for libel once a caricature had been published'.[65] This is significant as, given the growth of

56 Ibid.
57 Roberts (n 34) 495.
58 Ibid 497.
59 Ibid.
60 McConnell and Heneage (n 24). According to Alice Loxton, the Prince of Wales purchased '121 Gillray prints' in one year (Loxton (n 10) 116).
61 Roberts (n 34) 495.
62 McConnell and Heneage (n 23).
63 Bob Harris, 'Print Culture' in HT Dickinson (ed), *A Companion to Eighteenth-Century Britain* (Blackwell Publishing 2006) 284.
64 There was a strong belief in the importance of free press, and this held by 'amongst all stripes of political opinion' (Harris (n 63) 285). This view meant that regulation by the government would not be permitted. As Bob Harris argues, the rationale for '[p]olitical restrictions on the press were . . . weaker and the end of the century . . . [because] The final extinction of Jacobitism . . . made ministerial powers over the press more difficult to defend' (285).
65 Ibid.

print during the eighteenth century, there would always be too much printed to ever be censored once it had been published. The targets of the caricaturist did not have to like it, and even those in power had little real power to stop the caricaturist's abuse.

The problem for the authorities was that if they did prosecute a publisher or caricaturist, then the question of whether a cartoon amounted to libel would be determined by jurors. Given the popularity of caricatures, many jurors would have seen the print in question, or others like it before, and perhaps even had found it to be humourous. The government's solution was to require seditious libel to be, at a preliminary stage, dealt with in court by a judge, as this 'did not have to be heard before a grand jury'.[66] This preliminary stage would not determine guilt, but it was 'a very useful means of harassing the print trade . . . and was often employed without the case being prosecuted in court'.[67] An example of this was the arrest of Gillray and print sellers in January 1796, 'all being charged with selling Gillray's The Presentation, or, The Wise Men's Offering'.[68]

To understand the importance of caricature, it is also necessary to appreciate the social context. Prints were expensive, especially those coloured by the publishers. Only a few could afford them.[69] However, the prints were not only for the wealthy. They were publicly displayed in printshop windows and attracted audiences, although it is difficult to quantify just how many people there would have been, which meant that the prints were seen by more people than just those wealthy enough to purchase them.[70] The crowd gathered around the window of a printshop was seized upon by the caricaturists, with Piercy Roberts depicting crowds outside his premises viewing his prints.[71] Another earlier example is James Gillray's 'Very Slippy Weather',[72] which shows individuals admiring a range of his own caricatures in the window of Hannah Humphrey's print shop. We cannot prove that crowds gathered to view the windows of print shops. The caricatures by both Roberts and Gillray certainly show crowds admiring their caricatures, but as the artist they may have had a vested interest.

However, there is academic debate as to how realistic the popular image of crowds outside a print shop was and to what extent poorer individuals

66 Ibid 285.
67 Ibid.
68 McConnell and Heneage (n 23).
69 NG Howe notes that '[t]he cost of prints was generally placed at 6d. for a "plain" or "uncoloured" print, with the price rising upwards of 1s. for a "hand-coloured" print'. (Howe (n 1) 21).
70 Baer (n 8) 222–24.
71 Piercy Roberts, 'Caricature Shop' (Published by Piercy Roberts, 28 Middle Row, Holborn, September 1801).
72 (Published by Hannah Humphrey, 27 St James Street, 10 February 1808).

Figure 15.3 Caricature Shop
Source: © Yale University

interacted with the caricatures.[73] The literacy rates in the eighteenth century is an important consideration, as a degree of literacy was required to understand a print. But as Marc Baer informs us, 'the social reality of public viewing . . . prints were publicly scrutinized by patricians as well as the man and woman on the street'.[74]

The caricatures were popular and had a considerable impact on society. For Chiara Rolli, caricatures had a key impact on moulding contemporary British public opinion owing to the prints being circulated throughout the country.[75] Giving the example of the importance of caricatures during the impeachment of Warren Hastings, Rolli argues that the caricatures 'along with newspapers . . . formed and forged the national imagination with regard to the trial of Hastings'.[76] Diana Donald has a similar view, 'the scattered evidence . . . taken as a whole, indicates that satirical prints of the reign of George III must have

73 Howe (n 1) 21–22.
74 Marc Baer (n 8) 222.
75 Rolli (n 15) 126.
76 Ibid 126.

Figure 15.4 Very Slippy Weather

Source: © Yale University

permeated the national consciousness far more widely and deeply than has been suspected'.[77] In terms of raising awareness of constitutional issues of the day, Diana Donald observes that '[t]he craze for satirical prints was one indication among many of the extension of political participation and debate in late Georgian Britain'.[78] This was not just a London-centric phenomenon, although London-focused prints enjoyed regional and international popularity.[79]

What about the targets of the caricaturist's attack? The Whig elite was not easily insulted or offended by satire or critique.[80] Subject to frequent attacks, the 'Whigs could ignore the views of both kings and commoners',[81] and '[e]ven if their morals and ideas were adversely dissected in cartoons and pamphlets, this had no consequences. Their position in politics was assured'.[82] An example of such critique was Charles James Fox, who was the subject of approximately 821 prints between 1778 to 1791.[83] Fox 'collected cartoons himself. They were bound in folios for the amusements and edifications of visitors'.[84] Alice Loxton recounts the occasion that Fox hearing that Hannah Humphrey 'had published a particularly damning print of [him]' promptly visited the shop and purchased the print, but in doing so, clearly found it amusing and was kind to Hannah Humphrey.[85] Yet it was not just the elite who were the subjects of caricature, as Callum Smith has argued that despite being the subject of 33 known caricatures, the publican and Foxite Samuel House 'has been neglected by historians, despite his inclusion in more than 30 anti-Fox election prints, and his pre-eminence in his own constituency of Westminster as an active plebeian Foxite canvasser'.[86] House was chosen as a target 'by hostile caricaturists, likely in the employ of the government or its agents' in order to damage Fox's campaign to be re-elected in Westminster and tar Fox with 'House's stereotypical plebeian and drunken attributes'.[87]

* * *

We now examine five prints published between 1784 and 1819 during the reign of George III and examine them as leading works of the constitution. The caricatures reflect the key political and constitutional themes of the day. They represent how the population would have engaged with and understood

77 Diana Donald, *The Age of Caricature: Satirical Prints in the Reign of George III* (Yale University Press 1996) 21.
78 Ibid 2.
79 Ibid 20.
80 Mitchell (n 6) 22.
81 Ibid 22.
82 Ibid x.
83 Howe (n 1) 2.
84 Mitchell (n 6) 22.
85 Loxton (n 10) 165–66.
86 Callum D Smith, 'The 'Republican' Publican: "Honest" Sam House, Visual Culture, and the General Election of 1784' (2022) 41(2) Parliamentary History 240, 241.
87 Ibid 262.

the representation of contemporary constitutional events. The caricatures also illustrate wider and enduring constitutional themes concerning the allocation and exercise of political power and its scrutiny, the balance of power between different actors and institutions, and the tensions between them. There is also a distinct sense of change over time as the latter prints reflect wider developments, such as the impact of the French Revolution on Britain and the growing clamour from the working and middle classes for democracy and a broader franchise.

15.5 'A peep into Friar Bacon's study'

The first caricature is Thomas Rowlandson's 'A Peep into Friar Bacon's Study', which was published by William Humphrey (brother of Hannah) on 3 March 1784. Rowlandson, although highly talented, was new to political caricature, and this print forms part of his coverage of the constitutional and fraught events of 1784. The principal constitutional issue was the relationship and balance of power between the Crown and the Cabinet. At the time, it was still the personal prerogative of the monarch to appoint his own ministers.

The years 1783–84 were a turbulent time in British domestic politics. The government, which had come into power in April 1783, had been headed by the Whig Grandee the Duke of Portland, although the real power was exercised by Lord North and Charles James Fox. The government, a coalition between two political opponents, was known as the Fox-North ministry. Both men's decision to join in political union was lampooned by caricaturists.[88]

In December 1783, King George III dismissed this government and invited William Pitt the Younger to form what was popularly known as the Mince Pie Administration. What motivated King George III to use his prerogative power against his government which enjoyed the confidence of the House of Commons? Put simply, the King detested his ministers, especially Fox, and from the outset, resented having a Ministry imposed upon him. King George believed that he should be able to choose his ministers. At the time, the Crown's power of appointing and dismissing his ministers exceeded the importance of a government having a Commons majority.

Leslie Mitchell observes, '[s]o notorious was this union of recent enemies that it was ever after referred to as *the* Coalition. It was the unparalleled example of political opportunism'.[89] It was deemed to be a very unnatural

88 See, for example, George Dance's pair of caricatures published on the same day, the first entitled 'War' (published by Hannah Humphrey, 51 New Bond Street, London, 9 March 1783) depicts the men as enemies, with Fox declaring, 'I shold hold myself Infamous if I ever form'd a connection with him! – deserve the Ax! – disgrace! infamy! – shame! incapacity ignorance! corruption!'. The second, entitled 'Neither war nor peace', (published by Hannah Humphrey, 51 New Bond Street, London, 9 March 1783), with a subheading, 'The astonishing Coalition', shows Fox and North standing together, agreeing on the articles of peace.

89 Mitchell (n 10) 4.

Figure 15.5 A Peep into Friar Bacon's Study
Source: © Yale University

union. Rowlandson famously depicted this union in 'The Loves of the Fox and the Badger, or the Coalition Wedding',[90] which included Satan marrying the fox (Fox) and the badger (North). Another artist to parody the political union was Edward Topham's 'The Union – *Whom – Has Join'd, Let No Man put Asunder!*', which once again depicted the pair being married by Satan.[91]

Despite having a majority in the House of Commons, the coalition had earned more controversy owing to its planned reform of the East India Company. The previous reform to the East India Company by Lord North in 1773 had sought to fix the Company's problems, which included not being financially self-sufficient, failing to generate profit for the country, the company's corrupt practices, and the style of Warren Hastings, the Governor-General's, administration and his perceived personal failings.[92] As a minister within the coalition government, Edmund Burke enjoyed the support of his political ally Fox and took a keen interest in Indian affairs. It was Burke who drove the

90 Available at: <https://www.rct.uk/collection/810025/the-loves-of-the-fox-and-the-badger-or-the-coalition-wedding>.
91 Published by Elizabeth Darchery, St. James Street, 11 March 1783.
92 For the best account see PJ Marshall, *The Impeachment of Warren Hastings* (Oxford University Press 1965).

planned reform, which took the form of the India Bill in 1783, otherwise known as Fox's India Bill. The Company had considerable resources, and the Bill was seen by the coalition's opponents as a way to control the patronage and resources of the Company. The controversial nature of the India Bill has left a lasting legacy in the caricatures that have survived.

Eager to protect his own interests and prerogatives, the King engineered the defeat of the India Bill in the House of Lords, which then provided the pretext for dismissing his ministers. The constitutional appropriateness of the King dismissing his ministers is a moot point. The King, unlike his son William IV in 1834 when he dismissed Lord Melbourne, did not have to backtrack (due to the Commons supporting Melbourne) and reappoint the dismissed ministers. The reason was that George III, unlike his successors, had considerable patronage at his disposal, which enabled him to support his new Ministry. So, following the election in 1784, King George III emerged victorious from the crisis. Pitt was in government, the Coalition in opposition, albeit with a majority in the Commons, and there was an upcoming general election.

Against that background, we can consider Rowlandson's 'A Peep into Friar Bacon's Study', an interesting account of Britain's evolving constitutional arrangements. The central theme of the print is the use of 'Time is past', 'Time is', and 'Time was' to make an observation about the changing balance of power in the constitution.

Rowlandson's picture relies heavily upon its viewers being familiar with the nuances of Robert Greene's play, *Friar Bacon and Friar Bungay* (1589), which had been influenced by the life of Roger Bacon, the thirteenth-century philosopher.[93] The central character was Friar Bacon, who is portrayed by Greene 'as a patriotic and benevolent magician'.[94] The character was a magician, in the tradition of Merlin, and Friar Bacon 'is represented as a seer gifted with oracular powers which are used at the king's request in behalf of the state, a function and a service that recall Merlin's relations with Arthur'.[95] Bacon has the use of a Brazen Head, a legendary medieval automaton, which he tries to use to protect England by using the Brazen Head to create a brass wall. As Waldo McNeir observes,

> *The Famous Historie* emphasizes Bacon's patriotic purpose in wishing to learn from the Brazen Head how to encircle England with a wall of brass in order to make the island impregnable, and Greene attributes the same motive to his hero.[96]

93 Waldo F McNeir, 'Traditional Elements in the Character of Greene's Friar Bacon' (1948) 45(2) Studies in Philology 172, 172.
94 Ibid 177.
95 Ibid 176.
96 Ibid 177.

The Brazen Head was used by Friar Bacon to create a prophecy:

> Before the Brazen head that was to build the wall is mysteriously destroyed, its cryptic pronouncement shuts off consideration of the future at all, speaking only in the present and past tenses: 'time is', 'time was', and time is past' . . . . The failure of Bacon to gain control of the head and to harness its power marks the limits of his ability to control the future of the nation.[97]

Turning to the picture itself, King George III, wearing a monk's habit, is cast as Friar Bacon in his study. Above the King's head, there are three roundels, each of which is inscribed with the 'constitution'. Holding two wands, the King is pointing to the first roundel, which represents the old constitutional arrangements in which the King was all-powerful. There are also two hot air balloons representing the House of Commons and the House of Lords, thereby suggesting that the talk in Parliament is useless hot air. George III is sat on his throne resplendent with sunbeams – his royal powers – emanating from him.

In the second and third roundels, the word 'constitution' appears within what seems to resemble a wall. The purpose of Bacon's Brazen Head was to build a brass wall to protect England from its enemies, and this is reflected in the walls in the second and third roundels. The Brazen Head refers to the second roundel – 'Time is' – which depicts the present arrangements following the king's dismissal of the Fox-North coalition. In this roundel, King George is shown in the largest circle, sat on his throne, with a smaller circle depicting the House of Lords and the smallest circle depicting the House of Commons.

The third roundel – 'Time Was' – shows the King, the Lords, and the Commons as three equal-sized and balanced circles. This represents the state of the constitution before the dismissal of the coalition. Rowlandson's point is that the King's dismissal of the Fox-North ministry and his role in ensuring the defeat of the India Bill in the House of Lords has upset the balance of the constitution and increased royal power. This resonates with Dunning's famous resolution of 1780: 'the influence of the Crown has increased, is increasing, and ought to be diminished'. Given the fact that the King had been forced in April 1783 to accept the coalition, in December he was able to choose his next government despite the support the coalition enjoyed in the House of Commons. The shift in the third roundel represents an increase in the royal power, but the king is far from satisfied and wants to revert to the first roundel, that of unlimited monarchical power. The king is pointing with one wand to the House of Commons in the second roundel, while his other wand points to the

97 Brian Walsh, '"Deep Prescience": Succession and Politics of Prophecy in "Friar Bacon and Friar Bungay"' (2010) 23 Medieval & Renaissance Drama in England 63, 65.

king in the first roundel. He exclaims: 'What is this To This [?]'. King George clearly wants an unlimited monarchy.

On the periphery of the picture, politicians are jockeying for position. On the left-hand side, Fox, North, and Burke peep through the doorway with a warning: 'beware'. On the right-hand side, the new ministers are being led down a set of stairs towards the King, with a devil holding the hand of the first minister, Lord Temple. The second minister calls out 'we must destroy the coalition'. The third minister says, 'A Fig for the Resolutions', that is, the resolutions moved by Fox in order to dislodge Pitt, including those against the issuing of money from the Treasury.[98]

The 'Back Stairs' is a reference to royal intrigue. As Paul Kelly observes, in December 1783,

> opinion in the Commons seemed to be reacting sharply against the 'back-stairs' influence associated with Temple's interview with the king on 11 December and the way in which the king's name was subsequently used to influence the votes of members of the House of Lords on Fox's India bill.[99]

This secret manoeuvring is emphasised by Rowlandson and others. M Dorothy George, in her paper 'Fox's Martyrs; The General Election of 1784', writes that

> There can be no doubt that the constitutional issues were skilfully, and of course tendentiously, stated and widely circulated. They were cleverly embodied in pictorial satire. Foxite propaganda was also displayed in prints and in Westminster election squibs. Its topics were secret influence, the destruction of the Commons and Pitt's youth. Temple, holding the dark lantern of a conspirator, leads Pitt up the Back Stairs.[100]

Such was the controversial nature of back stairs machinations that, as the Duchess of Devonshire wrote in a letter to her mother, 'There was a new play last night in which the Back Stairs was introduced, it produced an angry riot and they would not allow them to proceed for a long time, however *we* got the better at last'.[101]

A closer study of the print suggests two somewhat subtler points, one perhaps intended by Rowlandson and the other not. First, the purpose of

98 See the commentary provided by the British Museum: <https://www.britishmuseum.org/collection/object/P_1851-0901-178>

99 Paul Kelly, 'The Pitt-Temple Administration: 19–22 December 1783' (1974) 17(1) The Historical Journal 157, 157.

100 M Dorothy George, 'Fox's Martyrs; The General Election of 1784' (1939) 21 Transactions of the Royal Historical Society 133, 153.

101 Ibid 150–51.

Bacon's Brazen Head was to build a brass wall to protect England from its enemies, but this wall is only present in the second and third roundels, i.e., those which represent the King's power being balanced, to varying degrees, with the Lords and Commons. Perhaps Rowlandson's point is that concentrating power solely in the King's hand would jeopardise the safety of the realm. If so, then this reinforces the warning from Burke and Fox about concentrating power solely in the King's hands. In the first roundel, the sun rays emanating from King George are reminiscent of Louis XIV, the Sun King.

The second point concerns the Brazen Head and the ultimate constitutional outcome of the tensions embodied in the picture. In Greene's play, Friar Bacon's Brazen Head only speaks three times – 'Time is', 'Time was', and 'Time is past' – and then falls to the floor and shatters. It does not speak about the future. Looking at the print at the time it was drawn, in many ways, it represents the last hurrah of royal power, the ability of the monarch to use his powers to choose his ministers and to protect his own position. George III's manoeuvring, with its 'questionable methods',[102] was controversial but was seen as legitimate by a large number of individuals,[103] although there is a clear message of caution against allowing the King to reclaim more power and thereby undermine the Whiggish evolution of the constitution toward a more balanced polity.

What Rowlandson and no one else at the time could possibly have known was that the King's triumphant victory was, in the long term, a pyrrhic one. Over time, the Crown's power diminished and eventually collapsed altogether. This process occurred in part as a result of the King's later bouts of insanity, Pitt's desire to arrogate power to himself, and the emergence of definite political issues, which required greater decision-making by the Cabinet.[104] These trends were then consolidated and reinforced by the extension of the franchise through the 1832 Great Reform Bill. The ending of the Crown's 'corrupt' influence reduced the sovereign's personal influence and his control over ministerial appointments in turn cleared the path for the strengthening and development of the cabinet.[105] The influence of the Crown was intimately bound up with the ancient electoral order, which was all swept away in 1832. After this fundamental reform, politics changed with the increase in the franchise, and the role of the monarch would be diminished during the nineteenth and early twentieth centuries. While Rowlandson's picture shows the King jubilant and wanting more power, ultimately, power shifted to the government and

102 Kelly (n 99) 157.

103 See Linda Colley, 'The Apotheosis of George III: Loyalty, Royalty and the British Nation' (1984) 102 Past & Present 94, 104 and George (n 100).

104 JP Mackintosh, *The British Cabinet* (3rd edn, Stevens 1977) 66–72.

105 Archibald S Foord, "The Waning of 'The Influence of the Crown'" (1947) 62 English Historical Review 484, 485.

Parliament, with the monarchy transformed from being politically active to a ceremonial constitutional monarchy.

15.6 'The Battle of Hastings'

William Dent's caricatures were crude in comparison to those of Gillray and Rowlandson. But in 'The Battle of Hastings' Dent manages to sum up the parliamentary debate leading up to the impeachment of Warren Hastings, the former Governor-General of Bengal who had returned home to Britain in 1785 (the caricature is available to view on the British Museum's website).[106] His tenure as Governor-General was controversial, and Hastings had returned to defend his conduct.

According to the British Museum's website, Dent '[d]esigned and coloured all his plates himself, but usually sold them through a number of other agents, who had no other connection with the print business'.[107] The rawness of his caricatures is compelling today and are to the point. The viewer, whether the purchaser or the public looking in through the print shop window, would have instantly understood the message – the political undertones of the impeachment and the magnitude of the issues at play.[108] The audience is taken into St Stephen's Chapel, where the House of Commons meets. Here, Dent is depicting a re-run of the famous Battle of 1066; however, this time, Hastings refers to Warren Hastings, the former Governor-General of Bengal, who is facing being impeached by the House of Commons. The battle is being fought with hot air. The speaker of the House of Commons declares, 'To be, or not to be, Impeachment is the question'. Beneath the title of the print, Dent has written 'Bella, horrida bella' – 'wars, savage wars'.

Stradling the centre of the picture stands Warren Hastings, who is depicted as an imagined caricature from Southeast Asia, wearing a turban and loin cloth. Hastings faces towards the left-hand side of the chamber, where government ministers sit wearing eastern clothing and ornate headpieces. They are the 'Bengal battalion'. From Hastings' right hand, mouth, and torso, a seemingly endless stream of coins is being dropped, spewed out, then readily devoured by the government benches. Standing at the forefront at the left-hand side of the picture, we have Henry Dundas, Pitt's key Scottish ally, who is depicted in Highland dress with a set of bagpipes (the Dress Act 1746, which had been repealed in 1782, had criminalised the wearing of Highland attire for civilians who were not members of the gentry). On the right-hand side is the British Battalion dressed in a romantic interpretation of knights in armour, literally banging the drum for Hastings' impeachment is Edmund Burke. It was Burke, allied with Richard Sheridan and Charles James Fox (who is sat next to Burke),

106 See: <https://www.britishmuseum.org/collection/object/P_1868-0808-5617>
107 Available at <https://www.britishmuseum.org/collection/term/BIOG25023>.
108 Published 9 February 1787.

who was instrumental in the impeachment. Sheridan is making the argument on behalf of the British Battalion; he is gifted with wit and humanity by Dent and shouts out 'truth', 'conviction', and 'justice'.

A number of points can be made. First, Hastings, having forgone his Britishness, has returned as a wealthy Eastern despot to corrupt a willing government with his loot plundered from India and thereby advance his own interests and those of the East India Company. He is wearing a sash with 'European Nabob' on it and has an axe on his person, with the axe head marked as 'a nabob's heart'. In the 1780s, there was genuine concern that returning servants who had abused their positions to make a private fortune could return to Britain with their wealth and purchase influence and a seat in the House of Commons. These servants were referred to as Nabobs. The theme of Hastings as corrupt and purchasing support in England was a common one. Burke, in particular, viewed the Nabobs as corrupting the constitution and the state.[109] Such was their wealth that some thought the Nabobs had bought the 1784 election for Pitt and the King.[110] The same theme was reflected in contemporary caricatures.[111]

Second, the government is both welcoming and protecting Hastings. Ministers are guzzling down the coinage and grasping it. One, under Hastings' right arm, has the face of a pig, thereby suggesting snouts in the trough. The corrupt influence of the Crown in the first print is here complemented by the corruption within Parliament. The King certainly liked Hastings,[112] and there

109 Philip Lawson and Jim Phillips, '"Our Execrable Banditti": Perceptions of Nabobs in Mid-Eighteenth Century Britain' (1984) 16(3) Albion: A Quarterly Journal Concerned with British Studies 225. As Lawson and Phillips observed, 'It is likely that attitudes towards nabobs before 1780 laid the groundwork for Burke's more consistent and developed critique of empire and contributed to the birth of notions of imperial responsibility in the late eighteenth century' (241).

110 See William Thomas Laprade, 'Public Opinion and the General Election of 1784' (1916) 31 (122) The English Historical Review 224, 234. Laprade argues that whilst 'The men who dominated the East India Company unquestionably furnished a large part of the money that was spent, though in many cases they probably nominated their own friends when they undertook the expenses of the election . . . . Since the Company was to profit by the change, however, it was no doubt reasonable that its members should bear a considerable share of the expenses incidental to bringing it about. But the information at hand does not enable us to say how much was spent by men connected with the Company or what proportion this amount constituted of the total expenses of the election'. See also Lucy S Sutherland, *The East India Company in Eighteenth-Century Politics* (Oxford University Press 1962) 410–12 for an assessment of the company's influence.

111 See, for example, Gillray's 'State-jugglers' (Published by SW Fores, 3 Piccadilly, London, 16 May 1788) and 'Opposition-Coaches' (Published by SW Fores, 3 Piccadilly, London, 20 May 1788), and William Dent's 'The Wise Man of the East Making His Offering' (Published by William Moore, 48 New Bond Street, London, 28 February 1788).

112 See GM Ditchfield, *George III: An Essay in Monarchy* (Palgrave Macmillan 2002): 'George III was clear in his view; it was reported that he disapproved of the part played by Henry Dundas in the impeachment proceedings and that "Off all the public characters that of Mr Hastings's stood highest in the King's estimation."' (135).

were caricatures depicting the King being purchased by Hastings, such as Gillray's 'Market-day'[113] and one George particularly found amusing, Joshua Kirby Baldrey's 'H-st-gs ho, rare H-st-gs!',[114] with its accompanying text 'What a Man buys he may sell'. The Lord Chancellor, Lord Thurlow, had been a school friend of Hastings at Westminster School. Thurlow was certainly an ally to his old friend. But how far does Dent's scene depict reality? Well, Dundas did not support Hastings, and he was certainly not playing the bagpipes in support of the Bengal Battalion. Dundas had chaired a Secret Committee on India since 1782 and played a key role in ensuring that Pitt and others voted to support some of the articles against Hastings.

A third point concerns the constitutional politics of scrutiny and accountability through the House of Commons and the inherently political nature of such scrutiny. There is a clash between impeaching Hastings 'for the honour of the nation' (as inscribed on Burke's drum) and the political and financial self-interest of the government and Hastings. The House of Commons voted to impeach Hastings in 1787, and he was then tried by the House of Lords, with the trial starting in 1788 and finally ending in 1795. Hastings was ultimately acquitted of all charges.

15.7 'The Vulture of the Constitution'

Our third picture is Gillray's 'The Vulture of the Constitution'. It addresses the Regency crisis of 1788–89, during which King George III had his first bout of serious illness, which incapacitated him. As Prime Minister, Pitt enjoyed a significant majority in the House of Commons and House of Lords and crucially had the support of the King. With the King unwell and unable to exercise royal power, there was a power vacuum, political paralysis, and uncertainty as to how the problem could be managed.

Two of the other key actors in the drama were Charles James Fox, Pitt's opponent and the leading Whig statesman, and Prince George, the Prince of Wales and the heir to the throne. Fox had been a prominent opponent of royal power and King George III, who Fox regarded as an aspiring tyrant. However, Fox, a friend of the spendthrift Prince of Wales, saw the Regency crisis as his chance to seize power. If Fox enabled the Prince to become Regent, then Fox would likely have been rewarded handsomely. Fox, therefore, changed his opinion about the Crown. In Fox's view, it was the Prince's absolute right, as heir to the Crown, to assume and exercise his father's powers. However, Pitt feared that if the Prince of Wales became regent, then he (Pitt) would be removed from office.

There was hypocrisy and personal ambition from both Pitt and Fox. The whole episode provided plenty of material for satirical prints. Both William

113 (Published by SW Fores, 3 Piccadilly, London, 2 May 1788).
114 (Published by J Doughty & Co, 19 Holborn, London, 12 February 1788).

Figure 15.6 The Vulture of the Constitution
Source: © Yale University

Dent and Thomas Rowlandson lampooned Fox for his hypocritical change of attitude toward the Crown and his support for Prince George, widely known for his reckless spending and extravagance. Fox, who had previously criticised the exercise of royal power, now argued that the Prince of Wales should become regent in order to restore royal authority. Dent's 'The Wonderful Word Eater' showed Fox eating his own words while trampling upon the rights of Parliament, the Bill of Rights, and Magna Carta. This was followed by Rowlandson's 'The Word Eater' in which Fox is depicted in the House of Commons using whatever arguments he can to his own personal advantage.[115]

Gillray responded first with 'Prince Pitt' in December 1788. Pitt is shown standing on the shoulders of two of his supporters, who are in turn standing on the Prince of Wales lying on the floor. Pitt then reaches for the crown and exclaims: 'The Prince of Wales has no more right to the regency than I have'. Pitt is depicted as both a usurper and a thief. Gillray then published 'The Vulture of the Constitution' on 3 January 1789. Here, Pitt's head is placed upon the body of an enormous vulture. Its bulging breast reads 'Treasury'. The formal title of the Prime Minister is the First Lord of the Treasury. The vulture's left claw stands upon the King's Crown and sceptre. Under the

115 Loxton (n 10) 84–100.

vulture's right claw, the coronet of the Prince of Wales is buckling and being crushed under the vulture's weight. Under the crown lies a shredded copy of 'Magna Charta'. As with Gillray's 'Prince Pitt', the traditional power hierarchy is reversed. Instead of Pitt being subservient to the King, in both prints he is standing upon and dominating the monarch. Moreover, the monstrous size of the vulture, its outstretched wings, large breast, and the length of its neck all suggest strength and muscular virility compared with the weakness of the Crown being trampled underneath.

Why is Pitt depicted as a vulture? In 1788, the trial of Warren Hastings attracted considerable public attention. Hastings' governorship of India and also British rule was often characterised as a vulture. The *London Templar* described Hastings' rule in India as akin to

> the protection of the vulture to the lamb, which covers while it devours its prey – which stretching its baleful pinions, and hovering in mid-air, disperses the hawks and kites, and saves the innocent and helpless victim from all talons but its own.[116]

The print's message is clear, direct, and lacking in subtlety. Pitt is the power-hungry vulture and the dominant actor in the constitution intent upon undermining and subverting established constitutional arrangements to attain political control for his own personal ends. Having taken control of the King's Crown, Pitt is now simultaneously crushing the coronet of the Prince of Wales and plucking out its feathers one by one. The symbol of the old constitution – Magna Carta – has been torn up and lies underneath the Crown. There is a new threat to the constitution – not the Crown – but Pitt's personal ambitions as Prime Minister.

The practical importance of the prints needs to be emphasised. As Reilly notes, both sides of the Regency controversy turned to the popular press to make their cases by commissioning 'cartoons, pamphlets, and handbills'.[117] Two days after Gillray's print was published, Pitt proposed a Regency Bill which enabled the Prince of Wales to act as regent ruling in his father's name. However, in something of a masterstroke, Pitt ensured that, as Regent, the Prince would only possess very limited powers. He would be unable to appoint new peers to the House of Lords, would have no powers of patronage, and could neither grant pensions nor manage the King's estates. Crucially, as Regent, the Prince would be obliged to keep the King's present government, i.e., Pitt would remain in office. The Prince wrote to the Cabinet and the Queen objecting to Pitt's plan on the ground that it would produce 'weakness, disorder and insecurity in every branch of the administration of affairs, a project for dividing the royal family from each other, from separating the

116 *London Templar*, 1 August 1788, p 15.
117 R Reilly, *William Pitt the Younger* (Putnam Publishing Group 1979) 206.

court from the state and thereby disjoining government from its natural and accustom'd support'.[118] In fact, Pitt had not explicitly crushed the Crown, although he had skilfully outmanoeuvred both the Prince and Fox. However, there had been the prospect of Prince George becoming Regent, and he was frivolous, reckless, selfish, and irresponsible. Affording him unbridled power would have come with many risks. In any event, the King's health improved before the Bill could be enacted.

Irrespective of the particular circumstances, 'The Vulture of the Constitution' can be seen as exemplifying a wider and deeper narrative of the constitution, which continues to this day, namely the risk of excessive power being concentrated in the hands of the Prime Minister. The print can be seen as a precursor to subsequent and more contemporary narratives of prime ministerial government, a power-grab and executive dictatorship that have become so common.

15.8 'Britannia between Scylla and Charbydis'

The fourth print is Gillray's 'Britannia between Scylla and Charbydis', published on 8 April 1793. The idiom is, of course, drawn from Homer's Odyssey; the two sea monsters reflect the dilemma of being caught between two equally unpleasant alternatives or opposite dangers. By 1793, the political and international situation had, by now, changed beyond recognition following the French Revolution. The overthrow of the French monarchy had produced consternation and prompted Edmund Burke to articulate his conservativism in his *Reflections on the Revolution in France* (1790). But the revolution was soon overtaken by massacres, the sans-culottes, the trial of King Louis XVI before the French National Convention, and then his execution in January 1793 and later the execution of his wife, Marie Antoinette, in October 1793. The quick collapse of the centuries-old structure of the French monarchy aroused concerns about the stability of the British monarchy. On the other hand, there were longstanding concerns in Britain about royal absolutism and the 'corrupt' powers and patronage of the Crown.

The dilemma for the government and Prime Minister Pitt was to avoid importing the violence of the French Revolution, but without reverting back to the arbitrary exercise of royal power and patronage. This is well-captured in Gillray's print. Sailing in choppy seas, Pitt is uncaricatured but implicitly cast as the wandering Homeric hero, Odysseus. He is steering a small boat, 'The Constitution'. Britannia holds her hands with some unease at the uncertainty of their predicament. The boat is being navigated through a dangerous strait toward the 'Haven of Public Happiness'. Pitt must seek to steer the ship of state between two conflicting forms of government. On the left, there is

118 M Brown, 'Letters Shed Light on Lovelorn Prince Who Became George IV' (*The Guardian*, 23 October 2019).

Figure 15.7 Britannia between Scylla and Charbydis

Source: © The Art Institute of Chicago

the rock of democracy with the lurking monster Scylla. On top of the rocky promontory is a bonnet rouge with a cocarde tricolore, which was worn by the French revolutionaries. If the boat crashes into the rock, then the risk is of revolutionary violence from the sans-culottes. But on the right, there is the whirlpool of arbitrary monarchical power (Charybdis). This is symbolised by what appears to be an upturned Crown, but is described as a 'jewelled Turkish turban'. This represents the nepotism, arbitrariness, and old corruption of monarchical government. The challenge for Pitt is to avoid both extremes, to chart a middle course. But the boat is being pursued by three sharks, the dogs of Scylla, namely, Sheridan, Fox, and Priestley, who sympathised with the French revolutionaries and were enthusiastic about importing their principles.

Britannia, hands aflutter, is looking with great trepidation to her right towards Scylla, thereby suggesting that the greater evil is the threat posed by French revolutionary principles than domestic arbitrary monarchy. The dogs of Scylla are, by implication, equally dangerous. In his 'A Democrat, or Reason & Philosophy' (1793), Gillray portrayed Fox as a sans-culotte revolutionist celebrating the execution of Louis XVI. The corruption and arbitrariness of Crown power would merely be a continuation of an autochthonous tradition, whereas Fox and the two other dogs of Scylla would import foreign and French terror.

The boat, 'The Constitution', needs to be navigated carefully, avoiding either extreme, and Britannia implicitly trusts Pitt as the man for the job. He is gazing intently upon the safety of the desired destination, the Haven of Happiness. The etching suggests success. The boat is well-balanced. 'The vessel of the Constitution' has been 'steered clear of the Rock of Democracy and the Whirlpool of the Arbitrary Power'. But yet, the boat is between the two risks. Success is not entirely guaranteed, and the sharks are following.

The print exemplifies a second perennial theme of British constitutionalism: the need for balance. This can take the form of a balance of powers between different institutions. It can also mean the need to achieve a balance between different competing forces. This is a tradition which emphasises both continuity and change in the constitution, modest and gradual reform as opposed to wholesale revolution.

The print can also be interpreted as reflecting deeper assumptions of politics as a practical activity, as articulated by Michael Oakeshott. As Oakeshott explained,

> In political activity . . . men sail a boundless and bottomless sea . . . . The enterprise is to keep afloat on an even keel; the sea is both friend and enemy; and the seamanship consists in using the resources of a traditional manner of behaviour in order to make a friend of every hostile occasion.[119]

Politics as an activity is a tradition of behaviour, something which is neither fixed nor finished; 'it has no changeless centre to which understanding can anchor itself'.[120] Instead, a tradition of behaviour is characterised by a principle of continuity; 'authority is diffused between past, present, and future; between the old, the new, and what is to come'.[121] One particular aspect of this tradition and the practical activity of politics is that those who practice it and seek to maintain continuity between the past, present, and future must be fully inculcated within the political tradition and be able to exercise their judgement wisely. As Gladstone noted, the British constitution 'presumes, more boldly than any other, the good faith of those who work it'.[122] This is Peter Hennessy's 'good chap' theory. This notion is often taken to refer to matters such as ministerial standards and the personal conduct of politicians, although

119 M Oakeshott, 'Political Education' in *Rationalism in Politics and Other Essays* (Methuen 1962) 127.
120 Ibid 128.
121 Ibid.
122 W Gladstone, *Gleanings of Past Years*, vol 1 (John Murray 1879) 243.

it should not necessarily be confined in this way. It can also be interpreted as including the conventions, values, wisdom, and exercise of judgement by leading politicians to navigate carefully forces which threaten the state.

15.9 'The British Constitution, 1819'

The final picture – 'The British Constitution, 1819' – is a much more viscerally raw, savagely brutal, and scathing critique and an implicit call to arms (the caricature is available to view on the National Archives' website).[123] By 1819, the repressive measures introduced in response to the French Revolution and internal discontent had been in place for many years. Given the hardships experienced by ordinary people and the problems caused by industrialisation and high food prices, there had been an increase in political meetings and public protests. The long Napoleonic wars had finished and were seen by some, such as William Cobbett, as highlighting the need for political and social reform and the opportunity for mass political activity and change. The ruling elite were preserving the interests of the wealthy, and there was a growing consciousness of this among the disenfranchised masses of people. Post-war demobilisation had led to high unemployment and declining wages. Following the end of the Napoleonic wars in 1815, there was economic dislocation. Corn prices had decreased, but then the Tory government introduced the Corn Laws, which restricted the importation of food and corn, thereby increasing prices for the poor and enhancing the profits and political power of the landed aristocracy and property owners. Rising discontent motivated increased calls for parliamentary reform. There was a significant increase in contentious gatherings.[124]

In 1818, the *Manchester Observer* (1818–1822) was established by its editor, James Wroe, along with John Knight, Joseph Johnson, and John Saxton. This was a self-consciously radical and anti-establishment newspaper which enjoyed a high circulation and was also sold in other industrial cities, including Birmingham, Leeds, and London. What was notable about the *Observer* was that its content was mainly concerned with radicalism on a national scale, as opposed to just local news stories. In early 1819, Wroe, Knight, and Johnson formed the Patriotic Union Society, which all the leading radicals and reformists in Manchester joined, with the principal aim of achieving parliamentary reform. The whole tenor of the febrile atmosphere is illustrated by a pamphlet, 'The Rights of the People. Unity or Slavery', published by Wroe's Observer Office in 1819. 'The right of resistance to oppression is inherent in the nature of man . . . . The means of popular resistance to arbitrary power consist in courage, intent and pecuniary resources'.

123 <https://images.nationalarchives.gov.uk/search/?searchQuery=The+British+Constitution%2C+1819%E2%80%99>

124 C Tilly, *Popular Contention in Great Britain 1758–1834* (Routledge 2005) 80–81.

The government responded with more repressive measures, spies, and criminal prosecutions in an attempt to quell the radicalism. In 1817, the Home Secretary, Lord Sidmouth, had led a crackdown on parliamentary reformers, that 'malignant spirit' and its agents by suspending Habeas Corpus.[125] Sidmouth was outraged that such seditious radicals had 'exaggerated calamity and fermented discontent' and had

> represented to the ignorant and credulous that their sufferings were to be attributed not merely to the ministers of the day but to defects in the Constitution. The efforts that have been made and nobly made to mitigate every cause of complaint have been treated as worse than nothing and as increasing the evil they were intended to remedy.

From the perspective of Sidmouth and the ruling class, the constitution was based upon the Glorious Revolution of 1688 and comprised a set of practices and arrangements that had been bequeathed to the country by providence. For Sidmouth, this evil agent – the seditious reformers – were seeking to achieve the 'deliberate purpose . . . to destroy all that is valuable' and that 'by open violence alone can their grievances be redressed'. The radicals had 'parliamentary reform in their mouths but rebellion and revolution in their hearts'.

The *Manchester Observer* had a wide circulation and was read aloud to those who could not read. However, printed words alone were insufficient, and 'The British Constitution, 1819' was etched with the clear aim of prompting discontent and action. Unlike Gillray's 'Britannia between Scylla and Charbydis', this picture was not meant to reassure but to expose the deep-seated hypocrisy and corruption inherent in the constitution and to incite protest and rebellion.

What then of the picture? It shows John Bull, the character that personified English liberty in contradistinction to the French revolutionaries and Napoleon.[126] However, deliberately contrary to his previous visual incarnations, this is not the well-fed and self-satisfied John Bull proud of his country and its traditions. Instead, there is a skeletal John Bull, a mere shadow of his former self. Like others, he is a victim of ministerial tyranny, corruption, and the mismanagement of the country. The text reads: 'Countrymen! Behold with Aching Hearts your once noble, fat and Jolly Kinsman Mr John Bull'. John Bull has suffered an enormous decline and there is no doubt at all who was responsible. The government was entirely to blame for his and the people's suffering.

125 G Cruikshank, 'Liberty Suspended! with the Bulwark of the Constitution!' March 1817; History Hub, 'Lord Sidmouth and the 1817 Crackdown on Parliamentary Reformers | Archives Alive: Peterloo', <https://youtu.be/2CFpadBqog8?si=IoMHSREhDDZvKxfr>

126 See Gillray's 'Bonaparte, 48 Hours after Landing!' (1803) in which John Bull is holding a hay fork with Napoleon's head.

John Bull's skeleton has been pierced by seven arrows in a way which is reminiscent of a St Sebastian or St Edmund Martyr. The arrows are: national debt and taxes; lost liberties (twice); despotism; officers of the Crown; butter and cheese laws; and the 'mortal stroke' of the Corn Laws. Five arrows merely touch Bull's bones, whereas two do not just puncture his body but go straight through it. The vertical arrow labelled 'national debt and taxes' seemingly enters the crown of Bull's skull and then goes down his neck and through his rib cage. The horizontal arrow represents the 'mortal stroke' of the Corn Laws. This is the largest, longest, and thickest arrow. John Bull is now a victim of ministerial corruption and violence. What, then, of traditional constitutional protections? They are not merely worthless but serve to protect the established order. In a biting tone, the print declares that 'the proud barriers to ministerial tyranny' have been 'overthrown for the convenience and shelter of villainous traitors'. The Bill of Rights 1688 is nothing but 'a bundle of waste papers', Habeas Corpus 'a child's plaything', and Magna Carta 'a mere empty scroll of musty parchment'.

There are a number of acute contrasts with the previous prints. They satirised the governing elite, King George, Pitt, Fox, and so on, thereby excluded the great mass of the people. By contrast, This print is not merely a satire of individual politicians but a damning overview of the entire system and the narrow interests that the constitution prioritised. It also presents a radical and scathing critique of the constitution as experienced by ordinary working people, the poor and disenfranchised. The constitution is an artifice in the hands of the powerful ruling elite and their class interests. By contrast, the poor are being hit hard by laws – such as the Corns Laws – in which they have no representation or participation at all. Furthermore, traditional liberties, such as Habeas Corpus, have been cynically eroded to maintain extant social power structures and to prevent change.

This is not Gillrayian satire about Pitt's desire for political power but a scathing and brutal demolition of the entire established constitutional order that lays bare its corruption and hypocrisy and the need for resistance to oppression. There is also a deep shift of perspective from the elite London-based royal court constitution of Pitt and the King to the lower ends of the social scale, the disenfranchised poor of Britain's growing industrial cities, in particular Manchester. This is the constitution as experienced and suffered by ordinary people. This is clearly signalled by the protagonist: the ordinary common man personified as John Bull, a figure that was readily recognisable and well-known. But, of course, this is not the rotund, well-fed, corpulent, and jovial John Bull but an eviscerated skeleton.

There is an inherent ambiguity in the picture. On the one hand, the 'mortal stroke' of the Corn Laws suggests John Bull has been lethally harmed. On the other hand, the speech bubble from his mouth contains one word: 'Resurgam' – 'I shall rise again'. Is John Bull still alive, speaking his last dying words, or is he already dead and speaking from beyond the grave? Will John Bull rise again? Is this a real or a false hope? Alternatively, Bull is symbolic of the ordinary people as a whole who may yet rise again. Perhaps the picture is implying that Bull's spirit could rise again through others – if they have the will. The ambiguity is deliberate. It presents these questions to the viewer and poses him or her with the dilemma. It is for the viewer to decide whether to admit defeat or to fight an oppressive and corrupt governing regime. The obvious answer is that the ordinary people must resist their oppression at the hands of the ruling elite and seek fair representation through parliamentary reform.

The picture was published by James Wroe of Great Ancoats Street, Manchester. Naturally enough, given the personal risks involved, the picture is anonymous, although it has been suggested that the author was by Wroe himself.[127] However, it does not seem that the print was ever published in the *Observer* or publicly disseminated. The government had its network of spies and informers. The print was sent to Sidmouth, the Home Secretary, by Colonel Fletcher of Hollins near Bolton-le-Moors on 25 February 1819, along with several other letters informing the Home Secretary about the establishment of a union room in Oldham.[128] Rooms were established for political meetings, which were seen as hotbeds of radicalism. Of the picture itself, Fletcher wrote: 'if the lower class can stand all these things it will be suppression indeed'.[129] Reactionary forces were then successful, and the radical cause suffered a major setback on 16 August 1819 during the Peterloo protest and massacre in Manchester. Some 18 people were killed, and between 400–700 were injured when the cavalry charged into a crowd of 60,000 people assembled in central Manchester to demand parliamentary reform.[130]

The print signalled a wide shift in political satire toward wholesale attacks on the parliamentary system and the need for reform. Consider, for instance, George Cruikshank's 'The "system" that "works so well"!! – or the boroughmongers grinding machine', published on 21 March 1831.[131] Here, Members of Parliament from rotten boroughs are snatching and hoarding gold coins – free public money – flowing out of Parliament, exclaiming: 'The System works well – Why should it be altered?!!'; 'We want no Reform – nothing can be better than the present System – why not let well alone?!!'; "We are indebted to this System for all the Blessings we enjoy!!!'; 'We must defend, Our Glorious Constitution!!'. Eventually, the message had an impact with the introduction of the Reform Act 1832. In his great speech of 7 October 1831,

127 R Poole, 'The Manchester Observer: Biography of a Radical Newspaper' (2019) 95 Bulletin of the John Rylands Library 30, 56.
128 HO 42/184 f33.
129 HO 42/184 f32.
130 M Bush, *The Casualties of Peterloo* (Carnegie Publishing 2005).
131 <https://www.britishmuseum.org/collection/object/P_1868-0808-9350#:~:text=From%20the%20greedy%20crowd%20rise,defend%2C%20Our%20Glorious%20Constitution!! https://www.britishmuseum.org/collection/object/P_1868-0808-9350>

arguing strenuously for the Bill, Lord Brougham comprehensively destroyed the argument that 'the system works well':[132]

> It works well, does it? For whom? For the Constitution? No such thing. For borough proprietors it works well, who can sell seats, or traffic in influence, and pocket the gains. Upon the Constitution it is the foullest stain, and eats into its very core.[133]

15.10 Conclusion

This chapter has examined political caricature as an important form of political and constitutional commentary during the late eighteenth and early nineteenth centuries. At the time, caricatures reached a relatively wide audience. They entertained ordinary people and enabled them to view political events in a different way. The prints examined here touch upon perennial themes of our evolving constitution: the balance of power between different actors and the risks incumbent upon power being accumulated in the hands of one person, the politics of scrutiny, the growth of democracy, and the need for reform. Above all these caricatures is an invitation for us to try and make sense of the past, and given their contemporary and now current importance, they must be regarded as leading commentaries on the political and constitutional controversies.

Bibliography

Baer M, *The Rise and Fall of Radical Westminster, 1780–1890* (Palgrave Macmillan 2012)

Baker K, *George III: A Life in Caricature* (Thames and Hudson 2007)

Baker K, 'The History of British Cartoons and Caricature' *Gresham College* (4 October 2010) <https://www.gresham.ac.uk/watch-now/history-british-cartoons-and-caricature>

Banks A, 'The Imperial Afterlife of Warren Hastings, 1818–1947' (2022) 50(3) The Journal of Imperial and Commonwealth History 498

Brown M, 'Letters Shed Light on Lovelorn Prince Who Became George IV' *The Guardian* (23 October 2019)

Bush M, *The Casualties of Peterloo* (Carnegie Publishing 2005)

Clayton T, 'Shells to Satire: The Career of Hannah Humphrey' in C S Martinez and C E Roman (eds), *Female Printmakers, Printsellers, and Print Publishers in the Eighteenth Century: The Imprint of Women, c. 1700–1830* (Cambridge University Press 2024)

Colley L, 'The Apotheosis of George III: Loyalty, Royalty and the British Nation' (1984) 102 Past & Present 94

Cust LH, revised by Smith EA, 'Sayers [Sayer], James' *Oxford Dictionary of National Biography* (23 September 2004)

Dickinson HT, *Caricatures and the Constitution 1760–1832* (Chadwyck-Healey 1986)

132 E Pearce, *Reform! The Fight for the 1832 Reform Act* (Pimlico 2004) 189–94.

133 Hansard HL Debs vol 8 col 260 7 October 1831.

Dickinson HT, *The Politics of the People in Eighteenth-Century Britain* (Macmillan Press 1994)
Ditchfield GM, *George III: An Essay in Monarchy* (Palgrave Macmillan 2002)
Donald D, *The Age of Caricature: Satirical Prints in the Reign of George III* (Yale University Press 1996)
Foord AS, 'The Waning of "The Influence of the Crown"' (1947) 62 English Historical Review 484
George MD, 'Fox's Martyrs; The General Election of 1784' (1939) 21 Transactions of the Royal Historical Society 133
George MD, *English Political Caricature: A Study of Opinion and Propaganda to 1792* (Oxford University Press 1959)
Gladstone W, *Gleanings of Past Years Volume 1* (John Murray 1879)
Harris B, 'Print Culture' in HT Dickinson (ed), *A Companion to Eighteenth-Century Britain* (Blackwell Publishing 2006)
Hayes J, 'Rowlandson, Thomas' *Oxford Dictionary of National Biography* (3 January 2008)
Howe NG, *Statesmen in Caricature: The Great Rivalry of Fox and Pitt the Younger in the Age of the Political Caricature* (IB Tauris 2019)
Kelly P, 'The Pitt-Temple Administration: 19–22 December 1783' (1974) 17(1) The Historical Journal 157
Laprade WT, 'Public Opinion and the General Election of 1784' (1916) 31(122) The English Historical Review 224
Lawson P and Phillips J, '"Our Execrable Banditti": Perceptions of Nabobs in Mid-Eighteenth Century Britain' (1984) 16(3) Albion: A Quarterly Journal Concerned with British Studies 225
Loxton A, *Uproar! Satire, Scandal and Printmakers in Georgian London* (Icon Books 2024)
Mackintosh JP, *The British Cabinet* (3rd edn, Stevens 1977)
Marshall PJ, *The Impeachment of Warren Hastings* (Oxford University Press 1965)
Masani Z, 'Warren Hastings, Governor-General of India' (2017) 67(11) History Today <https://www.historytoday.com/archive/warren-hastings-governor-general-india>
McNeir WF, 'Traditional Elements in the Character of Greene's Friar Bacon' (1948) 45(2) Studies in Philology 172
Mitchell L, *The Whig World* 1760–1837 (Hambledon and London 2005)
Oakeshott M, 'Political Education' in *Rationalism in Politics and Other Essays* (Methuen 1962)
Patten RL, 'Cruikshank [Crookshanks], Isaac' *Oxford Dictionary of National Bibliography* (23 October 2004)
Pearce E, *Reform! The Fight for the 1832 Reform Act* (Pimlico 2004)
Poole R, 'The Manchester Observer: Biography of a Radical Newspaper' (2019) 95 Bulletin of the John Rylands Library 30
Reilly R, *William Pitt the Younger* (Putnam Publishing Group 1979)
Roberts A, *George III: The Life and Reign of Britain's Most Misunderstood Monarch* (Allen Lane 2021)
Rolli C, *The Trial of Warren Hastings: Classical Oratory and Reception in Eighteenth-Century England* (Bloomsbury 2019)
Sherry J, 'Identifying a Gillray' <https://www.james-gillray.org/catalog_identifying.html>
Smith CD, 'The 'Republican' Publican: 'Honest' Sam House, Visual Culture, and the General Election of 1784' (2022) 41(2) Parliamentary History 240
Sutherland LS, *The East India Company in Eighteenth-Century Politics* (Oxford University Press 1962)
Tilly T, *Popular Contention in Great Britain 1758–1834* (Routledge 2005)

Torbert A, 'A Changing Industry: Women Publishing and Selling Prints in London, 1740–1800' in C S Martinez and C E Roman (eds), *Female Printmakers, Printsellers, and Print Publishers in the Eighteenth Century: The Imprint of Women, c. 1700–1830* (Cambridge University Press 2024)
Twiss H, *The Public and Private Life of Lord Chancellor Eldon, With Selections from His Correspondence*, vol 1 (John Murray 1844)
Walsh B, '"Deep Prescience": Succession and Politics of Prophecy in "Friar Bacon and Friar Bungay"' (2010) 23 Medieval & Renaissance Drama in England 63

16 Thomas Erskine May, *A Treatise upon the Law, Privileges, Proceedings and Usage of Parliament*

Colin Lee[1]

16.1 Introduction

In the summer of 1843, Thomas Erskine May, the 28-year-old Assistant Librarian of the House of Commons, sent the publisher Charles Knight a proposal reflecting May's 'desire to write a concise work' on the law and usages of Parliament, 'explaining principles and laying down rules of practice in the shortest way.' Knight replied to him in mid-November, stating that 'The work which you propose will, I have no doubt, be highly useful and I should think would have a considerable sale beyond Members of Parliament.'[2] Little more than six months later, the first edition of *A Treatise upon the Law, Privileges, Proceedings and Usage of Parliament* was published. The book was an immediate success. It served as a springboard for its author's career and wider influence. During May's lifetime, eight further editions of the *Treatise* were published, and such was the book's authority that further editions have continued to this day.

16.2 Describing parliamentary law and practice before Erskine May

Prior to May's *Treatise*, the description of parliamentary law was dominated by John Hatsell's *Precedents of Proceedings in the House of Commons.* Four books were published up to 1796, which were collected as a single four-volume work in 1818. Hatsell's work was based on long experience as Clerk of the House of Commons, combined with an in-depth study of the Journals of the House. Its status was reinforced by the practice of citing it in debate to settle disputes on the procedure, with MPs accepting its 'high authority'.[3] Despite its length,

1 The author is grateful to Sir William McKay, Sir David Natzler, Professor John McEldowney, Paul Evans, Dr Paul Seaward and Peter Aschenbrenner for comments on earlier drafts of this chapter.

2 TPA, ERM/10A/2-3, Draft Notes by May for Knight, undated, but summer 1843; TPA, ERM/10A/1, Knight to May, 18 November 1843.

3 C Lee and PJ Aschenbrenner, '"Upon a Greater Stage": John Hatsell and John Ley on Politics and Procedure, 1760–1796' (2021) 89 The Table 66–119, 75–80, 81–83, 87–98; *Parl Deb*,

DOI: 10.4324/9781032658698-17

the work had considerable gaps: privilege cases more recent than 1628 were not directly considered, and a projected volume on legislative proceedings never appeared. Over time, its weaknesses were increasingly felt. One reviewer of May's *Treatise* characterised Hatsell's work as 'an undigested collection . . . without methodical arrangement . . . overlaid and deformed by an enormous mass of notes.'[4] Hatsell's volumes nevertheless had important strengths. He drew upon his close relations with, and a firm understanding of the needs of, successive Speakers of the House of Commons, and his analysis of parliamentary procedure was underpinned by a keen sense of the delicate constitutional interplay between Crown and Parliament and a conviction that consistency in parliamentary practice served an important constitutional purpose.[5]

Most volumes on parliamentary practice between Hatsell and May had as their central focus proceedings on private bills – bills for the particular benefit of individuals, companies, or localities – reflecting the growth and procedural development of such private business. Many of these works, such as those published by Charles Ellis in 1799 and 1802, by John Halcomb in 1836, and Benjamin Lumley in 1838, were manuals for practitioners and did not aspire to a wider audience.[6] Some volumes, such as Anthony Hammond's *Summary Treatise on the Practice and Proceedings in Parliament* published in 1825, had wider ambitions. That work, however, lacked any sense of procedural change over time.[7] George Bramwell published a volume which sought to serve both as a short guide to procedure and an authoritative analysis and fell short in both aims. Precedents were placed at the end with no analysis.[8] In 1830, the barrister Fortunatis Dwarris published the first volume of *A General Treatise on Statutes*. The work sought to cover 'the present practice of Parliament', not only in passing bills, but also 'much of the regular routine of business, and

1st Series, vol 6, 31 Mar 1807, cols 621–22, 627; *Parl Deb*, 1st Series, vol 10, 4 Mar 1808, col 901; *Parl Deb*, 3rd Series, vol 35, 2 August 1836, cols 775–77.

4 *Dublin Evening Mail*, 26 March 1845, 3; P Seaward, 'Parliamentary Law in the Eighteenth Century: From Commonplace to Treatise' in P Evans (ed), *Essays on the History of Parliamentary Procedure in Honour of Thomas Erskine May* (Hart Publishing 2017) *Essays*, 97–114, 108.

5 J Hatsell, *Precedents of Proceedings in the House of Commons Under Separate Titles with Observations in Four Volumes* (Luke Hansard and Sons 1818), II.v–vii, I.v; III.v; Lee and Aschenbrenner (n 3) 81–87, 103–07, 117–19; WR McKay (ed), *Erskine May's Private Journal, 1883–1886* (HMSO, House of Commons Library Document No. 12 1984) viii; *Dublin Evening Mail*, 26 March 1845, 3.

6 DL Rydz, *The Parliamentary Agents: A History* (Royal Historical Society 1979) 42–49; OC Williams, *The Historical Development of Private Bill Procedure and Standing Orders in the House of Commons*, vol I (London 1948) 56–57; B Lumley, *Parliamentary Practice on Passing Private Bills* (London 1838), Preface, unpaginated.

7 A Hammond, *A Summary Treatise on the Practice and Proceedings in Parliament; the Passing of Public and Private Bills; and the Law of Elections* (Joseph Butterworth and Son 1825) 40, 71–73; Seaward (n 4) 113.

8 G Bramwell, *The Manner of Proceeding on Bills in the House of Commons* (James and Luke Hansard & Sons 1833) 77; Seaward (n 4) 112; *Morning Herald (London)* 3 April 1833, 8; *The Times*, 26 December 1833, 3.

somewhat of the peculiar law and custom of Parliament.' The work aspired to be 'a manual of parliamentary practice in ordinary cases', but remained largely derivative, relying hugely on Hatsell and Blackstone for the account of privilege and containing few recent precedents. Although it had some success, *The Times* reviewer termed it 'dry and didactic'.[9] Another precursor with a more limited scope was a manuscript work on committee proceedings of about 140 pages written by John Rickman, then Clerk Assistant, in the late 1830s, which was never published and no longer survives but was almost certainly known to May.[10]

All the published works prior to May's that sought in part to supersede Hatsell had shared weaknesses. They had a limited understanding of contemporary practice and, thus, of the drivers of procedural change. Dwarris acknowledged that 'a knowledge of the law and usage of Parliament, which regulates the proceedings in both Houses, can scarcely be attained without actual experience', which he lacked.[11] Furthermore, they were unable to draw wider lessons or ascertain clear patterns from the instances they identified. In 1835, the Speaker of the House of Commons, James Abercromby, observed of Dwarris and others: 'I do not attach any great weight to these authorities, because they do not rest their opinions on any rule or principle that can be adopted as a guide.'[12] The way remained open to a writer who could address such weaknesses.

16.3 The man and the first edition

Thomas Erskine May was born in London in 1815. His family background remains obscure, despite hints of an unspecified kinship with Thomas Erskine, the pre-eminent barrister of his generation who, as Lord Erskine, served as Lord Chancellor in 1806–07.[13] May was educated at Bedford School and offered an Exhibition at an Oxford College, but was unable to take up the place for unknown reasons.[14] Instead, at the age of 16, he became Assistant Librarian of the House of Commons in place of Thomas Vardon, who had just been

9 *ODNB*, Dwarris, Sir Fortunatus William Lilley; F Dwarris, *A General Treatise on Statutes . . . Part the First: Parliamentary* (1st edn, Saunders and Benning 1830) vi–vii, 67; *The Times*, 18 June 1830, 5; *Dublin Evening Mail*, 26 March 1845, 3.

10 Lee, 'May on Money: Supply Proceedings and the Functions of a Legislature' in P Evans (ed), *Essays on the History of Parliamentary Procedure in Honour of Thomas Erskine May* (Hart Publishing 2017) 171–87', 173, n 14. For an instance of May crediting Rickman, see *Treatise* (1st edn) 184, n 1.

11 Dwarris (n 9) vii.

12 *Parl Deb*, 3rd Series, vol 32, 23 March 1836, cols 503, 505.

13 WR McKay, 'A Sycophant of Real Ability: The Career of Thomas Erskine May' in P Evans (ed), *Essays on the History of Parliamentary Procedure in Honour of Thomas Erskine May* (Hart Publishing 2017) 21–32, 30–32; *ODNB*, Erskine, Thomas, first Baron Erskine.

14 D Holland and D Menhennet (eds), *Erskine May's Private Journal, 1857–1882: Diary of a Great Parliamentarian* (HMSO, House of Commons Library Document No. 9 1972) 35, 42.

promoted to the post of Librarian. The role involved research and indexing of papers and reports as well as the management of a book collection: in 1835, Vardon stated that 'there is no subject connected with parliamentary business, on finance, or the forms of the House, or the progress of Bills, or the content of Acts, on which I am not called upon to afford instant information.'[15] Along-side such work, May made amends for his lack of a university education by continuing 'to cherish my early habits of study'.[16] In 1838, he was called to the bar from the Middle Temple; he never practised, although he noted later that 'my studies had been always associated with the law and with legal history'.[17]

May's first published writings were a series of biographical sketches of characters such as John Wilkes and William Wilberforce for the publisher Charles Knight, whose ambition was to secure popular access to useful knowledge.[18] In 1841, May wrote an article on 'the Imperial Parliament' for *Knight's Store of Knowledge.* One reviewer termed this article 'a treatise on the history, the constitution, law, and usages of parliament . . . which condenses into sixteen agreeable and instructive pages more information than, we venture to say, the public ever before received in any one volume on the subject.' The matters it considered were dealt with 'luminously' so that 'nobody who reads a newspaper should be without it'.[19] In 1842, the article was published as a stand-alone pamphlet priced at fourpence, which May subsequently referred to as 'my little book'. Although the work was little more than 60 pages in length, even in its second form, it contained the kernel of some key components of the *Treatise.* Sections on the origins and constituent parts of Parliament and on the seminal case establishing the power of the Commons to determine the outcome of elections – *Ashby v White*[20] – first appeared in *The Imperial Parliament* and were transposed with little alteration to the *Treatise.* The analysis of privilege in the pamphlet also laid the foundations for that in the *Treatise.*[21]

This venture encouraged May to make the proposal described at the outset of this chapter. May was also able to draw upon another of his endeavours – 'a list of all general resolutions & standing orders which I made for the Speaker.'[22] The Speaker in question, Charles Shaw Lefevre, first chosen in 1839, had evidently identified May's ability, and the Preface to the First

15 *ODNB*, Vardon, Thomas; Holland and Menhennet (n 14) vi–vii; *Report from the Standing Committee on the Library*, Q 3.

16 Holland and Menhennet (n 14) viii, 42.

17 *ODNB*, May, Thomas Erskine, Baron Farnborough; McKay (n 13) 32; Holland and Menhennet (n 14) 35.

18 *ODNB*, Knight, Charles; McKay (n 5) vii–viii; TPA, ERM/18/1-4, manuscript articles.

19 TE May, *The Imperial Parliament* (Charles Knight & Co 1842); *Dublin Evening Mail*, 30 July 1841, 3.

20 (1703) 92 ER 126.

21 TPA, ERM/10A/2-3, Draft Notes by May for Knight, undated; May (n 19) 3–20, 26–28, 29–40, 45, 52–53; *Treatise* (1st edn) 1–29, 40–42.

22 TPA, ERM/10A/2-3, Draft Notes by May for Knight, undated.

Edition of May's *Treatise* noted how he was 'under peculiar obligations to Mr Speaker, with whose encouragement the work was undertaken, and by whose valuable suggestions it has been incalculably improved.'[23] As a consequence of the Speaker's patronage, the work from the outset had elements of an official endeavour. In outlining the proposed production timetable to Knight, May emphasised the need to enable his proposed text to be 'revised by the different officers of the House'.[24] It was nevertheless produced at great speed. The text managed to incorporate several precedents from 1844 and be published in the middle of May that year, a little more than six months after Knight's response to the book proposal.[25]

The title of May's new work was carefully chosen. The term 'treatise' reflected a contemporary vogue for treatises on particular branches of the law, charted by Professor Brian Simpson. May's work conformed to the model suggested by Simpson. Whereas Hatsell had enumerated precedents and then drawn observations from them, May set out rules and principles first, then authorities, and then 'brief statements of the general results of precedents', sometimes in categories, and noted exceptions. The reviewer in *The Times* characterised May's volume as 'the first successful attempt to reduce into order in one systematic treatise the chaos of Parliamentary precedents.' A review of the second edition noted that it was 'neither a mere treatise without the sanction of any precedent nor is it merely an index of cases. It combines the advantages of both.'[26]

Part of the success of the volume lay in the clarity of exposition and May's ability to distil complex issues into a short and memorable statement, epitomised by his summation of different constitutional roles with regard to public finance: 'Thus the Crown demands money, the Commons grant it, and the Lords assent to the grant.'[27] The reviewer in *The Times* commended the 'lucid' prose, also suggesting that it was 'a popular work, and one that will be prized by every gentleman that reads a newspaper, or dabbles in politics and Parliamentary debates.' Another reviewer noted that 'it seems to make popular, and almost familiar, that system of parliamentary technicalities which used to appear confused and chaotic.'[28]

23 Holland and Menhennet (n 14) 1; *Treatise* (1st edn), vii.

24 TPA, ERM/10A/2-3, Draft Notes by May for Knight, undated.

25 *Treatise* (1st edn) 145, 170, 410 n 3, 414 n 1; *Morning Post*, 21 May 1844, 8; McKay (n 5) viii.

26 AWB Simpson, 'The Rise and Fall of the Legal Treatise: Legal Principles and the Forms of Legal Literature' (1981) 48 University of Chicago Law Review 632–79, 633–34, 662–68; Seaward (n 4) 113; *Treatise* (1st edn), v–vi, 59–60, 131, 133, 154–55, 172, 195, 270; *The Times*, 15 October 1844, 8; *London Evening Standard*, 20 May 1851, 3.

27 *The Times*, 15 October 1844, 8; *Treatise* (1st edn) 324.

28 *The Times*, 15 October 1844, 8; *Globe*, 21 December 1844, 11; *Monthly Times*, 7 November 1844, 10.

This conception of the *Treatise* as a popular work was consistent with Knight's wider aims as a populariser of knowledge, and May had stipulated that 'a book of considerable price would not sell'. The cover price of 14 shillings was recognised as 'moderate'.[29] May described his own purpose as being 'to display Parliament in its present form'. By tapping into the growing market among those who followed parliamentary debates in the national and regional press, May was also reflecting his Whig political ideology, made explicit in a pamphlet he published a few years after the *Treatise* when he welcomed the 'publicity' given to parliamentary proceedings, which facilitated the 'free communication between the lawgivers and those for whose benefit the laws are made, which gives so great a moral weight to the Legislature.' The *Treatise* was a contribution to ensuring that there was an informed electorate to lend Parliament its legitimacy.[30]

The first of three 'books' in the *Treatise* categorised parliamentary privilege in ways that have stood the test of time. May's analysis reflected an understanding of contemporary concerns and priorities alongside historical precedents, identifying unresolved tensions between privilege and the general law and noting that precedents were 'contradictory' and the positions of the courts inconsistent. The tensions between the stances of the individual Houses as guardians of their privileges and the courts as guardians of the general law had recently come to the fore in the succession of legal cases and actions of the Commons arising from *Stockdale v Hansard*,[31] which May regarded as the most important privilege case in over a century. Legislation had resolved the immediate issue – the protection for publications ordered to be printed by either House against actions for libel – but left the tensions unresolved. May ended his analysis by describing this situation as 'unsatisfactory', and making the case for a 'well-considered statute' determining the scope of the privileges of the two Houses generally. One reviewer found that these difficult matters were 'treated with great impartiality', and viewed the proposal for a new statute as 'judicious'.[32]

In the second part, which considered the practice and proceedings of Parliament, May dealt with the Commons and Lords together; where their practice was the same, they were treated together; where those practices differed, the variation was explained. May described the modern practice as something that could only be known 'by personal experience, and by the daily practice of Parliament in the conduct of its various descriptions of business.' Contemporary practice relied upon what an 1861 select committee termed 'common consent' within a homogenous assembly in which Members had a shared sense of

29 TPA, ERM/10A/2-3, Draft Notes by May for Knight, undated; *The Times*, 13 May 1844, 10; *Globe*, 21 December 1844, 11.

30 *Treatise* (1st edn) 1–2; May, *Remarks*, 7.

31 (1839) 9 Ad & Ell 96.

32 *Treatise* (1st edn) 44, 48, 113–20, 125–130; *Dublin Evening Mail*, 26 Mar 1845, 3.

loyalty to the institution and a sense of respect for 'the written and the unwritten law of Parliament, which for ages has secured a good system of legislation, perfect freedom of debate, and a due regard for the rights of minorities.' The *Treatise* both described and buttressed this procedural system.[33]

The final book was concerned with private bills. In responding to May's original proposal, which had expressed some uncertainty about the likely readership for the work, Knight had advised him that there was a wider audience, 'especially if it were very complete in all matters relating to Private Bills'. May was very keen for rapid production of the work in part due to what he termed 'the constant changes in private business'.[34] He adopted the same methods as those applied earlier in the *Treatise*, but was faced, in this case, with the additional challenge of the number and complexity of standing orders in each House. He dealt extensively with the additional requirements for railway bills which were then reaching a peak. The reviewer in *The Times* thought that 'nothing so useful and so compendiously clear' as May's work had been produced on the subject of private bills, making intelligible the 'otherwise complex and embarrassing' standing orders of the two Houses 'about which every country solicitor and every shareholder in a railroad hears so much and comprehends so little.' Another reviewer pointed out that constant changes in standing orders had reduced this part of business to 'a mass of confusion', to which May had brought clarity and lucidity, invaluable for promoters of bills.[35]

16.4 Towards a work of reference: changes in the second and third editions

The second edition, which was published in April 1851, reflected the start of a change in the nature of the *Treatise*, from an accessible work for the general reader to a denser work of reference. May moved the publisher from Knight to Henry Butterworth, the chief London law publisher. The price for the second edition was 21 shillings, an increase of 50% compared with the first edition, and the price was to continue to rise.[36] The changing nature reflected in particular three aspects of May's professional development – in relation to private bills, elections, and his closeness to the Speaker.

33 *Treatise* (1st edn) 131; C Lee, 'Archibald Milman and the procedural response to obstruction, 1877–1888' (2015) 83 *The Table* 22–44, 25–27; *Report from the Select Committee on the Business of the House*, xi, iv.

34 TPA, ERM/10A/2-3, Draft Notes by May for Knight, undated; TPA, ERM/10A/1, Knight to May, 18 November 1843.

35 *Treatise* (1st edn) 385, 417–21, 443–44; OC Williams, *The Historical Development of Private Bill Procedure and Standing Orders in the House of Commons*, vol I (London 1948) 58–67; *The Times*, 15 October 1844, 8; *Dublin Evening Mail*, 26 March 1845, 3.

36 *Sun (London)* 14 April 1851, 5; *ODNB*, Henry Butterworth; *Morning Advertiser*, 29 November 1854, 1; *Morning Herald (London)* 29 January 1859, 8.

While still working in the Library, May was closely involved with the challenges of adapting to the exponential growth in railway bills. In the autumn of 1845, he sent Shaw Lefevre proposals on how to handle the 700 petitions for railway bills that threatened to overwhelm the House of Commons in the ensuing parliamentary session. The following year, May provided the Speaker with more detailed proposals for reform of private business.[37] At the heart of the reforms subsequently proposed by the Speaker was the creation of the role of Examiners of Petitions for Private Bills, determining the compliance of private bills with Standing Orders. May was appointed as one of the Examiners, and he found it a rewarding role, in part because this was what May characterised as 'a judicial office' requiring 'the exercise of considerable judgment', working in his own right rather than simply in support of Members. From 1847, he took on the additional role of Taxing Officer, determining the fees to be charged on private bills, which was described by the Speaker as 'by far the most laborious duty about the House, in consequence of the very heavy railway Bills which are brought in almost every Session.' Together, these two roles provided him with an income of £1,200 a year.[38] The chapters relating to private bills were far more extensively revised in the second edition than others, as May explained: 'The alterations in the mode of conducting Private business have been so great, during the last few years, that the third book may be regarded as a new treatise . . . embracing the most recent precedents.' The review in *The Times* praised May for his handling of 'a department of the law so very technical and complex that few even of the Lords and Commons themselves grapple successfully with its difficulties.' Again, in the third edition of 1855, May explained that 'The frequent changes of practice, especially in relation to Private Bills, have rendered necessary a careful revision of the entire Work; while much new matter, and very numerous references, have been added.' He provided a thorough account of the requirements expected of agents appearing before the Examiners.[39]

The second and third editions also reflected May's growing interest in the powers of the Commons in disputed elections. In 1850, he wrote a pamphlet, *On the Consolidation of the Election Laws*, contending that inconsistent statutes exacerbated the inconsistency of determinations by committees of the Commons on election petitions and tensions between the Commons and the courts. He argued that successful consolidation would mean that 'the law of elections will be more satisfactorily administered, the judicial character of parliamentary committees will stand higher in public estimation, and the

37 TPA, ERM/2/1-2, Shaw Lefevre to May, 1 November 1845; TPA, ERM/2/4-7, Shaw Lefevre to May, 14 November 1846.

38 *Treatise* (1st edn) 404; Holland and Menhennet (n 14) vii, 1, 56; BL, Add MS 72832 A, fos 29–30 v, May to Samuel Smith, 1 February 1871; Select Committee on Private Business, *First Report*, 3, 26; Williams (n 35) 74–76.

39 *Treatise* (2nd edn), v, 488–89, 501–03; *The Times*, 24 April 1851, 3; *Treatise* (3rd edn), v, 528–31, 541; Williams (n 35) 119–24.

exclusive jurisdiction of the House of Commons will not only be maintained but respected.' The second edition of the *Treatise* referred to this pamphlet and reflected recent contested election cases. Soon after the second edition was completed, May took on an additional temporary role in relation to election recognisances – sureties for election petitions – and this branch of parliamentary administration featured in subsequent editions.[40]

May's close collaboration with Shaw Lefevre as Speaker also influenced the evolution of the *Treatise*. Having established his professional position as Examiner in the Speaker's Department, May was able to gain intimate knowledge of the business of the House and the decisions of its presiding officer. In the second edition, May referred to the method which has applied to its revision ever since: '[T]he Work, as originally published, has been tested by constant reference and practical use.' That edition was 'the result of its continual revision, during the whole of that period', with 'all changes of practice and new precedents . . . noted, from day to day, as they happened.' The Speaker was again thanked for his 'invaluable information and assistance, which no one else could have afforded.' May was able to record significant rulings by Shaw Lefevre as Speaker – for example, on the information required to make a complaint of privilege in respect of a publication.[41] May was also involved in a further venture which came about due to the Speaker's initiative, in the form of a more systematic and modern index of the Journals of the House of Commons up to 1714.[42] It is evident from a letter from Shaw Lefevre to the Prime Minister, Lord John Russell, in September 1850 how far the Speaker believed that May's professional work would enhance the value of the *Treatise*:

> The book which he has published on the Proceedings & Usage of Parliament is very valuable as far as it goes, & may be made more complete when a new Edition is published, & from his having been engaged in framing the Index to the Journals from their very commencement & from the attention he has paid to the subject. He has more knowledge of the forms & practice of the House than any person I have known since the death of Mr Rickman.[43]

40 TE May, *On the Consolidation of the Election Laws* (Butterworths 1850) 3–7, 13–17, 22–23; TPA, ERM/8/62, draft of May to Lord Chelmsford, 7 November 1866; *Treatise* (2nd edn) 430 n1, 446–47; TPA, ERM/2/23-24, Shaw Lefevre to May, 23 December 1850; Select Committee on Private Business, *First Report*, 25; *Treatise* (4th edn) 562–66.

41 *Treatise* (2nd edn), v–vi, 88–89.

42 Report from the Select Committee on Miscellaneous Expenditure (HC 1847–48) 543) 65; T Vardon and TE May, *The General Index to the Journals of the House of Commons 1547–1714* (Henry Hansard 1852); *General Index*, v–vi; M Atkins, 'Persuading the House: The Use of the Commons Journals as a Source of Precedent' in P Evans (ed), *Essays on the History of Parliamentary Procedure in Honour of Thomas Erskine May* (Hart Publishing 2017) 69–85, 81–82.

43 TNA, PRO 30/22/8E/86, Shaw Lefevre to Lord John Russell, 3 September 1850 (fos 273–275v).

In December 1850, Shaw Lefevre asked May about the timing of the proofs of the Second Edition, as the Speaker wished 'to read it over in proof' in order 'to judge after reading it whether there are Omissions to be supplied or any other alterations to be made.'[44]

16.5 Becoming an authority

During the second half of May's life, the *Treatise,* which he had published as a young man, became recognised as an authority – the leading work on Parliamentary practice and on Parliamentary law as a distinct branch of constitutional law. In 1854, Sir John Pakington, the Chairman of a Select Committee on the Business of the House that had taken evidence from May, referred to May as someone 'whose work on Parliamentary forms and usages was looked upon as a standard authority upon the subject.'[45] The extent to which May's *Treatise* was increasingly recognised as an authority was a product of several factors alongside the textual development of the work itself, including May's role as a historian, May's professional career, his role in advising Speakers, cabinets, select committees and others, and the developing use of the *Treatise* in the chambers of the House of Commons and House of Lords.

In the early 1860s, May authored a two-volume book entitled *The Constitutional History of England since the Accession of Goerge III 1760–1860*, a work firmly in the Whig tradition, being designed to trace the process 'by which institutions have been improved, and abuses in the government corrected', underpinned by 'the earnest conviction that the development of popular liberties has been safe and beneficial'. The work was thematic in approach, and *The Times* reviewer referred to it as 'not so much a history of England as a series of historical essays on the political rights and privileges of Englishmen.' In 1871, May published a supplementary chapter which noted, in reference to Gladstone's General Election victory in 1868, 'the extraordinary power of a Government representing the popular will, under an extended franchise.'[46] In 1877, May published a further historical work entitled *Democracy in Europe: A History,* which attempted to explain the role of popular power in different European States, but sometimes substituting moral judgment for convincing causation. May himself conceded to Gladstone that 'I have fallen very short of my own ideal of such a work'. A review by May's friend Lord Acton observed that the work lacked any convincing synthesis, was weak on matters

44 TPA, ERM/2/23-24, Shaw Lefevre to May, 23 December 1850.

45 *Parl Deb*, 3rd Series, vol 133, 1 June 1854, col 1166.

46 Holland and Menhennet (n 14) 1, 3, 4; TE May, *The Constitutional History of England since the Accession of George the Third 1760–1860* (Longman, Green, Longman and Roberts, vol I, 1861, vol 2, 1863), I.v–vi, 477; *The Times*, 8 April 1863, 6; TE May, *The Constitutional History of England since the Accession of George the Third 1760–1860, with a Supplementary Chapter, 1861–1871*, 3 vols (5th edn, Longmans, Green & Co 1875), III. 430–42, 447; McKay (n 5) 26–27.

of ideology, and was uneven in execution.[47] May's historical work broadened his conception of Parliament's role. The man who in the 1840s and 1850s emphasised the machinery of the legislative process later argued, 'Ours is not a council of sages for framing laws, and planning amendments of the constitution; but a free and vigorous parliament.'[48] Although May's public reputation was initially forged by the *Treatise*, his historical works secured him what *The Times* called 'a literary reputation', and the *Constitutional History* was more popular than the *Treatise* could ever be.[49] The *Constitutional History* allowed him to restrain himself from including more than 'incidental allusions' to historical material in the *Treatise*.[50] May's historical research enabled his procedural and constitutional advice to command authority because he combined mastery of contemporary practice with an understanding of its origins and development. When May prepared a paper advising Gladstone early in 1874 about whether his appointment as Chancellor of the Exchequer and Prime Minister meant that his seat was vacated, Gladstone thanked him for his 'luminous paper . . . in which the spirit and qualifications of the historic student appear side by side with those of the constitutional lawyer.'[51]

From an early stage, there was a mutually reinforcing interaction between May's authorship and his career development. In 1850, Shaw Lefevre already viewed May as 'abundantly qualified' to be Clerk of the House, but the appointment was in the Prime Minister's gift, and when a vacancy arose that August, Lord John Russell gave the post to his political ally Sir Denis le Marchant.[52] In 1856, Shaw Lefevre was able to secure May the appointment as Clerk Assistant,

47 TE May, *Democracy in Europe: A History*, 2 vols (Longmans, Green and Co 1877), I.vii–viii, xxix, lxiii–lxiv, 327, II. 165–72; Holland and Menhennet (n 14) xiv, 15, 19, 21, 32, 44, 47, 48, 49; BL, Add MS 44154, fos 56–57, May to Gladstone, 13 November 1877; McKay (n 5) vii, 15–16; CUL, MS Add 8119/M148, May to Acton, 4 September 1877; CUL, MS Add 8119/M149, May to Acton, 8 October 1877; CUL, MS Add 8119/M149, May to Acton, 6 November 1877; Lord Acton, 'Sir Erskine May's *Democracy in Europe*' (1878) 145 The Quarterly Review 112–43, 113, 141–42.

48 Taylor, 'Parliamentary Representation' (2022) 65 The Historical Journal 1145–73, 1160, citing May (n 46) *Constitutional History* (1st edn), II.622.

49 Holland and Menhennet (n 14) 8, 41; *The Times*, 2 February 1871, 4; McKay (n 5) vii.

50 *Treatise* (4th edn), iii; *Treatise* (7th edn), iii.

51 Holland and Menhennet (n 14) 36–37. For the original paper, see TPA, ERM/8/125, Memorandum on the Offices of First Lord of the Treasury, and Chancellor of the Exchequer, 20 January 1874.

52 McKay (n 5) xi–xii; McKay (n 13) 21–24; TPA, ERM/2/16, Shaw Lefevre to May, 22 August 1850; TPA, ERM/2/17-18, 24 August 1850; TNA, PRO 30/22/8E/80, Labouchere to Lord John Russell, 25 August 1850 (fos 261–62); TNA, PRO 30/22/8E/81, Sir Denis Le Marchant to Lord John Russell, 26 August 1850 (fos 263–64); TNA, PRO 30/22/8E/82, Shaw Lefevre to Lord John Russell, 27 August 1850 (fos 265–66v); TPA, ERM/2/19-20, Shaw Lefevre to May, 28 August 1850; TPA, ERM/2/75-77, Shaw Lefevre to May, 31 August 1870; TNA, PRO 30/22/8E/86, Shaw Lefevre to Lord John Russell, 3 September 1850 (fos 273–75v); TNA, PRO 30/22/8E/107, Labouchere to Lord John Russell, 19 September 1850 (fos 333–33v); TNA, PRO 30/22/8E/111, Sir Denis Le Marchant to Lord John Russell, 24 September 1850 (fos 345–46).

and from this point, in his own words, May functioned as 'chief officer' of the House on points of parliamentary law and procedure.[53] This was implicitly acknowledged when Shaw Lefevre retired in 1857 by his successor, Evelyn Denison, in accepting the nomination:

> [U]nder [Shaw Lefevre's] immediate supervision, the rules and practice of Parliament have been digested and arranged by a Gentleman who now sits at that table (Mr. Erskine May, the Clerk Assistant) in a manner which cannot fail to afford material assistance to all who shall succeed to that chair.

May noted with satisfaction in his diary that the reference to him 'was readily understood and cheered by the House'.[54] May's professional advancement assisted him with the process of producing new editions of the *Treatise* 'decreed' by his publishers. With his position in the chamber and daily proximity to the Speaker, May was even better placed to identify what he termed 'every change and new precedent' meriting inclusion.[55] To accommodate these additions, the sixth edition was 'printed in a more condensed form', and May increasingly used footnotes to multiply precedents or to add unusual instances without revisiting the main text unless absolutely necessary.[56] May also involved colleagues in his enterprise. Thus, in 1868, when recommending Reginald Palgrave for the post of Second Clerk Assistant, May attested to the diligence and accuracy of Palgrave's researches 'while I was editing some of the editions of my "Law and Usage of Parliament".'[57]

When Le Marchant retired in 1870, May's claim to the post of Clerk of the House of Commons, based on what Gladstone termed 'his transcendent merits', was uncontested, and so May, in his own words, 'reached the top of this little ladder'. A tribute in *The Times* noted how May's *Treatise* 'at once placed him upon a level with Hatsell, and is now the recognized text book, not only in England, but in her Colonies, and wherever Parliamentary government is attempted'; but went on: 'It is with his official life that we are most concerned, and here his thorough mastery of Parliamentary lore and his readiness in every emergency have long been recognized. Still more, he enjoys the habitual confidence of all parties.'[58]

53 TPA, ERM/2/31-32, Shaw Lefevre to May, 4 December 1855; TPA, ERM/2/33-34, Shaw Lefevre to May, 10 December 1855; TPA, ERM/2/35-36, Shaw Lefevre to May, 16 December 1855; Holland and Menhennet (n 14) 24.

54 *Parl Deb*, 3rd Series, vol 145, 30 April 1857, col 9; Holland and Menhennet (n 14) 2.

55 Holland and Menhennet (n 14) 6, 8, 14, 20.

56 *Treatise* (6th edn), iii; Treatise (7th edn) 284 n1, 319 n2.

57 BL, Add MS 44154, fos 29–30, Memorandum on Mr Palgrave's services, 28 December 1868.

58 TPA, ERM/1/16, Gladstone to May, 12 August 1870; Holland and Menhennet (n 14) 22–24; BL, Add MS 72832 A, fos 29–30 v, May to Samuel Smith, 1 February 1871; *The Times*, 2 February 1871, 4.

The value of May's advice on matters of parliamentary law was established well before his professional apotheosis. When a select committee had considered the case for a Deputy Speaker in 1853, May was the first witness. He was examined at length, and invited to read the text of a bill he had drafted to enable a Deputy Speaker to perform almost all of the functions of the Speaker. The Speaker was the only other witness and endorsed May's evidence. Despite initial caution attributed by May to the House's 'continued reluctance to change', a subsequent Standing Order and Statute closely mirrored May's proposals.[59] In his first edition, May had regretted that 'the penalties of perjury do not attach to false testimony before the House of Commons', so that the matter could only be proceeded with as a breach of privilege. Soon after this alleged lacuna was highlighted in a debate in 1869, during which May's views were cited, a select committee was established to consider the matter. The committee treated his evidence on history as 'exhaustive' and happily endorsed his recommendation for a statutory provision as their own, which was duly enacted in 1871.[60]

Some of the revisions to the *Treatise* directly reflected matters on which he had been involved in giving advice to ministers, for example, on enabling Queen Victoria to attend the State Opening but not read the speech from the Throne and on handling Disraeli's resignation in 1868 shortly before a new session was due to start and when the new ministers would be absent seeking re-election.[61] In 1870, when someone serving a sentence of penal servitude for life was elected as MP for Tipperary, May advised Gladstone on 'the most summary method of repudiating' the MP's election by declaring him incapable of being elected or returned. During the ensuing debate, May found that, not for the last time, his *Treatise* was referred to for cases which called into question the House's power to do this, even though he himself believed that the power existed. In 1875, the electors of Tipperary again chose a convicted felon, this time someone who had escaped from prison, as one of their representatives. May persuaded Disraeli, as he had Gladstone, to make a motion of incapacity, a decision whose legality was subsequently upheld in the courts.[62]

59 *Treatise* (1st edn) 154–55; *Report from the Select Committee on Office of the Speaker*, iii, xiv, 1, 10–11, 16–17; TE May, 'The Machinery of Parliamentary Legislation' (1854) 94 The Edinburgh Review 243–82, 246–47; *Treatise* (3rd edn) 203–04; *Treatise* (4th edn) 222–24; Holland and Menhennet (n 14) 16; *Treatise* (6th edn) 222–23; *Treatise* (7th edn) 232.

60 *Treatise* (1st edn) 245; *Parl Deb*, 3rd Series, vol 196, 5 May 1869, col 241; Select Committee on Witnesses (House of Commons), *Report*, iii–iv, 1–14; *Parl Deb*, 3rd Series, vol 208, 10 August 1871, col 1399; Holland and Menhennet (n 14) 21; *Treatise* (7th edn) 428–29.

61 Holland and Menhennet (n 14) 15–16, 20; *Treatise* (6th edn) 197–98; *Treatise* (7th edn) 204–05, 186–87.

62 Holland and Menhennet (n 14) 46; *Parl Deb*, 3rd Series, vol 199, 10 February 1870, cols 123–52; *Parl Deb*, 3rd Series, vol 222, 18 February 1875, cols 493–539; *Tipperary Election: Return to an Order of the House of Commons dated 3 June 1875*, HC (1875) 241.

The Times observed in 1874 in relation to the *Treatise* that 'a book which becomes identified with the working system of a powerful institution becomes thereby a living influence'.[63] This was especially apparent in matters of privilege. In April 1873, the Attorney General, Sir John Coleridge, in seeking to contest a claim of privilege, referred to May's *Treatise* as 'the book which is always referred to as the authority on questions of this kind.' In February 1880, another Attorney General argued that

> The law of Parliament affecting the question under discussion was laid down with the greatest possible clearness in the work of Sir Erskine May, who was a great authority on Parliamentary law.
>
> In later editions, May sought to capture the seeming inconsistencies of decisions about the precedence for debate on matters of privilege, which depended upon context and were ultimately a judgment for the Speaker. In the contested instance of 1880, Lord Hartington, the Leader of the Opposition, noted that the *Treatise*, 'to which we always refer on these occasions . . . shows that innumerable cases of this sort have been brought before the House, and with very different results.' In 1881, a Member cited May's *Treatise* in arguing that a topic should not have priority as a matter of privilege, only for the Speaker to respond directly with a citation from the same source as the basis of his contrary ruling.[64]

On matters of procedure, May's *Treatise* was also recognised as being of great value, but May sought to convey the difficulties of establishing clear rules on complex matters.[65] May's work was described as authoritative when a precedent could be found which suited the argument of the person deploying it, but this could frequently rebound on them. In 1882, a Member praying in aid of the *Treatise* about the rights of those who formally seconded a motion was slapped down by the Speaker for confusing a substantive motion with an adjournment motion.[66] In the late 1870s and early 1880s, Charles Stewart Parnell and other Irish Home Rule MPs frequently cited May's *Treatise* but had no success in persuading the Speaker or the House about their deductions from it.[67] In 1894, in the first edition of the *Treatise* published after

63 *The Times*, 15 January 1874, 4.

64 *Treatise* (7th edn) 266–67, 268–69; *Parl Deb*, 3rd Series, vol 215, 3 April 1873, col 536; *Parl Deb*, 3rd Series, vol 250, 20 February 1880, cols 1122–23; *Parl Deb*, 3rd Series, vol 245, 17 April 1879, col 517; *Parl Deb*, 3rd Series, vol 250, 17 February 1880, col 806; *Parl Deb*, 3rd Series, vol 261, 13 May 1881, cols 430–31.

65 *Parl Deb*, 3rd Series, vol 229, 9 June 1876, cols 1622–30; *Parl Deb*, 3rd Series, vol 231, 11 August 1876, col 1119; *Parl Deb*, 3rd Series, vol 231, 11 August 1876, cols 1159–60; *Treatise* (7th edn) 300–02, 670–76.

66 *Parl Deb*, 3rd Series, vol 267, 14 March 1882, cols 893–94.

67 *Parl Deb*, 3rd Series, vol 243, 24 February 1879, col 1694; *Parl Deb*, 3rd Series, vol 241, 2 July 1878, cols 592–96; *Parl Deb*, 3rd Series, vol 266, 26 February 1882, cols 1805–11.

May's death, Palgrave observed how the book was often 'caught up from the Table of the House to parry an objection, or to perplex an antagonist'.[68]

May had advocated reforms of public business with little success for 30 years, often drawing upon his historical research and his experience of private business.[69] From 1877, the shared understanding of, and loyalty to, the customary practice of the House began to break down, principally under the strain of systematic obstruction, pursued initially by Parnell and his supporters but then taken up by others. In the eighth edition in 1879, May noted how the House's rules 'of late . . . have been strained and perverted . . . for purposes of obstruction'. He was confident that 'rules will be devised for vindicating the authority of Parliament, and repressing a serious political evil'. May was then instrumental in the process of seeking to overcome resistance through the introduction of a panoply of new temporary and standing orders in 1881 and 1882, dealing with disciplinary powers, measures to curtail debate – through the closure and 'guillotine' – measures to improve financial procedures and steps to delegate some legislative functions to Standing Committees.[70] In January 1883, Butterworths had informed him that copies of the eighth edition had 'melted away during the last few months much faster than we could have expected they would', perhaps partly as a result of heightened political interest in procedural matters, and May took on the task of a new edition with limited enthusiasm, although perhaps comforted by the offer of an initial payment at the time of publication of £400, and an increase in a print run from 750 to 1,000.[71]

As Sir William McKay has noted, by 1883, 'the structure of the *Treatise*. . . was beginning to creak under the load of piecemeal amendment'. In the ninth edition produced that year, May described recent procedural reforms but struggled to recast his *Treatise* to take account of the fundamental transition now underway in public business, from customary law to Standing Orders. His account was vitiated by his reluctance to make structural changes and by his desire to combine description with advocacy so that he was caught between the original conception based on description and the temptations

68 *Treatise* (10th edn) xi.

69 WR McKay, 'The Principle of Progress: May and Procedural Reform' in P Evans (ed), *Essays on the History of Parliamentary Procedure in Honour of Thomas Erskine May* (Hart Publishing 2017) 157–70, 158–67; C Lee, 'May on Money' (n 10), 171–79; TE May, *Remarks and Suggestions with a View to Facilitate the Dispatch of Public Business in Parliament* (2nd edn, James Ringway, Piccadilly 1849) 16, 19, 21, 23; P Evans and A Ninkovic, 'From Manual to Authority: The Life and Times of the *Treatise*' in P Evans (ed), *Essays on the History of Parliamentary Procedure in Honour of Thomas Erskine May* (Hart Publishing 2017) 115–28, 116; P Salmon, 'Parliament' in DS Brown, R Crowcroft and G Pentland (eds), *The Oxford Handbook of Modern British Political History, 1800–2000* (Oxford University Press 2018) 83–102, 91–94.

70 *Treatise* (8th edn) 351–52; McKay (n 69) 162–69; Lee (n 69) 175–87; C Lee, 'Archibald Milman and the Evolution of the Closure – Part 1: Origins to 1881' (2020) 88 The Table 5–54, 25–54; C Lee, 'Archibald Milman and the Evolution of the Closure – Part 2: 1882–1885' (2021) 89 The Table 5–55, 7–18; C Lee, 'Archibald Milman and the Crisis of Legislation' (2023) 91 The Table 139–81, 141–54, 163–66.

71 TPA, ERM/10A/102-103, Butterworths to May, 6 January 1883.

of prescription.[72] In the field of parliamentary privilege, the ninth edition described what May termed the 'perplexing case' concerning Charles Bradlaugh and the parliamentary oath. This led to Bradlaugh bringing legal action against the Deputy Serjeant-at-Arms, during which May's *Treatise* was cited. The outcome of that case was, in some senses, a vindication of May's account of privilege, with the courts shying away from any interference in the powers and privileges of the House of Commons, although the definitiveness of the judicial position arguably weakened May's case for a statute to delineate parliamentary privilege.[73]

During a conversation with Denison in 1858, Albert, the Prince Consort, referred to the importance of May's *Treatise* in having 'first systematised the Proceedings'. Nearly 30 years later, in his own tribute to May, his successor, Palgrave, told May that 'You have done more than any one to strengthen & consolidate the Parliamentary system'. The structure of parliamentary practice based overwhelmingly on custom and unwritten laws was greatly strengthened by May's ability to describe it. By systematising, May also succeeded in providing clarity not only within Parliament, but also well beyond. As the last Speaker whom he served, Arthur Peel, said in announcing May's retirement: 'The work which he published in the year 1844, on the privileges, the customs, and not only a household word in this House, but it has been the model for many other Legislatures'. Gladstone, in his tribute, also identified the wider audience for 'the great classic of Parliamentary lore and learning', who were able 'to derive from his pages assistance not less valuable than that which he has given to us in the conduct of our high functions'.[74]

16.6 Becoming a book

The most enduring testament to the status of the *Treatise* was its continuation after his death. After some delicate negotiations with May's widow, Palgrave published a new edition in 1894 with May's name as author and Palgrave's as editor. Palgrave sought to retain as much of May's text as possible while also observing how much procedure had changed in the preceding decade, so that 'An attempt to engraft into a treatise framed on the easy-going lines of 1844 the complex procedure of 1893, without some alteration of structure, proved, consequently, of no avail'.[75]

72 McKay (n 5) viii–ix; *Treatise* (9th edn) 381–85, 444–45.

73 *Treatise* (9th edn) 210–15, 190–91; *The Times*, 19 December 1882, 5 *Bradlaugh v Gossett* [1884] EWHC 1 (QB).

74 TPA, ERM/3/144-145, Denison to May, undated [? Summer 1858]; TPA, ERM/10B/290-291, Palgrave to May, 5 May 1886; *Parl Deb*, 3rd Series, vol 304, 15 April 1886, col 1633; *Parl Deb*, 3rd Series, vol 304, 16 April 1886, cols 1775–76.

75 TPA, ERM/10A/107-108, Palgrave to Lady Farnborough, 19 September 1892; TPA, ERM/10A/109-110, Palgrave to Lady Farnborough, 26 September 1892; *Treatise* (10th edn) v–vii.

The *Treatise* had already acquired a dual identity as a description of current practice and as an embodiment of the parliamentary and legal opinions of one man. When May's work was cited during the debate in the House of Lords in 1860 prior to the rejection of the Paper Duty Bill, May's recognition of the right of the Lords to reject a money bill was felt to have especial value because May's wider sympathies were assumed to be with the financial privileges of the Commons.[76] In the second edition, May had ventured an opinion on the use of financial resolutions as the authority for levying taxes and duties prior to them being given statutory effect, which he viewed as 'not strictly legal'. He subsequently resisted pressure to revise that opinion, but the 11th edition produced in 1906 contended that 'an anticipatory authority is imparted by usage to the resolutions of the committee of ways and means which impose or alter taxation'. When dispute on the same matter came to the fore in 1910, one Member, Thomas Gibson Bowles, claimed that there was 'no higher authority than Sir Erskine May on the legal validity of proceedings in this House', citing 'the 1879 edition of his book, before it was revised by scholiasts', in his support. In 1912, Bowles succeeded in a legal action to establish that the resolutions had no legal force pending the enactment of a Finance Bill, leading to the passage of what became the Provisional Collection of Taxes Act 1913.[77]

For some time after May's death, there was a tendency to attribute citations from the *Treatise* to Erskine May the man. He was invested with a personal authority in this afterlife which was not given to him as a serving official, with one Member even referring in 1900 to 'a ruling by Sir Erskine May'. In 1902, Charles Ritchie, the Chancellor of the Exchequer, made a point of referring to an earlier edition of the treatise, which still had May's personal authority. Sometimes, Members fell into the trap of attributing to the man opinions which were added in the tenth or subsequent editions, including David Lloyd George as Chancellor of the Exchequer, referring to the statement about the authority of financial resolutions which had been added to the 11th edition as if it had the authority of the original author.[78]

The reflected glory of May the man may have been a factor in the marked reluctance of May's successors to make radical changes to the structure or

76 *Parl Deb*, 3rd Series, vol 158, 21 May 1860, cols 1475, 1477–78.

77 C Lee, 'Archibald Milman and the 1894 Finance Bill' (2018) 86 The Table 10–39, 34–37; *Treatise* (2nd edn) 406, 427; *Parl Deb*, 3rd Series, vol 160, 25 August 1860, cols 1827–28; *Treatise* (7th edn) 573–74; *Treatise* (8th edn) 593–94; *Treatise* (11th edn) 589, n3; *HC Deb*, 5th Series, vol 15, 21 March 1910, cols 806–07; J Jaconelli, 'The "Bowles Act" – Cornerstone of the Fiscal Constitution' (2010) 69 Cambridge Law Journal 582–608, 582–608; M Daunton, 'Thomas Gibson Bowles v Bank of England (1913): A Modern John Hampden?' in J Snape and D de Cogan (eds), *Landmark Cases in Revenue Law* (Hart Publishing 2019) 93–118.

78 *Parl Deb*, 4th Series, vol 30, 22 February 1895, col 1416; *Parl Deb*, 4th Series, vol 87, col 972; *Parl Deb*, 4th Series, vol 114, 4 November 1902, cols 108–09; *Parl Deb*, 4th Series, vol 79, 22 February 1900, cols 824–25 (citing *Treatise* (10th edn) 214; *HC Deb*, 5th Series, vol 51, 8 April 1913, col 1082 (citing *Treatise* (11th edn) 589, n3).

text of the *Treatise*. Palgrave's changes were relatively limited, given the fundamental transformation in the nature of the procedure. His successor as editor, Thomas Lonsdale Webster, primarily responsible for the 11th edition in 1906 and for two further editions in 1917 and 1924, positively celebrated the 'endeavour to preserve the balance of the work precisely as it was', with restructuring avoided even when significant procedural changes had taken place. One reviewer noted how the 1906 edition embodied the idea that it was 'best to keep the old familiar form for the sake of easy reference', even when 'some improvement might have been possible'. There then followed a 22-year gap before the next edition. Only with Sir Gilbert Campion, who produced the 14th edition published in 1946, did the *Treatise* find an editor willing 'to expound a developing system rather than to edit a text, however classical.' He noted that 'the changing balance of procedure, in particular the relation between the old ground-work of practice and the novel accretion of standing orders' meant that 'the original statement of the rules has become overweighted with qualifications – to the extent, in some places, that the original text was in danger of becoming a historical introduction to footnotes.' The work was almost completely recast to reflect modern procedure, beginning with a new exposition on the sources and content of parliamentary law and procedure, followed by a synthesis of modern work on the origin and development of Parliament, drawing on the 'advice and authority' of a distinguished historian of medieval England, Helen Cam, and finally excising May's text on the Saxon origins of Parliament, which had remained essentially unchanged since 1841. In abandoning most of May's superstructure, Campion went some way to return the work to the ambitions of the 1844 edition by expounding clear rules or principles at the outset. Campion's shift from purporting to be the authoritative work of one individual to becoming the focus of an institutional effort was reinforced by Sir Barnett Cocks in the 18th edition of 1971, who best summed up the modern status of the work:

> Texts like Erskine May's cannot be scriptural in their authority. Only Parliament itself can synthesize the sometimes opposing interests of rule and practice at particular times in particular circumstances. It is for each new edition of this work, by assimilating the actions of the past, to help with the decisions of the future . . . 'Erskine May', although still sometimes appealed to in debate as an authority with a separate existence, is in fact no more than a convenient appellation for the contemporary work and corporate memory of Clerks in both Houses of Parliament.[79]

79 *Treatise* (11th edn) vii–xii; *Treatise* (12th edn) vii–ix; *Treatise* (13th edn), *Treatise* (13th edn) vii; AG Porritt, 'Review: A Treatise of the Laws, Privileges, and Usages of Parliament' (1908) 2 The American Political Science Review 320–25, 325; *Treatise* (14th edn) vi–vii, xlvii–lvi, 3–7; *ODNB*, Cam, Helen Maud; *Treatise* (18th edn) v.

Bibliography

Primary sources

Acton Lord, 'Sir Erskine May's Democracy in Europe' (1878) 145 The Quarterly Review 112–43

BL, Add MS 72832 A, Clough-Shore Smith Papers, Vol ix a

Bramwell G, *The Manner of Proceeding on Bills in the House of Commons* (James and Luke Hansard & Sons 1833)

British Library [BL], Add MS 44154, Gladstone Papers, Vol LXIX

British Newspaper Archive, for all newspapers cited other than *The Times*

Cambridge University Library [CUL], MS Add 8119/M144–M153, Letters from May to Sir John, later Lord, Acton

Campion G (ed), *Treatise* (14th edn, Butterworth & Co 1946)

Cocks B (ed), *Treatise* (18th edn, Butterworth & Co 1971)

Dwarris F, *A General Treatise on Statutes . . . Part the First: Parliamentary* (1st edn, Saunders and Benning 1830)

Hammond A, *A Summary Treatise on the Practice and Proceedings in Parliament; The Passing of Public and Private Bills; and the Law of Elections* (Joseph Butterworth and Son 1825)

Hatsell J, *Precedents of Proceedings in the House of Commons Under Separate Titles With Observations in Four Volumes* (Luke Hansard and Sons 1818)

Holland D and Menhennet D (eds), *Erskine May's Private Journal, 1857–1882: Diary of a Great Parliamentarian* (HMSO, House of Commons Library Document No. 9 1972)

House of Commons Debates (*HC Deb*) Fifth Series

Lumley B, *Parliamentary Practice on Passing Private Bills* (London 1838)

May TE, 'The Imperial Parliament' in *Knight's Store of Knowledge for All Readers* (Charles Knight & Co 1841) vol 7, 97–112

May TE, *The Imperial Parliament* (Charles Knight & Co 1842)

May TE, *A Treatise upon the Law, Privileges, Proceedings and Usage of Parliament* [*Treatise*] (1st edn, Charles Knight & Co 1844)

May TE, *Remarks and Suggestions with a View to Facilitate the Dispatch of Public Business in Parliament* (2nd edn, James Ringway, Piccadilly 1849)

May TE, *On the Consolidation of the Election Laws* (Butterworths 1850)

May TE, *Treatise* (2nd edn, Butterworths 1851)

May TE, 'The Machinery of Parliamentary Legislation' (1854) 94 The Edinburgh Review 243–82

May TE, *Treatise* (3rd edn, Butterworths 1855)

May TE, *Treatise* (4th edn, Butterworths 1859)

May TE, *The Constitutional History of England Since the Accession of George the Third 1760–1860* (Longman, Green, Longman and Roberts, vol I, 1861, vol 2, 1863)

May TE, *Treatise* (5th edn, Butterworths 1863)

May TE, *Treatise* (6th edn, Butterworths 1868)

May TE, *Treatise* (7th edn, Butterworths 1873)

May TE, *The Constitutional History of England Since the Accession of George the Third 1760–1860, with a Supplementary Chapter, 1861–1871*, 3 vols (5th edn, Longmans, Green & Co 1875)

May TE, *Democracy in Europe: A History*, 2 vols (Longmans, Green and Co 1877)

May TE, *Treatise* (8th edn, Butterworths 1879)

May TE, *Treatise* (9th edn, Butterworths 1883)

McKay WR (ed), *Erskine May's Private Journal, 1883–1886* (HMSO, House of Commons Library Document No. 12 1984)

The National Archives [TNA], PRO 30/22/8E, Lord John Russell Papers, Correspondence and Papers, 29 May–30 September 1850
Palgrave RFD and Bonham-Carter A (eds), *Treatise* (10th edn, William Clowes and Sons Limited 1893)
The Parliamentary Archives [TPA], ERM, Papers of Thomas Erskine May, Baron Farnborough
Parliamentary Debates (*Parl Deb*) 1st Series (1803–1820), 2nd Series (1820–1830) 3rd Series (1830–1891) 4th Series (1892–1908)
Porritt AG, 'Review: A Treatise of the Laws, Privileges, and Usages of Parliament (1908) 2 The American Political Science Review 320–25
Select Committee on the Business of the House, *Report* (HC (1861) 173)
Select Committee on Miscellaneous Expenditure, *Report* (HC (1847–48) 543)
Select Committee on Office of the Speaker, *Report* (HC (1852–53) 478)
Select Committee on Private Business, *First Report* (HC (1851) 35)
Select Committee on Witnesses (House of Commons), *Report* (HC (1868–69) 305)
Standing Committee on the Library of the House of Commons, *Report* (HC (1835) 104)
The Times Digital Archive
Tipperary Election: Return to an Order of the House of Commons Dated 3 June 1875, HC (1875) 241
Vardon T and May TE, *The General Index to the Journals of the House of Commons 1547–1714* (Henry Hansard 1852)
Webster TL (ed), *Treatise* (12th edn, Butterworth and Co 1917)
Webster TL (ed), *Treatise* (13th edn, Butterworth and Co 1924)
Webster TL and Grey WE (eds), *Treatise* (11th edn, William Clowes and Sons Limited 1906)

Secondary sources

Atkins M, 'Persuading the House: The Use of the Commons Journals as a Source of Precedent' in P Evans (ed), *Essays on the History of Parliamentary Procedure in Honour of Thomas Erskine May* (Hart Publishing 2017) 69–85
Daunton M, 'Thomas Gibson Bowles v Bank of England (1913): A Modern John Hampden?' in J Snape and D de Cogan (eds), *Landmark Cases in Revenue Law* (Hart Publishing 2019) 93–118
Evans P (ed), *Essays on the History of Parliamentary Procedure in Honour of Thomas Erskine May* (Hart Publishing 2017)
Evans P and Ninkovic A, 'From Manual to Authority: The Life and Times of the *Treatise*' in P Evans (ed), *Essays on the History of Parliamentary Procedure in Honour of Thomas Erskine May* (Hart Publishing 2017) 115–28
Jaconelli J, 'The "Bowles Act" – Cornerstone of the Fiscal Constitution' (2010) 69 Cambridge Law Journal, 582–608
Lee C, 'Archibald Milman and the Procedural Response to Obstruction, 1877–1888' (2015) 83 The Table 22–44
Lee C, 'May on Money: Supply Proceedings and the Functions of a Legislature' in P Evans (ed), *Essays on the History of Parliamentary Procedure in Honour of Thomas Erskine May* (Hart Publishing 2017) 171–87
Lee C, 'Archibald Milman and the 1894 Finance Bill' (2018) 86 The Table 10–39
Lee C, 'Archibald Milman and the Evolution of the Closure – Part 1: Origins to 1881' (2020) 88 The Table 5–54
Lee C, 'Archibald Milman and the Evolution of the Closure – Part 2: 1882–1885' (2021) 89 The Table 5–55

Lee C, 'Archibald Milman and the Crisis of Legislation' (2023) 91 The Table 139–81
Lee C and Aschenbrenner PJ, '"Upon a Greater Stage": John Hatsell and John Ley on Politics and Procedure, 1760–1796' (2021) 89 The Table 66–119
McKay WR, 'The Principle of Progress: May and Procedural Reform' in P Evans (ed), *Essays on the History of Parliamentary Procedure in Honour of Thomas Erskine May* (Hart Publishing 2017a) 157–70
McKay WR, 'A Sycophant of Real Ability: The Career of Thomas Erskine May' in P Evans (ed), *Essays on the History of Parliamentary Procedure in Honour of Thomas Erskine May* (Hart Publishing 2017b) 21–32
Oxford Dictionary of National Biography online [*ODNB*]
Rydz DL, *The Parliamentary Agents: A History* (Royal Historical Society 1979)
Salmon P, 'Parliament' in DS Brown, R Crowcroft and G Pentland (eds), *The Oxford Handbook of Modern British Political History, 1800–2000* (Oxford University Press 2018) 83–102
Seaward P, 'Parliamentary Law in the Eighteenth Century: From Commonplace to Treatise' in P Evans (ed), *Essays on the History of Parliamentary Procedure in Honour of Thomas Erskine May* (Hart Publishing 2017) *Essays*, 97–114
Simpson AWB, 'The Rise and Fall of the Legal Treatise: Legal Principles and the Forms of Legal Literature' (1981) 48 University of Chicago Law Review 632–79
Taylor M, 'Parliamentary Representation in Modern Britain: Past, Present, and Future' (2022) 65 The Historical Journal 1145–73
Williams OC, *The Historical Development of Private Bill Procedure and Standing Orders in the House of Commons*, vol I (London 1948)

17 The Government of India Act 1858

*N.C. Fleming**

17.1 Introduction

On 2 August 1858, Queen Victoria gave her assent to the Act for the Better Government of India. It marked the end of the East India Company's role in governing India and redefined, rationalised, and strengthened the constitutional basis of the United Kingdom's sovereignty on the subcontinent and over its two hundred million inhabitants. It was enacted at the tail end of a long and bloody revolt across north India that had begun on 10 May 1857 with the sepoy mutiny at Meerut. It was the third attempt by Parliament in 1858 to legislate on the future government of India, the previous two bills having been discarded. Scholarly assessments of the Act's significance are mixed. On the one hand, it is presented as far-reaching; as the constitutional aspect of the 'new order' established in the wake of the mutiny-revolt that transformed the British from 'outsiders' to 'insiders'; that it changed 'the very political and legal foundations of colonialism' in India; that it 'constituted . . . the seizure of power by a centralized bureaucratic state from the "aristocratic republicans" of the East India Company'; and that it brought into existence the South Asian state that 89 years later achieved independence as the Union of India and the Dominion of Pakistan.[1] On the other hand, the Act is depicted as having 'very little political significance'; and that 'the change from Company to Crown was largely a matter of nomenclature'.[2] A related tendency portrays it

* The author acknowledges the helpful advice of Professor Arvind Elangovan.

1 Bernard S Cohn, 'Representing Authority in Victoria India' in Eric Hobsbawm and Terence Ranger (eds), *The Invention of Tradition* (first published 1983, Canto 1992) 165 and 178; Naveen Kanalu, 'The Pure Reason of *Lex Scripta*: Jurisprudential Philology and the Domain of Instituted Laws during Early British Colonial Rule in India (1770s–1820s)' in Edward Cavanagh (ed), *Empire and Legal Thought: Ideas and Institutions from Antiquity to Modernity* (Brill 2020) 483; Anthony Pagden, *Lords of All the World: Ideologies of Empire in Spain, Britain and France, c. 1500–c. 1800* (Yale University Press 1995); Burton Stein, *A History of India* (Blackwell 1998) 239.

2 Thomas R Metcalf, *The Aftermath of Revolt: India, 1857–1870* (Princeton University Press1965) ix; Percival Spear, *The Oxford History of Modern India 1740–1975* (2nd edn, Oxford University Press 1974) 232. See also Karl de Schweinitz, *The Rise and Fall of British India:*

DOI: 10.4324/9781032658698-18

as preordained or the inevitable culmination of Parliament's increasing scrutiny of company rule.[3]

Whichever way it is presented, the 1858 Act has long been overshadowed, even upstaged, by the Queen's proclamation that announced its implementation on 1 November. It is not uncommon for survey histories to skip over the Act in favour of the proclamation.[4] Likewise, a primer on the post-independence Indian constitution has no cause to mention the Act but does refer to the proclamation.[5] That reverses the constitutional significance of the two documents; some even appear to attribute to the proclamation the full transfer of power to the crown.[6] Without a doubt, the Act was not wide-ranging; Parliament in 1858 was primarily concerned with the restoration and preservation of order in India.[7] The Act merely signalled, for example, Parliament's future intention to reform the Indian Civil Service and the Indian armed forces. The expansion and modification of the system of governors-in-council was likewise undertaken subsequently by separate legislation. Even the Governor-General's designation as Viceroy was conferred by the proclamation, not the Act.[8] The latter's legalistic language, along with its preoccupation with financial and personnel matters, compares unfavourably to the Queen's seemingly personal and all-embracing proclamation 'to the Princes, Chiefs and People'. Publicised with fanfare across India in the closing months of a brutal conflict, it was the proclamation that became the totemic marker of the transition to crown government. It was the proclamation, not the Act, which declared that all religions would enjoy the equal protection of the law, and it was through the proclamation that Victoria held herself 'bound to the Natives of Our Indian Territories by the same obligations of duty which bind us to all Our other subjects'. It contained the 'unconditional pardon' for those 'in arms against the Government', and it made clear the

---

Imperialism and Inequality (Methuen 1983) 176; Timothy H Parsons, *The Rule of Empires: Those Who Built Them, Those Who Endured Them, and Why They Always Fall* (Oxford University Press 2010) 224.

3 Lionel J Trotter, *History of India Under Queen Victoria from 1836 to 1880*, vol II (WH Allen 1886) 108; R Palme Dutt, *India To-Day* (Victor Gollancz 1940) 138; Metcalf, *Aftermath of Revolt*, ix; Denis Judd, *The Lion and the Tiger: The Rise and Fall of the British Raj, 1600–1947* (Oxford University Press 2004) 87; William Dalrymple, *The Anarchy: The Relentless Rise of the East India Company* (Bloomsbury 2020) 314, 391.

4 See, for example, HG Keene, *History of India: From the Earliest Times to the End of the Nineteenth Century*, vol II (rev. edn, John Grant 1910) 236–37; Jon Wilson, *India Conquered: Britain's Raj and the Chaos of Empire* (Simon and Schuster 2016) 262. See also Piers Brendon, *The Decline and Fall of the British Empire, 1781–1997* (Vintage 2008) 135–36.

5 Brij Kishore Sharma, *Introduction to the Constitution of India* (11th edn, Asoke K Ghosh 2022) 1.

6 See, for example, Mithi Mukherjee, *India in the Shadows of Empire: A Legal and Political History, 1774–1950* (Oxford University Press 2010) 77.

7 Douglas M Peers, 'State, Power and Colonialism' in Douglas M Peers and Nandini Gooptu (eds), *India and the British Empire* (Oxford University Press 2012) 16–43, at 20–25.

8 Sarvepalli Gopal, *British Policy in India 1858–1905* (Cambridge University Press 1965) 3.

crown's intention to recast its relationship with India's princes in the language of mutual obligation.[9] As a result, the 'soothing, promising and reassuring' words of the Queen 'were turned to over and again' by Indians during her lifetime in order to make British rule more accountable.[10] Thereafter, the failure of the British to live up to its 'noble' intentions was cited by Indian nationalists to corrode 'popular confidence in the benevolent character of British rule'.[11]

This chapter presents the 1858 Act as a leading work in the history of the constitution. As such, it recognises that the constitution had an 'imperial life', and that this provides an important way of understanding it 'that a UK-centred vantage point does not itself deliver'.[12] The decision to terminate John Company's role in the government of India was not inevitable or straightforward; it took a widespread, bloody, and costly rebellion to make it happen. Not only did the abolition of the company run counter to the ingrained attitudes of many Whig and Conservative parliamentarians, but passing a measure on India in 1858 was not regarded by some as urgent or even necessary. Such legislation was further hampered by the peculiarly fissiparous, unstable, and shifting party calculations and alignments that then pertained in Parliament, and the strained ability of two governments in succession – Whig and Conservative – to command the House of Commons. When the third India bill introduced that year finally made it to the statute book, the legislation was far more than an incremental development of the previous acts that had gradually increased parliamentary oversight of the company. The termination of company rule went hand in hand with abolishing the archaic constitutional construction which it inhabited in India, namely the vestigial power and potent symbolism of the Mughal emperor as universal ruler. In its place, the British crown became the paramount sovereign authority in India and of a bounded territory that thereafter would be treated, in effect, as a unitary state. The attendant expansion in the application of the royal prerogative increased the involvement of the British Queen in Indian affairs, and more consequentially,

9 Frederick Madden and David Fieldhouse (eds), *The Dependent Empire and Ireland, 1840–1900: Advance and Retreat in Representative Self-Government: Select Documents on the Constitutional History of the British Empire and Commonwealth*, vol V (Greenwood 1991) 73.

10 Ram Parkash Sikka, 'The Royal Proclamation of 1858 and the Civil Service Question in India' (1983) 32(2) Indian Archives 27–44, at 28; Miles Taylor, *Empress: Queen Victoria and India* (Yale University Press 2018) 116, 270–71.

11 BR Nanda, *Gokhale: The Indian Moderates and the British Raj* (Oxford University Press 1977) 67, 182; Bipan Chandra, Mridula Mukherjee, Aditya Mukherjee, KN Panikkar, and Sucheta Mahajan, *India's Struggle for Independence 1857–1947* (Penguin 1989) 98. See also Shashi Tharoor, *Inglorious Empire: What the British Did to India* (Penguin 2017) 47.

12 H Kumarasingham, 'Constitution and Empire' in Peter Cane and H Kumarasingham (eds), *The Cambridge Constitutional History of the United Kingdom, Volume II: The Changing Constitution* (Cambridge University Press 2023) 497, 527–28. For developments in Indian constitutional history, see Arvind Elangovan, 'A Political Turn? New Developments in Indian Constitutional Histories' (2022) 20(8) History Compass.

it placed overarching power into the hands of her Secretary of State at the newly created India Office.

17.2 Double government

In 1765, Shah Alam II conferred the *diwani* of Bengal, Bihar, and Orissa on the East India Company. Concern at Westminster about the company's role as the emperor's financial administrator, along with the chequered reputation of its servants, encouraged greater parliamentary interest in its activities.[13] In what appears, in retrospect, to be a long-drawn-out process, Parliament from the 1770s periodically attempted to redress perceived defects or abuses in the company. These reforms had two aspects, though in practice, legislation typically dealt with both. The first, not examined here, gradually eroded the company's monopoly and trading privileges and opened the Indian economy to the forces of free trade.[14] The second instituted and enhanced the constitutional means through which Parliament oversaw and scrutinised the company's policies and activities in India. It is understandable that some see the resulting system of 'double government' as a process that reached its climax with the 1858 Act. But, assigning a teleological meaning to these developments all too easily overlooks the fact that for almost 90 years, successive acts of Parliament preserved the existence of the company and its peculiar place in the British constitution. The tendency in historiography to explain these interventions as tackling a doomed anachronism overlooks why the successive reforms happened when they did and what options were perceived to be available on each occasion to ministers and Parliament.[15] The constitution, Costin and Watson aver, 'is flexible in the sense of being found in the minds and practice of each generation'.[16] Or, to put it another way, the 'conventions of the constitution . . . have meaning only when they are looked at against a background of continuous political change'.[17] In the long view, double government might have all the appearance of an ineluctable process, but on each occasion that Parliament considered the company's future before 1858, sound and ultimately

13 DA Washbrook, 'India, 1818–1860: The Two Faces of Colonialism' in Andrew Porter (ed), *The Oxford History of the British Empire, Volume III: The Nineteenth Century* (Oxford University Press 1999) 395–421.

14 Anthony Webster, *The Twilight of the East India Company: The Evolution of Anglo-Asian Commerce and Politics 1790–1860* (Boydell Press 2009) 129–50.

15 Ged Martin, *Past Futures: The Impossible Necessity of History* (University of Toronto Press 2004) 4–5.

16 WC Costin and J Steven Watson (eds), *The Law and Working of the Constitution: Documents 1660–1914, Volume II: 1784–1914* (Adam and Charles Black 1952) vii.

17 GHL Le May, *The Victorian Constitution: Conventions, Usages and Contingencies* (Duckworth 1979) 21. See also H Kumarasingham, 'The Historical Constitution' in Peter Cane and H Kumarasingham (eds), *The Cambridge Constitutional History of the United Kingdom, Volume I: Exploring the Constitution* (Cambridge University Press 2023) 9.

persuasive reasons prevailed for maintaining its core function in the government of India. Even after it was excised from the constitution, the new arrangements established by the 1858 Act arguably conformed to the principle of double government.[18]

Double government usually refers to a distinct phase in the relationship between the crown, or the crown in Parliament, and the company, inaugurated by the India Act 1784. The original company's first royal charter, issued by Elizabeth I in 1600, was based on the crown's prerogative to regulate its chartered companies' activities overseas. The early concession of limited legislative powers to the East India Company concerning its small settlements and its transoceanic trade was comparable to the customary powers given to local municipal or corporate bodies. This modest and practical arrangement, however, did not yet give the company the power to legislate for and govern territory. The reign of Charles II witnessed several innovations that had the effect of moving in that direction. The company was granted the authority to fortify its territorial enclaves, to raise and command its own military and naval forces, to declare martial law, and to make war and peace. These concessions were made with the proviso that the crown preserved its right to interpose in the company's affairs and that it retained ultimate sovereignty over the company's forts and plantations. The king's acquisition of Bombay from Portugal in 1661 meant that crown sovereignty was now established over a specific territory. The powers to make laws for the island's good government were soon after entrusted to the company. During the reign of George II, the company's military victories over Indian and European rivals led the crown to concede the right to all booty captured from the king's and company's enemies. The company also acquired the freedom to make treaties that disposed of property, including territory, acquired by conquest from any Indian prince. In these ways, the doctrine was upheld that conquest vested sovereignty and proprietary rights in the crown, even as it delegated these to the company, and as a corollary, that the peaceful acquirement of territory vested the crown with sovereignty but not proprietary rights.[19]

The lack of effective parliamentary oversight that accompanied these developments gave way after 1765 to growing unease among parliamentarians about the company's capability and competence to assume the functions of a state in Bengal, Bihar, and Orissa.[20] At first, concerns about the easy fortunes acquired by the company's servants induced Parliament to demand large

18 Robin J Moore, 'Imperial India, 1858–1914' in Andrew Porter (ed), *The Oxford History of the British Empire, Volume III: The Nineteenth Century* (Oxford University Press 1999) 422–46, at 425.

19 A Berriedale Keith, *A Constitutional History of India 1600–1935* (2nd edn, Barnes & Noble 1969) 1–20.

20 HV Bowen, 'British India, 1765–1813: The Metropolitan Context' in PJ Marshall (ed), *The Oxford History of the British Empire, Volume II: The Eighteenth Century* (Oxford University Press 1998) 530–51, at 532.

payments in return for its adherence to the new dispensation in India.[21] Crown government was certainly discussed among parliamentarians and even senior figures in the company, but intervention of a more effective kind was initially held in check by a number of factors. It was generally accepted that in comparison to the company's executive, the Court of Directors, Parliament lacked the requisite expertise and resources to administer British interests in India. Not only would crown government infringe on the sanctity of property rights, but it would also require the rights attached to the *diwani* to be defined and clarified in such a way as to avoid George III appearing to be a delegate of the Mughal emperor. The former's dignity, after all, could only be preserved at the expense of the latter's.[22] And any attempt to negative Shah Alam's sovereignty would provoke great resentment in India and further destabilise relations with other European powers during a period of acute international turbulence.[23] There was also the matter of Whiggish concern that placing British-controlled India in the hands of the king and his ministers would result in an alarming increase in crown patronage.[24]

The collapse of the company's finances in 1772 provided the pretext for Parliament to change its tack. It agreed to make a loan to the company on certain conditions about repayment and the company's economic practices. More significantly, Parliament passed the Regulating Act 1773. It altered the structure of the company at home and in India, all with the intention of giving Parliament greater influence over its deliberations and actions. At home, changes were made to the election of directors.[25] In India, the 1773 Act appointed the governor of Fort William, Calcutta, and it elevated the office above the governors of the Bombay and Madras presidencies with the new designation of governor-general. Four councillors were also named in the Act to assist the

21 Ben Gilding, '"A New Tide of Corruption": Economical Reform and the Regulation of the East India Company, 1765–84' in Ian Cawood and Tom Crook (eds), *The Many Lives of Corruption: The Reform of Public Life in Modern Britain, c. 1750–1950* (Manchester University Press 2022) 75–95, at 80–81.

22 A means of avoiding this scenario had been in practice in Europe, where the House of Hanover's assumption of the British throne in 1714 required British diplomats to stress the separation of the crowns of Hanover and Great Britain; *inter alia*, the Prince Elector's nominal subordination to the Holy Roman Emperor did not apply to the King of Great Britain. See TCW Blanning, '"That Horrid Electorate" or "Ma Patrie Germanique"? George III, Hanover, and the *Fürstenbund* of 1785' (1977) 20(2) Historical Journal 311–44; Torsten Riotte, 'George III and Hanover' in Brendan Simms and Torsten Riotte (eds), *The Hanoverian Dimension in British History, 1714–1837* (Cambridge University Press 2007) 58–85.

23 Keith (n 19) 69; GJ Bryant, *The Emergence of British Power in India 1600–1784: A Grand Strategic Interpretation* (Boydell Press 2013) 1–34.

24 Conor Cruise O'Brien, *The Great Melody: A Thematic Biography and Commented Anthology of Edmund Burke* (Sinclair-Stevenson 1992) 270.

25 At home, the election of six directors each year, for four-year terms, was substituted for the annual election of all 24 directors. Only those shareholders with £1,000 of stock, assembled in the Court of Proprietors, could vote for the directors; an alteration that inevitably concentrated power in the hands of the wealthiest stockholders.

governor-general for terms of five years; only the king could recall them on the recommendation of the Court of Directors. The governor-general and council were vested with responsibility for the good government of the presidency's territorial acquisitions as well as the revenues of Bengal, Bihar, and Orissa. The governor-general and council were subject to orders issued by the Court of Directors. Advice on revenues received by the Court of Directors from India was to be relayed to the Treasury and to the appropriate secretary of state on civil and military matters. The 1773 Act also provided for a judiciary in British India that derived its authority from the crown; the supreme court of judicature at Calcutta was given the responsibility for registering and approving all rules, regulations, and ordinances made by the governor-general and council.[26]

The 1773 Act was a departure and, as such, received criticism in certain quarters, but it failed to ensure effective ministerial scrutiny, let alone tackle the concerns that it was meant to address. An effort was made to remedy this in 1781 when the regular scrutiny of the company's dispatches to India was made a condition of its charter renewal that year. Less than a decade later, however, the company's major shareholders, the Court of Proprietors, defied the House of Commons by refusing to recall the Governor-General, Warren Hastings. In doing so, the company demonstrated that Parliament would have to go to extraordinary lengths to assert its authority on contentious matters of Indian policy.[27] The company's need for financial relief in 1783 provided Parliament with its opportunity to redress the 1773 Act's defects. Charles James Fox introduced a bill that year which substituted a board of seven commissioners for the Court of Directors and the Court of Proprietors. Sitting in London, it was to be given control of British revenues and territories in India, the power to inspect company minutes, and control of company patronage. Passed in the House of Commons, the bill was defeated in the House of Lords after George III let it be known that any peer voting for it would be considered his enemy.[28] Legislation introduced by William Pitt the following year borrowed the essential element of oversight contained in Fox's bill, but it left the controversial matter of patronage in the hands of the company. The Court of Directors and Court of Proprietors were likewise preserved.[29]

The India Act 1784 created a Board of Six Commissioners for the Affairs of India. Comprised of privy councillors and known soon after as the Board of Control, it was meant to oversee all civil and military matters of government in British India, to have access to all dispatches to and from India, and to approve all outgoing dispatches. The Court of Proprietors was forbidden

26 Keith (n 19) 68–76.

27 PJ Marshall, *The Impeachment of Warren Hastings* (Oxford University Press 1965).

28 The India bill provided George III with the opportunity to successfully undermine the coalition ministry, which he had reluctantly admitted to office in April 1783.

29 Keith (n 19) 94–95.

from amending decisions reached by the Court of Directors which had been approved by the Board of Control. The Court of Directors appointed the governor-general and the governors of the Bombay and Madras presidencies, as well as the three councillors now assigned to each presidency. The power to recall these officers was vested in both the Court of Directors and the crown. The subordination of the Bombay and Madras presidencies to Bengal was further elaborated, and all were forbidden from declaring war or making treaties without the approval of the Court of Directors. Undoubtedly, the 1784 Act gave Parliament the 'upper hand' in its relationship with the company.[30] But, the Board of Control was a revising body, not an originating body, and its capacity to properly oversee the company was compromised by its duties falling to one member, its president. Moreover, the company's commercial functions were beyond the Board of Control's remit, with the Court of Directors further protected by a right of appeal to the king in council. As Michael Bentley pithily observes, 'the Company led and the government followed'.[31] Even so, the President of the Board of Control was an office of significance, equivalent to a secretary of state and typically carrying cabinet rank, which meant that ministers could more effectively consider Indian affairs.[32] The inevitable tensions that arose over the respective remits of the Board of Control and the Court of Directors, especially in the early years, were a testament to the determination of both to exert their authority.[33]

The Charter Act 1833 altered the powers and remit of the company in several ways. Most significantly, its commercial transactions were wound up, and its remaining trade monopoly terminated, though the company continued to be a pugnacious, if embattled, defender of British investors in eastern trade.[34] But, the liberal principles that produced this outcome also ensured that the constitutional role of the company within the government of India was sustained for the 20-year period of the renewed charter. The secretary of the Board of Control, Thomas Babington Macaulay, defended its retention with the decades-old argument that the Court of Directors – since 1784 augmented by the Board of Control – was more capable than Parliament in managing the government of India.[35] Likewise, there was the enduring Whig concern about

30 Bowen (n 20) 545–46.

31 Michael Bentley, *Politics without Democracy 1815–1914: Perception and Preoccupation in British Government* (2nd edn, Blackwell 1999) 105.

32 Keith (n 19) 95–99.

33 William Foster, 'The India Board (1784–1858)' (1917) 11 Transactions of the Royal Historical Society 61–85; AK Ghosal, 'Constitutional Relations between the Court of Directors and the Board of Control with Special Reference to the Dispute Over Fort William College' (1942) 4(2) Indian Journal of Political Science 170–82.

34 Webster (n 14) 129–50.

35 See Catherine Hall, *Macaulay and Son: Architects of Imperial Britain* (Yale University Press 2012).

placing too much patronage in the hands of the crown. Any countervailing check held out by the expansion of the Board of Control was never fulfilled as, in practice, its management continued to remain in the President's hands. In India, power was further centralised to the governor-general of India – the new title properly reflecting the remit of the office – and his council; and now, when these convened as a legislature, a fourth member was added.[36] Still, Whig distaste for concentrating power to individuals ensured the continued existence of separate presidencies for Bombay and Madras.[37] Percival Spear concludes that the 1833 Act rendered the crown 'the effective ruler of India in all but name', but as even he concedes, in 1844, the Court of Directors was still able to recall the governor-general, the second Baron Ellenborough, in defiance of the cabinet.[38] As such, it is more helpful to see the company as having become integral to the constitution. The initiative in public business remained with the Court of Directors, and its expertise could not be easily set aside by politicians.[39]

The Charter Act 1853 contained a number of provisions that made some further inroads into the company's remaining authority. The Court of Directors was reduced in size from 24 to 18, with six selected by the crown. The Board of Control was to oversee the substitution of competitive examinations in place of the company's long-coveted control of patronage. The crown's sanction was required for all appointments to the three presidency councils. The governor-general-in-council was expanded to include, among others, representatives of the presidencies, and the legislative member was permitted to sit and vote in all council business.[40] What is more remarkable about the 1853 Act is the political context in which it was passed. To be sure, the principle of double government remained attractive to Whigs who revered the mixed constitution.[41] Nevertheless, the Whig conception of the constitution as checks and balances was losing its wider hold on Parliament.[42] Radicals demanded the abolition of the company on the basis that double government went against the principle of ministerial accountability to Parliament. Given the loose party connection between Whigs, Liberals, and Radicals, the bill's author, Sir Charles Wood, President of the Board of Control, sent mixed signals about the lack of an expiry date in the charter. To some, he suggested that

36 Keith (n 19) 131–32.

37 Eric Stokes, *The English Utilitarians and India* (rev. edn, Oxford University Press 1963) 255–56.

38 Spear (n 2) 83, 229; Albert H Imlah, *Lord Ellenborough: A Biography of Edward Law, Earl of Ellenborough, Governor-General of India* (Harvard University Press 1939) 226.

39 Wilson (n 4) 212; Keith (n 19) 140.

40 Keith (n 19) 137–38.

41 RJ Moore, *Sir Charles Wood's Indian Policy 1853–66* (Manchester University Press 1966) 23–32.

42 HJ Hanham, *The Nineteenth Century Constitution: Documents and Commentary* (Cambridge University Press 1969) 3, 13.

it allowed for the company's dissolution well before the customary 20-year term. To others, that the bill permitted the charter's indefinite renewal. But it seems likely that Wood had no intention of following the former course. His skilful handling of the Court of Directors, and preparedness to sidestep it by bringing Indian business before the cabinet and Parliament, inclined him to see only the benefits of double government.

The Radicals, however, were not the only party to signal their dissent. The Conservatives' leader in the House of Commons, Benjamin Disraeli, defied his party leader in the House of Lords, the fourteenth Earl of Derby, by collaborating with the leading Radical MP, John Bright, in opposing the charter's renewal. Derby warned Disraeli that many Conservatives looked on the company as 'a good Tory body', but 140 Conservatives, almost half the party's MPs in the House of Commons, joined Disraeli in opposing the bill.[43] Disraeli had a distinctly Tory rationale for doing away with the company, namely its complicity in promoting 'liberal democracy, capitalism, and scientific rationalism', and for undermining India's 'rural, aristocratic, propertied, and religious institutions'.[44] He was also convinced that its aggressive annexationist policies had harmed the Indian economy. Disraeli returned to these arguments four years later, following the mutiny at Meerut, accusing the Whigs of overseeing the destruction of native authority, the disturbance of property rights, and tampering with religion and society.[45]

The mutiny-revolt of 1857–58 shook British liberalism to its core. Whig and Liberal MPs might outwardly take issue with Disraeli's analysis, but most came to share it. It had been evident for some time, of course, that Christian missionaries were unable to effect any tangible transformation of Indian society.[46] But the revolt seemed to be nothing less than a wholesale rejection of the company's Westernising policies; the voices of its leaders were, in any case,

43 Robert Blake, *Disraeli* (St Martin's Press 1967) 356–57; Angus Hawkins, *The Forgotten Prime Minister: The 14th Earl of Derby, Volume II: Achievement: 1851–1869* (Oxford University Press 2008) 73. On the company being 'Tory', James Vaughn contends that its extractive imperialism was symptomatic of the victory of conservative-reactionary forces over radical-Whiggery in the 1750s–60s. See James M Vaughn, *The Politics of Empire at the Accession of George III: The East India Company and the Crisis and Transformation of Britain's Imperial State* (Yale University Press 2019). The Whig governor-general, Lord William Bentinck, in 1834, remarked of India and the company's servants that 'Ultra-Toryism prevails here in its purest sense'. John Rosselli, *Lord William Bentinck: The Making of a Liberal Imperialist 1774–1838* (Chatto & Windus for Sussex University Press 1974) 187.

44 Matthew Stubbings, 'British Conservatism and the Indian Revolt: The Annexation of Awadh and the Consequences of Liberal Empire, 1856–1858' (2016) 55(4) Journal of British Studies, 728–49, at 729.

45 Ann Pottinger Saab, 'Disraeli, India, and the Indians: 1852–58' in Wolfgang Elz and Sonke Neitzel (eds), *Internationale Beziehungen Im 19. Und 20* (Ferdinand Schöningh Verlag 2003) 37–52.

46 CA Bayly, *The New Cambridge History of India, Part II, Volume I: Indian Society and the Making of the British Empire* (Cambridge University Press 1988) 202.

largely unheard due to British military success and repression.[47] Liberals perceived the revolt as a blow to their presumption that all peoples were rational and capable of being improved. In its place, they became disposed to the view that Indian people were irrational and unsuited to European-style modernity.[48] What the revolt did not do was encourage any serious examination of the United Kingdom's right to rule India.[49] Instead, the most conspicuous reaction was outrage at the mutinous sepoys and their allies. Consequently, the third Viscount Palmerston's ministry – recently victorious at the general election held prior to the mutiny – was under no pressure to urgently address the constitutional basis of British rule in India. The preparedness of the opposition Conservatives to treat the revolt as a national crisis and not a political crisis also helped.[50] It appears that the prime minister was only drawn to address the matter by growing concern about its potential to increase the vulnerability of British finance in an already turbulent international economic context.[51] Even then, the pace was slow. In September 1857, Palmerston asked the fourth Earl of Clarendon, who was attending the Queen at Balmoral, 'While you are shaving or taking a walk or ride, turn over in your mind what will be the best thing to do as to the future government of India'. Amused by the method of expression, the Foreign Secretary still understood that the prime minister had 'made up his mind to throw over the East India Company'.[52] In October, Palmerston tested the attitude of the cabinet.[53] The latter's approval was secured on 25 November, and by the middle of December, a plan was in place to assume crown control through a president and council.[54]

17.3 Three India bills

Palmerston introduced his India bill to the House of Commons on 12 February 1858. He did so in defiance of those in his own party, such as the third Earl Grey, who strongly deprecated any attempt to do away with the

47 Ira Klein, 'Materialism, Mutiny and Modernization in British India' (2000) 34(3) Modern Asian Studies 545–80, at 561.

48 Thomas R Metcalf, *The New Cambridge History of India, Part III, Volume IV: Ideologies of the Raj* (Cambridge University Press 1998) 44–49.

49 Christopher Herbert, *War of No Pity: The Indian Mutiny and Victorian Trauma* (Princeton University Press 2008) 56.

50 Angus Hawkins, *Parliament, Party and the Art of Politics in Britain, 1855–59* (Stanford University Press 1987) 85–87.

51 David Brown, *Palmerston: A Biography* (Yale University Press 2012) 407.

52 Quoted in James Chambers, *Palmerston: 'The People's Darling'* (John Murray 2004) 437. On shaving and Indian government, it is noteworthy that the former governor-general, Lord Ellenborough, looking back on his time in that post, remarked that the only leisure time he had 'in which to throw his mind on the whole administration of the country was when shaving'. Imlah (n 37) 182.

53 Angus Hawkins, 'British Parliamentary Party Alignment and the Indian Issue, 1857–1858' (1984) 23(2) Journal of British Studies, 79–105, at 86.

54 Brown (n 50) 407–08.

company. There was also suspicion and anger in Liberal and Radical ranks that Palmerston prioritised the bill to further delay parliamentary reform. Increasingly vulnerable, Palmerston could no longer count on the Conservatives' quiescence on Indian matters.[55] Introducing his bill, the prime minister cast it as a measure to make the system of Indian government more efficient. He attached no blame to the company, but he replaced its operations in London with a council of eight members nominated for eight years, chaired by a president of cabinet rank, empowered with the final decision on all matters, and assisted by a secretary also sitting in Parliament. The company's remaining patronage was to pass to the council. J.S. Mill's famous defence of the company certainly spoke for some Whigs and Liberals, but others were satisfied that its plea for the merits of double government was addressed by the new president being assisted by a council.[56] Palmerston's great rival, Lord John Russell, recognised the urgent need for such a measure, but the former prime minister avoided endorsing the bill's contents in the knowledge that it could be modified or even voted down in the upper house.[57] His hesitancy was, to some extent, borne out at a critical division held on 18 February.[58] The government secured a large majority, 318 to 173, but its success on this occasion rested on shifting sands, given that 37 Whigs, Liberals, and Radicals – and four Peelites – voted with the opposition, and 27 Conservatives voted with the government.[59]

The following day, 89 Whigs, Liberals, and Radicals voted with the Conservatives on an unrelated matter. The government resigned and was succeeded by a Conservative administration under Derby. Though a minority government, the open fissures on the opposition benches meant that the Conservatives were the single largest party in the House of Commons, and Derby hoped to further stimulate his opponents' difficulties by proposing moderate measures and policies.[60] On India, it meant accepting the principle of Palmerston's bill but setting it aside to frame a measure that could also command the support of his own party. Ellenborough's longstanding support for transferring the government to the crown no doubt made it appropriate that he be given the task of framing the new bill, even if it overlooked his recent claim that no legislation should be introduced until the last of the revolt was stamped out.[61] India bill

55 Hawkins (n 49) 89, 102; Denis Judd, *Palmerston* (Weidenfeld and Nicolson 1975) 134.

56 Douglas M Peers, 'Imperial Epitaph: John Stuart Mill's Defence of the East India Company' in Martin I Moir, Douglas M Peers, and Lynn Zastoupil (eds), *J.S. Mill's Encounter with India* (University of Toronto Press 1999) 198–220; Verney Lovett, 'The Home Government, 1858–1918' in H Dodwell (ed), *The Cambridge History of the British Empire, Volume VI: The Indian Empire, 1858–1918* (Cambridge University Press 1932) 206–25, at 206.

57 Hawkins (n 49) 103.

58 *House of Commons Debates*, 18 February 1858, vol 148, cols 1607–715.

59 Hawkins (n 49) 104, 329.

60 Hawkins (n 43) 169.

61 Imlah (n 37) 41–42, 50, 164, 168–70, 190; Robin Wilson, *The Life and Times of Queen Victoria*, vol II (Cassell 1888) 8.

no. 2, as it became known, resembled its predecessor in so far as it replaced the company with a president and 'Council of India'. The latter, however, was to be expanded to eighteen members, with half appointed by the crown and the other half elected. Among the latter cohort, four were to be chosen by those who had been resident in India and who met certain requirements concerning their employment or assets there, a constituency of around 5,000.[62] As for the remaining elected seats, Ellenborough originally intended to assign these to large cities in India, to give those in charge of Indian government a sense of responsibility to its people, but he was persuaded by the cabinet to transfer these to British commercial centres and to increase their number to five.[63]

The complex and cumbrous structure of the council's elective element attracted concern and mockery, not least among Conservatives.[64] Even the Queen warned that the selection of London, Glasgow, Liverpool, Manchester, and Belfast appeared arbitrary and would lead to claims for representation from other cities. She likewise questioned the suitability of elections in determining the course of imperial policy, not least because the proposed electors knew so little about India.[65] More consequently, the Radical MPs that Derby and Ellenborough had hoped to win over with the elective element came out against it as an absurdity, arguing that it would diminish the role of the House of Commons in scrutinising India policy.[66] But their criticisms were not pressed too hard lest these hasten the return of another Palmerston-led government. Like Russell, they wanted the Conservatives to remain in office to bide time for the emergence of an alliance of Whigs, Liberals, and Radicals committed to parliamentary reform. Through an intermediary, Bright signalled that he could support a measure in which the council of India was reduced to 12, all to be nominated by the crown and subject to parliamentary scrutiny. On 2 April, Disraeli received word from another intermediary, almost certainly speaking for Russell, suggesting that a senior figure on the opposition benches could move a series of resolutions that would command support across the House of Commons. Three days later, Derby publicly announced his desire to work across party lines and his willingness to drop the elective element of the second India bill.[67] The upshot of the recent subterranean exchanges was played out in the House of Commons on 12 April, when Russell and Disraeli concurred that the house should proceed by discussing a series of resolutions that would frame a new bill. However, another Whig, Charles Wood, intervened to chide Disraeli's assent to the proposal as an abdication of ministerial responsibility. Having already received a copy of Russell's resolutions, Disraeli

62 Hawkins (n 49) 123.

63 Imlah (n 37) 248.

64 Edmond Fitzmaurice, *The Life of Granville George Leveson Gower, Second Earl Granville KG 1815–1891*, vol I (Longmans Green 1906) 299; Hawkins (n 43) 169–70.

65 Wilson (n 60) 15–16.

66 Keith Robbins, *John Bright* (Routledge and Keegan Paul 1979) 135.

67 Hawkins (n 49) 128–29.

was able to deflect Wood's attack by agreeing to move them on behalf of the government.[68]

Ministers and Parliament considered the resolutions throughout the remainder of April.[69] Having outflanked the opposition, there were still tensions among Conservative parliamentarians about the degree to which they were prepared to go in winning support across the House of Commons.[70] The government's progress was interrupted the following month by a highly public row involving Ellenborough and the governor-general of India, the second Viscount Canning, which in the end was diffused by the former's resignation.[71] Derby's son, Lord Stanley, now took the reins at the Board of Control and introduced what was inevitably called India bill no. 3 to the House of Commons on 17 June. The resulting debate continued into July, with Stanley's skill and success in maintaining discipline among Conservatives in marked contrast to the ill-tempered rows and weakness of cohesion on the opposition benches.[72] The latter were exacerbated by Stanley's willingness to tactically withdraw should a clause fail to command a majority in the Commons and by the public disagreements between Palmerston and Russell.[73] As the Liberal MP, Sir Charles Trelawny, noted in his diary, 'The fact is, while we think we are gravely discussing the India Bill, we are merely the stage on which a fencing match or triangular duel is taking place between the great party leaders opposed to the Ministry'.[74] The government was further helped by Bright's decision not to oppose the bill, despite his reservations about its capacity to measure up to the immense and complex task of governing India. In so doing, he joined the Peelite MP, William Gladstone, as one of the very few parliamentarians to express some doubt about the wisdom of trying to govern the subcontinent.[75] Bright's own scheme, for India to be divided into five independent presidencies of equal rank, satisfied his Radical credentials but otherwise had no impact on the bill.[76] The bill passed its third reading on 8 July and went to the House of Lords, where Derby had to see off an attempt by the Archbishop of Canterbury to sharpen the Christian mission of British rule in India. The Queen, too, required Derby's reassurances before her assent was granted on 2 August.[77]

68 *House of Commons Debates*, 12 April 1858, vol 149, cols 858–771; Hawkins (n 49) 131.

69 Hawkins (n 49)133.

70 Derby to Disraeli, 30 April 1858, in Costin and Watson (n 16) 406–07; Hawkins, *Derby*, p 174.

71 Michael Maclagan, *'Clemency' Canning: Charles John, 1st Earl Canning, Governor-General and Viceroy of India 1856–1862* (Macmillan 1962) 166–211.

72 Hawkins (n 43) 179.

73 Hawkins (n 49) 145.

74 Trelawny, diary, 6 July 1858, TA Jenkins (ed), 'The Parliamentary Diaries of Sir John Trelawny, 1858–1865' (1990) 40 Royal Historical Society Camden Fifth Series 55.

75 *House of Commons Debates*, 3 April 1858, vol 149, cols 1585–85, 1596–98; *House of Commons Debates*, 26 April 1858, vol 149, cols 1680–87.

76 Robbins (n 65) 136–37.

77 Trotter (n 3) 102–04; Taylor (n 10) 773.

17.4 Westminster and crown government

'Parliament is, from the legal point of view, the absolute sovereign of the British Empire'. Sidney Low immediately follows this statement with the observation that the 'electorate is the real "sovereign" in England [*sic*], and the conventions of the Constitution are supposed to maintain its supremacy'.[78] The first proposition is almost word for word what is contended by the more famous exponent of parliamentary supremacy, A.V. Dicey.[79] The second raises an issue that, for three generations, contributed to the survival of the Court of Directors and which was a factor in bringing down India bill no. 2. Walter Bagehot addresses it indirectly in his observations that 'the British Empire is a miscellaneous aggregate, and each bit of the aggregate brings its bit of business to the House of Commons', and that a 'perfectly inexperienced man, so far as Indian affairs go', is able as Secretary of State for India to rule 'all our Indian Empire'.[80] It is the very tenacity of this concern among ministers, of Whig and Conservative stripes, which meant that each of the three India bills introduced in 1858 provided for a council to work alongside the responsible minister.[81] As established by the 1858 Act, the Council of India contained eight members nominated by the crown and seven elected by the Court of Directors from among themselves or their predecessors.[82] Thereafter, future vacancies among the nominees were to be filled by the crown and among the elected cohort through co-options.

Section 3 of the 1858 Act provided that 'One of her Majesty's Principal Secretaries of State shall have and perform all such or the like Powers and duties in anywhere relating to the Government or Revenue of India'. In practice, an additional secretary of state was created and placed at the head of the India Office, with Stanley its first holder. The Secretary of State for India, or India Secretary, in some ways resembled the President of the Board of Control. The obligation under Section 53 of the 1858 Act – that the minister present an annual financial statement to Parliament – formalised a relatively recent innovation in which the president performed the same task, though the obligation was now widened to encompass the 'moral and material progress' of India. But, there was a significant difference in the authority and powers of the president and secretary of state. Whereas the Court of Directors initiated policy and the Board of Control served as a check, the roles were reversed by

78 Sidney Low, *The Governance of England* (2nd impression, T Fisher Unwin 1906) 172.

79 AV Dicey, *Introduction to the Study of the Law of the Constitution* (8th edn, Macmillan 1915) 425.

80 Walter Bagehot, *The English Constitution* (Chapman and Hall 1867) 141 and 215.

81 William Roy Smith, *Nationalism and Reform in India* (first published 1938, Kennikat Press 1973) 14.

82 The company existed for another 15 years before closing in 1874. 'Like so many of her peasants and workers who are born in debt', KS Shelvankar observes of the compensation to stockholders from Indian revenues provided for by Section 42 of the 1858 Act, 'India entered the modern world as a debt-slave.' KS Shelvankar, *The Problem of India* (Penguin 1940) 50.

the 1858 Act. The secretary of state was the initiator of policy and was placed in a commanding position over the Council of India. The latter was not able to act on any issue until required to do so by the minister. The conduct of business on the council, including the decision to establish committees, was a matter for the minister's discretion, and only he could bring a matter discussed in committee before the full council. Despatches sent to India were in the name of the minister.

Not that the council was without influence. Members were to be chosen for their long experience of India, which could not be easily set aside by a minister with comparatively little or no experience, and the self-electing status of seven council members allowed for a measure of independence.[83] When matters were brought before the council, all 15 were entitled to give an opinion and even to submit in writing their dissent from its decisions. And with the exception of urgent and diplomatic affairs, all orders of the secretary of state had to be brought before the council before they were issued. Nevertheless, the minister could overrule the council on all matters except expenditure, for which he was required to secure a majority. There were also aspects of policymaking that were the preserve of the cabinet and Parliament, including the framing and passage of legislation. In such cases, it was only after decisions were taken, and only if these required the secretary of state to issue orders, that the council was consulted. Stanley was only in post for nine months before the fall of Derby's ministry. His successor at the India Office, Charles Wood, quickly gained the impression that Stanley had left too much initiative in the hands of the council.[84] Matters came to a head in 1860 when he dealt with the sensitive question of army reform without consulting the council. Section 56 of the 1858 Act transferred the military and naval forces of the company to the Queen. It also stipulated that the obligations, privileges, and pay of the company's European officers would remain the same 'as if they had continued in the Service of the said Company'. Disbelief that these two policies could be reconciled led to the so-called 'white mutiny' among officers in India. Not unexpectedly, the old India hands on the Council of India were sympathetic to the officers' grievance and were long used to the Court of Directors having greater initiative in the area of policy. But, sticking to the letter of the 1858 Act, Wood succeeded in holding his ground that it was a matter for the cabinet and Parliament.[85]

The controversy also highlighted another constitutional question that had attended the three India bills, albeit behind the scenes. In contrast to the prevailing view on the Council of India, the Queen demanded the fulfilment of Section 56; as the head of the army, she expected that the company's soldiers would serve under her. Palmerston and Derby, when overseeing their

83 Donovan Williams, 'The Formation of Policy in the India Office 1858–69: A Study in the Tyranny of the Past' (1973) 51 Journal of Indian History 873–92.

84 Moore (n 40) 34–35, 38.

85 Moore (n 40) 37–38, 206–07.

respective legislative measures through Parliament, had been left in no doubt by Victoria that she envisaged the crown having a greater role in India, from viewing dispatches to patronage. Both men responded by highlighting that their bills substantially increased the crown's prerogative powers.[86] They were correct, of course, and such reassurances appear to have succeeded in winning her around. But the Queen's ministers, Whig then Conservative, intended in practice to use the crown's prerogative powers themselves. This was not only in keeping with accepted constitutional practice, but it was in line with Parliament's active role in Indian constitutional reform since the Regulating Act 1773.[87] It is hardly surprising then that Victoria was jealous of the Council of India, especially as it represented a new and additional check on the use of her prerogative powers.[88] But, if she and the council pulled in opposite directions over Indian army reform, the 1858 Act ensured that the India Secretary had the upper hand throughout.[89] Still, Victoria's keen interest in India did not abate. Her distrust of Parliament's capability of handling its affairs meant that she actively used her prerogative powers within the accepted constitutional limits, and that she hardly ever missed a despatch in the years that followed.[90]

17.5 India and crown government

The abolition of the 330-year-old Mughal dynasty ended decades of uncertainty about the constitutional status of India.[91] On the one hand, the tenacity of its politico-religious culture, centred on the universal sovereignty of the Mughal emperor, had long defied European conceptions of the international state system.[92] On the other, the English then British crown's claim that it retained ultimate sovereignty over company-controlled India stretched a principle once intended for small settlements to the vast territories annexed in the late eighteenth and early nineteenth centuries.[93] The original legal basis of the company's rule in Bengal, Bihar, and Orissa, the *diwani* granted in 1765 by Shah Alam II, further complicated matters, as did the company's begrudging and progressively attenuated acknowledgment of his dignity and that of his successors, Akbar II and Bahadur Shah II. The company's military conquest and economic dominance of much of India in the second half of the

86 Taylor (n 10) 8, 75–77.
87 Vernon Bogdanor, *The Monarchy and the Constitution* (Clarendon Press 1997) 66; AC Banerjee, *English Law in India* (Shakti Malik 1984) 269. See also John F McEldowney, *Public Law* (Sweet & Maxwell 1994) 65–73.
88 Moore (n 180) 425.
89 Moore (n 40) 35–36.
90 Taylor (n 10) 78, 116.
91 John Darwin, *Unfinished Empire: The Global Expansion of Britain* (Allen Lane 2012) 77, 125, 173.
92 Keith (n 19) 111.
93 A Berriedale Keith, *Speeches and Documents on Indian Policy 1750–1921*, vol I (Oxford University Press 1922) xix.

eighteenth century undoubtedly gave it paramountcy by 1802–03. But, in an age when the indigenous empires of Asia remained largely intact, the company found it convenient to continue operating within the 'framework of Mughal legitimacy'.[94] As Amar Farooqui observes, the 'Company-as-state could not have sought legitimacy merely by referring to the metropolitan constitutional framework to which it owed its existence as a commercial and political entity'.[95]

The uncertainty that stemmed from the 'twofold' origin of British authority in India tended to be compounded rather than resolved by successive agreements, treaties, and legislation.[96] The *diwani*, although conferred in the shadow of the emperor's defeat in 1764 at the battle of Buxar, was presented by Shah Alam as a gift and not the result of bargaining in order to preserve his dignity.[97] Similarly, as it had since the battle of Plassey in 1757, the company continued to use puppet nawabs to serve as figureheads.[98] The Regulating Act 1773 and Pitt's India Act 1784 might have treated company-controlled India as subject to British sovereignty, but the position of the crown was conspicuously evaded.[99] And although the Charter Act 1813 did refer to the crown's 'undoubted sovereignty', it applied only to the company's territory in India, and it did not stop the latter's officials from continuing to recognise and honour the emperor.[100] The company's conquest of certain princely states and their survival as distinct entities further complicated the matter, such as the administrative takeover of Mysore in 1831 and Hyderabad in 1853, which left in place their respective rulers' sovereignty.[101] As Sudipta Sen argues, the 'very ad hoc nature of military exploits, and persistent ambiguities in the application of the laws of conquest stymied a precise expression of imperial sovereignty'.[102] It is true that successive governors-general had little time for the emperor. In 1835, Akbar II's image on company coins was replaced with that of William IV. The following decade, Lord Ellenborough defied the Court of Directors by ceasing to present the customary gifts to Bahadur Shah II on behalf of the

94 John Darwin, *After Tamerlane: The Rise and Fall of Global Empires* (Penguin 2007) 110; Rajat Kanta Ray, 'Indian Society and the Establishment of British Supremacy, 1765–1818' in PJ Marshall (ed), *The Oxford History of the British Empire, Volume II: The Eighteenth Century* (Oxford University Press 1998) 508–29, at 510.

95 Amar Farooqui, 'Governance, Corporate Interest and Colonialism: The Case of the East India Company' (2007) 35(9/10) Social Science, 44–51, at 44.

96 Courteny Ilbert, *The Government of India: Being a Digest of the Statute Law Relating Thereto* (2nd edn, Oxford University Press 1907) 1.

97 Wilson (n 4) 110.

98 Narendra Krishna Sinha and Anil Chandra Banerjee, *History of India* (7th edn, Mukherjee 1956) 505–10.

99 Keith (n 19) 101–02.

100 Banerjee (n 86) 2–5.

101 Rosselli (n 43) 225; Keith (n 19) 124.

102 Sudipta Sen, 'Unfinished Conquest: Residual Sovereignty and the Legal Foundations of the British Empire in India' (2012) 9(2) Law, Culture and the Humanities 227–42, at 237–38.

company.[103] Condescending British references to Bahadur Shah as the 'king of Delhi' were likewise calculated to play down his status, as well as reflect the reality that his territorial power was confined to the precincts of Delhi's Red Fort. The result, Kaye and Malleson conclude, was a 'political paradox', in which the 'Great Mughul' was to be 'a King, yet no King – a something and yet a nothing – a reality and a sham at the same time'.[104]

The most aggressively expansionist governor-general, the tenth Earl of Dalhousie, tried to end the paradox. He pressed the Court of Directors to agree that Bahadur Shah's title should lapse on his death, but doubts about such a course led Dalhousie to reach an agreement with the heir apparent, Fakhr-ud-din Mirza, that he could retain the title on condition that he treat the governor-general as an equal and that he departed the Red Fort. The plan expired with the prince's death in 1856.[105] Dalhousie's successor, Lord Canning, took a slightly different tack. He was prepared to recognise Bahadur Shah's new heir, but with the condition that on succession, he would resign his royal title and live away from Delhi.[106] Had the mutiny-revolt and the 1858 Act not resolved the issue decisively, it is tempting to see Canning's actions as the last word on the subject. However, the status of the House of Babur remained a sensitive matter in India. Combined with the hesitation of the Court of Directors and concern among sections of Conservative opinion about the company's attitude to Indian rulers, it is possible that further equivocations could have been conceived. After all, the company had long had it both ways; in India, outwardly posing as the emperor's vassal; and at home, claiming to be 'the representative of the British government' whose responsibilities included the protection of Bahadur Shah as a 'subject' and 'pensioner'.[107] Despite his reduced circumstances, the residual importance of Bahadur Shah was recognised by both sides during the mutiny-revolt. He provided the rebellion with its titular leadership, and this in turn provided the

103 Keith (n 19) 120–21.

104 John W Kaye and George B Malleson, *Kaye's and Malleson's History of the Indian Mutiny of 1857–8*, vol II (2nd edn, Longmans, Green 1892) 4.

105 Edwin Arnold, *The Marquess of Dalhousie's Administration of British India*, vol II (Saunders, Ottley 1865) 203–06; Keith (n 19) 124.

106 Maclagan (n 70) 65.

107 FW Buckler argues that the emperor's authority 'was primarily religious, and political authority fell within the sphere of religious authority', and that the company recognised this in practice in India but suggested otherwise in London. On this basis, he argues that 'If there were any mutineer, it was the East India Company'. FW Buckler, 'The Political Theory of the Indian Mutiny' (1922) 5 Transactions of the Royal Historical Society, fourth series, 71–100. The subtlety of Buckler's argument appears to be overlooked by his critics, see Douglas Dewar and HL Garrett, 'A Reply to Mr F.W. Buckler's "The Political Theory of the Indian Mutiny"' (1924) 7 Transactions of the Royal Historical Society, fourth series, 131–65. On the trial of Bahadur Shah as a breach of international law, see Lucinda Downes Bell, 'The 1858 Trial of the Mughal Emperor Bahadur Shah II "Zafar" for "Crimes Against the State"' (PhD thesis, University of Melbourne 2004).

British with a convenient pretext to de-sanctify the 'old order'. As Bernard Cohn argues, the 'new order' established by the 1858 Act brought to an end the 'contradictions and difficulties' long faced by the company 'in defining a symbolic-cultural constitution'.[108] In its place, according to Mithi Mukherjee, Victoria was cast 'as a denationalized and deterritorialized figure who stood above the identity and interests of England', for the purpose of masking 'the foreign origin of the colonial state'.[109] This re-conquest of India could now be openly rationalised as such.[110]

It need hardly be said that actual sovereignty over the vast territory of the Indian subcontinent could not simply be made real or effective by an Act of Parliament.[111] As Lauren Benton highlights, Europe's overseas empires did not 'cover space evenly but composed a fabric that was full of holes, stitched together out of pieces, a tangle of strings'.[112] This is especially so in the case of the approximately 560 princely states that survived the mutiny-revolt. Although the 1858 Act made no direct reference to them, Section 67 committed the crown to observe all treaties made by the company, which in effect meant recognising treaties agreed with native states. At the same time, the Act effectively ruled out any notion that international law might determine their relationship with the British crown.[113] The royal proclamation that announced the Act elaborated that 'We desire no extension of Our present Territorial Possessions . . . We shall respect the rights, dignity and honour of Native Princes as Our own'. In practice, the Indian princes were now the Queen's feudatories and were expected to express their allegiance to her through her Viceroy, the governor-general. Strategic and economic factors dictated their preservation, yet little serious consideration was given to their future until 1859–60.[114]

108 Cohn (n 1) 176–79. In contrast to Metcalf's dismissive attitude to the 1858 Act, he subsequently cited Cohn's analysis without demur, see Metcalf (n 47) 50.

109 Mukherjee (n 6) xx.

110 Jon Wilson and Andrew Dilley, 'The Incoherence of Empire. Or, the Pitfalls of Ignoring Sovereignty in the History of the British Empire' (2023) 1 Transactions of the Royal Historical Society, seventh series, 191–217. It is arguable that *de jure* sovereignty was assumed unambiguously by the British just prior to the 1858 Act, through the declaration of martial law in large swathes of north India, the brutal punishments meted out to 'rebels', and the trial of the emperor. See Alastair McClure, 'Sovereignty, Law, and the Politics of Forgiveness in Colonial India, 1858–1903' (2018) 38(3) Comparative Studies of South Asia, Africa and the Middle East 385–401.

111 Antoinette Burton, *The Trouble with Empire: Challenges to Modern British Imperialism* (Oxford University Press 2015) 63; Wilson (n 4) 498–99.

112 Lauren Benton, *A Search for Sovereignty: Law and Geography in European Empires* (Cambridge University Press 2009) 2. See also Douglas M Peers and Nandini Gooptu, 'Introduction' in Douglas M Peers and Nandini Gooptu (eds), *India and the British Empire* (Oxford University Press 2012) 1–15, at 2.

113 Keith (n 19) 125; Ajit K Neogy, *The Paramount Power and the Princely States of India, 1858–1881* (KP Bagchi 1979) 4.

114 Bhupen Qanungo, 'A Study of British Relations with the Native States of India, 1858–62' (1969) 26 Journal of Asian Studies 251–65; Ian Copland, *The British Raj and the Indian Princes: Paramountcy in Western India 1857–1930* (Orient Longman 1982) 93.

Their survival raises the question of whether it is more appropriate to interpret the 1858 Act as asserting *paramount* sovereignty. Sen argues that the princely states possessed an 'indissoluble residuum of [their] former dignity [as] the traditional rulers of India'. He sees this 'residual sovereignty' as a feature of the longer pattern of expansion of British power that 'left unresolved certain questions of conquest, sovereignty and subjecthood', and which made it difficult to establish a consistent, self-contained theory of sovereignty.[115] It is even borne out by subsequent developments, for the contractual relationship between the crown and princes established in 1858 had the effect, in theory, of limiting paramountcy. As a result, a new theory emerged at the end of the nineteenth century to dissolve such limitations on British power based on 'usage' and 'sufferance'.[116]

The demise of the Mughal dynasty had another important result, one confirmed by the royal proclamation's explicit use of the term viceroy. It left the governor-general the exclusive locus of all authority in India.[117] The 1858 Act provided that his appointment and that of his council, as well as the governors and councils of Bombay and Madras, respectively, be transferred from the Court of Directors to the crown.[118] As before 1858, these 'non-sovereign legislative bodies' remained subordinate to Acts of Parliament; their laws and regulations could be annulled by the crown, and unlike the United Kingdom's courts, Indian courts could still declare laws to be unconstitutional.[119] Yet, the importance given to the crown by the 1858 Act cannot disguise the fact that the years which immediately followed witnessed a return to the parliamentary habit of inattention to Indian affairs.[120] In part, as the advocates of double government had long argued, because the necessary level of scrutiny required an amount of interest and expertise that was lacking in Parliament but not in an especially appointed council.[121] But also, as Derby observed when addressing India bill no. 3 in the House of Lords, because

> the Government of India must, as cannot be too often repeated, be on the whole carried on in India . . . the less interference there is on the part

115 Sen, 'Unfinished Conquest' 227–42. The idea of paramount sovereignty appears to have been in Disraeli's mind later, during the 1876 parliamentary debates about Victoria assuming the title of empress of India, see Cohn (n 1) 184. The company's use of the doctrine of lapse, to annex or otherwise take control of princely states, revived a Mughal practice in which the emperor's deputy determined succession. See Buckler, 'Political Theory' 96.

116 Copland (n 113) 309–10.

117 Cohn (n 1) 180.

118 Herbert Cowell, *The History and Constitution of the Courts and Legislative Authorities in India* (5th edn, Thacker, Spink 1905) 60–66.

119 Dicey (n 78) 95–98. Subsequently, the Indian Councils Act 1861 permitted councils to increase their respective memberships when convening as legislatures.

120 Bayly (n 45) 196–97. See Justin McCarthy, *A History of Our Own Times*, vol III (Caxton 1910) 134.

121 John P Mackintosh, *The British Cabinet* (3rd edn, Stevens & Sons 1977) 268.

of Parliament the better prospect will there be of securing happiness and contentment of the people of India.[122]

17.6 Conclusion

The 1858 Act terminated the peculiar place of the East India Company in the British constitution and the remaining symbolism of Mughal authority. Out went the system of double government through which the Board of Control had the upper hand over the Court of Directors, but which still, in effect, left much of the initiative in the hands of the latter. In its place, there was an echo of those arrangements in the form of the India Secretary and the Council of India, with the minister and cabinet now given the upper hand. Outwardly, the structure of power in India appeared largely unchanged, not least the governor-general and governors and their respective councils and the patchwork of princely states that straddled the subcontinent. But the constitutional underpinnings of this power had without doubt changed. The 1858 Act swept away all ambiguity about sovereignty; the British crown was now unequivocally the singular source of all constitutional and judicial authority and the basis of British relations with the princely states. Moreover, these arrangements, and the Act's commitment to the preservation of treaties made by the company, established a unitary state with fixed boundaries; a constitutional entity, as Burton Stein observes, 'which could in the future be taken over *en bloc* by other bodies'.[123]

To adopt this interpretation is not to reject the notion that the 1858 Act was an exercise in political expediency. Parliament and the company had been jointly implicated in the government of India since 1784 and were effectively intertwined from 1833. Little wonder, then, that the termination of 'company rule' appeared to some contemporaries to be a self-serving distraction from the failings of Whitehall and Westminster.[124] If there had long been pressure from some quarters to take this step, there were stronger forces in Parliament which, in the case of Whigs and Liberals, defended the principle of double government, and in the case of many, though not all Conservatives, that defended the company. Even during the crisis of 1857–58, there was little sense of urgency in Parliament about overhauling the constitutional arrangements for governing India; the pace was largely determined by party

122 'Lord Derby's Speech on the Government of India Bill, 1858' in Anil Chandra Banerjee (ed), *Indian Constitutional Documents, 1757–1947, Volume II: 1858–1917* (3rd edn, A. Mukherjee 1961) 22–23. See also Anil Seal, *The Emergence of Indian Nationalism: Competition and Collaboration in the Later Nineteenth Century* (Cambridge University Press 1971) 3; Peter Robb, *A History of India* (Palgrave Macmillan 2002) 153. For contrasting emphasis, see KM Panikkar, *Asia and Western Dominance: A Survey of the Vasco de Gama Epoch of Asian History 1498–1945* (George Allen and Unwin 1953) 111–12.

123 Stein (n 1) 239.

124 Trotter (n 3) 94, 97.

calculations, and for many months, it was by no means certain that a measure would be passed.[125] As ever in imperial affairs, constitutional change 'was the junior partner to politics'.[126]

Likewise, to present the 1858 Act as a landmark in the history of the constitution is not to suggest that it utterly transformed the practical business of ruling India or even that it gave it an obvious shape or sense of direction.[127] Even so, parliamentary inattention did not become a permanent feature after 1858. And as Judith Brown avers, the fact that 'India now lay open' to the 'gaze and influence' of Parliament meant that it was 'exposed to the force of British racial and political sentiment to an unprecedented degree', with the result that how Parliament handled Indian affairs became the source of 'political disquiet in India'.[128] In parallel to the increasing prominence of Indian affairs in Parliament, the Council of India came to be seen as a hindrance to the government of India, as the vaunted experience of the India Secretary's advisers was, over time, perceived as limiting their ability to assess new currents of opinion.[129] The two developments came together at the first meeting of the Indian National Congress in 1885 when it called for the council's abolition and the opening up of India's legislative councils to Indians.[130] As these developments demonstrate, the 1858 Act was more than a holding measure but less than an Indian constitution. It was, in fact, the constitutional foundation on which British-Indian relations were practised and redefined through to independence in 1947.

Bibliography

Arnold E, *The Marquess of Dalhousie's Administration of British India, Volume II* (Saunders, Ottley 1865)

Bagehot W, *The English Constitution* (Chapman and Hall 1867)

Banerjee AC (ed), *Indian Constitutional Documents, 1757–1947, Volume II: 1858–1917* (3rd edn, A. Mukherjee 1961)

Banerjee AC, *English Law in India* (Shakti Malik 1984)

Bayly CA, *The New Cambridge History of India, Part II, Volume I: Indian Society and the Making of the British Empire* (Cambridge University Press 1988)

125 Hawkins (n 52) 79.

126 Kumarasingham, 'Constitution and Empire' 504.

127 See Metcalf (n 47) 51–52. Ira Klein convincingly disrupts the neat binary often made between liberal interventionism before 1857 and a conservative direction of travel thereafter. Klein (n 46) 545–80.

128 Judith M Brown, *Modern India: The Origins of an Asian Democracy* (2nd edn, Oxford University Press 1994) 96–97.

129 Spear (n 2) 230. See also Andrew Roberts, *Salisbury: Victorian Titan* (Phoenix 2000) 83. The Council of India's declining reputation helped successive governors-general to protect the latitude of independence achieved by their forbears. See Donovan Williams, 'The Council of India and the Relationship between the Home and Supreme Governments, 1858–70' (1966) 81(318) English Historical Review 56–73.

130 Wilson (n 4) 334.

Bell LD, 'The 1858 Trial of the Mughal Emperor Bahadur Shah II "Zafar" for "Crimes Against the State"', PhD thesis (University of Melbourne 2004)
Bentley M, *Politics without Democracy 1815–1914: Perception and Preoccupation in British Government* (2nd edn, Blackwell 1999)
Benton L, *A Search for Sovereignty: Law and Geography in European Empires* (Cambridge University Press 2009)
Blake R, *Disraeli* (St Martin's Press 1967)
Blanning TCW, '"That Horrid Electorate" or "Ma Patrie Germanique"? George III, Hanover, and the *Fürstenbund* of 1785' (1977) 20(2) Historical Journal 311–44
Bogdanor V, *The Monarchy and the Constitution* (Clarendon Press 1997)
Bowen HV, 'British India, 1765–1813: The Metropolitan Context' in PJ Marshall (ed), *The Oxford History of the British Empire, Volume II: The Eighteenth Century* (Oxford University Press 1998) 530–51
Brendon P, *The Decline and Fall of the British Empire, 1781–1997* (Vintage 2008)
Brown D, *Palmerston: A Biography* (Yale University Press 2012)
Brown JM, *Modern India: The Origins of an Asian Democracy* (2nd edn, Oxford University Press 1994)
Bryant GJ, *The Emergence of British Power in India 1600–1784: A Grand Strategic Interpretation* (Boydell Press 2013)
Buckler FW, 'The Political Theory of the Indian Mutiny' (1922) 5 Transactions of the Royal Historical Society, fourth series, 71–100
Burton A, *The Trouble with Empire: Challenges to Modern British Imperialism* (Oxford University Press 2015)
Chambers J, *Palmerston: 'The People's Darling'* (John Murray 2004)
Chandra B, Mukherjee M, Mukherjee A, Panikkar KN and Mahajan S, *India's Struggle for Independence 1857–1947* (Penguin 1989)
Cohn BS, 'Representing Authority in Victoria India' in E Hobsbawm and T Ranger (eds), *The Invention of Tradition* (first published 1983, Canto 1992) 165–209
Copland I, *The British Raj and the Indian Princes: Paramountcy in Western India 1857–1930* (Orient Longman 1982)
Costin WC and Steven Watson J (eds), *The Law and Working of the Constitution: Documents 1660–1914, Volume II: 1784–1914* (Adam and Charles Black 1952)
Cowell H, *The History and Constitution of the Courts and Legislative Authorities in India* (5th edn, Thacker, Spink 1905)
Dalrymple W, *The Anarchy: The Relentless Rise of the East India Company* (Bloomsbury 2020)
Darwin J, *After Tamerlane: The Rise and Fall of Global Empires* (Penguin 2007)
Darwin J, *Unfinished Empire: The Global Expansion of Britain* (Allen Lane 2012)
de Schweinitz K, *The Rise and Fall of British India: Imperialism and Inequality* (Methuen 1983)
Dewar D and Garrett HL, 'A Reply to Mr F.W. Buckler's 'The Political Theory of the Indian Mutiny' (1924) 7 Transactions of the Royal Historical Society, fourth series, 131–65
Dicey AV, *Introduction to the Study of the Law of the Constitution* (8th edn, Macmillan 1915)
Dutt RP, *India To-Day* (Victor Gollancz 1940)
Elangovan A, 'A Political Turn? New Developments in Indian Constitutional Histories' (2022) 20(8) History Compass
Farooqui A, 'Governance, Corporate Interest and Colonialism: The Case of the East India Company' (2007) 35(9/10) Social Science 44–51
Fitzmaurice E, *The Life of Granville George Leveson Gower, Second Earl Granville KG 1815–1891, Volume I* (Longmans Green 1906)

Foster W, 'The India Board (1784–1858)' (1917) 11 Transactions of the Royal Historical Society 61–85

Ghosal AK, 'Constitutional Relations between the Court of Directors and the Board of Control with Special Reference to the Dispute over Fort William College' (1942) 4(2) Indian Journal of Political Science 170–82

Gilding B, '"A New Tide of Corruption": Economical Reform and the Regulation of the East India Company, 1765–84' in I Cawood and T Crook (eds), *The Many Lives of Corruption: The Reform of Public Life in Modern Britain, c. 1750–1950* (Manchester University Press 2022) 75–95

Gopal S, *British Policy in India 1858–1905* (Cambridge University Press 1965)

Hall C, *Macaulay and Son: Architects of Imperial Britain* (Yale University Press 2012)

Hanham HJ, *The Nineteenth Century Constitution: Documents and Commentary* (Cambridge University Press 1969)

Hawkins A, 'British Parliamentary Party Alignment and the Indian Issue, 1857–1858' (1984) 23(2) Journal of British Studies 79–105

Hawkins A, *Parliament, Party and the Art of Politics in Britain, 1855–59* (Stanford University Press 1987)

Hawkins A, *The Forgotten Prime Minister: The 14th Earl of Derby, Volume II: Achievement: 1851–1869* (Oxford University Press 2008)

Herbert C, *War of No Pity: The Indian Mutiny and Victorian Trauma* (Princeton University Press 2008)

Ilbert C, *The Government of India: Being a Digest of the Statute Law Relating Thereto* (2nd edn, Oxford University Press 1907)

Imlah AH, *Lord Ellenborough: A Biography of Edward Law, Earl of Ellenborough, Governor-General of India* (Harvard University Press 1939)

Jenkins TA (ed), 'The Parliamentary Diaries of Sir John Trelawny, 1858–1865' (1990) 40 Royal Historical Society Camden Fifth Series 55

Judd D, *Palmerston* (Weidenfeld and Nicolson 1975)

Judd D, *The Lion and the Tiger: The Rise and Fall of the British Raj, 1600–1947* (Oxford University Press 2004)

Kanalu N, 'The Pure Reason of *Lex Scripta*: Jurisprudential Philology and the Domain of Instituted Laws During Early British Colonial Rule in India (1770s–1820s)' in E Cavanagh (ed), *Empire and Legal Thought: Ideas and Institutions from Antiquity to Modernity* (Brill 2020)

Kaye JW and Malleson GB, *Kaye's and Malleson's History of the Indian Mutiny of 1857–8, Volume II* (2nd edn, London: Longmans, Green 1892)

Keene HG, *History of India: From the Earliest Times to the End of the Nineteenth Century, Volume II* (rev edn, John Grant 1910)

Keith AB, *Speeches and Documents on Indian Policy 1750–1921, Volume I* (Oxford University Press 1922)

Keith AB, *A Constitutional History of India 1600–1935* (2nd edn, Barnes & Noble 1969)

Klein I, 'Materialism, Mutiny and Modernization in British India' (2000) 34(3) Modern Asian Studies 545–80

Kumarasingham H, 'Constitution and Empire' in P Cane and H Kumarasingham (eds), *The Cambridge Constitutional History of the United Kingdom, Volume II: The Changing Constitution* (Cambridge University Press 2023a)

Kumarasingham H, 'The Historical Constitution' in P Cane and H Kumarasingham (eds), *The Cambridge Constitutional History of the United Kingdom, Volume I: Exploring the Constitution* (Cambridge University Press 2023b)

Le May GHL, *The Victorian Constitution: Conventions, Usages and Contingencies* (Duckworth 1979)

Lovett V, 'The Home Government, 1858–1918' in HH Dodwell (ed), *The Cambridge History of the British Empire, Volume VI: The Indian Empire, 1858–1918* (Cambridge University Press 1932) 206–25

Low S, *The Governance of England* (2nd impression, T Fisher Unwin 1906)
Mackintosh JP, *The British Cabinet* (3rd edn, Stevens & Sons 1977)
Maclagan M, *'Clemency' Canning: Charles John, 1st Earl Canning, Governor-General and Viceroy of India 1856–1862* (Macmillan 1962)
Madden F and Fieldhouse D (eds), *The Dependent Empire and Ireland, 1840–1900: Advance and Retreat in Representative Self-Government: Select Documents on the Constitutional History of the British Empire and Commonwealth, Volume V* (Greenwood 1991)
Marshall PJ, *The Impeachment of Warren Hastings* (Oxford University Press 1965)
Martin G, *Past Futures: The Impossible Necessity of History* (University of Toronto Press 2004)
McCarthy J, *A History of Our Own Times, Volume III* (Caxton 1910)
McClure A, 'Sovereignty, Law, and the Politics of Forgiveness in Colonial India, 1858–1903' (2018) 38(3) Comparative Studies of South Asia, Africa and the Middle East 385–401
McEldowney JF, *Public Law* (Sweet & Maxwell 1994)
Metcalf TR, *The Aftermath of Revolt: India, 1857–1870* (Princeton University Press 1965)
Metcalf TR, *The New Cambridge History of India, Part III, Volume IV: Ideologies of the Raj* (Cambridge University Press 1998)
Moore RJ, *Sir Charles Wood's Indian Policy 1853–66* (Manchester University Press 1966)
Moore RJ, 'Imperial India, 1858–1914' in A Porter (ed), *The Oxford History of the British Empire, Volume III: The Nineteenth Century* (Oxford University Press 1999) 422–46
Mukherjee M, *India in the Shadows of Empire: A Legal and Political History, 1774–1950* (Oxford University Press 2010)
Nanda BR, *Gokhale: The Indian Moderates and the British Raj* (Oxford University Press 1977)
Neogy AK, *The Paramount Power and the Princely States of India, 1858–1881* (KP Bagchi 1979)
O'Brien CC, *The Great Melody: A Thematic Biography and Commented Anthology of Edmund Burke* (Sinclair-Stevenson 1992)
Pagden A, *Lords of All the World: Ideologies of Empire in Spain, Britain and France, c. 1500–c. 1800* (Yale University Press 1995)
Panikkar KM, *Asia and Western Dominance: A Survey of the Vasco de Gama Epoch of Asian History 1498–1945* (George Allen and Unwin 1953)
Parsons TH, *The Rule of Empires: Those Who Built Them, Those Who Endured Them, and Why They Always Fall* (Oxford University Press 2010)
Peers DM, 'Imperial Epitaph: John Stuart Mill's Defence of the East India Company' in MI Moir, DM Peers and L Zastoupil (eds), *J.S. Mill's Encounter with India* (University of Toronto Press 1999) 198–220
Peers DM, 'State, Power and Colonialism' in DM Peers and Nandini G (eds), *India and the British Empire* (Oxford University Press 2012) 16–43
Peers DM and Nandini G, 'Introduction' in DM Peers and Nandini G (eds), *India and the British Empire* (Oxford University Press 2012) 1–15
Qanungo B, 'A Study of British Relations with the Native States of India, 1858–62' (1969) 26 Journal of Asian Studies 251–65
Ray RK, 'Indian Society and the Establishment of British Supremacy, 1765–1818' in PJ Marshall (ed), *The Oxford History of the British Empire, Volume II: The Eighteenth Century* (Oxford University Press 1998) 508–29
Riotte T, 'George III and Hanover' in Simms B and Riotte T (eds), *The Hanoverian Dimension in British History, 1714–1837* (Cambridge University Press 2007) 58–85
Robb P, *A History of India* (Palgrave Macmillan 2002)

Robbins K, *John Bright* (Routledge and Keegan Paul 1979)
Roberts A, *Salisbury: Victorian Titan* (Phoenix 2000)
Rosselli J, *Lord William Bentinck: The Making of a Liberal Imperialist 1774–1838* (Chatto & Windus for Sussex University Press 1974)
Saab AP, 'Disraeli, India, and the Indians: 1852–58' in W Elz and S Neitzel (eds), *Internationale Beziehungen Im 19. Und 20* (Ferdinand Schöningh Verlag 2003) 37–52
Seal A, *The Emergence of Indian Nationalism: Competition and Collaboration in the Later Nineteenth Century* (Cambridge University Press 1971)
Sen S, 'Unfinished Conquest: Residual Sovereignty and the Legal Foundations of the British Empire in India' (2012) 9(2) Law, Culture and the Humanities 227–42
Sharma BK, *Introduction to the Constitution of India* (11th edn, Asoke K Ghosh 2022)
Shelvankar KS, *The Problem of India* (Penguin 1940)
Sikka RP, 'The Royal Proclamation of 1858 and the Civil Service Question in India' (1983) 32(2) Indian Archives 27–44
Sinha NK and Banerjee AC, *History of India* (7th edn, Mukherjee 1956)
Smith WR, *Nationalism and Reform in India* (first published 1938, Kennikat Press 1973)
Spear P, *The Oxford History of Modern India 1740–1975* (2nd edn, Oxford University Press 1974)
Stein B, *A History of India* (Blackwell 1998)
Stokes E, *The English Utilitarians and India* (rev edn, Oxford University Press 1963)
Stubbings M, 'British Conservatism and the Indian Revolt: The Annexation of Awadh and the Consequences of Liberal Empire, 1856–1858' (2016) 55(4) Journal of British Studies
Taylor M, *Empress: Queen Victoria and India* (Yale University Press 2018)
Tharoor S, *Inglorious Empire: What the British Did to India* (Penguin 2017)
Trotter LJ, *History of India under Queen Victoria from 1836 to 1880, Volume II* (WH Allen 1886)
Vaughn JM, *The Politics of Empire at the Accession of George III: The East India Company and the Crisis and Transformation of Britain's Imperial State* (Yale University Press 2019)
Washbrook DA, 'India, 1818–1860: The Two Faces of Colonialism' in A Porter (ed), *The Oxford History of the British Empire, Volume III: The Nineteenth Century* (Oxford University Press 1999) 395–421
Webster A, *The Twilight of the East India Company: The Evolution of Anglo-Asian Commerce and Politics 1790–1860* (Boydell Press 2009)
Williams D, 'The Council of India and the Relationship between the Home and Supreme Governments, 1858–70' (1966) 81(318) English Historical Review 56–73
Williams D, 'The Formation of Policy in the India Office 1858–69: A Study in the Tyranny of the Past' (1973) 51 Journal of Indian History 873–92
Wilson J, *India Conquered: Britain's Raj and the Chaos of Empire* (Simon and Schuster 2016)
Wilson J and Dilley A, 'The Incoherence of Empire. Or, the Pitfalls of Ignoring Sovereignty in the History of the British Empire' (2023) 1 Transactions of the Royal Historical Society, seventh series, 191–217
Wilson R, *The Life and Times of Queen Victoria, Volume II* (Cassell 1888)

18 Comparative perspectives on the historical legacy of the English constitution

Anne Twomey

18.1 Introduction

To understand law, one must understand its history. This is particularly challenging when the law is transplanted into a new territory where it has no roots and does not form part of the territory's tradition or history. Even when a local legislature has been established by colonists to make domestic laws suitable to their circumstances, it has tended to operate within a matrix of laws, that arrived with the colonists, many of which are ancient.

This was certainly the case in lands 'settled' by the British in the age of Empire. To make sense of this imposed system of law, it was necessary to have recourse to fundamental statutes that were 'received' as law within the colony, as well as legal works such as those by Coke, Blackstone, and Holdsworth, which not only explained the legal development of the law, but imposed a logical structure upon it.[1] Such works were highly influential in the early days of the development of the legal and political systems in former colonies. In some cases, their terms were replicated in fundamental constitutional documents, and in other cases, the law in its received form continued to apply.

Article 9 of the Bill of Rights 1689, for example, which grants freedom of speech or debate in Parliament, continues to be relevant today in many countries, including Australia,[2] the Bahamas,[3] Fiji,[4] India,[5] New Zealand,[6]

1 See, for example, Joseph's list of 'commentaries of persuasive authority' in New Zealand: Philip A Joseph, *Joseph on Constitutional and Administrative Law* (5th edn, Thomson Reuters 2021) 46.

2 *Egan v Willis* [1998] HCA 71, (1998) 195 CLR 424 [129] (Kirby J): '[T]he Bill of Rights is part of the constitutional heritage of Australia'. See also: *Rowley v O'Chee* [1997] QCA 401, [2000] 1 Qd R 207; *Erglis v Buckley* [2003] QSC 440.

3 *Bahamas District of the Methodist Church in the Caribbean v Symonette* [2000] UKPC 31, [2000] 5 LRC 196.

4 *Butadroka v Attorney-General* [1993] FJLawRp 24, (1993) 39 FLR 115 (High Court of Fiji).

5 *Kalpana Mehta v Union of India* [2018] INSC 441, AIR 2018 Supreme Court 2493; *Markandey Katju v Lok Sabha* [2016] INSC 888, AIR 2017 Supreme Court 1379 (reflecting the equivalent freedom in Article 105 of the Constitution of India).

6 *Buchanan v Jennings* [2004] UKPC 36, [2005] 1 AC 115; *Leigh v Attorney-General* [2010] NZCA 624, [2011] 2 NZLR 148.

DOI: 10.4324/9781032658698-19

Saint Vincent and the Grenadines,[7] and Sri Lanka.[8] This is because Article 9 formed part of the British law received by that country when it was formerly a colony or because its statute law or Constitution replicated the terms of Article 9. In Canada, aspects of the Bill of Rights 1689 and parliamentary privilege have been applied by the courts due to the statement in the Preamble to the Constitution Act 1867 (Can) that the provinces united into one Dominion 'with a Constitution similar in principle to that of the United Kingdom'.[9] Even in the Republic of Ireland, Article 9 remains relevant due to its status as the predecessor of article 15.13 of the Irish Constitution and jurisprudence on Article 9 is still used for comparative purposes.[10]

Other aspects of the Bill of Rights also remain significant. For example, a New Zealand Prime Minister found that his post-election announcement that compulsory superannuation contributions were no longer required[11] breached the Bill of Rights 1689 because it had the purported effect of suspending the application of a law without Parliament's consent.[12] Chief Justice Wild observed:

> It is a graphic illustration of the depth of our legal heritage and the strength of our constitutional law that a statute passed by the English Parliament nearly three centuries ago to extirpate the abuses of the Stuart Kings should be available on the other side of the earth to a citizen of this country which was then virtually unknown in Europe and on which no Englishman was to set foot for almost another hundred years. And yet it is not disputed that the Bill of Rights is part of our law.[13]

As there are countless examples that could be drawn upon, this Chapter addresses the impact outside the United Kingdom of Magna Carta,[14] Blackstone's *Commentaries on the Laws of England*,[15] Bryce's *The American Commonwealth*,[16]

7 *Toussaint v Attorney-General (Saint Vincent and the Grenadines)* [2007] UKPC 48, [2007] 1 WLR 2825.
8 *Gomes v Mohamed, Speaker of Parliament* [1991] LKCA 12, (1991) 2 Sri LR 408.
9 *Re Resolution to amend the Constitution* [1981] 1 SCR 753, 785; *New Brunswick Broadcasting Co v Nova Scotia (Speaker of the House of Assembly)* [1993] 1 SCR 319; *Ontario English Catholic Teachers' Association v Ontario (Attorney-General)* [2001] 1 SCR 470, [69].
10 *Ahern v Judge Mahon & Ors* [2008] IEHC 119, [2008] 4 IR 704; and *Howlin v Morris* [2003] IEHC 55.
11 The announcement stated that legislation would be enacted in the next parliamentary session to repeal the compulsory contributions, with retrospective effect back to the date of the announcement.
12 *Fitzgerald v Muldoon* [1976] 2 NZLR 615.
13 *Fitzgerald v Muldoon* [1976] 2 NZLR 615, 622 (Wild CJ). See also: Joseph (n 1) 226–27.
14 Magna Carta 1297, 25 Edw I, c 1, which is the version commonly received as part of the law of British colonies.
15 William Blackstone, *Commentaries on the Laws of England* (Clarendon Press 1765–1769) vols I-IV (hereafter Blackstone's *Commentaries*).
16 James Bryce, *The American Commonwealth*, vols I and II (3rd edn, Macmillan & Co 1893).

and Erskine May's *Treatise on the Law, Privileges, Proceedings and Usage of Parliament.*[17] It takes an Antipodean focus but includes some other comparative examples.

18.2 Magna Carta

Arguably, the most influential document of English law has been Magna Carta.[18] As an agreement to settle a dispute between King John and his barons, it contained some very particular provisions[19] relevant to the circumstances of the time, as well as some limited legal protections that applied in the context of feudal law. Claims that Magna Carta is the source of the right to trial by jury, due process of law, the rule of law, and habeas corpus have often been debunked,[20] but Magna Carta remains a convenient origin myth that is embroidered anew by successive generations.

Indeed, at times, the 'rights' conferred by Magna Carta have veered from the aspirational into the realm of the fanciful. After a wedding guest in colonial Sydney was assaulted for singing a song that insulted tailors and butchers, a magistrate, in committing his assailants to trial, claimed that Magna Charta[21] gave an Englishman the undoubted right to sing and that his attackers were no true friends to the Constitution.[22]

But it can also be claimed that Magna Carta and subsequent laws that sought to give effect to it[23] provided the catalyst for rights that were later proclaimed in the French Declaration of the Rights of Man and the Citizen, the United States Bill of Rights,[24] the Universal Declaration of Human Rights, the

17 Thomas Erskine May, *A Treatise on the Law, Privileges, Proceedings and Usage of Parliament* (Charles Knight & Co 1844) (hereafter Erskine May's *Treatise*).

18 Magna Carta 1215: <https://www.nationalarchives.gov.uk/education/resources/magna-carta/british-library-magna-carta-1215-runnymede/>.

19 See, e.g., Chapters 58 and 59 of Magna Carta 1215 regarding the return of hostages.

20 See, e.g., Anthony Arlidge and Igor Judge, *Magna Carta Uncovered* (Hart Publishing 2014) 58–66; David Clark, 'The Icon of Liberty: The Status and Role of *Magna Carta* in Australian and New Zealand Law' (2000) 24 MULR 866, 882–85; *Kingswell v The Queen* [1985] HCA 72, (1985) 159 CLR 264, 299 (Deane J); *Adler v District Court of New South Wales* (1990) 19 NSWLR 317, 346 (Priestley JA) and BH McPherson, *The Reception of English Law Abroad* (Supreme Court of Queensland Library 2007) 224.

21 Note that Magna Carta was often referred to in the past as Magna Charta, but that after debate on the matter in the Westminster Parliament, it was settled upon as 'Magna Carta' in the British Museum Act 1946 (UK).

22 'Police Reports' (*The Sydney Gazette and New South Wales Advertiser*, 10 August 1827) 3 <https://trove.nla.gov.au/newspaper/article/2188733?browse=ndp%3Abrowse%2Ftitle%2FS%2Ftitle%2F3%2F1827%2F08%2F10%2Fpage%2F496013%2Farticle%2F2188733>.

23 See, e.g., 28 Edw 3, c 3 (1354) and 42 Edw 3, c 3 (1368) regarding 'due process of law'.

24 Note that aspects of Magna Carta had previously been enacted in the statutes of American colonies, such as the Maryland Act for the Liberties of the People 1639, or as part of their Constitutions: McPherson (n 20) 215–16.

Constitution of India and the Canadian Charter of Rights and Freedoms. As Kirby J noted in *Newcrest Mining (WA) v Commonwealth*, Magna Carta has contributed to human rights on an international scale.[25]

18.3 The legal application of Magna Carta in Australia and New Zealand

The original Magna Carta of June 1215 was annulled later that year. Other versions of it were issued by different monarchs, with the last being enacted under Edward I in 1297 as an Act of Parliament with an ongoing legal application. Little of it survives as part of the law of the United Kingdom today.[26]

The Australian and New Zealand colonies received remnants of the 1297 Magna Carta in their law upon settlement or a later reception date, to the extent that it was part of the law of England at the time and was suitable for application in the colony. In New Zealand, New South Wales, Victoria, Queensland, and the Australian Capital Territory, statutes have since preserved Chapter 29[27] and repealed the rest.[28] The preservation of Chapter 29 was regarded by the New South Wales Law Reform Commission as being for chiefly 'sentimental' reasons, given its historical significance.[29] In New Zealand, it was preserved due to a 'desire to recognise the constitutional and historical heritage' of the nation rather than any intention for it to have legal effect.[30]

In Western Australia, South Australia, Tasmania, and the Northern Territory, Magna Carta became law upon the relevant date of reception.[31] Only so much of Magna Carta would have been received as continued to apply in the United Kingdom at the time, and only to the extent that it was relevant and applicable in Australia. Hence, provisions regarding the liberties of the Church of England and the City of London, for example, would not have applied. As

25 *Newcrest Mining (WA) v Commonwealth* [1997] HCA 38, (1997) 190 CLR 513, 658–59.

26 In addition to implied repeal due to later inconsistent statutes, much of Magna Carta was formally repealed by *Statute Law Revision Act 1863* (26 & 27 Vict c 125). For the four remaining provisions, see: *Magna Carta 1297*, 25 Edw 1, c 9: <https://www.legislation.gov.uk/aep/Edw1cc1929/25/9/data.pdf>.

27 Chapter 29 of the 1297 Magna Carta is the equivalent of clauses 39 and 40 of the 1215 Magna Carta – both concerning rights of persons not to be imprisoned or to have their liberties destroyed but by lawful judgement of their peers or the law of the land.

28 Imperial Laws Application Act 1988 (NZ), s 3(1) and Sched 1; Imperial Acts Application Act 1969 (NSW), s 6; Imperial Acts Application Act 1980 (Vic), s 8; Imperial Acts Application Act 1984 (Qld), s 5; Imperial Acts Application Ordinance 1986 (ACT), sch 3.

29 New South Wales Law Reform Commission, *Report of the Law Reform Commission on the Application of Imperial Acts* (Report No 4, 1967) 62.

30 Clark (n 20) 870.

31 The reception dates were 1 June 1829 in Western Australia; 28 December 1836 in South Australia; 25 July 1828 in Tasmania; and 28 December 1836 in the Northern Territory.

the Western Australian Law Reform Commission noted, Chapter 29 was the only remaining relevant provision, 'the others being either obsolete, superseded or never having been a part of the law of the jurisdiction'.[32] It also observed that the preservation of Chapter 29 does not make the rights it contains inalienable because later inconsistent statutes enacted by the States would operate to repeal Chapter 29.[33] Magna Carta is not constitutionally entrenched in Australia or New Zealand, and its terms can, therefore, be displaced by subsequent enacted statutes.[34]

Nonetheless, Magna Carta has become a magnet for pseudo law adherents who rely on it to argue that they do not have to pay taxes,[35] repay their mortgage,[36] or pay speeding fines[37] and cannot be convicted for possessing an unlicensed weapon.[38] In all cases, they failed. In the case concerning unlicensed weapons, McPherson JA of the Queensland Court of Appeal wearily observed:

> I suppose it will help no one to be told that as a matter of history Magna Carta did not guarantee trial by jury because, at the time Magna Carta was introduced, there was no such thing as a jury. But that is history, and is really, in a sense, beside the point. The simple fact is that it is enough to say here that the legislatures of the Australian States . . . have complete power to repeal Magna Carta or to amend it, either expressly or by passing legislation like the Weapons Act 1990 that is or may be inconsistent with it.[39]

A claim of a legal right to a speedy trial, relying on the assertion in Chapter 29 of Magna Carta that to no one will we deny or delay right or justice, has also failed in Australia. The High Court of Australia recognised a right to a fair trial and considered that delay could be considered in that context, but that Magna Carta was not a source of a legal right to a speedy trial.[40] Brennan J

32 Law Reform Commission of Western Australia, *United Kingdom Statutes in Force in Western Australia* (Project No 75, October 1994) 21.
33 Ibid.
34 *Chia Gee v Martin* [1905] HCA 70, (1905) 3 CLR 649, 653 (Griffith CJ); *Kable v Director of Public Prosecutions (NSW)* [1996] HCA 24, (1996) 189 CLR 51, 73 (Dawson J); *Carnes v Essenberg* [1999] QCA 339.
35 *Bishop v Australian Taxation Department* (1996) 32 ATR 644; *Skyring v Federal Commissioner of Taxation* (1991) 23 ATR 84.
36 *Arnold v State Bank of South Australia* [1992] FCA 554, (1992) 38 FCR 484.
37 *MacDonald v County Court of Victoria* [2013] VSC 109 [38].
38 *R v Essenberg* [2002] QCA 4.
39 Ibid 2. See also: *Skyring v ANZ Banking Group Ltd* [1994] QCA 143; and *Flowers v New South Wales [No 5]* [2021] NSWSC 887 [69].
40 *Jago v District Court (NSW)* [1989] HCA 46 (1989) 168 CLR 23. Compare the express right in s 25(b) of the *New Zealand Bill of Rights Act 1990* (NZ) to be tried without undue delay.

noted that this provision of Magna Carta, as interpreted by Coke, sets out the qualities of justice to which the courts aspire but does not give rise to a legal right or a power in the courts to refuse to exercise their jurisdiction due to delay.[41]

But there have been rare occasions in Australia where Magna Carta has resulted in rights surviving because subsequent legislation has been interpreted as not being intended to restrict them. One example involved public fishing rights, which were held not to have been intended to be limited by the statutory grant of Aboriginal land rights over the relevant tidal waters.[42]

18.4 Magna Carta and the rights of British subjects

New Zealand courts have also recognised a link between Magna Carta and the Treaty of Waitangi. The third article of the Treaty provides that Her Majesty extended to Māori people her royal protection and 'all the rights and privileges of British subjects', which included article 29 of Magna Carta.[43]

Similarly, charters were granted to the earliest settlements in North America and royal instructions were given to their colonial governors, which also granted colonial subjects the same liberties as those born within England.[44] While these liberties were subject to law, colonial laws could be disallowed for breaching fundamental rights[45] or treated as invalid due to repugnancy to British law.[46] After the revolution, many of those liberties were later entrenched in the United States Bill of Rights.

Even though Magna Carta does not apply as a binding law in the way that litigants seem to think, it remains a relevant touchstone for courts in many countries. In *Ex parte Walsh and Johnson; Re Yates*, Isaacs J of the High Court of Australia saw in Magna Carta the proposition that 'every free man has an inherent individual right to his life, liberty, property and citizenship', but that this was still subject to the law of the land which is necessary to adjust the individual and social rights and duties of the members of the state.[47]

41 *Jago v District Court (NSW)* [1989] HCA 46 (1989) 168 CLR 23, 42 (Brennan J). See also 66–67 (Toohey J) and 78 (Gaudron J).

42 *Arnhemland Aboriginal Land Trust v Director of Fisheries (Northern Territory)* [2000] FCA 165.

43 *Kohu v Police* [1989] NZHC 449, (1989) 5 CRNZ 52, 54 (Anderson J).

44 See, for example, a clause to this effect in the first Virginia Charter of 1606 and the royal instructions for Nova Scotia, discussed in: McPherson (n 20) 208–12.

45 Ibid 212–13.

46 Ibid 214.

47 *Ex parte Walsh and Johnson; In Re Yates* [1925] HCA 53, (1925) 37 CLR 36, 79. See also *Re Stanbridge's Application* (1996) 70 ALJR 640, 642 (Kirby J); and *Momcilovic v The Queen* [2011] HCA 34, (2011) 245 CLR 1, 177 (Heydon J).

18.5 Blackstone

Timing and availability are significant factors when it comes to the influence of leading works in the history of the English Constitution upon colonies developing new systems of government. In the United States, Blackstone's *Commentaries* appeared at a critical point of American constitutional development. The four volumes of Blackstone's *Commentaries* were first printed in the United States in 1772, before the Declaration of Independence. They have, therefore, been drawn upon as a compendium of the common law in America prior to the revolution. Their availability and the lack of alternative legal sources gave them greater influence in America than in Blackstone's native England.[48]

Blackstone himself was 'no friend to the American Revolution', although his *Commentaries* were deployed by both sides to support their legal arguments.[49] From 1803, separate American editions with their own annotations and explanations applicable to law in the United States were produced – sometimes with additional annotations concerning the law of a particular State. The existence of these many different American editions of the work, produced over a long period, makes it difficult to treat Blackstone's *Commentaries* as one cohesive text.[50] Nonetheless, both as a work of historical importance and an evolving American text, it has had a major impact on jurisprudence.[51]

Blackstone played a personal role in influencing the British legislation that led to the transportation of convicts to Australia.[52] The common law of England arrived in Australia with the First Fleet in 1788, not just as a matter of English legal theory, being the birthright[53] of the convicts who stumbled off the ships, but also physically in the form of Blackstone's *Commentaries*, in the baggage of the Judge-Advocate, David Collins.[54] At a time when the first judges were not even legally trained, the common law principles and history set out in Blackstone's *Commentaries* provided authoritative guidance in the new colony.

48 Albert W Alschuler, 'Rediscovering Blackstone' (1996) 145 University of Pennsylvania Law Review 1, 5–7.

49 Wilfrid Prest, *William Blackstone – Law and Letters in the Eighteenth Century* (OUP 2008) 292.

50 Michael Hoeflich, 'American Blackstones' in Wilfred Prest (ed), *Blackstone and His Commentaries: Biography, Law, History* (Hart Publishing 2009) 173.

51 Alschuler (n 48) 2, describing Blackstone's *Commentaries* as 'the most influential law book in Anglo-American history'. See also Blackstone's importance in the Caribbean: Sir Fred Phillips, *Commonwealth Caribbean Constitutional Law* (Cavendish Publishing 2002) 2.

52 Prest (n 49) 296–97.

53 Sir Edward Coke, *The First Part of the Institutes of the Laws of England* (vol I) p 142a; and *Calvin's Case* (1608) 7 Co Rep 1a, 18a, 77 ER 377, 398.

54 Bruce Kercher, *An Unruly Child: A History of Law in Australia* (Allen & Unwin 1995) xii; Wilfrid Prest, 'Antipodean Blackstone: The *Commentaries* "Down Under"' (2003) 6 Flinders Journal of Law Reform 151, 155.

In the 1803 case of *Lord v Palmer*,[55] the only record of 'sophisticated legal reasoning' came from a convict barrister, George Crossley,[56] who relied upon Blackstone.[57] The passage concerned, which continues to be controversial, asserted that when an:

> uninhabited country be discovered and planted by English subjects, all the English laws are immediately there in force. For as the law is the birthright of every subject, so wherever they go they carry their law with them.[58]

Whether this meant English law governed internal Indigenous conflicts remained a matter of dispute for some time until it was held in *R v Murrell and Bummaree*, again drawing on Blackstone, that the Indigenous peoples of New South Wales were not recognised as sovereign states governed by their own laws.[59] The Supreme Court concluded that English law applied equally to Indigenous peoples, giving them protection and sanctuary from offences being committed upon them by their own people and preventing murder with impunity.[60] The imposition of English law on Indigenous Australians remains a hotly contested issue.[61]

Blackstone later qualified his assertion about the application of British law in new colonies by adding in the fourth volume of his work, published in 1769, that 'the colonists carry with them only so much of English law as is applicable to their own situation, and the condition of an infant colony'.[62] This qualification led to many cases about whether British statutes applied to the circumstances of the colony.[63]

55 [1803] NSWKR 3. Blackstone was also quoted as authority in the earlier case of *Atkins v Harris* [1799] NSWKR 4.

56 Crossley had been an attorney in England before being transported to Australia after being convicted of the crime of perjury.

57 Bruce Kercher, 'The Foundation of Judicial Methods in Early New South Wales' in *Enduring Courts in Changing Times – Celebrating the 2024 Bicentenaries of the Supreme Courts of New South Wales and Tasmania* (Australian Academy of Law 2024) 86, 89.

58 Blackstone (n 15) vol I, 104–05. Note the extensive references to Blackstone in *Mabo v Queensland (No 2)* (1992) 175 CLR 1 concerning whether Australia was 'terra nullius' at the time of British settlement. Compare the status of conquered and ceded lands, and the consequential influence of Blackstone in Quebec: Michel Morin, 'Blackstone and the Birth of Quebec's Distinct Legal Culture 1765–1867' in Wilfrid Prest (ed), *Re-Interpreting Blackstone's Commentaries* (Hart Publishing 2005) 105–24.

59 *R v Murrell and Bummaree* [1836] NSWSupC 35; (1836) 1 Legge 72, 73 (Burton J).

60 Ibid. Murrell was later acquitted. See further: *Love v Commonwealth; Thoms v Commonwealth* [2020] HCA 3, (2020) 270 CLR 152, [267] (Nettle J).

61 See, e.g., Irene Watson, 'Aboriginal Laws and Colonial Foundation' (2017) 26(4) Griffith Law Review 469.

62 This supplement is now included in the reprint of vol I of the 1765 edition: Blackstone (n 15) vol I, Supplement, ii–iii. See further: Prest (n 54) 158.

63 See, e.g., *MacDonald v Levy* (1833) 1 Legge 39, 52 (Forbes CJ).

In the early years of the colony of New South Wales, proposed laws were first vetted by the Chief Justice, who was required to certify that they were not repugnant to the law of England and were as consistent with such laws as local circumstances would admit before they were put to the Legislative Council for enactment. On one notable occasion, the Chief Justice, Francis Forbes, decided that the main clauses of Governor Darling's 1827 *Bill for Regulating the Publication of Newspapers* were repugnant to the constitutional privilege of liberty of the press as recognised in the law of England.[64] Darling had claimed that the licensing and censorship of the press were necessary for the safety of the colony because local newspapers 'persevered in their mischievous endeavours to bring the Government into hatred and contempt and, in fact, succeeded in exciting a strong spirit of discontent amongst the Prisoners'.[65] The Act would have made it a criminal offence to publish a newspaper without a licence, and provided for licences to be granted and revoked at the will of the Governor. In identifying the fundamental laws of England, Forbes relied[66] on a passage from Blackstone, which he set out as follows:

> The liberty of the press consists in laying no previous restraint upon publications, and not in freedom from censure for criminal matter when published. Every free man has an undoubted right to lay what sentiments he pleases before the public – to forbid this is to destroy the freedom of the press. To subject the press to the restrictive power of a *licenser*, as was formerly done, both before and since the revolution, is to subject all freedom of sentiment to the prejudices of one man, and to make him the arbitrary and infallible judge of all controverted points in learning, religion and government.[67]

On this basis, Forbes refused to certify the Bill, preventing its enactment.[68] Blackstone has also been quoted in India as an authority in relation to pre-censorship of the press.[69]

64 Letter by Chief Justice Forbes to Earl Bathurst, 1 May 1827, attaching 'Reasons assigned by the Chief Justice of New South Wales for not certifying certain clauses of a proposed law or ordinance for restraining the freedom of the press, laid before him by the Governor in pursuance of the New South Wales Act', *Historical Records of Australia,* Series I, vol 13, p 289, at 293–94.

65 Letter by Governor Darling to Chief Justice Forbes, 14 April 1827, *Historical Records of Australia,* Series I, vol 13, 281.

66 Letter by Chief Justice Forbes to Earl Bathurst, 1 May 1827, attaching 'Reasons assigned by the Chief Justice of New South Wales for not certifying certain clauses of a proposed law or ordinance for restraining the freedom of the press, laid before him by the Governor in pursuance of the New South Wales Act', *Historical Records of Australia,* Series I, vol 13, p 289, at 292–93.

67 The quote as set out by Forbes leaves out some wording. Compare: William Blackstone (n 15) vol IV, 151–52.

68 See further: Enid Campbell, 'Colonial Legislation and the Law of England' (1965) 2(2) University of Tasmania Law Review 148, 157–59.

69 *Brij Bhushan v Delhi* (1950) SCR 605, 608.

Blackstone's influence in Australian jurisprudence was always stronger in relation to basic principles and rights than in relation to the day-to-day application of the law, as his work was already out of date by the 1830s. It is primarily used today in the higher courts of Australia when judgments seek to trace back the history or explore the basis of particular legal principles. This is reflected in studies of the use of secondary sources in courts, where lower courts tend to refer to current practical works, but higher courts are more inclined to reference historical legal works, such as Blackstone and Holdsworth, which add 'gravitas to the reasoning of the judge'.[70]

Blackstone's early significance in Australia is notably preserved in a stained glass window depicting him in the Great Hall of the University of Sydney, which was opened in 1859. Few legal academics are accorded such an honour, especially in a foreign country.[71]

18.6 Bryce's *The American Commonwealth*

A more unusual example of an influential English constitutional work is Bryce's book, *The American Commonwealth*. While not strictly a work on the English Constitution, its value lies in its analysis of the American Constitution through English eyes, identifying the English foundations of the Constitution's operation.

The profound influence of this book in Australia is again attributable to timing. Published in 1888, it was seized upon by those in the Australian colonies who were advocating for federation. At the preliminary 1890 Conference in Melbourne on whether to pursue federalism, Alfred Deakin pointed to *The American Commonwealth* as the primary work for the critical examination of the federal system in the United States.[72] At the ensuing Constitutional Conventions of 1891 and 1897–8, where successive drafts of the Commonwealth Constitution were debated, Bryce's *The American Commonwealth* was not only the 'compulsory reading' for the framers of the Constitution[73] but also the subject of 'extensive, unparalleled and usually deferential' citation.[74]

As Australia was a British colony, one would have assumed that it would have followed the Canadian approach to federalism. It was Bryce, however, who effectively translated the American federal system into terms that were

70 Russell Smyth and Ingrid Nielsen, 'The Citation Practices of the High Court of Australia, 1905–2015' (2019) 47(4) Federal Law Review 655, 677.

71 A different stained glass window of Blackstone from 1891 was removed from the Hall of All Souls College, Oxford, for its protection during World War II and later installed in the Marshall-Wythe Law School at the College of William and Mary in Williamsburg, Virginia: Wilfrid Prest (n 49) 1 and illustration 20.

72 *Official Record of the Proceedings and Debates of the Australasian Federation Conference, 1890* (Government Printer, Melbourne 1890) 89.

73 JA LaNauze, *The Making of the Australian Constitution* (MUP 1972) 18.

74 Nicholas Aroney, *The Constitution of a Federal Commonwealth – The Making and Meaning of the Australian Constitution* (CUP 2009) 79.

not only comprehensible but attractive to the Australian framers of the Constitution.[75] He did so by tracing back many of its provisions and some of its nomenclature[76] to colonial arrangements, making them more familiar and less revolutionary in perception. Even the choice of the name 'Commonwealth of Australia', to which Queen Victoria objected due to its republican overtones,[77] was influenced by its association with Bryce's *The American Commonwealth*.[78]

For Bryce, federalism was a 'means of uniting commonwealths into one nation under one national government without extinguishing their separate administrations, legislatures and local patriotisms'.[79] It was, therefore, ideal for bringing together existing colonies while preventing the development of a 'despotic central government'.[80]

But Bryce did not sugar-coat the failings of the American political system. One of his most interesting chapters is entitled 'Why great men are not chosen Presidents'.[81] Amongst the many reasons he suggested was that to a political party, it is better that the nominee be a good candidate so as to win the election than to be a good President.[82] Bryce also observed that a President 'need not be a man of brilliant intellectual gifts'. He considered that the personal qualities required of a President were '[f]irmness, common sense, and most of all, honesty, an honesty above all personal interest'.[83] He concluded that great men are not chosen Presidents 'first because great men are rare in politics; secondly, because the method of choice does not bring them to the top; thirdly, because they are not, in quiet times, absolutely needed'.[84] The framers of the Commonwealth Constitution, while adopting a federal system, declined to adopt a Presidential system of government.

75 John SF Wright, 'Anglicizing the United States Constitution: James Bryce's Contribution to Australian Federalism' (2001) 31(4) Publius: The Journal of Federalism 107, 112; and Stephen Gageler, 'James Bryce and the Australian Constitution' (2015) 43 Federal Law Review 177, 187.

76 This included terms such as President, Senate and Congress: Gageler (n 75) 185.

77 Queen Victoria noted in her journal that she objected to the term Commonwealth and would have preferred 'Dominion', but that Mr Chamberlain has told her that the term did not imply anything like a republic, and that the Australians only wanted to distinguish themselves from the Dominion of Canada: Queen Victoria, *Journals* (Princess Beatrice Copies) 27 June 1900, 226.

78 J Quick and RR Garran, *The Annotated Constitution of the Australian Commonwealth* (Angus and Robertson 1901) 314; Sir W Harrison Moore, *The Constitution of the Commonwealth of Australia* (2nd edn, Maxwell 1910) 66; Gageler (n 75) 182–83.

79 Bryce (n 16) vol I, 350.

80 Ibid 351. See also: Aroney (n 74) 86.

81 Bryce (n 16) 78–85.

82 Ibid 80.

83 Ibid 81.

84 Ibid 84.

Despite the significant influence of Bryce upon the framers of the Commonwealth Constitution, Bryce's work has not had much of an ongoing influence on the operation and interpretation of the Constitution thereafter. Perhaps that is because, unlike the work of his contemporary, A V Dicey, which was republished and updated through many editions, Bryce's *The American Commonwealth* remained a static description of a system of government at a particular point in time. It provided an explanation of why choices were made, but it did not go further to explain how those choices should operate in the future.

18.7 Erskine May's *Treatise upon the Law, Privileges, Proceedings and Usage of Parliament*

In terms of practical use, the most influential leading work in former British colonies would have to be the various editions of Erskine May's *Treatise upon the Law Privileges, Proceedings and Usage of Parliament.* It has provided the precedents and rules of operation for legislatures throughout the former Empire for well over a century, and in some cases, it still does.

Fledgling legislatures in territories without a history of democracy had great need of a work that could explain the history and customs of Parliament, as well as give practical guidance about the operation of the procedural rules of its Houses. Until local legislatures could build up and publish their own precedents in equivalent works of guidance, Erskine May remained the primary work on the table of each House of a Westminster-style Parliament, consulted by the Clerks, the Presiding Officers, and Members alike.

In Australia, Erskine May's first edition of 1844 was well-timed to aid the first representative legislature in the colony of New South Wales, which had recently commenced operation in 1843. The Speaker of the Legislative Council wrote to Erskine May in 1851, observing that it was impossible 'to overrate the advantages which have resulted from the employment of your work in the colonial legislature'.[85] By the time of federation in 1901, Erskine May's *Treatise* was a key resource for the determination of disputes about parliamentary procedure. In addition, the first Standing Orders for the House of Representatives included a default rule that if a matter was not addressed by the Sessional or other Orders of the House, resort shall be had to the rules, forms, and practice of the House of Commons.[86] This increased the relevance of Erskine May's explication of those rules in relation to the House of Representatives.

85 D Natzler, D Bagnall, J-P Brochu, and P Fowler, 'Controversy at the Antipodes (and Elsewhere)' in P Evans (ed), *Essays on the History of Parliamentary Procedure: In Honour of Thomas Erskine May* (Bloomsbury 2020) 129, 148.

86 Australia, House of Representatives, Standing Order 1. A form of this Standing Order remained in place until 2004.

Erskine May's *Treatise* maintained its pre-eminence at the federal level in Australia until the publication of Odgers' *Australian Senate Practice* in 1953.[87] The House of Representatives did not produce its own equivalent work, *House of Representatives Practice,* until 1981.[88]

Erskine May's *Treatise* remains a significant reference work for Australian Houses at the Commonwealth, State, and Territory levels but is now primarily used as a source of comparison[89] to see how a similar legislature deals with common issues (such as how to discipline Members of Parliament who have engaged in bullying or sexual harassment).

There is, however, a continuing constitutional relevance to Erskine May's *Treatise* in Australia. Section 49 of the Commonwealth Constitution provides that:

> The powers, privileges, and immunities of the Senate and of the House of Representatives, and of the members and the committees of each House, shall be such as are declared by the Parliament, and until declared shall be those of the Commons House of Parliament of the United Kingdom, and of its members and committees, at the establishment of the Commonwealth.

As these powers, privileges, and immunities are tied to those of the House of Commons at a particular date – the establishment of the Commonwealth on 1 January 1901 – this makes the tenth edition of Erskine May's *Treatise*, published in 1893 of continuing relevance to Australia. It is the most authoritative source for ascertaining what those powers, privileges, and immunities were at that time. While this was only intended to be a temporary measure, until the Commonwealth Parliament enacted legislation declaring the powers, privileges, and immunities of its Houses, no comprehensive legislation has been enacted on this subject.[90] Hence, the tenth edition of Erskine May's *Treaties* retains constitutional significance in Australia.

New Zealand followed a similar track, with significant reliance on Erskine May's *Treatise* until McGee's *Parliamentary Practice in New Zealand* was first published in 1985.[91] Indeed, the 1865 Standing Orders were largely copied from Erskine May's companion manual of *Rules, Orders, and Forms of*

87 JR Odgers (ed), *Australian Senate Practice* (Australian Government Publishing Service 1953).

88 JA Pettifer (ed), *House of Representatives Practice* (Australian Government Publishing Service 1981).

89 Natzler (n 85) 129, 151.

90 The Parliamentary Privileges Act 1987 (Cth) makes some minor alterations to the existing powers, privileges and immunities of the Houses, including the removal of the power to expel Members, but it otherwise leaves the substance of those powers, privileges, and immunities to be ascertained by reference to those of the House of Commons on 1 January 1901.

91 David McGee, *Parliamentary Practice in New Zealand* (Government Printer 1985).

Proceeding of the House of Commons, with appropriate alterations to adapt them to the New Zealand institutions of government.[92] In addition, the Parliamentary Privileges Act 1865 (NZ)[93] conferred upon the New Zealand General Assembly all the powers and privileges held by the House of Commons as of 1 January 1865. As in Australia, this made the relevant edition of Erskine May's *Treatise* essential to determine the scope of those powers and privileges.[94]

In Canada, however, there were some quite early works on Canadian parliamentary procedure, such as Todd's *The Practice and Privilege of the Two Houses of Parliament*, first published in 1840,[95] and Bourinot's *Parliamentary Procedure and Practice in the Dominion of Canada*, first published in 1884.[96] This lessened the influence of Erskine May's *Treatise*, at least to the extent that local precedents and variations on procedural rules were readily accessible. In practice, 'precedence is given to Bourinot over May, as it provides examples from Canadian practice', but 'May can still be relied on to clarify more complex procedural rules' and the historical context of rules.[97] As in Australia and New Zealand, there is still a tie between the privileges, powers, and immunities of the Houses and those of the House of Commons.[98]

18.8 Conclusion

English constitutional history forms part of the constitutional history of many former British colonies across the globe. That history also underpins the Constitutions, bills of rights, and other legislation of those countries, which often encapsulate complex modern concepts within much older terms and phrases, such as 'due process of law', 'trial by jury', and the 'freedom of speech and debates or proceedings in Parliament'. Knowledge of that history can give context to these provisions and enrich understanding of them, although it cannot dictate their meaning and operation today.

The degree of influence of certain English legal works in those former colonies was affected by their availability and the timing of their publication at critical stages in a colony's constitutional development. Appeal courts throughout

92 Natzler (n 85) 129, 136.

93 See later: Legislature Act 1908 (NZ), s 242; and Parliamentary Privilege Act 2014 (NZ), s 8.

94 See, e.g., *Peters v Collinge* [1993] 2 NZLR 554, 573 (Fisher J); *Television New Zealand Ltd v Prebble* [1993] 3 NZLR 513, 527–28; *Buchanan v Jennings* [2002] 3 NZLR 145, [25], [32] and [149].

95 Alpheus Todd, *The Practice and Privileges of the Two Houses of Parliament* (Rogers & Thompson 1840).

96 JG Bourinot, *Parliamentary Procedure and Practice with an Introductory Account of the Origin and Growth of Parliamentary Institutions in the Dominion of Canada* (Dawson Brothers 1884).

97 Natzler (n 85) 145.

98 Constitution Act 1867, s 18, as amended; and Parliament of Canada Act 1985 (Can), s 4.

the common law world still draw upon them when seeking to clarify the origins and progressive development of rights and legal principles. These works continue to spread light on fundamental constitutional concepts, retaining their value for future generations.

Bibliography

Alschuler AW, 'Rediscovering Blackstone' (1996) 145 University of Pennsylvania Law Review 1

Arlidge A and Judge I, *Magna Carta Uncovered* (Hart Publishing 2014)

Aroney N, *The Constitution of a Federal Commonwealth – The Making and Meaning of the Australian Constitution* (CUP 2009)

Blackstone W, *Commentaries on the Laws of England* (Clarendon Press 1765–1769)

Bourinot JG, *Parliamentary Procedure and Practice With an Introductory Account of the Origin and Growth of Parliamentary Institutions in the Dominion of Canada* (Dawson Brothers 1884)

Bryce J, *The American Commonwealth* (3rd edn, Macmillan & Co 1893)

Campbell E, 'Colonial Legislation and the Law of England' (1965) 2(2) University of Tasmania Law Review 148

Clark D, 'The Icon of Liberty: The Status and Role of *Magna Carta* in Australian and New Zealand Law' (2000) 24 MULR 866

Coke E, *The First Part of the Institutes of the Laws of England* (Vol I) p 142a; and *Calvin's Case* (1608) 7 Co Rep 1a, 18a, 77 ER 377

Erskine May T, *A Treatise on the Law, Privileges, Proceedings and Usage of Parliament* (Charles Knight & Co 1844)

Gageler S, 'James Bryce and the Australian Constitution' (2015) 43 Federal Law Review 177

Harrison Moore W, The Constitution of the Commonwealth of Australia (2nd edn, Maxwell 1910)

Hoeflich M, 'American Blackstones' in W Prest (ed), *Blackstone and His Commentaries: Biography, Law, History* (Hart Publishing 2009)

Joseph PA, *Joseph on Constitutional and Administrative Law* (5th edn, Thomson Reuters 2021)

Kercher B, *An Unruly Child: A History of Law in Australia* (Allen & Unwin 1995)

Kercher B, 'The Foundation of Judicial Methods in Early New South Wales' in *Enduring Courts in Changing Times – Celebrating the 2024 Bicentenaries of the Supreme Courts of New South Wales and Tasmania* (Australian Academy of Law 2024)

LaNauze JA, *The Making of the Australian Constitution* (MUP 1972)

McGee D, *Parliamentary Practice in New Zealand* (Government Printer 1985)

McPherson BH, *The Reception of English Law Abroad* (Supreme Court of Queensland Library 2007)

Natzler D, Bagnall D, Brochu JP and Fowler P, 'Controversy at the Antipodes (and Elsewhere)' in P Evans (ed), *Essays on the History of Parliamentary Procedure: In Honour of Thomas Erskine May* (Bloomsbury 2020)

Odgers JR (ed), *Australian Senate Practice* (Australian Government Publishing Service 1953)

Pettifer JA (ed), *House of Representatives Practice* (Australian Government Publishing Service 1981)

Phillips F, *Commonwealth Caribbean Constitutional Law* (Cavendish Publishing 2002)

Prest W, 'Antipodean Blackstone: The *Commentaries* "Down Under"' (2003) 6 Flinders Journal of Law Reform 151

Prest W (ed), *Re-Interpreting Blackstone's Commentaries* (Hart Publishing 2005)

Prest W, *William Blackstone – Law and Letters in the Eighteenth Century* (OUP 2008)
Quick J and Garran RR, *The Annotated Constitution of the Australian Commonwealth* (Angus and Robertson 1901)
Smyth R and Nielsen I, 'The Citation Practices of the High Court of Australia, 1905–2015' (2019) 47(4) Federal Law Review 655
Todd A, *The Practice and Privileges of the Two Houses of Parliament* (Rogers & Thompson 1840)
Watson I, 'Aboriginal Laws and Colonial Foundation' (2017) 26(4) Griffith Law Review 469
Wright JSF, 'Anglicizing the United States Constitution: James Bryce's Contribution to Australian Federalism' (2001) 31(4) Publius: The Journal of Federalism 107

Index

Papier | Fördert gute Waldnutzung
FSC® C083411

Kolibri 360 GmbH
Ferdinand-Jühlke-Straße 7
99095 Erfurt, Deutschland
produktsicherheit@kolibri360.de